# *Mathematical Models*

# Mathematical Models

## Mechanical Vibrations, Population Dynamics, and Traffic Flow

(AN INTRODUCTION TO APPLIED MATHEMATICS)

Richard Haberman

*Department of Mathematics*
*Rutgers University*

PRENTICE-HALL, INC., *Englewood Cliffs, New Jersey 07632*

*Library of Congress Cataloging in Publication Data*

HABERMAN, RICHARD, (Date)
    Mathematical models in mechanical vibrations,
population dynamics, and traffic flow.

    Includes bibliographies and index.
    1. Mathematics—1961-   2. Mathematical
models.   3. Vibration—Mathematical models.
4. Ecology—Mathematical models.   5. Traffic flow
—Mathematical models.   I. Title.
QA37.2.H2          001.4'24        76-48911
ISBN   0-13-561738-3

Prentice-Hall International, Inc., *London*
Prentice-Hall of Australia Pty. Limited, *Sydney*
Prentice-Hall of Canada, Ltd., *Toronto*
Prentice-Hall of India Private Limited, *New Delhi*
Prentice-Hall of Japan, Inc., *Tokyo*
Prentice-Hall of Southeast Asia Pte. Ltd., *Singapore*
Whitehall Books Limited, *Wellington, New Zealand*

# *Contents*

*(Starred sections may be
omitted without loss of continuity.)*

# Population Dynamics—
# Mathematical Ecology  *117*

# *Preface*

I believe the primary reason for studying mathematics lies in its applications. By studying three diverse areas in which mathematics has been applied, this text attempts to introduce to the reader some of the fundamental concepts and techniques of applied mathematics. In each area, relevant observations and experiments are discussed. In this way a mathematical model is carefully formulated. The resulting mathematical problem is solved, requiring at times the introduction of new mathematical methods. The solution is then interpreted, and the validity of the mathematical model is questioned. Often the mathematical model must be modified and the process of formulation, solution, and interpretation continued. Thus we will be illustrating the relationships between each area and the appropriate mathematics. Since one area at a time is investigated in depth in this way, the reader has the opportunity to understand each topic, not just the mathematical techniques.

Mechanical vibrations, population dynamics, and traffic flow are chosen as areas to investigate in an introduction to applied mathematics for similar reasons. In each, the experiments and common observations necessary to formulate and understand the mathematical models are relatively well known to the average reader. We will not find it necessary to refer to exceedingly technical research results. Furthermore these three topics were chosen for inclusion in this text because each serves as an introduction to more specialized investigations. Here we attempt only to introduce these various topics and leave the reader to pursue those of most interest. Mechanical vibrations (more specifically the motion of spring-mass systems and pendulums) is naturally followed by a study of other topics from physics; mathematical ecology (involving the population growth of species interacting with their environment) is a possible first topic in biomathematics; and traffic flow (investigating the fluctuations of traffic density along a highway) introduces the reader in a simpler context to many mathematical and physical concepts common in various areas of engineering, such as heat transfer and fluid dynamics. In addition, it is hoped that the reader will find these three topics as interesting as the author does.

A previous exposure to physics will aid the reader in the part on mechanical vibrations, but the text is readily accessible to those without this background. The topics discussed supplement rather than substitute for an introductory physics course. The material on population dynamics requires no background in biology; experimental motivation is self-contained. Similarly, there is sufficient familarity with traffic situations to enable the reader to thoroughly understand the traffic models that are developed.

This text has been written with the assumption that the reader has had the equivalent of the usual first two years of college mathematics (calculus and some elementary ordinary differential equations). Many critical aspects of these prerequisites are briefly reviewed. More specifically, a knowledge of calculus including partial derivatives is required, but vector integral calculus (for example, the divergence theorem) is never used (nor is it needed). Linear algebra and probability are also not required (although they are briefly utilized in a few sections which the reader may skip). Although some knowledge of differential equations is required, it is mostly restricted to first and second order constant coefficient equations. A background in more advanced techniques is not necessary, as they are fully explained where needed.

Mathematically, the discussion of mechanical vibrations and population dynamics proceed in similar ways. In both, emphasis is placed on the nonlinear aspects of ordinary differential equations. The concepts of equilibrium solutions and their stability are developed, considered by many to be one of the fundamental unifying themes of applied mathematics. Phase plane methods are introduced and linearization procedures are explained in both parts. On the other hand, the mathematical models of traffic flow involve first-order (nonlinear) partial differential equations, and hence is relatively independent of the previous material. The method of characteristics is slowly and carefully explained, resulting in the concept of traffic density wave propagation. Throughout, mathematical techniques are developed, but equal emphasis is placed on the mathematical formulation of the problem and the interpretation of the results.

I believe, in order to learn mathematics, the reader must take an active part. This is best accomplished by attempting a significant number of the included exercises. Many more problems are included than are reasonable for the average reader to do. The exercises have been designed such that their difficulty varies. Almost all readers will probably find some too easy, while others are quite difficult. Most are word problems, enabling the reader to consider the relationships between the mathematics and the models.

Each major part is divided into many subsections. However, these sections are not of equal length. Few correspond to as much as a single lecture. Usually more than one (and occasionally, depending on the background of the reader, many) of the sections can be covered in an amount of time equal to that of a single lecture. In this way the book has been designed to be substantially covered in one semester. However, a longer treatment of these subjects will be beneficial for some. Furthermore, with material added by individual instructors, this text may be used as the basis of a full year's introduction to applied mathematics. For others, a second semester of applied mathematics could consist of, for example, the heat, wave and Laplace's equation (and the mathematics of Fourier series as motivated by separation of variables of these partial differential equations).

This text is a reflection of my own philosophy of applied mathematics. However, anyone's philosophy is strongly influenced by one's exposure. For my own education, the applied mathematics group at the Massachusetts Institute of Technology must be sincerely thanked. Any credit for much of this book must be shared with them in some ill-defined way.

A course has been offered for a few years based on preliminary versions of this text. Student comments have been most helpful as have been the insights given to me by Dr. Eugene Speer and Dr. Richard Falk who have co-taught the material with me. Also I would like to express my appreciation to Dr. Mark Ablowitz for his many thoughtful and useful suggestions.

For the opportunity and encouragement to develop an applied mathematics course for which this text was written, I wish sincerely to thank Dr. Terry Butler. Furthermore his interest in the needs of students reinforced my own attitudes and resulted in this text.

Besides the usual gratitude to one's wife, my thanks to Liz for the thankless task of helping in rewriting the many drafts. Having no interest or knowledge in mathematics, this was an exceptionally difficult effort.

My appreciation to the typists of the manuscript (originally class notes), especially Mrs. Annette Roselli whose accurate work was second only to her patience with the numerous revisions.

RICHARD HABERMAN

# Mechanical Vibrations

# 1. Introduction to Mathematical Models in the Physical Sciences

Science attempts to establish an understanding of all types of phenomena. Many different explanations can sometimes be given that agree qualitatively with experiments or observations. However, when theory and experiment quantitatively agree, then we can usually be more confident in the validity of the theory. In this manner mathematics becomes an integral part of the scientific method.

Applied mathematics can be said to involve three steps:

1. the formulation of a problem—the approximations and assumptions, based on experiments or observations, that are necessary to develop, simplify, and understand the mathematical model;
2. the solving of realistic problems (including relevant computations);
3. the interpretation of the mathematical results in the context of the nonmathematical problem.

In this text, we will attempt to give equal emphasis to all three aspects.

One cannot underestimate the importance of good experiments in developing mathematical models. However, mathematical models are important in their own right, aside from an attempt to mimic nature. This occurs because the real world consists of many interacting processes. It may be impossible in an experiment to entirely eliminate certain undesirable effects. Furthermore one is never sure which effects may be negligible in nature. A mathematical model has an advantage in that we are able to consider only certain effects, the object being to see which effects account for given observations and which effects are immaterial.

The process of applying mathematics never ends. As new experiments or observations are made, the mathematical model is continually revised and improved. To illustrate this we first study some problems from physics involving mechanical vibrations.

A spring-mass system is analyzed, simplified by many approximations including linearization (Secs. 2–9). Experimental observations necessitate the consideration of frictional forces (Secs. 10–13). A pendulum is then analyzed (Secs. 14–16) since its properties are similar to those of a spring-mass system. The nonlinear frictionless pendulum and spring-mass systems are briefly studied, stressing the concepts of equilibrium and stability (Secs. 17–18), before energy principles and phase plane analysis are used (Secs. 19–20). Examples of nonlinear frictionless oscillators are worked out in detail (Secs. 21–25). Nonlinear systems which are damped are then discussed (Secs. 26–28). Mathematical models of increasing difficulty are formulated; we proceed in the following manner:

1. linear systems (frictionless).
2. linear systems with friction.
3. nonlinear systems (frictionless).
4. nonlinear systems with friction.

## 2.  Newton's Law

To begin our investigations of mathematical models, a problem with which most of you are somewhat familiar will be considered. We will discuss the motion of a mass attached to a spring as shown in Fig. 2-1:

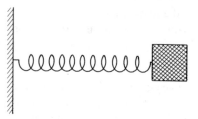

Figure 2-1   Spring-mass system.

Observations of this kind of apparatus show that the mass, once set in motion, moves back and forth (oscillates). Although few people today have any intrinsic interest in such a spring-mass system, historically this problem played an important part in the development of physics. Furthermore, this simple spring-mass system exhibits behavior of more complex systems. For example, the oscillations of a spring-mass system resemble the motions of clock-like mechanisms and, in a sense, also aid in the understanding of the up-and-down motion of the ocean surface.

*Physical problems cannot be analyzed by mathematics alone.* This should be the first fundamental principle of an applied mathematician (although apparently some mathematicians would frequently wish it were not so). A spring-mass system cannot be solved without formulating an equation which describes its motion. Fortunately many experimental observations culminated in **Newton's second law of motion** describing how a particle reacts to a force. Newton discovered that the motion of a point mass is well described by the now famous formula

$$\vec{F} = \frac{d}{dt}(m\vec{v}),\tag{2.1}$$

where $\vec{F}$ is the vector sum of all forces applied to a point mass of mass $m$. The forces $\vec{F}$ equal the rate of change of the **momentum** $m\vec{v}$, where $\vec{v}$ is the velocity of the mass and $\vec{x}$ its position:

$$\vec{v} = \frac{d\vec{x}}{dt}. \tag{2.2}$$

If the mass is constant (which we assume throughout this text), then

$$\boxed{\vec{F} = m\frac{d\vec{v}}{dt} = m\vec{a},} \tag{2.3}$$

where $\vec{a}$ is the vector acceleration of the mass

$$\vec{a} = \frac{d\vec{v}}{dt} = \frac{d^2\vec{x}}{dt^2}. \tag{2.4}$$

Newton's second law of motion (often referred to as just **Newton's law**), equation 2.3, states that the force on a particle equals its mass times its acceleration, easily remembered as "$F$ equals $ma$." The resulting acceleration of a point mass is proportional to the total force acting on the mass.

At least two assumptions are necessary for the validity of Newton's law. There are no point masses in nature. Thus, this formula is valid only to the extent in which the finite size of a mass can be ignored.* For our purposes, we will be satisfied with discussing only point masses. A second approximation has its origins in work by twentieth century physicists in which Newton's law is shown to be invalid as the velocities involved approach the speed of light. However, as long as the velocity of a mass is significantly less than the speed of light, Newton's law remains a good *approximation*. We emphasize the word approximation, for although mathematics is frequently treated as a science of exactness, mathematics is applied to models which only approximate the real world.

# EXERCISES

**2.1.** Consider Fig. 2-2, which shows two masses ($m_1$ and $m_2$) attached to the opposite ends of a rigid (and massless) bar:

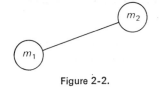

Figure 2-2.

---

*Newton's second law can be applied to finite sized rigid bodies if $\vec{x}$, the position of the point mass, is replaced by $\vec{x}_{cm}$, the position of the center of mass (see exercise 2.1).

$m_1$ is located at $\vec{x}_1$ and $m_2$ is located at $\vec{x}_2$. The bar is free to move and rotate due to imposed forces. The bar applies a force $\vec{F}_1$ to mass $m_1$ and also a force $\vec{F}_2$ to $m_2$ as seen in Fig. 2-3:

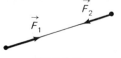

Figure 2-3.

Newton's third law of motion, stating that the forces of action and reaction are equal and opposite, implies that $\vec{F}_2 = -\vec{F}_1$.

(a)   Suppose that an external force $\vec{G}_1$ is applied to $m_1$, and $\vec{G}_2$ to $m_2$. By applying Newton's second law to each mass, show the law can be applied to the rigid body consisting of both masses, if $\vec{x}$ is replaced by the center of mass $\vec{x}_{cm}$ [i.e., show $m(d^2\vec{x}_{cm}/dt^2) = \vec{F}$, where $m$ is the total mass, $m = m_1 + m_2$, $\vec{x}_{cm}$ is the center of mass, $\vec{x}_{cm} = (m_1\vec{x}_1 + m_2\vec{x}_2)/(m_1 + m_2)$, and $\vec{F}$ is the sum of forces applied, $\vec{F} = \vec{G}_1 + \vec{G}_2$]. The motion of the center of mass of the rigid body is thus determined. However, its rotation remains unknown.

(b)   Show that $\vec{x}_{cm}$ lies at a point on the rigid bar connecting $m_1$ to $m_2$.

**2.2.**   Generalize the result of exercise 2.1 to a rigid body consisting of $N$ masses.

**2.3.**   Figure 2-4 shows a rigid bar of length $L$:

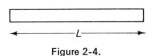

Figure 2-4.

(a)   If the mass density $\rho(x)$ (mass per unit length) depends on the position along the bar, then what is the total mass $m$?

(b)   Using the result of exercise 2.2, where is the center of mass $\vec{x}_{cm}$? [Hint: Divide the bar up into $N$ equal pieces and take the limit as $N \rightarrow \infty$.]

(c)   If the total force on the mass is $\vec{F}$, show that

$$m\frac{d^2\vec{x}_{cm}}{dt^2} = \vec{F}.$$

# 3.   Newton's Law as Applied to a Spring-Mass System

We will attempt to apply Newton's law to a spring-mass system. It is assumed that the mass moves only in one direction, call it the $x$ direction, in which case the mass is governed by

$$m\frac{d^2x}{dt^2} = F \tag{3.1}$$

If there were no forces $F$, the mass could move only at a constant velocity. (This statement, known as Newton's first law, is easily verifiable—see exercise 3.1.) Thus the observed variability of the velocity must be due to forces probably exerted by the spring. To develop an appropriate model of the spring force, one should study the motions of spring-mass systems under different circumstances. Let us suppose a series of experiments were run in an attempt to measure the spring force. At some position the mass could be placed and it would not move; there the spring exerts no force on the mass. This place at which we center our coordinate axis, as we see in Fig. 3-1, $x = 0$, is called the **equilibrium** or unstretched position of the spring*:

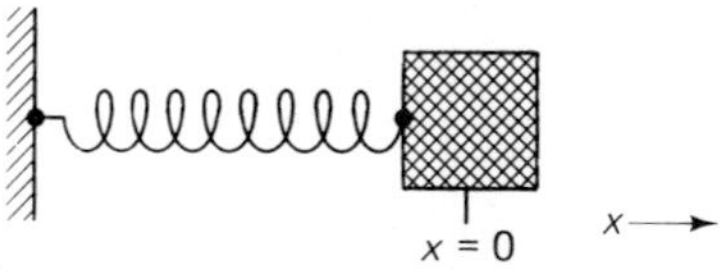

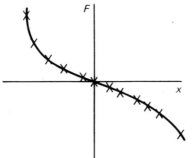

Figure 3-1   Equilibrium: no force exerted by the spring.

$x = 0$   $x \longrightarrow$

The distance $x$ is then referred to as the displacement from equilibrium or the amount of stretching of the spring. If we stretch the spring (that is let $x > 0$), then the spring exerts a force pulling the mass back towards the equilibrium position (that is $F < 0$). Similarly, if the spring is contracted ($x < 0$), then the spring pushes the mass again towards the equilibrium position ($F > 0$). Such a force is called a **restoring** force. Furthermore, we would observe that as we increase the stretching of the spring, the force exerted by the spring would increase. Thus we might obtain the results shown in Fig. 3-2, where a curve is smoothly drawn connecting the experimental data points marked with an "$x$":

$F$

$x$

Figure 3-2   Experimental spring force.

We have assumed that the force only depends on the amount of stretching of the spring; the force does not depend on any other quantities. Thus, for example, the force is assumed to be the same no matter what speed the mass is moving at.

---

*Throughout this text, we assume that the width of the mass is negligible.

A careful examination of the experimental data shows that the force depends, in a complex manner, on the stretching. However, for stretching of the spring which is not too large (corresponding to at most a moderate force), Fig. 3-3 shows that this curve can be approximated by a straight line:

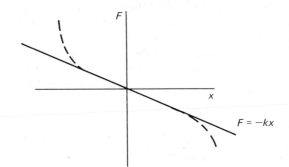

Figure 3-3   Hooke's Law: approximation of experimental spring force.

Thus

$$F = -kx$$   (3.2)

is a good approximation for the spring-force as long as the mass is not very far from its equilibrium position. $k$ is called the spring constant. It depends on the elasticity of the spring. This linear relationship between the force and the position of the mass was discovered by the seventeenth century physicist Hooke and is thus known as **Hooke's law**. Doubling the displacement, doubles the force.

Using Hooke's law, Newton's second law of motion yields

$$m \frac{d^2x}{dt^2} = -kx,$$   (3.3)

the simplest mathematical model of a spring-mass system.

# EXERCISES

**3.1.**   Newton's first law states that with no external forces a mass will move along a straight line at constant velocity.

(a)   If the motion is only in the $x$ direction, then using Newton's second law ($m(d^2x/dt^2) = F$), prove Newton's first law.

    (b)  If the motion is in three dimensions, then using Newton's second law $(m(d^2\vec{x}/dt^2) = \vec{F})$, prove Newton's first law. (Why is the motion in a straight line?)

**3.2.**  If a spring is permanently deformed due to a large force, then do our assumptions fail?

# 4.  Gravity

In Sec. 3, we showed that the differential equation

$$m\,\frac{d^2x}{dt^2} = -kx \tag{4.1}$$

describes the motion of a spring-mass system. Some of you may object to this model, since you may find it difficult to imagine a horizontally oscillating spring-mass system such as that shown in Fig. 4-1:

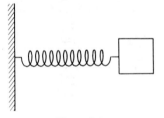

Figure 4-1.

It may seem more reasonable to consider a vertical spring-mass system as illustrated in Fig. 4-2:

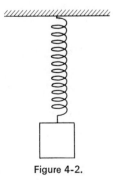

Figure 4-2.

The derivation of the equation governing a horizontal spring-mass system does not apply to the vertical system. There is another force—gravity. We approximate the gravitational force as a constant* $-mg$, the mass $m$ times the acceleration due to gravity $-g$. The two forces add vectorially and hence Newton's law becomes

$$m\frac{d^2y}{dt^2} = -ky - mg, \qquad (4.2)$$

where $y$ is the vertical coordinate. $y = 0$ is the position at which the spring exerts no force.

Is there a position at which we could place the mass and it would not move, what we have called an *equilibrium position*? If there is, then it follows that $dy/dt = d^2y/dt^2 = 0$, and the two forces must balance:

$$0 = -ky - mg.$$

Thus we see

$$y = -\frac{m}{k}g$$

is the equilibrium position of this spring-mass-gravity system (represented by Fig. 4-3), not $y = 0$:

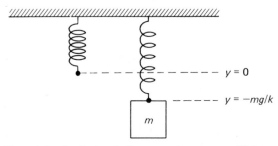

Figure 4-3    Gravitational effect on spring-mass equilibrium.

---

*Actually, a gravitational force of attraction $\vec{F}$ exists directed between any two point masses $m_1$ and $m_2$. Its magnitude is inversely proportional to the square of the distance between them, $r$,

$$|\vec{F}| = \frac{Gm_1m_2}{r^2},$$

the so-called **inverse-square law**, where $G$ is a universal constant determined experimentally. If the earth is spherically symmetric, then the force due to the earth's mass acting on any point mass is directed towards the center of the earth (or downwards). Thus the radial component of the gravitational force on a mass $m$ is

$$F = \frac{-GmM}{r^2},$$

where $M$ is the mass of the earth. If the displacement of the spring is small as compared to the radius of the earth $r_0$ (not a very restrictive assumption!), then the gravitational force

Only at that position will the force due to gravity balance the upward force of the spring. The spring sags downwards a distance $mg/k$ when the mass is added, a result that should not be surprising. For a larger mass, the spring sags more. The stiffer the spring ($k$ larger), the smaller the sag of the spring (also quite reasonable).

It is frequently advantageous to translate coordinate systems from one with an origin at $y = 0$ (the position of the unstretched spring) to one with an origin at $y = -mg/k$ (the equilibrium position with the mass). Let $Z$ equal the **displacement** from this equilibrium position:

$$Z = y - \left(-\frac{mg}{k}\right) = y + \frac{mg}{k}.$$

Upon this substitution, equation 4.2 becomes

$$m\frac{d^2Z}{dt^2} = -kZ.$$

This is the same as equation 4.1. Thus the mass will move vertically around the new vertical equilibrium position in the same manner as the mass would move horizontally around its horizontal equilibrium position. For this reason we may continue to study the horizontal spring-mass system even though vertical systems are more commonplace.

# EXERCISES

**4.1.** A mass $m$ is thrown upward with initial speed $v_0$. Assume that gravity is constant. How high does the mass go before it begins to fall? Does this height depend in a reasonable way on $m$, $v_0$, and $g$?

**4.2.** A mass $m$ is rolled off a table (at height $h$ above the floor) with horizontal speed $v_0$. Where does the mass land? What trajectory did the mass take?

**4.3.** A mass $m$ is thrown with initial speed $v_0$ at an angle $\theta$ with respect to the horizon. Where does the mass land? What trajectory did the mass take? For what angle does the mass land the farthest away from where it was thrown (assuming the same initial speed)?

---

can be approximated by $-GmM/r_0^2$, a constant. Thus the universal constant $G$ is related to $g$ by

$$g = \frac{GM}{r_0^2}.$$

The rotation of the earth only causes very small modifications of this result. In addition, since the earth is not spherically symmetric, there are local variations to this formula. Furthermore, inhomogeneities in the earth's internal structure cause measurable variations, (which are useful in mineral and oil exploration).

# 5. Oscillation of a Spring-Mass System

We now proceed to analyze the differential equation describing a spring-mass system,

$$m \frac{d^2x}{dt^2} = -kx. \tag{5.1}$$

The restoring force is proportional to the stretching of the spring. Although this equation has been derived using many approximations and assumptions, it is hoped that the understanding of its solution will aid in more exact investigations (some of which we will pursue). Equation 5.1 is a second-order linear differential equation with constant coefficients. As you should recall from a course in differential equations, the general solution of this differential equation is

$$x = c_1 \cos \omega t + c_2 \sin \omega t, \tag{5.2}$$

where

$$\omega^2 = \frac{k}{m}$$

and where $c_1$ and $c_2$ are arbitrary constants. However, for those readers who did not recognize that equation 5.2 is the general solution of equation 5.1, a brief review of the standard technique to solve constant coefficient linear differential equations is given. The general solution of a second-order linear homogeneous differential equation is a linear combination of two homogeneous solutions. For constant coefficient differential equations, the homogeneous solutions are usually in the form of simple exponentials, $e^{rt}$. The specific exponential(s) are obtained by directly substituting the assumed form $e^{rt}$ into the differential equation.

If $e^{rt}$ is substituted into equation 5.1, then a quadratic equation for $r$ results,

$$mr^2 = -k.$$

The two roots are imaginary,

$$r = \pm i\omega$$

where $\omega = \sqrt{k/m}$. Thus the general solution is a linear combination of $e^{i\omega t}$ and $e^{-i\omega t}$,

$$x = ae^{i\omega t} + be^{-i\omega t}, \tag{5.3}$$

where $a$ and $b$ are arbitrary constants. However, the above solution involves the exponential function of an imaginary argument. The displacement $x$ must be real. To show how equation 5.3 can be expressed in terms of real functions, we must recall that

$$e^{i\omega t} = \cos \omega t + i \sin \omega t \qquad\qquad (5.4a)$$

as is derived in exercise 5.6 using the Taylor series of sines, cosines, and exponentials. A similar expression for $e^{-i\omega t}$, can be derived from equation 5.4a by replacing $\omega$ by $-\omega$. This results in

$$e^{-i\omega t} = \cos \omega t - i \sin \omega t \qquad\qquad (5.4b)$$

where the evenness of the cosine function $[\cos(-y) = \cos y]$ and the oddness of the sine function $[\sin(-y) = -\sin y]$ has been used. Equations 5.4a and 5.4b are called *Euler's formulas*, which when applied to equation 5.3 yield

$$x = (a + b) \cos \omega t + i(a - b) \sin \omega t.$$

The desired result

$$x = c_1 \cos \omega t + c_2 \sin \omega t$$

follows, if the constants $c_1$ and $c_2$ are defined by

$$c_1 = a + b$$
$$c_2 = i(a - b).$$

The constants $c_1$ and $c_2$ are arbitrary since given any value of $c_1$ and $c_2$, there exists values of $a$ and $b$, namely

$$a = \tfrac{1}{2}(c_1 - ic_2)$$
$$b = \tfrac{1}{2}(c_1 + ic_2).$$

Since the algebra is a bit involved, it is useful to *memorize* the result we have just derived:

An arbitrary linear combination of $e^{i\omega t}$ and $e^{-i\omega t}$,

$$x = ae^{i\omega t} + be^{-i\omega t},$$

is equivalent to an arbitrary linear combination of $\cos \omega t$ and $\sin \omega t$,

$$x = c_1 \cos \omega t + c_2 \sin \omega t.$$

In the above manner you should now be able to state without any hesitation that the general solution of

$$m \frac{d^2x}{dt^2} = -kx$$

is

$$x = c_1 \cos \omega t + c_2 \sin \omega t,$$

where $\omega = \sqrt{k/m}$ and $c_1$ and $c_2$ are arbitrary constants. The general solution is a linear combination of two oscillatory functions, a cosine and a sine. An *equivalent* expression for the solution is

$$\boxed{x = A \sin (\omega t + \phi_0).} \tag{5.5}$$

This is shown by noting

$$\sin (\omega t + \phi_0) = \sin \omega t \cos \phi_0 + \cos \omega t \sin \phi_0,$$

in which case

$$c_1 = A \sin \phi_0$$
$$c_2 = A \cos \phi_0.$$

If you are given $c_1$ and $c_2$, it is seen that both $A$ and $\phi_0$ can be determined. Dividing the two equations yields an expression for $\tan \phi_0$, and using $\sin^2 \phi_0 + \cos^2 \phi_0 = 1$ results in an equation for $A^2$:

$$A = (c_1^2 + c_2^2)^{1/2}$$

$$\phi_0 = \tan^{-1} \frac{c_1}{c_2}.$$

The expression, $x = A \sin (\omega t + \phi_0)$, is especially convenient for sketching the displacement as a function of time. It shows that the sum of any multiple of $\cos \omega t$ plus any multiple of $\sin \omega t$ is itself a sinusoidal function as sketched in Fig. 5-1:

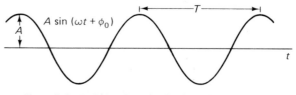

Figure 5-1   Period and amplitude of oscillation.

$A$ is called the **amplitude** of the oscillation; it is easily computed from the above equation if $c_1$ and $c_2$ are known. The **phase** of oscillation is $\omega t + \phi_0$,

$\phi_0$ being the phase at $t = 0$. In many situations, this agrees with the observed motion of a spring-mass system.

This motion is referred to as **simple harmonic motion**. The mass oscillates sinusoidally around the equilibrium position $x = 0$. The solution is periodic in time. As illustrated in Fig. 5-1, the mass after reaching its maximum displacement ($x$ largest), again returns to the same position $T$ units of time later. The entire oscillation repeats itself every $T$ units of time, called the **period** of oscillation. Mathematically a function $f(t)$ is said to be periodic with period $T$ if

$$f(t + T) = f(t).$$

To determine the period $T$, we recall that the trigonometric functions are periodic with period $2\pi$. Thus for a complete oscillation, as $t$ increases to $t + T$, from equation 5.5 $\omega t + \phi_0$ must change by $2\pi$:

$$\omega(t + T) + \phi_0 - \omega t - \phi_0 = 2\pi.$$

Consequently the period $T$ is

$$T = \frac{2\pi}{\omega} = 2\pi\sqrt{\frac{m}{k}}. \tag{5.6}$$

$\omega$, called the **circular frequency** (as is explained in exercise 5.7), is the number of periods in $2\pi$ units of time:

$$\omega = \frac{2\pi}{T} = \sqrt{\frac{k}{m}}. \tag{5.7}$$

The number of oscillations in one unit of time is the **frequency** $f$,

$$f = \frac{1}{T} = \frac{\omega}{2\pi} = \frac{1}{2\pi}\sqrt{\frac{k}{m}},$$

measured in cycles per second (sometimes known as a Hertz). Since a spring-mass system normally oscillates with frequency $1/2\pi\sqrt{k/m}$, this value is referred to as the *natural frequency* of a spring-mass system of mass $m$ and spring constant $k$. Other physical systems have natural frequencies of oscillation. Perhaps in a subsequent course you will determine the natural frequencies of oscillation of a vibrating string or a vibrating drum head!

# EXERCISES

**5.1.** Sketch $x = 2 \sin (3t - \pi/2)$.

**5.2.** If $x = -\cos t + 3 \sin t$, what is the amplitude and phase of the oscillation? Sketch this function.

**5.3.** If $x = -\cos t + 3 \sin (t - \pi/6)$, what is the amplitude of the oscillation?

**5.4.** If $x = -\sin 2t$, what is the frequency, circular frequency, period, and amplitude of the oscillation? Sketch this function.

**5.5.** It was shown that $x = ae^{i\omega t} + be^{-i\omega t}$ is equivalent to $x = c_1 \cos \omega t + c_2 \sin \omega t$. Show that if $c_1$ and $c_2$ are real (that is if $x$ is real), then $b$ is the complex conjugate of $a$.

**5.6.** The Taylor series for $\sin x$, $\cos x$, and $e^x$ are well known for real $x$:

$$\sin x = x - \frac{x^3}{3!} + \frac{x^5}{5!} - \frac{x^7}{7!} + \cdots$$

$$\cos x = 1 - \frac{x^2}{2!} + \frac{x^4}{4!} - \frac{x^6}{6!} + \cdots$$

$$e^x = 1 + x + \frac{x^2}{2!} + \frac{x^3}{3!} + \cdots$$

The above Taylor expansions are also valid for complex $x$.
(a) Show that $e^{i\omega t} = \cos \omega t + i \sin \omega t$, for $\omega$ real.
(b) Show that $e^{-i\omega t} = \cos \omega t - i \sin \omega t$, for $\omega$ real.

**5.7.** Consider a particle moving around a circle, with its position designated by the polar angle $\theta$. Assume its **angular velocity** $d\theta/dt$ is constant, $d\theta/dt = \omega$. Show that the $x$ component of the particle's position executes simple harmonic motion (and also the $y$ component). $\omega$ is measured in radians per unit of time or revolutions per $2\pi$ units of time, the **circular frequency**.

**5.8.** (a) Show that $x = c_1 \cos \omega t + c_2 \sin \omega t$ is the general solution of $m(d^2x/dt^2) = -kx$. What is the value of $\omega$?
(b) Show that an equivalent expression for the general solution is $x = B \cos (\omega t + \theta_0)$. How do $B$ and $\theta_0$ depend on $c_1$ and $c_2$?

# 6. Dimensions and Units

In the previous section, the formula for the circular frequency of a simple spring-mass system was derived,

$$\omega = \sqrt{\frac{k}{m}}.$$

As a check on our calculations we claim that the dimensions of both sides of this equation agree. Checking formulas by dimensional analysis is an important general procedure you should follow. Frequently this type of check will detect embarrassing algebraic errors.

In dimensional analysis, brackets indicate the dimension of a quantity. For example, the notation [x] designates the dimension of $x$, which is a length

$L$, i.e., $[x] = L$, measured in units of feet, inches, miles, meters, or smoots.*
In any calculation to eliminate possible confusion only one unit of length
should be used. In this text we will use metric units in the *m–k–s* system, i.e.,
*meters* for length, *kilogram* for mass, and *seconds* for time. However, as an
aid in conversion to those familiar with the British–American system the
equivalent length in feet or miles and the equivalent mass in pounds will
appear afterwards in parentheses.

What is the dimension of $dx/dt$, the velocity? Clearly,

$$\left[\frac{dx}{dt}\right] = \frac{L}{\tau},$$

a length $L$ divided by a time $\tau$. Mathematically we note that

$$\left[\frac{dx}{dt}\right] = [x]/[t].$$

The dimensions of a derivative of any quantity is always the ratio of the
dimension of that quantity divided by the dimension of the variable which we
are differentiating with respect to. This is shown in general directly from the
definition of a derivative,

$$\frac{dy}{dz} = \lim_{\Delta z \to 0} \frac{y(z + \Delta z) - y(z)}{\Delta z}.$$

The dimensions of the two sides must agree. The right-hand side is the
difference between two values of $y$ (hence having the dimension of $y$) divided
by a small value of $z$ (having the dimension of $z$). Thus,

$$\left[\frac{dy}{dz}\right] = [y]/[z].$$

This result can be used to determine the dimensions of an acceleration:

$$\left[\frac{d^2x}{dt^2}\right] = \frac{[x]}{[t]^2} = \frac{L}{\tau^2}.$$

Note that

$$\left[\frac{d^2x}{dt^2}\right] \neq \frac{L^2}{\tau^2}.$$

This is obvious from a physical point of view. However, this result is shown
below (since sometimes the dimension of a quantity might not be as obvious

---

*Units are chosen to facilitate communication and understanding of the magnitudes of
quantities. Meters (and the other metric units) are familiar to all of the world except the
general public in the United States, who seem reluctant to change. At the other extreme, a
smoot is a unit of length only used to measure the distance across the Charles River in
Boston on the frequently walked Harvard Bridge. Local folklore says that this unit was the
length of a slightly inebriated student as he was rolled across the bridge by some "friends".

as it is in this problem):

$$\frac{d^2x}{dt^2} = \frac{d}{dt}\left(\frac{dx}{dt}\right).$$

Thus,

$$\left[\frac{d^2x}{dt^2}\right] = \frac{\left[\dfrac{dx}{dt}\right]}{[t]} = \frac{L/\tau}{\tau} = \frac{L}{\tau^2}.$$

Since $g$ is an acceleration, the units will be a length per unit of time squared. As discussed in Sec. 4, $g$ is only an approximation, the value we use is $g = 9.8$ meters/sec$^2$ (32 feet/sec$^2$). Everywhere at the surface of the earth, the gravitational acceleration is within 1 percent of this value.

What is the dimension of $k$? Since $F = -kx$, then

$$[k] = \frac{[F]}{[x]} = \frac{\left[m\dfrac{d^2x}{dt^2}\right]}{[x]} = \frac{ML/\tau^2}{L} = \frac{M}{\tau^2},$$

where $M$ is a unit of mass. In this way $\omega$ can be shown to have the same dimension as $\sqrt{k/m}$ (see exercise 6.1).

## EXERCISES

**6.1.** (a)  What is the dimension of $\omega$?

(b)  Show that $\omega$ has the same dimensions as $\sqrt{k/m}$.
You will probably need to note that a radian has no dimension. The formula $(d/d\theta) \sin \theta = \cos \theta$ shows this to be true.

**6.2**  Suppose a quantity $y$ having dimensions of time is *only* a function of $k$ and $m$.

(a)  Give an example of a possible dependence of $y$ on $k$ and $m$.

(b)  Can you describe the most general dependence that $y$ can have on $k$ and $m$?

# 7. Qualitative and Quantitative Behavior of a Spring-Mass System

To understand the predictions of the mathematical model of a spring-mass system, the effect of varying the different parameters is investigated. An important formula is the one derived for the period of oscillation,

$$T = 2\pi\sqrt{\frac{m}{k}}. \tag{7.1}$$

Suppose that we use a firmer spring, that is one whose spring constant $k$ is larger, with the same mass. Without relying on the mathematical formula, what differences in the motion should occur? Let us compare two different springs represented in Fig. 7-1:

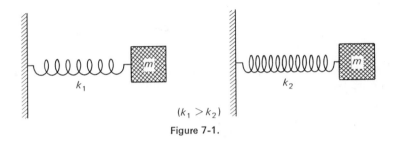

$(k_1 > k_2)$

Figure 7-1.

The one which is firmer has a larger restoring force and hence it returns more quickly to its equilibrium position. Thus we suspect that the larger $k$ is, the shorter the period. Equation 7.1 also predicts this qualitative feature. On the other hand, if the mass is increased using the same spring, then the formula shows that the period increases. The system oscillates more slowly (is this reasonable?).

In any problem we should compare as much as possible our intuition about what should happen with what the formula predicts. If the two agree, then we expect that our formula gives us the quantitative effects for the given problem—one of the major purposes for using mathematics. In particular for a spring-mass system, we might have suspected without using any mathematics that increasing the mass increases the period, but it is doubtful that we could have known that quadrupling the weight results in an increase in the period by a factor of two!

In mathematical models, usually the qualitative effects are at least partially understood. Quantitative results are often unknown. When quantitative results are known (perhaps due to precise experiments), then mathematical models are desirable in order to discover which mechanisms best account for the known data, i.e., which quantities are important and which can be ignored. In complex problems sometimes two or more effects interact. Although each by itself is qualitatively and quantitatively understood, their interaction may need mathematical analysis in order to be understood even qualitatively.

If our intuition about a problem does not correspond to what a mathematical formula predicts, then further investigations of the problem are necessary. Perhaps the intuition is incorrect, in which case the mathematical formulation and solution has aided in directly improving one's qualitative understanding. On the other hand, it may occur that the intuition is correct and consequently that either there was a mathematical error in the derivation of the formula or the model upon which the analysis is based may need improvement.

## EXERCISES

**7.1.**  A .227 kilogram ($\frac{1}{2}$ pound) weight is observed to oscillate 12 times per second. What is the spring constant? If a .91 kilogram (two pound) weight was placed on the same spring, what would be the resulting frequency?

**7.2.**  A weight (of unknown mass) is placed on a vertical spring (of unknown spring constant) compressing it by 2.5 centimeters (one inch). What is the natural frequency of oscillation of this spring-mass system?

# 8.  *Initial Value Problem*

In the previous sections, we have shown that

$$x = c_1 \cos \omega t + c_2 \sin \omega t \tag{8.1}$$

is the general solution of the differential equation describing a spring-mass system,

$$m \frac{d^2 x}{dt^2} = -kx, \tag{8.2}$$

where $c_1$ and $c_2$ are arbitrary constants and $\omega = \sqrt{k/m}$. The constants $c_1$ and $c_2$ will be determined from the initial conditions of the spring-mass system.

One way to initiate motion in a spring-mass system is to strike the mass. A simpler method is to pull (or push) the mass to some position (say $x_0$) and then let go. Mathematically we wish to determine the solution of equation 8.2 which satisfies the initial conditions that the mass is at $x_0$ at $t = 0$,

$$x(0) = x_0,$$

and at $t = 0$, the velocity of the mass, $dx/dt$, is zero,

$$\frac{dx}{dt}(0) = 0.$$

**8.3.**   Consider a spring-mass system initially at rest with initial displacement $x_0$. Show that the maximum and minimum displacements occur halfway between times at which the mass passes its equilibrium position.

# 9.   A Two-Mass Oscillator

In the previous sections we carefully developed a mathematical model of a spring-mass system. We analyzed the resulting oscillations which occur when the force can be approximated as being simply proportional to the stretching of the spring.   Before discussing modifications to this model, as an example let us consider a more complicated spring-mass system. Suppose instead of attaching a spring and a mass to a rigid wall, we attach a spring and a mass to another mass which is also free to move. Let us assume that the two masses are $m_1$ and $m_2$, while the connecting spring is known to have an unstretched length $l$ and spring constant $k$. We insist that the system is constrained to move only horizontally (as might occur if both masses slide along a table) as shown in Fig. 9-1:

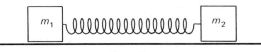

Figure 9-1.

We wish to know the manner in which the two masses, $m_1$ and $m_2$, move.

To analyze that question, we must return to fundamental principles; we must formulate Newton's law of motion for *each* mass. The force on each mass equals its mass times its acceleration. In order to obtain expressions for the accelerations, we introduce the position of each mass (for example, in Fig. 9-2, $x_1$ and $x_2$ are the distances each mass is from a fixed origin):

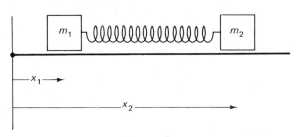

Figure 9-2.

Although the unstretched length of the spring is $l$, it is *not* necessary that $x_2 - x_1 = l$, for in many circumstances the spring may be stretched or compressed. Certainly, for example, we may impose initial conditions such that initially $x_2 - x_1 \neq l$. Now from Newton's law of motion, it follows that if $F_1$ is the force on mass $m_1$ and if $F_2$ is the force on mass $m_2$, then

$$m_1 \frac{d^2 x_1}{dt^2} = F_1 \quad \text{and} \quad m_2 \frac{d^2 x_2}{dt^2} = F_2.$$

To complete the derivation of the equations of motion, we must determine the two forces, $F_1$ and $F_2$. The only force on each mass is due to the spring. Each force is an application of Hooke's law; the force is proportional to the *stretching* of the spring (it is *not* proportional to the length of the spring). The stretching of the spring is the length of the spring $x_2 - x_1$ minus the unstretched length $l$: $x_2 - x_1 - l$. The magnitude of the force is just the spring constant $k$ times the stretching, but the direction of the force is quite important. An error may be made if we are not careful. If, for example, the spring is stretched ($x_2 - x_1 - l > 0$), then the mass $m_1$ is being pulled to the right. The force is in the positive $x_1$ direction, $k(x_2 - x_1 - l)$. In any situation the force on mass $m_1$ is $k(x_2 - x_1 - l)$ and thus

$$\boxed{m_1 \frac{d^2 x_1}{dt^2} = k(x_2 - x_1 - l).} \qquad (9.1)$$

However, although the magnitude of the force on mass $m_2$ is the same, the spring force acts in the opposite direction. Thus

$$\boxed{m_2 \frac{d^2 x_2}{dt^2} = -k(x_2 - x_1 - l).} \qquad (9.2)$$

Having derived the equations describing the motion of this system of two masses coupled by a spring, we have only begun the process of applying mathematics to this physical situation. We must now proceed to solve these equations. At first glance, we have a difficult task in front of us for although equation 9.1 is a linear equation for $x_1$, it contains $x_2$ which is at present unknown! A similar predicament appears in equation 9.2. Equations 9.1 and 9.2 form a linear system of two coupled second order ordinary differential equations involving the two unknowns $x_1$ and $x_2$. The direct analysis of such a system is not difficult.

However, we prefer to approach the solution of this problem in a different way; one which in fact yields a solution more easily interpreted. By inspection we note that the equations simplify if they are added together. In that manner

$$m_1 \frac{d^2x_1}{dt^2} + m_2 \frac{d^2x_2}{dt^2} = 0. \tag{9.3}$$

The sum of the two forces vanishes (since one force is minus the other). Equation 9.3 can be re-expressed as

$$\frac{d^2}{dt^2}(m_1x_1 + m_2x_2) = 0. \tag{9.4}$$

Thus the center of mass of the system, $(m_1x_1 + m_2x_2)/(m_1 + m_2)$, (as discussed in exercise 2.1a), does not accelerate, but moves at a constant velocity (determined from initial conditions). If this system of two masses attached to a spring is viewed as a single entity, then since there are no external forces on it, the system obeys Newton's first law and will not accelerate. By saying there is no acceleration, we have shown that we mean that the center of mass of the system of two masses moves at a constant velocity.

The simple expression for the motion of the center of mass is quite interesting, but hardly aids in understanding the possibly complex behavior of each individual mass. Try subtracting equation 9.2 from equation 9.1; you will soon discover that although adding the two equations results in a significant simplification, subtracting the two is not helpful. Instead we note that the force only depends on the stretching of the spring, $x_2 - x_1 - l$. Perhaps we can directly determine a differential equation for the stretching of the spring. We see this can be accomplished by dividing each equation by the mass (i.e., equation 9.1 by $m_1$ and equation 9.2 by $m_2$) and then subtracting rather than by subtracting right away. Through this subtle trick* we discover that

$$\frac{d^2}{dt^2}(x_2 - x_1) = -\frac{k}{m_2}(x_2 - x_1 - l) - \frac{k}{m_1}(x_2 - x_1 - l).$$

Letting $z$ be the stretching of the spring

$$z = x_2 - x_1 - l, \tag{9.5}$$

we see that

$$\boxed{\frac{d^2z}{dt^2} = -k\left(\frac{1}{m_1} + \frac{1}{m_2}\right)z.} \tag{9.6}$$

By this rather lucky manipulation, we see the remarkable result that the stretching of the spring executes simple harmonic motion. The circular frequency is $\sqrt{k(1/m_1 + 1/m_2)}$.

---

*You should note that we did not use any mathematical motivation for these steps. Instead as often occurs in applied mathematics, the solution of the mathematical equation of interest simplifies if we use insight gained from the physical problem.

We also note that this is the same type of oscillation that would result if a certain mass $m$ were placed on the *same* spring, that is one with spring constant $k$ but fixed at the other end. The mass $m$ necessary for this analogy is such that

$$\boxed{\frac{1}{m} = \frac{1}{m_1} + \frac{1}{m_2}.}$$  (9.7)

This mass $m$ is less than either $m_1$ or $m_2$ (since $1/m > 1/m_1$ and $1/m > 1/m_2$); it is thus called the **reduced mass**:

$$\boxed{m = \frac{1}{\dfrac{1}{m_1} + \dfrac{1}{m_2}} = \frac{m_1 m_2}{m_1 + m_2}.}$$  (9.8)

Attaching a spring-mass system to a movable mass reduces the effective mass; the stretching of the spring executes simple harmonic motion as though a smaller mass was attached. But don't forget that the entire system may move, i.e., the center of mass moves at a constant velocity!

We could discuss more complex spring-mass systems. Instead, we will return in the next sections to the study of a single mass attached to a spring.

# EXERCISES

**9.1.**  Suppose that the initial positions and initial velocities were given for a spring-mass system of the type discussed in this section:

$$x_1(0) = \alpha \qquad \frac{dx_1}{dt}(0) = \gamma$$

$$x_2(0) = \beta \qquad \frac{dx_2}{dt}(0) = \delta.$$

Determine the position of each mass at future times. [Hint: See equations 9.4, 9.5, and 9.6.]

**9.2.**  Consider two masses (of mass $m_1$ and $m_2$) attached to a spring (of unstretched length $l$ and spring constant $k$) in a manner similar to that discussed in this section. However, suppose the system is aligned vertically (rather than horizontally) and that consequently a constant gravitational force is present. Analyze this system and compare the results to those of this section.

**9.3.–9.6.**

In the following exercises consider two springs, each obeying Hooke's law; one spring with spring constant $k_1$ (and unstretched length $l_1$) and the other with spring constant $k_2$ (and unstretched length $l_2$) as shown in Fig. 9-3:

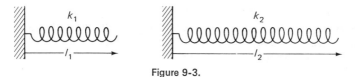

Figure 9-3.

**9.3.** Suppose that a mass $m$ were attached between two walls a distance $d$ apart (refer to Figures 9-3 and 9-4):

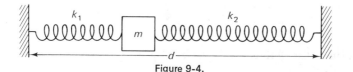

Figure 9-4.

(a)  Briefly explain why it is *not* necessary for $d = l_1 + l_2$.
(b)  What position of the mass would be called the equilibrium position of the mass? If both springs are identical, where should the equilibrium position be? Show that your formula is in agreement.
(c)  Show that the mass executes simple harmonic motion about its equilibrium position.
(d)  What is the period of oscillation?
(e)  How does the period of oscillation depend on $d$?

**9.4.** Suppose that a mass $m$ were attached to two springs in **parallel** (refer to Figs. 9-3 and 9-5):

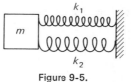

Figure 9-5.

(a)  What position of the mass would be called the equilibrium position of the mass?
(b)  Show that the mass executes simple harmonic motion about its equilibrium position.
(c)  What is the period of oscillation?
(d)  If the two springs were to be replaced by one spring, what would be the unstretched length and spring constant of the new spring such that the motion would be *equivalent*?

**9.5.** Suppose a mass $m$ were attached to two springs in **series** (refer to Figs. 9-3 and 9-6):

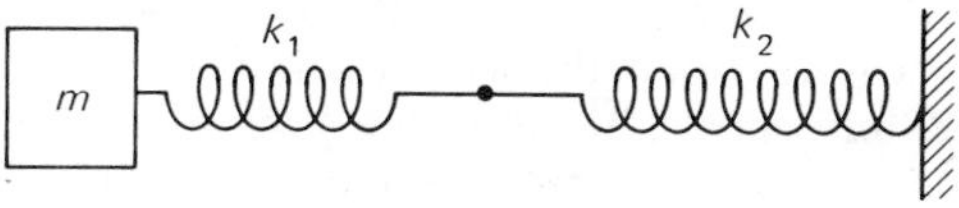

Figure 9-6.

Answer the same questions as in exercise 9.4a–d. [Hint: Apply Newton's law also to the massless point at which the two springs are connected.]

**9.6.** Consider two masses each of mass $m$ attached between two walls a distance $d$ apart (refer to Figs. 9-3 and 9-7):

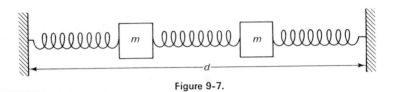

Figure 9-7.

Assume that all three springs have the same spring constant and unstretched length.

(a) Suppose that the left mass is a distance $x$ from the left wall and the right mass a distance $y$ from the right wall. What position of each mass would be called the equilibrium position of the system of masses?

(b) Show that the distance between the masses oscillates. What is the period of that oscillation?

(c) Show that $x-y$ executes simple harmonic motion with a period of oscillation different from (b).

(d) If the distance between the two masses remained constant, describe the motion that could take place both qualitatively and quantitatively.

(e) If $x = y$, describe the motion that could take place both qualitatively and quantitatively.

**9.7.** Consider a mass $m_1$ attached to a spring (of unstretched length $d$) and pulled by a constant force $F_2$, $F_2 = m_2 g$, as illustrated in Fig. 9-8.

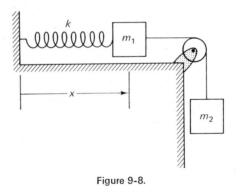

Figure 9-8.

(a) Suppose that the system is in equilibrium when $x = L$. Is $L > d$ or is $L < d$? If $L$ and $d$ are known, what is the spring constant $k$?

(b) If the system is at rest in the position $x = L$ and the mass $m_2$ is suddenly removed (for example, by cutting the string connecting $m_1$ and $m_2$), then what is the period and amplitude of oscillation of $m_1$?

# 10. *Friction*

Our mathematical model shows that the displacement of a simple spring-mass system continues to oscillate for all time. The amplitude of oscillation remains constant; the mass never stops completely nor does the amplitude even decay! Does this correspond to our experience? If we displaced the mass to the right, as shown in Fig. 10-1, then we would probably expect the mass to oscillate in the manner sketched in Fig. 10-2. We suspect that the mass oscillates around its equilibrium position with smaller and smaller magnitude until it stops.

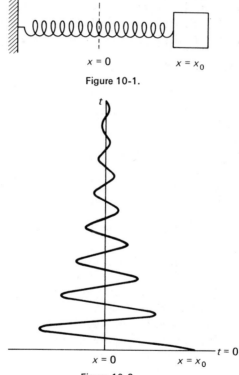

$x = 0$         $x = x_0$

**Figure 10-1.**

$x = 0$         $x = x_0$    $t = 0$

**Figure 10-2.**

Must we reject a mathematical model that yields perfect periodic motion? Absolutely not, for we can at least imagine a spring-mass system that exhibits *many* oscillations before it finally appears to significantly decay. In this case the mathematical model of a spring-mass system,

$$m \frac{d^2x}{dt^2} = -kx,$$

is a good approximation *for times that are not particularly long*. Furthermore, the importance of simple harmonic motion is in its aid in understanding more complicated periodic motion.

How can we improve our model to account for the experimental observation that the amplitude of the mass decays? Perhaps when the restoring force was approximated by Hooke's law, the possibility of decay was eliminated. However, in later sections we will show that this is not the case as the equation $m(d^2x/dt^2) = -f(x)$, representing any restoring force, never has oscillatory solutions that decay in time.

In order to account for the observed decay, we must include other forces. What causes the amplitude of the oscillation to diminish? Let us conjecture that there is a **resistive** force, that is, a force preventing motion. When the spring is moving to the right, then there is a force exerted to the left, as shown in Fig. 10-3, resisting the motion of the mass. Figure 10-4 shows that when the spring is moving to the left, then there is a force exerted to the right.

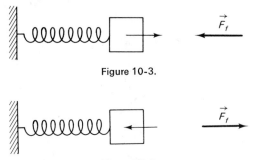

Figure 10-3.

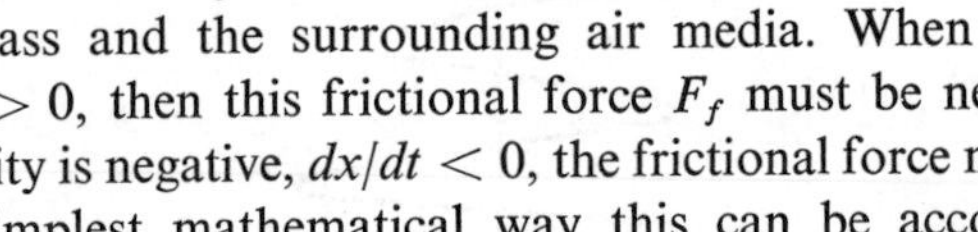

Figure 10-4.

For example, we can imagine this kind of force resulting from the "friction" between the mass and the surrounding air media. When the velocity is positive, $dx/dt > 0$, then this frictional force $F_f$ must be negative, $F_f < 0$. When the velocity is negative, $dx/dt < 0$, the frictional force must be positive, $F_f > 0$. The simplest mathematical way this can be accomplished is to assume that the frictional force is linearly dependent on the velocity:

$$F_f = -c\frac{dx}{dt}$$

(10.1)

where $c$ is a *positive* constant ($c > 0$) referred to as the friction coefficient. This force-velocity relationship is called a **linear damping force**; a damped oscillation meaning the same as an oscillation which decays. The accuracy of this assumed form of the force-velocity relationship should be verified experimentally. Here we claim that in some situations (but certainly not all) this is a good approximate expression for the force resulting from the resistance between an object and its surrounding fluid (liquid or gas) media (especially if the velocities are not too large). Independent forces add vectorially; hence, the differential equation describing a spring-mass system with a linear damping force and a linear restoring force is

$$m\frac{d^2x}{dt^2} = -kx - c\frac{dx}{dt}$$

or equivalently

$$\boxed{m\frac{d^2x}{dt^2} + c\frac{dx}{dt} + kx = 0.}$$ (10.2)

The force corresponding to the friction between a spring-mass system and a table, illustrated in Fig. 10-5, does not act in the way previously described, $F_f \neq -c(dx/dt)$. Instead, experiments indicate that once the mass is moving

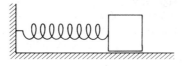

Figure 10-5.

the friction force is resistive but has a magnitude which is approximately constant independent of the velocity. We model this experimental result by stating

$$F_f = \begin{cases} \gamma & \text{for } dx/dt < 0 \\ -\gamma & \text{for } dx/dt < 0, \end{cases}$$ (10.3)

as sketched in Fig. 10-6 (see exercise 10.4). $\gamma$ depends on the roughness of the surface (and the weight of the mass). In later sections exercises will discuss the mathematical solution of problems involving this type of friction, called

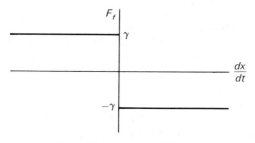

Figure 10-6  Coulomb friction.

**Coulomb friction**. However, in this text for the most part, we will limit our discussion to linear damping,

$$F_f = -c\frac{dx}{dt}.$$

# EXERCISES

**10.1.** Suppose that an experimentally observed frictional force is approximated by $F_f = \alpha(dx/dt)^3$, where $\alpha$ is a constant.
  (a)  What is the sign of $\alpha$?
  (b)  What is the dimension of $\alpha$?
  (c)  Show that the resulting differential equation is nonlinear.

**10.2.** From the differential equation for a spring-mass system with linear damping, show that $x = 0$ is the only equilibrium position of the mass.

**10.3.** What is the dimension of the constant $c$ defined for linear damping?

**10.4.** Consider Coulomb friction, equation 10.3.
  (a)  What is the sign of $\gamma$?
  (b)  What is the dimension of $\gamma$?
  (c)  Assume that if $dx/dt = 0$, then $F_f$ could be any value such that $|F_f| \leq \gamma$. What values of $x$ are then equilibrium positions of the spring-mass system?

**10.5.** Assume the same form of friction as in exercise 10.4. If initially $x = x_0 > 0$ and the velocity is $v_0 > 0$, then at what time does the mass of a spring-mass system first stop moving to the right? Will the mass continue to move after that time?

**10.6.** In some problems *both* linear damping and Coulomb friction occur. In this case, sketch the total frictional force as a function of the velocity.

**10.7.** In certain physical situations the damping force is proportional to the velocity squared, known as **Newtonian damping**. In this case show that

$$m\frac{d^2x}{dt^2} = -kx - \alpha\frac{dx}{dt}\left|\frac{dx}{dt}\right|,$$

where $\alpha > 0$.

**10.8.** If gravity is approximated by a constant and if the frictional force is proportional to the velocity, show that a free-falling body (i.e., no restoring force) approaches a **terminal** velocity. [You may wish to think about this effect for raindrops, meteorites, or parachutes. An excellent brief discussion is given by Dickinson, *Differential Equations, Theory and Use in Time and Motion*, Reading, Mass.: Addison-Wesley, 1972.]

**10.9.** A particle not connected to a spring, moving in a straight line, is subject to a *retardation* force of magnitude $\beta(dx/dt)^n$, with $\beta > 0$.
  (a)  Show that if $0 < n < 1$, the particle will come to rest in a finite time. How far will the particle travel, and when will it stop?

   (b)   What happens if $n = 1$?
   (c)   What happens if $1 < n < 2$?
   (d)   What happens if $n > 2$?

**10.10.**   Consider Fig. 10-7, which shows a glass of mass $m$ starting at $x = 0$ and sliding on a table of length $H$:

Figure 10-7.

   (a)   For what initial velocities $v_0$ will the glass fall off the table on the right if the only force is Coulomb friction, equation 10.3?
   (b)   Suppose that the frictional force instead is

$$F_f = \begin{cases} -\gamma - c\dfrac{dx}{dt} & \text{if } \dfrac{dx}{dt} > 0 \\[2ex] \gamma - c\dfrac{dx}{dt} & \text{if } \dfrac{dx}{dt} < 0. \end{cases}$$

   Describe physically what $F_f$ represents. Answer the same question as in part (a).
   (c)   Compare the results of parts (a) and (b).

# 11.   Oscillations of a Damped System

A spring-mass system with no forces other than a spring force and friction is governed by

$$m\frac{d^2x}{dt^2} + c\frac{dx}{dt} + kx = 0. \qquad (11.1)$$

It must be verified that solutions to this equation behave in a manner consistent with our observations. If this is not true then perhaps a spring-mass system decays as a result of forces other than a linear damping force.

   In order to solve a constant coefficient homogeneous ordinary differential equation recall that the two linearly independent solutions "almost always" can be written in the form of exponentials $e^{rt}$, where $r$ satisfies the **characteris-**

**tic equation** obtained by direct substitution,

$$mr^2 + cr + k = 0. \qquad (11.2)$$

The two roots of this equation are

$$r = \frac{-c \pm \sqrt{c^2 - 4mk}}{2m}. \qquad (11.3)$$

From a dimensional point of view, this shows that $c^2$ and $mk$ must have the same dimensions (as you can easily verify). The three cases $c^2 \gtreqless 4mk$ must be distinguished. A different form of the general solution corresponds to each case, since the roots are respectively real and unequal, real and equal, and complex.

## EXERCISES

**11.1.** Show that $c^2$ has the same dimension as $mk$.

**11.2.** What dimension should the roots of the characteristic equation have? Verify that the roots have this dimension.

## 12.  *Underdamped Oscillations*

If $c^2 < 4mk$, then the coefficient of friction is small; the damping force is not particularly large. We call this the **underdamped** case. In this case, the roots of the characteristic equation are complex conjugates of each other (see equation 11.3)

$$r = -\frac{c}{2m} \pm i\omega,$$

where

$$\omega = \frac{\sqrt{4mk - c^2}}{2m} = \sqrt{\frac{k}{m} - \frac{c^2}{4m^2}}.$$

Thus the general solution of the differential equation (11.1) is

$$x = ae^{[(-c/2m)+i\omega]t} + be^{[(-c/2m)-i\omega]t}.$$

By factoring $e^{-ct/2m}$, we see

$$x = e^{-ct/2m}(ae^{i\omega t} + be^{-i\omega t}).$$

Recalling that an arbitrary linear combination of $e^{i\omega t}$ and $e^{-i\omega t}$ is equivalent to an arbitrary linear combination of $\cos \omega t$ and $\sin \omega t$, we observe that the motion of a linearly damped spring-mass system in the underdamped case $(c^2 < 4mk)$ is described by

$$x = e^{-ct/2m}(c_1 \cos \omega t + c_2 \sin \omega t)$$

or

$$\boxed{x = Ae^{-ct/2m} \sin (\omega t + \phi_0).} \qquad (12.1)$$

A sketch of the solution is most easily accomplished using the latter form. The solution is the product of an exponential and a sinusoidal function (each sketched in Fig. 12-1). At the maximum value of the sinusoidal function,

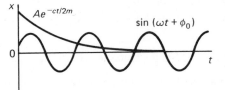

Figure 12-1.

$x$ equals the exponential alone, while at the minimum value of the sinusoidal function, $x$ equals minus the exponential. Thus we first sketch the exponential $Ae^{-ct/2m}$ and its negative $-Ae^{-ct/2m}$ in dashed lines. Periodically at the "$x$'s" the solution lies on the two exponential curves drawn in Fig. 12-2 (exactly where depends on the phase $\phi_0$):

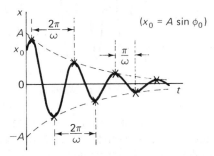

Figure 12-2   Underdamped oscillation.

Halfway between the marks, the function is zero. It varies smoothly throughout. Thus in the figure we sketch in a solid line the motion of a spring-mass system in the slightly damped case*. The exponential $Ae^{-ct/2m}$ is called the amplitude of the oscillation. Thus the amplitude exponentially decays. Indeed this seems quite similar to what we expect to observe in the case of a

---

*Although the zeroes are easy to locate, the maxima and minima are not halfway between the appropriate zeroes.

spring-mass system with **sufficiently small friction**. However, the mass never absolutely stops.

As long as there is friction ($c > 0$), no matter how small, it cannot be ignored as the amplitude of the oscillation will diminish in time only with friction. In this case though the solution is not exactly periodic, we can speak of an approximate circular frequency

$$\omega = \sqrt{\frac{k}{m} - \frac{c^2}{4m^2}}. \tag{12.2}$$

Notice this expression for the frequency reduces to the frictionless value if there is no friction, $c = 0$, $\omega = \sqrt{k/m}$.

We will show that for some time the solution behaves as though there were no friction if

$$c^2 \ll 4mk \qquad \text{(read "much less than")}.$$

The friction of a spring-mass system is said to be **negligible** if during many oscillations the amplitude remains approximately the same as is represented in Fig. 12-3.

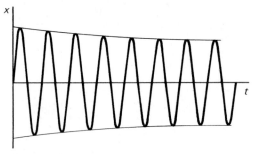

Figure 12-3    Oscillation with negligible damping.

It is equivalent to say the friction is negligible if after one "period" the amplitude of the oscillation has remained approximately constant. Thus we wish to determine the amplitude of oscillation after one period. The period of oscillation follows from equations 12.1 and 12.2 and is

$$T = \frac{2\pi}{\sqrt{k/m - c^2/4m^2}} = \frac{2\pi}{\sqrt{k/m[1 - (c^2/4mk)]}}.$$

However if $c^2 \ll 4mk$, we can approximate the period by its frictionless value:

$$T \approx \frac{2\pi}{\sqrt{k/m}} \qquad \text{(read "approximately equals")}.$$

This is the first term in a Taylor series expansion of the period.* In this manner we can roughly estimate the amplitude of oscillation after one period,

$$Ae^{-ct/2m} \approx Ae^{-2\pi[c/2m\sqrt{(k/m)}]} = Ae^{-2\pi(c^2/4mk)^{1/2}}.$$

Since $e^{-x}$ approximately equals 1 if $x$ is small, it follows that if $c^2 \ll 4mk$, then the exponential has not decayed much in one "period."

Using a numerical criteria, the damping might be said to be negligible if after one "period" the mass returns to at least 95 percent of its original position, that is if

$$e^{-2\pi(c^2/4mk)^{1/2}} \geq .95.$$

Taking the natural logarithm of both sides, yields

$$-2\pi\left(\frac{c^2}{4mk}\right)^{1/2} \geq \log(.95)$$

or

$$\frac{c^2}{4mk} \leq \left[\frac{-\log(.95)}{2\pi}\right]^2.$$

The natural logarithm of .95 can be obtained from a mathematical table. However, the natural logarithm near 1 may be accurately approximated using the Taylor series formula

$$\log(1 - x) \approx -x.$$

Using this formula, damping is negligible (with a 95 percent criteria) if

$$\frac{c^2}{4mk} \leq \left(\frac{.05}{2\pi}\right)^2 = \frac{.0025}{4\pi^2} \approx .00006.$$

This calculation has been simplified using the rough numerical approximation $\pi^2 \approx 10$, since $\pi^2 = 9.8696 \ldots$.

# EXERCISES

**12.1.**  If friction is sufficiently small ($c^2 < 4mk$), it has been shown that

$$x = Ae^{-ct/2m}\sin(\omega t + \phi_0),$$

where

$$\omega = \sqrt{\frac{k}{m} - \frac{c^2}{4m^2}}.$$

(a)  Show that $\omega = \sqrt{\frac{k}{m}}\sqrt{1 - \frac{c^2}{4mk}}$.

(b)  Determine the first few terms of the Taylor series for small $z$ of $(1 - z)^{1/2}$. [Hint: Use the binomial expansion (see page 89).]

---

*Improvements to this approximation of the period are suggested in the exercises.

(c)   Using the result of (b), improve the approximation

$$\omega \approx \sqrt{\frac{k}{m}} \qquad \text{valid if } c^2 \ll 4mk.$$

**12.2.**   At what time has the amplitude of oscillation of a spring-mass system with negligible friction decayed to $1/e$ of its original value? Does this time depend in a reasonable way on $k$, $m$, and $c$?

**12.3.**   Show that the ratio of two consecutive local maximum displacements is a constant.

**12.4.**   If $c < 0$, the force is called a negative friction force.
(a)   In this case, show that $x \longrightarrow \infty$ as $t \longrightarrow \infty$.
(b)   If in addition $c^2 < 4mk$, then roughly sketch the solution.

**12.5.**   Determine the motion of an underdamped spring-mass system which is initially at its equilibrium position ($x = 0$) with velocity $v_0$. What is the amplitude of the oscillation?

**12.6.**   Show that the local maximum or minimum for the displacement of an underdamped oscillation does *not* occur halfway between the times at which the mass passes its equilibrium position. However, show that the time period between successive local maxima (or minima) is constant. What is that period?

**12.7.**   Consider a spring-mass system with linear friction (but without gravity). Suppose that there is an additional force, $B \cos \omega_0 t$, a periodic forcing function. Assume that $B$ and $\omega_0$ are known.
(a)   If the coefficient of friction is zero (i.e., $c = 0$), then determine the general solution of the differential equation. Show that the solution is oscillatory if $\omega_0 \neq \sqrt{k/m}$. Show that the solution algebraically grows in time if $\omega_0 = \sqrt{k/m}$ (this is called **resonance** and occurs if the forcing frequency $\omega_0$ is the same as the natural frequency $\sqrt{k/m}$).
(b)   If $c^2 < 4mk$, show that the general solution consists of the sum of oscillatory terms (of frequency $\omega_0$) and terms which exponentially decay in time. Thus for sufficiently large times the motion is accurately approximated by an oscillation of constant amplitude. What is that amplitude? Note it is independent of initial conditions.
(c)   If $c^2 \ll 4mk$, show that for large times the oscillation approximately obeys the following statements: If the forcing frequency is less than the natural frequency ($\omega_0 < \sqrt{k/m}$), then the mass oscillates "in phase" with the forcing function (i.e., when the forcing function is a maximum, the stretching of the spring is a maximum, and vice versa). On the other hand, if the forcing frequency is greater than the natural frequency ($\omega_0 > \sqrt{k/m}$), then the mass oscillates "180 degrees out of phase" with the forcing function (i.e., when the forcing function is a maximum, the compression of the spring is a maximum and vice versa).
(d)   In part (b) the ratio of the amplitude of oscillation of the mass to the amplitude of the forcing function is called the **response**. If $c^2 \ll 4mk$, then at what frequency is the response largest?

**12.8.**   Consider the effect of striking the mass of a spring-mass system that is initially at rest. The problem is to solve

$$m\frac{d^2x}{dt^2} + c\frac{dx}{dt} + kx = f(t),$$

subject to the initial conditions

$$x(0) = x_0$$

$$\frac{dx}{dt}(0) = 0,$$

where $f(t)$ is the force due to the striking. Assume that $f(t)$ is approximately constant for some short length of time $\Delta t$, and then zero thereafter:

$$f(t) = \begin{cases} f_0 & 0 \le t \le \Delta t \\ 0 & t > \Delta t. \end{cases}$$

(a) Show that if $c^2 < 4mk$, then

$$x = \frac{f_0}{k} + \left(x_0 - \frac{f_0}{k}\right)e^{-ct/2m}\left(\cos \omega_0 t + \frac{c}{2m\omega_0}\sin \omega_0 t\right)$$

for $0 \le t \le \Delta t$.

(b) Calculate the position and velocity of the mass at $t = \Delta t$.

(c) Assume that the force is large for the short length of time $\Delta t$, i.e., as $\Delta t \to 0$, $f_0 \to \infty$. Further assume that as $\Delta t \to 0$, $f_0 \Delta t \to I$ (called the **impulse**). Calculate the limit of part (b) as $\Delta t \to 0$, and show that as $\Delta t \to 0$,

$$x(\Delta t) \longrightarrow x_0$$

$$\frac{dx}{dt}(\Delta t) \longrightarrow \frac{I}{m}.$$

(d) Briefly explain the following conclusion: the effect of an impulsive force is only to instantaneously increase the velocity by $I/m$. This explains a method by which a nonzero initial velocity occurs.

**12.9.** Reconsider exercise 12.8 for an alternate derivation.

(a) Show that for $0 \le t \le \Delta t$,

$$m\frac{dx}{dt} + cx - cx_0 + k\int_0^t x\, d\bar{t} = f_0 t.$$

(b) If $\Delta t$ is small, show that

$$m\frac{dx}{dt}(\Delta t) \approx f_0\, \Delta t.$$

[Hint: Use Taylor expansions.]

(c) If (as before) $\Delta t \to 0$ and $f_0 \to \infty$ such that $f_0\, \Delta t \to I$, show that the new initial conditions after the impulse are $x(0) = x_0$ and $(dx/dt)(0) = I/m$.

# 13.  Overdamped and Critically Damped Oscillations

On the other hand, if the **friction is sufficiently large**, then

$$c^2 > 4mk,$$

and we call the system **overdamped**. The motion of the mass is no longer a decaying oscillation. The solution of equation 11.1 is

$$x = c_1 e^{r_1 t} + c_2 e^{r_2 t}, \qquad (13.1)$$

where $r_1$ and $r_2$ are real and both negative,

$$r_1 = \frac{-c + \sqrt{c^2 - 4mk}}{2m}$$

$$r_2 = \frac{-c - \sqrt{c^2 - 4mk}}{2m}.$$

If the friction is sufficiently large, we should expect that the mass decays to its equilibrium position quite quickly. Exercise 13.1 shows that it does not oscillate. Instead, the mass either decays to its equilibrium position as seen in Fig. 13-1(a) or (b), or it shoots past the equilibrium position exactly once before returning monotonically towards the equilibrium position as seen in Fig. 13-1(c):

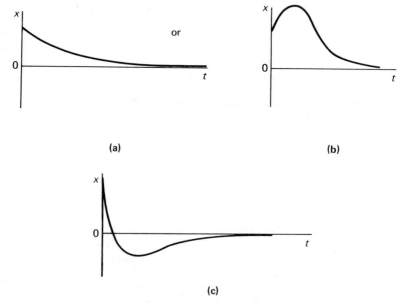

(a)

(b)

(c)

Figure 13-1   Overdamped oscillations.

It cannot cross the equilibrium position more than once. The mass crosses its equilibrium position only if the initial velocity is sufficiently negative (assuming that the initial position is positive).

When $c^2 = 4mk$, the spring-mass system is said to be **critically damped**. Mathematically $c^2 = 4mk$ requires a separate discussion since both exponential solutions become the same. However, from a physical point of view this case is *insignificant*. This is because the quantities $c$, $m$, and $k$ are all experimentally measured quantities—there is no possibility that these measurements could be such that $c^2 = 4mk$ exactly. Any small deviation from equality will result in either of the previous two cases. For mathematical completeness, the solution in this case is

$$x = e^{-ct/2m}(At + B). \qquad (13.2)$$

Although there is an algebraic growth $t$, the solution still returns to its equilibrium position as $t \to \infty$ since the exponential decay is much stronger than an algebraic growth. A sketch would indicate no qualitative difference between this case and the overdamped case. In particular, the solution may go through the equilibrium position once at most.

# EXERCISES

**13.1.** Assume that friction is sufficiently large ($c^2 > 4mk$).
 (a) Show that the mass either decays to its equilibrium position (without passing through it), or that the mass shoots past its equilibrium position exactly once before returning monotonically towards its equilibrium position.
 (b) If the initial position $x_0$ of the mass is positive, then show that the mass crosses its equilibrium position only if the initial velocity is sufficiently negative. What is the value of this critical velocity? Does it depend in a reasonable way on $x_0$, $c$, $m$, and $k$?

**13.2.** Do exercise 13.1 for the critically damped case $c^2 = 4mk$.

**13.3.** Assume that friction is extremely large ($c^2 \gg 4mk$).
 (a) If the mass is initially at $x = 0$ with a positive velocity, then roughly sketch the solution you expect by physical reasoning.
 (b) Estimate the characteristic roots if $c^2 \gg 4mk$.
 (c) Based on part (b), sketch the approximate solution. What is the approximate maximum amplitude?

**13.4.** Assume that friction is extremely large ($c^2 \gg 4mk$).
 (a) If the mass is initially at $x = x_0$ with velocity $v_0$, then approximate the solution. [Hint: Use the result of exercise 13.3b.]
 (b) Solve the differential equation governing the spring-mass system (with friction) if the mass term can be neglected. Show that the two initial

conditions cannot be satisfied. Why not? Applying which one of the two initial conditions yields a result consistent with (a)? Show that the solutions obtained in (a) and (b) are quite similar except for small times.

(c)   Solve the differential equation governing the spring-mass system (with friction) if the restoring force term can be neglected. Show that the two initial conditions can be satisfied. Show that this solution does not approximate very well the solution to (a) for all time.

**13.5.**   Assume that $c^2 > 4mk$.
(a)   Solve the initial value problem, that is, at $t = 0$, $x = x_0$ and $dx/dt = v_0$.
(b)   Take the limit of the solution obtained in (a) as $c^2 \longrightarrow 4mk$. Show that the limiting solution is the same as for the case $c^2 = 4mk$. [Hint: Let $r_1 \longrightarrow r_2$.]

**13.6.**   (a)   Using a computer, determine the motion of an overdamped spring-mass system (let $m = 1$, $k = 1$, $c = 3$), satisfying the initial conditions $x(0) = 1$ and $(dx/dt)(0) = v_0$ for various *negative* initial velocities.
(b)   Show that the mass crosses its equilibrium position only if the initial velocity is sufficiently negative.
(c)   Estimate this critical velocity.
(d)   Compare your result to exercise 13.1b.

**13.7.**   Consider a vertical spring-mass system with linear friction. Suppose two additional forces are present, gravity and any other force $f_1(t)$ only depending on time. Show that the motion is the same as that which would occur without gravity, but with a spring of greater length with the same spring constant.

**13.8.**   Assume

$$m \frac{d^2x}{dt^2} + c \frac{dx}{dt} + kx = f(t)$$

and also assume a particular solution is known. Show that the difference between the exact solution and the particular solution tends towards zero as $t \longrightarrow \infty$ (if $c > 0$) independent of the initial conditions.

# 14.   A Pendulum

We have investigated in some depth a spring-mass system which is governed by a linear differential equation. We may now be wondering what effect the neglected nonlinear terms may have. To give us additional motivation to analyze nonlinear problems, we now discuss a common physical system whose mathematical formulation results in a specific nonlinear equation.

Consider a pendulum of length $L$, shown on the next page in Fig. 14-1. At one end the pendulum is attached to a fixed point and is free to rotate about it. A mass $m$ is attached at the other end as illustrated below. We know from observations that a pendulum oscillates in a manner at least qualitatively

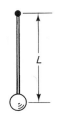

Figure 14-1   A pendulum.

similar to a spring-mass system. To make the problem easier, we assume the mass *m* is large enough so that, as an approximation, we state that all the mass is contained at the bob of the pendulum (that is the mass of the rigid shaft of the pendulum is assumed negligible). Again we apply Newton's second law of motion,

$$\vec{F} = m\vec{a}.$$

The pendulum moves in two dimensions (unlike the spring-mass system which was constrained to move in one dimension). However, a pendulum also involves only one degree of freedom as it is constrained to move along the circumference of a circle of radius *L*. This is represented in Fig. 14-2.

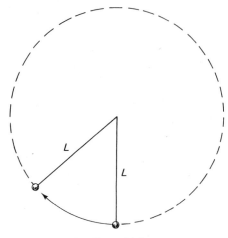

Figure 14-2.

Consequently, we will now develop the form Newton's law takes in polar coordinates. In two or three dimensions, Newton's law for a mass *m* is

$$m\frac{d^2\vec{x}}{dt^2} = \vec{F},$$

where $\vec{x}$ is the position vector of the mass (the vector from the origin to the mass). (In 3-dimensional rectangular coordinates, $\vec{x} = x\hat{i} + y\hat{j} + z\hat{k}$, the acceleration is given by

$$\frac{d^2\vec{x}}{dt^2} = \frac{d^2x}{dt^2}\hat{i} + \frac{d^2y}{dt^2}\hat{j} + \frac{d^2z}{dt^2}\hat{k},$$

since $\hat{i}, \hat{j}, \hat{k}$ are unit vectors which not only have fixed magnitude but also have fixed directions.) In polar coordinates (centered at the fixed vertex of the pendulum), the position vector is pointed outward with length $L$,

$$\vec{x} = L\hat{r}, \tag{14.1}$$

where $\hat{r}$ is the radial unit vector. The polar angle $\theta$ is introduced such that $\theta = 0$ corresponds to the pendulum in its "natural" position.* (See Fig. 14-3.)

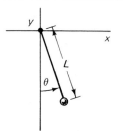

Figure 14-3.

$L$ is constant since the pendulum does not vary in length. Thus

$$\boxed{\frac{d^2\vec{x}}{dt^2} = L\frac{d^2\hat{r}}{dt^2}.} \tag{14.2}$$

However, although the magnitude of $\hat{r}$ is constant ($|\hat{r}| = 1$), its direction varies in space. To determine the change in the radial unit vector $\hat{r}$, we express it in terms of the Cartesian unit vectors. From Fig. 14-5

$$\boxed{\hat{r} = \sin\theta\,\hat{i} - \cos\theta\,\hat{j}.} \tag{14.3a}$$

Note the minus sign. You can easily verify that $\hat{r}$ is a unit vector. The $\theta$-unit vector is perpendicular to $\hat{r}$ and of unit length (and is in the direction of

---

*Be careful—this definition of the polar angle differs from the standard one shown in Fig. 14-4.

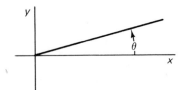

Figure 14-4.

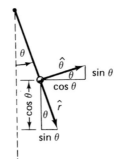

Figure 14-5   Radial and angular unit vectors.

increasing $\theta$). Thus also from Fig. 14-5:

$$\hat{\theta} = \cos\theta\,\hat{i} + \sin\theta\,\hat{j}. \qquad\qquad (14.3b)$$

In order to calculate the acceleration vector $d^2\vec{x}/dt^2$, the velocity vector $d\vec{x}/dt$ must first be calculated:

$$\frac{d\vec{x}}{dt} = L\frac{d\hat{r}}{dt} + \frac{dL}{dt}\hat{r}.$$

Since $L$ is a constant for a pendulum, $dL/dt = 0$, and hence

$$\frac{d\vec{x}}{dt} = L\frac{d\hat{r}}{dt}.$$

From equation 14.3a,

$$\frac{d\hat{r}}{dt} = \frac{d\theta}{dt}(\cos\theta\,\hat{i} + \sin\theta\,\hat{j}),$$

which we note in general is more simply written as

$$\frac{d\hat{r}}{dt} = \frac{d\theta}{dt}\hat{\theta}. \qquad\qquad (14.4a)$$

Similarly,

$$\frac{d\hat{\theta}}{dt} = -\frac{d\theta}{dt}\hat{r}. \qquad\qquad (14.4b)$$

Thus the velocity vector is in the direction of $\hat{\theta}$,

$$\frac{d\vec{x}}{dt} = L\frac{d\theta}{dt}\hat{\theta}.$$

The magnitude of the velocity is $L(d\theta/dt)$, if motion lies along the circumference of a circle. Why is it obvious that if $L$ is constant, then the velocity is in the $\theta$ direction? [Answer: If $L$ is constant, then in a short length of time the position vector has changed only a little, but the change must be in the $\theta$ direction (see Fig. 14-6). In fact we see geometrically that

$$\frac{d\vec{x}}{dt} \approx \frac{\vec{x}(t + \Delta t) - \vec{x}(t)}{\Delta t} \approx \frac{L\Delta\theta\,\hat{\theta}}{\Delta t} \approx L\frac{d\theta}{dt}\hat{\theta}. \Big]$$

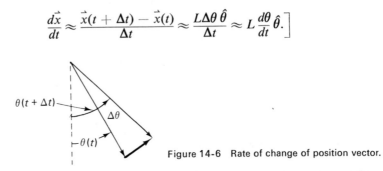

Figure 14-6   Rate of change of position vector.

The $\theta$ component of the velocity is the distance $L$ times the **angular velocity** $d\theta/dt$. The acceleration vector is obtained as the derivative of the velocity vector:

$$\frac{d^2\vec{x}}{dt^2} = L\frac{d}{dt}\Big(\frac{d\theta}{dt}\hat{\theta}\Big) = L\Big[\frac{d^2\theta}{dt^2}\hat{\theta} - \Big(\frac{d\theta}{dt}\Big)^2\hat{r}\Big].$$

The angular component of the acceleration is $L(d^2\theta/dt^2)$. It exists only if the angle is accelerating. If $L$ is constant, the radial component of the acceleration, $-L(d\theta/dt)^2$, is always directed inwards. It is called the centripetal acceleration and will occur even if the angle is only steadily increasing (i.e., even if the angular velocity $d\theta/dt$ is constant).

For *any* forces $\vec{F}$, when a mass is constrained to move in a circle, Newton's law implies

$$mL\frac{d^2\theta}{dt^2}\hat{\theta} - mL\Big(\frac{d\theta}{dt}\Big)^2\hat{r} = \vec{F}. \tag{14.5}$$

For a pendulum, what are the forces? Clearly, there is a gravitational force $-mg\hat{j}$, which should be expressed in terms of polar coordinates. From the definitions of $\hat{r}$ and $\hat{\theta}$, equation 14.3,

$$\begin{array}{l} \hat{i} = \phantom{-}\hat{r}\sin\theta + \hat{\theta}\cos\theta \\ \hat{j} = -\hat{r}\cos\theta + \hat{\theta}\sin\theta. \end{array} \tag{14.6}$$

Thus the gravitional force,

$$m\vec{g} = -mg\hat{j} = mg\cos\theta\,\hat{r} - mg\sin\theta\,\hat{\theta}.$$

Perhaps this is more readily seen by breaking the direction $-\hat{j}$ into its polar components, as is done in Fig. 14-7.

Are there any other forces on the mass? If there were no other forces, then the mass would not move along the circle. The mass is held by the rigid shaft of the pendulum, which exerts a force $-T\hat{r}$ towards the origin of as yet

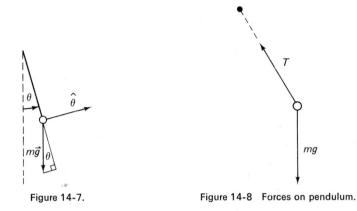

Figure 14-7.                Figure 14-8   Forces on pendulum.

unknown magnitude $T$ (and, as will be shown, of nonconstant magnitude). The forces on the bob of the pendulum are illustrated in Fig. 14-8. This results in motion along the circle. Thus

$$mL\frac{d^2\theta}{dt^2}\hat{\theta} - mL\left(\frac{d\theta}{dt}\right)^2\hat{r} = mg\cos\theta\hat{r} - mg\sin\theta\,\hat{\theta} - T\hat{r}.$$

Each component of this vector force equation yields an ordinary differential equation:

$$mL\frac{d^2\theta}{dt^2} = -mg\sin\theta \qquad\qquad \textbf{(14.7a)}$$

$$-mL\left(\frac{d\theta}{dt}\right)^2 = mg\cos\theta - T. \qquad\qquad \textbf{(14.7b)}$$

(A two-dimensional vector equation is equivalent to two scalar equations.) $T$ could be obtained from the second equation (if desired, which it frequently isn't), after determining $\theta$ from the first equation. Equation 14.7a implies that the mass times the $\theta$ component of the acceleration must balance the $\theta$ component of the gravitational force.

The mass $m$ can be cancelled from both sides of equation 14.7a. Thus, the motion of the pendulum does not depend on the magnitude of the mass $m$ attached to the pendulum. Only varying the length $L$ (or $g$) will affect the motion. This qualitative fact has been determined even though we have not as yet solved the differential equation. Furthermore, only the ratio $g/L$ is important as from equation 14.7a

$$\frac{d^2\theta}{dt^2} = -\frac{g}{L}\sin\theta. \qquad\qquad \textbf{(14.8)}$$

(This is an advantageous procedure whenever possible in applied mathematics

—the determination of the important parameters. In fact for a spring-mass system, $m(d^2x/dt^2) = -kx$, it is not the two parameters $k$ and $m$ that are important, but only their ratio $k/m$, since $d^2x/dt^2 = -(k/m)x$. Again a conclusion is reached without solving the equation.)

The pendulum is governed by a nonlinear differential equation, equation 14.8, and hence is called a **nonlinear pendulum**. The restoring force $-mg \sin \theta$ does not depend linearly on $\theta$, the unknown! Nonlinear problems are usually considerably more difficult to solve than linear ones. Before pursuing this nonlinear problem (and others), we recall from calculus that for $\theta$ small,

$$\sin \theta \approx \theta.$$

Geometrically the functions $\sin \theta$ and $\theta$ are nearly identical for small $\theta$ ($\theta$ being the linearization of $\sin \theta$ around the origin as seen in Fig. 14-9):

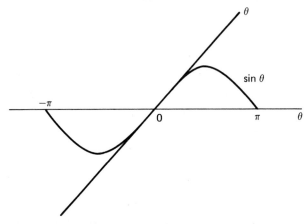

Figure 14-9   For $\theta$ small, $\theta$ approximates $\sin \theta$.

Using that approximation, the differential equation becomes

$$\frac{d^2\theta}{dt^2} = -\frac{g}{L}\theta \qquad\qquad \textbf{(14.9)}$$

called the equation of a **linearized pendulum**. This is the same type of differential equation as the one governing a linearized spring-mass system without friction. Hence a linearized pendulum also executes simple harmonic motion. The pendulum oscillates with circular frequency

$$\omega = \sqrt{\frac{g}{L}} \qquad\qquad \textbf{(14.10)}$$

and period $T = 2\pi\sqrt{L/g}$, *as long as $\theta$ is small*. This result can be checked as to its dimensional consistency. The effect of changing the length of the pendulum (or changing the magnitude of gravity) can be qualitatively and quantitatively determined immediately. Again the period of oscillation is independent of amplitude (as an approximation for small amplitude oscillations). Apparently this was first realized by Galileo, who observed the swinging of lamps suspended from long cords (i.e., a pendulum) in churches. You must remember that these observations were made before accurate clocks existed, and thus Galileo used his pulse to measure time!

In later sections we will investigate what happens if $\theta$ is *not* small.

# EXERCISES

**14.1.** Consider the differential equation of a pendulum. Show that the period of *small amplitude* oscillations (around its natural position) is $T = 2\pi\sqrt{L/g}$. Briefly discuss the dependence of the period on $L$, $g$, and $m$.

**14.2.** Consider a mass $m$ located at $\vec{x} = x\hat{i} + y\hat{j}$, where $x$ and $y$ are unknown functions of time. The mass is free to move in the $x$–$y$ plane without gravity (i.e., it is *not* connected to the origin via the shaft of a pendulum) and hence the distance $L$ from the origin may vary with time.
   (a) Using polar coordinates as introduced in Sec. 14, what is the velocity vector?
   (b) Show that the acceleration vector $\vec{a} = (d^2/dt^2)\vec{x}$ is

$$\vec{a} = \left(L\frac{d^2\theta}{dt^2} + 2\frac{dL}{dt}\frac{d\theta}{dt}\right)\hat{\theta} + \left(\frac{d^2L}{dt^2} - L\left(\frac{d\theta}{dt}\right)^2\right)\hat{r}.$$

   (c) If $L$ is independent of $t$ and $d\theta/dt$ is constant, sketch the trajectories. What direction is $\vec{a}$. Is this reasonable?
   (d) If $\theta$ is independent of $t$, sketch possible trajectories. From part (b), show that the acceleration is in the correct direction.

**14.3.** Consider a mass $m$ located at $\vec{x} = x\hat{i} + y\hat{j}$ and only acted upon by a force in the direction of $\hat{r}$ with magnitude $-g(L)$ depending only on $L \equiv |\vec{x}|$, called a **central force**.
   (a) Derive the differential equations governing the angle $\theta$ and the distance $L$ [Hint: Use the equation for $\vec{a}$ determined in exercise 14.2b].
   (b) Show that $L^2(d\theta/dt)$ is constant [Hint: Differentiate $L^2(d\theta/dt)$ with respect to $t$]. This law is called **Conservation of Angular Momentum.**

**14.4.** A particle's angular momentum around a fixed point is defined as a vector, the cross-product of the position vector and the momentum:

$$\vec{x} \times m\frac{d\vec{x}}{dt}$$

where $\vec{x}$ is the position vector relative to the fixed point. If all forces are in the direction of the fixed point (called **central forces**, see exericse 14.3), then show that angular momentum is conserved, i.e., show

$$\frac{d}{dt}\left(\vec{x} \times m\frac{d\vec{x}}{dt}\right) = 0.$$

**14.5.** Find an approximate expression for the radial force exerted by the shaft of the pendulum in the case of small oscillations. Show that the tension $T \approx mg$. Is this reasonable? Improve that approximation, and show that the radial force is *not* constant in time.

**14.6.** Consider a *swinging spring* of unstretched length $L_0$ and of spring constant $k$ attached to a mass $m$ as illustrated in Fig. 14-10.

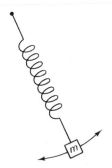

Figure 14-10   A swinging spring.

Show that the only force in addition to gravity acting on the mass is $-k(L - L_0)\hat{r}$. Derive the differential equations governing the motion of the mass. [Hint: Use the result of exercise 14.2].

**14.7.** One of **Kepler's laws of planetary motion** states that the radius vector drawn from the sun to a planet describes equal areas in equal times, that is, the rate of change of the area is a constant. Prove this using the result of exercise 14.3. [Hint: The differential area subtended is $dA = \frac{1}{2}L^2\,d\theta$ (Why?), and thus what is $dA/dt$?].

**14.8.** Newton knew an experimentally determined value of $g$, the radius of the earth, and the distance the moon is from the center of the earth. Using this information and assuming the moon moves in a circular orbit, estimate how long it takes the moon to go around the earth. [Hint: Recall $g = GM/r_0^2$]. Newton in the seventeenth century essentially used the preceeding ideas to help verify the inverse-square universal law of gravitation.

**14.9.** Consider an object resting on the equator. It obviously moves in a circle with a radius of approximately 4000 miles.
(a)   Estimate the velocity of the object.
(b)   There are two forces holding the object from moving radially: the force exerted by the surface of the earth and the gravitational force. Show that the radial acceleration of the object is much less than the gravitational acceleration.

**14.10.** Refer to exercise 14.9. Since most of you do not live at the equator, approximately calculate your present acceleration. In what direction is it?

**14.11.** From equation 14.3, show that $\hat{r}$ is perpendicular to $\hat{\theta}$.

**14.12.** Consider any nonconstant vector $\vec{f}$ of constant length. Show that $d\vec{f}/dt$ is perpendicular to $\vec{f}$.

**14.13.** Consider a pendulum whose length is varied in a prescribed manner, as shown in Fig. 14-11, i.e., $L = L(t)$ is known:

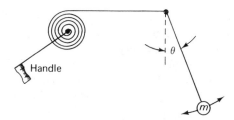

Figure 14-11   A variable length pendulum.

Derive the differential equation governing the angle $\theta$. [Hint: Use the result of exercise 14.2.]

**14.14.** Show that $d\hat{\theta}/dt = -\hat{r}(d\theta/dt)$.


# 15.   How Small is Small?

The nonlinear ordinary differential equation describing the motion of a pendulum was simplified to a linear one by using the approximation

$$\sin \theta \approx \theta.$$

Is this a good approximation? The Taylor series of $\sin \theta$,

$$\sin \theta = \theta - \frac{\theta^3}{3!} + \frac{\theta^5}{5!} - \frac{\theta^7}{7!} + \cdots,$$

is valid for all $\theta$. What error is introduced by neglecting all the nonlinear terms? An application of an extension of the mean value theorem (more easily remembered as the Taylor series with remainder*), yields

$$\sin \theta = \theta - \frac{\theta^3}{3!} \cos \bar{\theta},$$

---

*The formula for the Taylor series (with remainder) of $f(x)$ around $x = x_0$ is

$$f(x) = \sum_{n=0}^{N-1} \frac{f^{(n)}(x_0)}{n!}(x - x_0)^n + f^{(N)}(\bar{x})\frac{(x - x_0)^N}{N!},$$

where $\bar{x}$ is an intermediate point ($x_0 < \bar{x} < x$ if $x > x_0$), but $\bar{x}$ is otherwise unknown. The underlined expression is the first $N$ terms of the Taylor series. The remainder appears like the $N + 1$st term except that the $N$th derivative is evaluated at the unknown intermediate point $\bar{x}$ rather than at the point $x_0$. The above formula is valid as long as $f(x)$ is continuous in the interval and the derivatives of $f(x)$ through the $N$th derivative are also continuous.

where $\bar{\theta}$ is such that $0 < \bar{\theta} < \theta$, but $\bar{\theta}$ is otherwise unknown. The error $E$ in our approximation, $E = -(\theta^3/6) \cos \bar{\theta}$, is bounded by $\theta^3/6$,

$$|E| < \frac{\theta^3}{6},$$

since $|\cos \bar{\theta}| < 1$. (The percentage error is $\theta^2/6$.) At $\theta$ equal one radian, the error is at most 16 percent, (not too bad an approximation considering one radian is about 57° which is not a very small angle). At $\theta$ equal $\frac{1}{2}$ radian, the error is reduced to at most about 4 percent, yet even $\frac{1}{2}$ radian is not a particularly small angle. In fact, in Fig. 15-1 we compare $\theta$ to $\sin \theta$ using a set of tables. It is seen that $\sin \theta \approx \theta$ is a good approximation, even for angles that are not too small. However, we must still investigate whether the solution to the linear equation, $d^2\theta/dt^2 = -(g/L)\theta$, is a good approximation to the solution to the more difficult nonlinear equation, $d^2\theta/dt^2 = -(g/L) \sin \theta$! Approximate equations do not *always* have solutions that are a good approximation to the solution of the exact equation. As an oversimplified example we know that $(1000.5)\pi$ in some sense approximately equals $1000\pi$, but $\cos (1000\pi)$ is not a good approximation to $\cos (1000.5\pi)$, (since $\cos (1000\pi)$ $= 1$ and $\cos (1000.5\pi) = 0$).

| $\theta$ (degrees) | $\theta$ (radians) | $\sin \theta$ |
|:---:|:---:|:---:|
| 1 | 0.0174533 | 0.0174524 |
| 5 | 0.08726 | 0.08716 |
| 10 | 0.17453 | 0.17365 |
| 15 | 0.26179 | 0.25882 |
| 20 | 0.34907 | 0.34202 |
| 25 | 0.43633 | 0.42262 |
| 30 | 0.52360 | 0.50000 |
| 35 | 0.61087 | 0.57358 |
| 40 | 0.69813 | 0.64279 |

Figure 15-1.

# EXERCISES

**15.1.** For what angles is $\sin \theta \approx \theta$ a valid approximation with an error guaranteed to be less than 10 percent?

**15.2.** (a) Using the Taylor series with remainder, what is the maximum percent error that occurs when $\sin \theta$ is approximated by $\theta$ for $\theta = 30°$?

(b) For $\theta = 30°$, what is the actual percent error?

(c) Compare part (a) to part (b).

# 16.   A Dimensionless Time Variable

Returning to the equation of a nonlinear pendulum,

$$\frac{d^2\theta}{dt^2} = -\frac{g}{L}\sin\theta,$$

let us suppose that we need to compute solutions to this equation numerically. Initial conditions are needed to solve a differential equation on the computer. In general,

$$\theta(0) = \theta_0$$

$$\frac{d\theta}{dt}(0) = \Omega_0.$$

This suggests three parameters of significance in the calculation, $\theta_0$, $\Omega_0$, and $g/L$. To determine all solutions to the differential equation, it appears we must vary these *three* parameters. However, if time is measured in a certain way, then we will show that only two parameters are important. Let us **scale** the time $t$ by any constant time $Q$, by which we mean let

$$t = Q\tau.$$

Using the chain rule

$$\frac{d}{dt} = \frac{1}{Q}\frac{d}{d\tau},$$

yields the differential equation

$$\frac{d^2\theta}{d\tau^2} = -\frac{g}{L}Q^2\sin\theta,$$

to be solved with the modified initial conditions:

$$\theta(0) = \theta_0$$

$$\frac{d\theta}{d\tau}(0) = Q\Omega_0.$$

$Q$ is chosen such that there are less parameters necessary in the problem. For example, let $(g/L)Q^2 = 1$ or $Q = \sqrt{L/g}$, in which case

$$\boxed{\begin{aligned} &\frac{d^2\theta}{d\tau^2} = -\sin\theta \\[4pt] &\theta(0) = \theta_0 \\[4pt] &\frac{d\theta}{d\tau}(0) = \Omega_0\sqrt{\frac{L}{g}}. \end{aligned}}$$

$$(16.1)$$

This resulting problem has only two parameters of significance, $\theta_0$ and $\Omega_0\sqrt{L/g}$. To obtain numerical solutions, we only have to vary these two parameters.

Let us describe what this scaling of time represents physically. The circular frequency of small amplitude oscillations is $\omega_0 = \sqrt{g/L}$ and thus

$$\tau = \sqrt{\frac{g}{L}}t = \omega_0 t.$$

(16.2)

The variable $\tau$ has no dimensions, and is thus called a **dimensionless** time variable! The only important parameters in the nonlinear problem (if we measure time based on the frequency of a small oscillation) is $\theta_0$, the initial amplitude of the pendulum, and

$$\Omega_0\sqrt{\frac{L}{g}} = \frac{\Omega_0}{\omega_0},$$

the ratio of the initial angular velocity $\Omega_0$ to the circular frequency of small oscillations!

## EXERCISES

**16.1.** Using an appropriate dimensionless time variable, what equation governs a frictionless spring-mass system with a linear restoring force?

**16.2.** Consider a linearized pendulum. Show, by independently scaling both time and the angle $\theta$, that the three parameters $\theta_0$, $\Omega_0$, and $g/L$ reduce to one parameter. Why doesn't this work for the nonlinear pendulum?

**16.3.** Show that $\Omega_0/\omega_0$ is a dimensionless parameter.

# 17.  Nonlinear Frictionless Systems

For a spring-mass system without friction, we have shown

$$m\frac{d^2x}{dt^2} = -f(x).$$

(17.1)

Here the force, $-f(x)$, depends only on the position of the mass. If the equilibrium position is $x = 0$, then the spring exerts no force there, $f(0) = 0$.

We assume that $f(x)$ is such that it can be expanded in a Taylor series,

$$f(x) = f(0) + xf'(0) + \frac{x^2}{2!}f''(0) + \cdots.$$

Since $f(0) = 0$,

$$m\frac{d^2x}{dt^2} = -kx - \frac{f''(0)}{2}x^2 - \cdots,$$

where $k = f'(0)$. If the force is a restoring force, then $f(x)$ is positive for positive $x$ (and vice versa), and hence $k$ is positive. Thus the result *for small amplitudes of oscillation* in which the nonlinear terms can be neglected, is Hooke's law (the linearized spring-mass equation).

We will now consider motions of a spring-mass system such that the amplitudes are not necessarily small. Then equation 17.1 is appropriate. The nonlinear pendulum also satisfies a differential equation of that form, since

$$L\frac{d^2\theta}{dt^2} = -g \sin \theta. \tag{17.2}$$

Before solving these nonlinear ordinary differential equations, what properties do we expect the solution to have? For small amplitudes the solution most likely oscillates periodically. For larger amplitudes oscillations are still expected, at least for the nonlinear pendulum. Futhermore, there are certain equilibrium positions for the nonlinear pendulum, that is, if the pendulum is in that position and at rest it will stay there. For $\theta = \theta_E$ to be an equilibrium position, $\theta = \theta_E$ must solve the differential equation 17.1. Since $\theta_E$ is a constant $d\theta_E/dt = d^2\theta_E/dt^2 = 0$, and thus equation 17.2 implies

$$\sin \theta_E = 0.$$

Consequently, $\theta_E = 0, \pi$. (Other mathematical solutions to this equilibrium problem are physically equivalent.) $\theta_E = 0$ is the "natural" position of a pendulum, as shown in Fig. 17-1, while $\theta_E = \pi$ as demonstrated in Fig. 17-2 is the "inverted" position of a pendulum:

Figure 17-1    Natural equilibrium position
of a pendulum.

Figure 17-2    Inverted equilibrium position
of a pendulum.

It is only at these two positions that the forces will balance, yielding no motion. However, there is a fundamental difference between these solutions that is immediately noticeable. Although both are equilibrium positions,

$\theta_E = 0$ is stable and $\theta_E = \pi$ is very unstable! Any mathematical solution must illustrate this striking difference between these two equilibrium positions.

In general if equation 17.1 is valid then there is an equilibrium position at any value of $x$ such that $f(x) = 0$.

# 18. Linearized Stability Analysis of an Equilibrium Solution

The concept of the stability of solutions is considered to be one of the fundamental aspects of applied mathematics. Now we are pursuing this subject with respect to the stability of the equilibrium positions of a pendulum. In the discussion of population dynamics later in the text, we will investigate the stability of equilibrium populations. Other areas in which stability questions are important include, for example, economics, chemistry, and widely diverse fields of engineering and physics.

As illustrated by the two equilibrium positions for a nonlinear pendulum, the concept of stability is not a difficult one. Basically, an equilibrium solution of a time-dependent equation is said to be **stable** if the (usually time-dependent) solution stays "near" the equilibrium solution for *all* initial conditions "near" the equilibrium. More precise mathematical definitions of different kinds of stability can be given. (See, for example, W. Boyce and R. DiPrima, *Elementary Differential Equations and Boundary Value Problems*, New York: John Wiley & Sons, 1969.) In a precise discussion, what is meant by "near" is carefully defined. However, for our purposes the abstractness of the rigorous definitions of stability is unnecessary. When an equilibrium solution is not stable, it is said to be **unstable**. For example, even if only one initial condition exists for which the solution tends "away" from the equilibrium, then the equilibrium is unstable. On the other hand an equilibrium is not stable just because there exists one initial condition such that the solution stays near the equilibrium. We repeat, to be stable it must stay near for *all* initial conditions. In summary, an equilibrium solution is unstable if solutions tend "away" from the equilibrium and stable if solutions either tend "toward" the equilibrium or stay the same "distance away" (for example, for the natural position of the linearized pendulum the amplitude of oscillation remains the same; in some sense the solution does not tend towards the equilibrium, but stays the same "distance away".)

In this section, we give a mathematical method to distinguish between stable and unstable equilibrium solutions. If a mass $m$ is acted upon by a force $-f(x)$, then

$$m \frac{d^2x}{dt^2} = -f(x).$$

(18.1)

$x = x_E$ is an equilibrium position if

$$f(x_E) = 0.$$

(18.2)

To analyze the stability of this equilibrium position, we investigate positions $x$ of the mass near its equilibrium position. For $x$ near to $x_E$, the function $f(x)$ can be approximated using the first few terms of its Taylor series around $x = x_E$:

$$f(x) = f(x_E) + (x - x_E)f'(x_E) + \frac{(x - x_E)^2}{2!}f''(x_E) + \cdots$$

Thus

$$m \frac{d^2x}{dt^2} = -f(x_E) - (x - x_E)f'(x_E) - \frac{(x - x_E)^2}{2!}f''(x_E) - \cdots$$

Since $x = x_E$ is an equilibrium position, $f(x_E) = 0$ and thus

$$m \frac{d^2x}{dt^2} = -(x - x_E)f'(x_E) - \frac{(x - x_E)^2}{2!}f''(x_E) - \cdots$$

For $x$ sufficiently near to $x_E$, $(x - x_E)^2$ is much smaller than $x - x_E$ and consequently the quadratic term $[(x - x_E)^2 f''(x_E)/2!]$ can be ignored, as well as the higher-order terms of the Taylor series (if $f'(x_E) \neq 0$). As an approximation

$$m \frac{d^2x}{dt^2} = -(x - x_E)f'(x_E).$$

Although this equation can be explicitly solved, it is more convenient to introduce the **displacement from equilibrium** $y$:

$$y = x - x_E.$$

Using $y$ as the new dependent variable

$$m \frac{d^2y}{dt^2} = -f'(x_E)y.$$

(18.3)

The coefficient $f'(x_E)$ is a *constant*; the displacement from equilibrium $y$ approximately satisfies the above linear differential equation with constant coefficients.

We say the equilibrium solution is **stable** if for initial conditions sufficiently near the equilibrium solution, the solution stays close to the equilibrium solution. Otherwise the equilibrium solution is said to be **unstable**. Thus the stability of the equilibrium solution is determined by the time dependence of the displacement from equilibrium. A simple analysis of equation 18.3, known as a **linearized stability analysis**, shows that:

1. If $f'(x_E) > 0$, then the mass executes simple harmonic motion (about its equilibrium position). In this case we say the equilibrium position is **stable**.* This shows the importance of simple harmonic motion as it will describe motion near a stable equilibrium position. For slight departures from equilibrium, in this case the force tends to restore the mass.

2. If $f'(x_E) < 0$, then the system has some exponential decay and some exponential growth. Since the solution consists of a combination of these two effects, the displacement from equilibrium will exponentially grow for most initial conditions. Thus in this case the equilibrium point is said to be **unstable**. If displaced from equilibrium, the force will push it further away.

3. If $f'(x_E) = 0$, then this linearized stability analysis is inconclusive as additional terms of the Taylor series need to be calculated.

As an example, let us investigate the linearized stability of the equilibrium positions of a nonlinear pendulum:

$$L \frac{d^2\theta}{dt^2} = -g \sin \theta.$$

The equilibrium positions are $\theta_E = 0$ and $\theta_E = \pi$. $f(\theta) = g \sin \theta$, and therefore $f'(\theta) = g \cos \theta$. We note that

$$f'(0) = \quad g > 0$$
$$f'(\pi) = -g < 0.$$

Thus, as we know by our experience with pendulums, $\theta_E = 0$ is a stable equilibrium position of a nonlinear pendulum, while $\theta_E = \pi$ is an unstable equilibrium position.

An *equivalent* method known as a **perturbation method** is sometimes used to investigate the linearized stability of an equilibrium solution. To facilitate remembering that $x$ is near to $x_E$, a small parameter $\epsilon$ is introduced, $0 < \epsilon \ll 1$, such that

$$x(t) = x_E + \epsilon x_1(t).$$

$\epsilon x_1(t)$ is now the displacement from equilibrium (also known as the amount the position is perturbed or the perturbation). If this expression is substituted into the differential equation

$$m \frac{d^2x}{dt^2} = -f(x),$$

---

*The term **neutrally stable** is sometimes used, indicating that the solution does not tend to equilibrium as $t \longrightarrow \infty$.

then

$$\epsilon m \frac{d^2 x_1}{dt^2} = -f(x_E + \epsilon x_1)$$

results, since $x_E$ is a constant. Again using the Taylor series it is seen that

$$\epsilon m \frac{d^2 x_1}{dt^2} = -f(x_E) - \epsilon x_1 f'(x_E) - \frac{\epsilon^2 x_1^2}{2!} f''(x_E) - \cdots$$

By neglecting the $O(\epsilon^2)$* terms, this reduces to equation 18.3. Using either method, the difficult to solve nonlinear differential equation is approximated by an easily analyzed linear differential equation.

# EXERCISES

**18.1.**   In this problem we will investigate the stability of circular planetary orbits. In exercises 14.2 and 14.3 it was shown that

$$m\left[\frac{d^2 L}{dt^2} - L\left(\frac{d\theta}{dt}\right)^2\right] = -g(L)$$

$$L^2 \frac{d\theta}{dt} = \text{constant} \equiv H_0.$$

(a)   Show that $m[(d^2L/dt^2) - L^{-3}H_0^2] = -g(L)$, a second-order differential equation. In parts (b) and (c) assume the radial force is an inverse-power law, i.e.,

$$g = \frac{c}{L^n} \quad \text{with } c > 0.$$

(b)   What is the radius $L_0$ of an allowable *circular* orbit? [Hint: $L_0 = \{c/[m(d\theta/dt)^2]\}^{1/(n+1)}$.]

(c)   Using a linearized stability analysis, show that this circular orbit is stable only if $n < 3$ (i.e., for an inverse-square law, a circular orbit is stable).

**18.2.**   Assume that $x = x_0$ is a *stable* equilibrium point of equation 18.1. What is the period of small oscillations around that equilibrium point?

**18.3.**   Suppose

$$\frac{d^2 x}{dt^2} = x - x^2$$

(a)   Determine all possible equilibrium solutions. [Hint: The answer is $x = 0$ and $x = 1$.]

---

*The symbol $O(\epsilon^2)$ is read as "order $\epsilon^2$." It indicates that the order of magnitude of the most important neglected term is $\epsilon^2$. A more careful treatment of this symbol can be developed. The author believes this is unnecessary in this text.

(b)   Is $x = 0$ a stable equilibrium solution?

(c)   Is $x = 1$ a stable equilibrium solution?

**18.4.**   Consider a spring-mass system with a nonlinear restoring force satisfying

$$m\frac{d^2x}{dt^2} = -kx - \alpha x^3,$$

where $\alpha > 0$. Which positions are equilibrium positions? Are they stable?

**18.5.**   Consider a system which satisfies

$$m\frac{d^2x}{dt^2} = -kx + \alpha x^3,$$

where $\alpha > 0$.

(a)   Show that the force does not always restore the mass towards $x = 0$.

(b)   Which positions are equilibrium positions? Are they stable?

**18.6.**   Consider a stranded moonship of mass $m_s$ somewhere directly between the moon (of mass $m_m$) and the earth (of mass $m_e$). The gravitational force between any two masses is an *attractive* force of magnitude $G(m_1 m_2/r^2)$, (where $G$ is a universal gravitational constant, $m_1$ and $m_2$ are the two masses, and $r$ is the distance between the masses).

(a)   If the moonship is located at a distance $y$ from the center of the earth, show that

$$m_s\frac{d^2y}{dt^2} = -G\frac{m_e m_s}{y^2} + G\frac{m_m m_s}{(r_0 - y)^2},$$

where $r_0$ is the constant distance between the earth and moon. (Assume that the earth has no effect on the moon, i.e., assume that both are fixed in space.)

(b)   Calculate the equilibrium position of the moonship.

(c)   Is the equilibrium position stable? Is your conclusion reasonable?

(d)   Compare this problem to exercise 18.7.

**18.7.**   Consider an isolated positive electrically charged particle of charge $q_e$ (and mass $m_e$) located directly between two fixed positive charged particles of charge $q_{p_1}$ and $q_{p_2}$ respectively. The electrical force between two charged particles is $-F(q_1 q_2/r^2)$ (alike charges repel and different charges attract), where $F$ is a universal electrical constant, $q_1$ and $q_2$ are the two charges, and $r$ is the distance between the two charges.

(a)   If the middle particle is located at a distance $y$ from one of the particles, show that

$$m_e\frac{d^2y}{dt^2} = F\frac{q_e q_{p_1}}{y^2} - F\frac{q_e q_{p_2}}{(r_0 - y)^2},$$

where $r_0$ is the approximately constant distance between the two positively charged particles.

(b)   Calculate the equilibrium position of the positively charged particle.

(c)   Is the equilibrium position stable? Is your conclusion reasonable?

(d)   Compare this problem to exercise 18.6.

**18.8.**   Consider a mass $m$ attached to the exact middle of a stretched string of length $l$.

(a) Suppose that the mass when attached forms in equilibrium a 30°–30°–120° triangle (due to gravity $g$) as in Fig. 18-1.

Figure 18.1   Vertically vibrating mass.

Calculate the *tension T* in the string. (The tension is the force exerted by the string.)

(b) Assume that the tension remains the same when the mass is displaced vertically a *small* distance $y$. Calculate the period of oscillation of the mass.

**18.9.** Consider a nonlinear pendulum. Using a linearized stability analysis, show that the inverted position is unstable. What is the exponential behavior of the angle in the neighborhood of this unstable equilibrium position?

**18.10.** Suppose

$$m\frac{d^2x}{dt^2} = \alpha(e^{\beta x} - 1) \quad \text{with } \alpha > 0 \text{ and } \beta > 0.$$

(a) What are the dimensions of $\alpha$ and $\beta$?

(b) Determine all equilibrium positions.

(c) Describe the motion in the neighborhood of the equilibrium position, $x = 0$.

**18.11.** Consider equation 18.3. If $f'(x_E) > 0$, show that the amplitude of the oscillation is small if the initial displacement from equilibrium *and* the initial velocity are small.

# 19.   Conservation of Energy

In the previous section, we were able to analyze the solution of

$$\boxed{m\frac{d^2x}{dt^2} = -f(x)} \tag{19.1}$$

in the neighborhood of an equilibrium position. Here we continue the investigation of this nonlinear equation representing a spring-mass system without friction. We are especially interested now in determining the behavior of solutions to equation 19.1 valid far away from an equilibrium position.

The general solution to a second-order differential equation (even if nonlinear) contains two arbitrary constants. One of these constants can be obtained in a manner to be described. First multiply both sides of equation

19.1 by the velocity $dx/dt$,

$$m \frac{dx}{dt} \frac{d^2x}{dt^2} = -f(x) \frac{dx}{dt}.$$

The left-hand side is an exact derivative, since

$$\frac{d}{dt}\left[\frac{1}{2}\left(\frac{dx}{dt}\right)^2\right] = \frac{dx}{dt} \frac{d^2x}{dt^2}.$$

Thus,

$$m \frac{d}{dt}\left[\frac{1}{2}\left(\frac{dx}{dt}\right)^2\right] = -f(x) \frac{dx}{dt}.$$

After multiplying by $dt$,

$$md\left[\frac{1}{2}\left(\frac{dx}{dt}\right)^2\right] = -f(x)\,dx.$$

Both sides of this equation can now be integrated. If there is a function $F(x)$ such that $dF/dx = f$ (i.e., $F(x) = \int^x f(\bar{x})\,d\bar{x}$), then *indefinite* integration yields

$$\frac{1}{2}m\left(\frac{dx}{dt}\right)^2 = -F(x) + E$$

or

$$\boxed{\frac{1}{2}m\left(\frac{dx}{dt}\right)^2 + F(x) = E,} \qquad \text{(19.2a)}$$

where $E$ is a constant of integration. The quantity $\frac{1}{2}m(dx/dt)^2 + F(x)$, which we will show is the total energy, remains the same throughout the motion; it is said to be **conserved**.

Especially in cases in which $f(x)$ does not have a simple integral, it is often more advantageous to do a *definite* integration from the initial position $x_0$ with initial velocity $v_0$, i.e.,

$$x(t_0) = x_0$$

$$\frac{dx}{dt}(t_0) = v_0.$$

Thus

$$\frac{1}{2}m\left(\frac{dx}{dt}\right)^2 - \frac{1}{2}mv_0^2 = -\int_{x_0}^x f(\bar{x})\,d\bar{x}.$$

This expression corresponds to the one obtained by indefinite integration if $E = \frac{1}{2}mv_0^2$. An alternate expression, more easily interpreted, can be derived by noting

$$\int_{x_0}^x f(\bar{x})\,d\bar{x} = \int_{x_0}^{x_1} f(\bar{x})\,d\bar{x} + \int_{x_1}^x f(\bar{x})\,d\bar{x},$$

where $x_1$ is any fixed position. Then

$$\frac{1}{2}m\left(\frac{dx}{dt}\right)^2 + \int_{x_1}^{x} f(\bar{x})\,d\bar{x} = \frac{1}{2}mv_0^2 + \int_{x_1}^{x_0} f(\bar{x})\,d\bar{x} \equiv E. \qquad \text{(19.2b)}$$

The quantity

$$\frac{1}{2}m\left(\frac{dx}{dt}\right)^2 + \int_{x_1}^{x} f(\bar{x})\,d\bar{x}$$

is again said to be **conserved**, since it is constant throughout the motion, being initially equal to

$$\frac{1}{2}mv_0^2 + \int_{x_1}^{x_0} f(\bar{x})\,d\bar{x}.$$

This constant of the motion is called the **total energy**. Part of it

$$\frac{1}{2}m\left(\frac{dx}{dt}\right)^2 = \frac{1}{2}mv^2$$

is called the **kinetic energy**; it is that portion of energy due to the *motion* of the mass (hence the term kinetic). $\int_{x_1}^{x} f(\bar{x})\,d\bar{x}$ is the work* necessary to raise the mass from $x_1$ to $x$. The force necessary to raise the mass is minus the external force [for example, with gravity $-mg\hat{j}$, the force necessary to raise a mass is $+mg\hat{j}$]. Thus if the external force is $-f(x)$, i.e., $m(d^2x/dt^2) = -f(x)$, then the work necessary to raise the mass from $x_1$ to $x$ is $\int_{x_1}^{x} f(x)\,dx$. It is thus in essence the work or energy that is stored in the system for "potential" usage, and hence is called the **potential energy** (relative to the position $x = x_1$). Equation 19.2 is called the equation of **conservation of energy** or the **energy equation**. The total energy is shared between kinetic energy and potential energy. For example, as a mass speeds up it must gain its kinetic energy from the potential energy already stored in the system. Often (but not always) it is convenient to measure potential energy relative to an equilibrium position (i.e., let $x_1 = x_E$).

The principle of **conservation of energy** is frequently quite useful (and always important). As an example, consider an object being thrown vertically subject only to the force of gravity. Newton's law implies

$$m\frac{d^2y}{dt^2} = -mg,$$

---

*The definition of work $W$ is the force times the distance (i.e., for a variable force $g$, $w = \int_{x_1}^{x} g\,ds$). In two or three spatial dimensions if the force is $\vec{g}$, the work done by the force is $W = \int_{x_1}^{x} \vec{g}\cdot d\vec{s}$.

where $y$ is the height above the ground. Suppose the object is initially at $y = 0$, but thrown upward with velocity $v_0$ (the initial velocity $dy/dt = v_0$). A reasonable question is: What is the highest point the object reaches before it falls back to the ground. Although it is not difficult to directly solve this differential equation (integrate twice!) and then determine the highest point (as was done in exercise 4.1), conservation of energy more immediately yields the result. The potential energy relative to the ground level (a convenient position since there is no equilibrium for this problem) is

$$F(y) = \int_0^y mg \, d\bar{y} = mgy.$$

Conservation of energy implies that the sum of the kinetic energy and the potential energy does not vary in time,

$$\frac{1}{2} m \left(\frac{dy}{dt}\right)^2 + mgy = E.$$

The constant $E$ equals the initial kinetic energy,

$$E = \frac{1}{2} mv_0^2,$$

because initially the potential energy is zero since initially $y = 0$. Furthermore at the highest point $y = y_{\max}$, the velocity must equal zero, $dy/dt = 0$ at $y = y_{\max}$. Hence at the highest point the kinetic energy must be zero. At that point all of the energy must be potential energy. Thus conservation of energy implies

$$mgy_{\max} = E = \frac{1}{2} mv_0^2.$$

Consequently the highest point is

$$y_{\max} = \frac{v_0^2}{2g}.$$

Other applications are considered in the exercises.

Suppose the potential energy relative to a position $x = x_1$ is known

$$F(x) = \int_{x_1}^x f(\bar{x}) \, d\bar{x}$$

and is sketched, yielding (for example) Fig. 19-1. The derivative of the potential energy is $f(x)$,

$$\frac{dF(x)}{dx} = f(x).$$

The applied force is $-f(x)$. Thus *the derivative of the potential energy is minus the force.* Since $f(x_E) = 0$, potential energy at an equilibrium position has an extremum point $dF/dx = 0$ (a relative minimum if $f'(x_E) > 0$, a relative

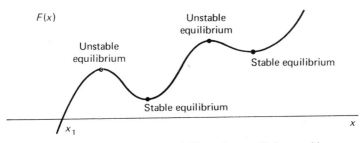

Figure 19-1   Potential energy $F(x)$ illustrating equilibrium positions.

maximum if $f'(x_E) < 0$, and if $f'(x_E) = 0$ either a relative minimum, a relative maximum, or a saddle point). Recall in studying the linearized stability of an equilibrium position, it was determined that an equilibrium position is stable if $f'(x_E) > 0$ and unstable if $f'(x_E) < 0$. Thus the potential energy has a relative minimum at a stable equilibrium position. Similarly at an unstable equilibrium position, the potential energy has a relative maximum. It is easy to remember these results as they are the same as would occur if a ball were placed on a mountain shaped like the potential energy curve. These facts are noted in Fig. 19-1.

From conservation of energy, equation 19.2, an expression for the velocity, $dx/dt$, can be obtained,

$$\frac{dx}{dt} = \pm\sqrt{\frac{2E}{m} - \frac{2}{m}\int_{x_1}^{x} f(\tilde{x})\,d\tilde{x}}.$$

The sign of the square root must be chosen appropriately. It is positive if the velocity is positive and vice versa. Furthermore, this first order differential equation is separable:

$$\frac{dx}{\pm\sqrt{\dfrac{2E}{m} - \dfrac{2}{m}\displaystyle\int_{x_1}^{x} f(\tilde{x})\,d\tilde{x}}} = dt.$$

Integrating from $t = t_0$ (where $x = x_0$), yields an implicit solution

$$t = t_0 + \int_{x_0}^{x} \frac{d\tilde{x}}{\pm\sqrt{\dfrac{2E}{m} - \dfrac{2}{m}\displaystyle\int_{x_1}^{\tilde{x}} f(\tilde{x})\,d\tilde{x}}},$$

where the appropriate sign again must be chosen in the integrand depending on whether the velocity is positive or negative. However, this equation solves for $t$ as a function of $x$. We usually are more interested in the position $x$ as a function of $t$. Furthermore, this formula is not particularly helpful in understanding the qualitative behavior of the solution.

# EXERCISES

**19.1.**  Consider the equation of a nonlinear pendulum:

$$L \frac{d^2\theta}{dt^2} = -g \sin \theta.$$

(a)  What are the two equilibrium positions?

(b)  Define the potential energy as

$$F(\theta) \equiv \int_0^\theta g \sin \bar{\theta} \, d\bar{\theta}.$$

Evaluate this potential and formulate conservation of energy.

(d)  Show that this potential energy (as a function of $\theta$) has a relative minimum at the stable equilibrium position and a relative maximum at the unstable equilibrium position.

**19.2.**  The equation of a linearized pendulum is $L(d^2\theta/dt^2) = -g\theta$. By multiplying by $d\theta/dt$ and integrating, determine a quantity which is a constant of motion.

**19.3.**  In general show that the potential energy when a mass is at rest equals the total energy.

**19.4.**  A linear spring-mass system (without friction) satisfies $m(d^2x/dt^2) = -kx$.

(a)  Derive that

$$\frac{m}{2}\left(\frac{dx}{dt}\right)^2 + \frac{k}{2}x^2 = \text{constant} \equiv E.$$

(b)  Consider the initial value problem such that at $t = 0$, $x = x_0$ and $dx/dt = v_0$. Evaluate $E$.

(c)  Using the expression for conservation of energy, evaluate the maximum displacement of the mass from its equilibrium position. Compare this to the result obtained from the exact explicit solution.

(d)  What is the velocity of the mass when it passes its equilibrium position?

**19.5.**  Derive an expression for the potential energy if the only force is gravity.

**19.6.**  Suppose a mass $m$ located at $(x, y)$ is acted upon by a force field, $\vec{F}$ (i.e., $m(d^2\vec{x}/dt^2) = \vec{F}$). The kinetic energy is defined as

$$\frac{m}{2}\left[\left(\frac{dx}{dt}\right)^2 + \left(\frac{dy}{dt}\right)^2\right];$$

it again equals $\frac{1}{2}mv^2$. The potential energy is defined as

$$-\int_{\vec{x}_1}^{\vec{x}} \vec{F} \cdot d\vec{s},$$

where $\vec{x}_1$ is any fixed position. If there exists a function $\phi(x, y)$ such that

$$\vec{F} = -\nabla\phi,$$

then show that the total energy (kinetic energy plus potential energy) is conserved. Such a force field $\vec{F}$ is called a **conservative force field**. In this case show that the potential energy equals $\phi(\vec{x}) - \phi(\vec{x}_1)$.

**19.7.** A mass $m$ is thrown upwards at velocity $v_0$ against the inverse-square gravitational force $(F = -GmM/L^2)$.
   (a)   How high does the mass go?
   (b)   Determine the velocity at which the mass does not return to earth, the so-called **escape velocity**.
   (c)   Estimate this value in kilometers per hour (miles per hour).

**19.8.** Using a computer, numerically integrate any initial value problem for a frictionless spring-mass system with a linear restoring force. Is the energy constant?

## 20.  Energy Curves

In the previous section a complex expression was derived for the motion of a spring-mass system. A better understanding of the solution can be obtained by analyzing the energy equation 19.2,

$$\frac{1}{2} m \left(\frac{dx}{dt}\right)^2 + \int_{x_1}^{x} f(\bar{x}) \, d\bar{x} = \frac{1}{2} m v_0^2 + \int_{x_1}^{x_0} f(\bar{x}) \, d\bar{x},$$

representing conservation of energy.

Let us consider $x$ and $dx/dt$ as variables rather than $x$ and $t$. In this manner conservation of energy yields a relationship between $x$ and $dx/dt$, namely

$$\frac{1}{2} m \left(\frac{dx}{dt}\right)^2 + F(x) = E, \tag{20.1}$$

where the potential energy only depends on the position,

$$F(x) = \int_{x_1}^{x} f(\bar{x}) \, d\bar{x}, \tag{20.2}$$

and the total energy is constant,

$$E = \frac{1}{2} m v_0^2 + \int_{x_1}^{x_0} f(\bar{x}) \, d\bar{x} = \text{constant}. \tag{20.3}$$

Graphing equation 20.1 as in Fig. 20-1 will yield some curve in the $dx/dt$ vs. $x$ space, for each value of $E$:

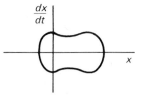

Figure 20-1   Typical energy curve.

For each time, the solution $x(t)$ corresponds to one point on this curve since if $x(t)$ is known so is $dx/dt$. As time changes, the point corresponding to the solution changes, sketching a curve in the $dx/dt$ vs. $x$ space. Along this curve energy is conserved. This coordinate system is called the **phase plane**, since we have expressed the equation in terms of the two variables $x$ and $dx/dt$, referred to as the two phases of the system (position and velocity). The curve sketching the path of the solution is called the **trajectory** in the phase plane.

The actual graph of the curves of constant energy (corresponding to different constant values of $E$) depends on the particular potential energy function, equation 20.2. For example, if $f(x) = kx$ (let $x_1 = 0$), then

$$F(x) = \frac{kx^2}{2}.$$

Sketching the potential energy and the total constant energy yields Fig. 20-2. Since the kinetic energy is positive ($\frac{1}{2}m(dx/dt)^2 \geq 0$), the total energy is

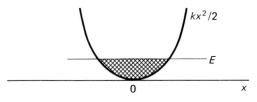

Figure 20-2.

greater than the potential energy, $E \geq kx^2/2$ as sketched in the hatched region. The values of $x$ are restricted. For these values of $x$ there will be two possible values of $dx/dt$, determined from conservation of energy,

$$\frac{1}{2}m\left(\frac{dx}{dt}\right)^2 + k\frac{x^2}{2} = E.$$

In the next sections we will illustrate how to use this information to sketch the phase plane.

Suppose *part* of one such energy curve in the phase plane relating $x$ and $dx/dt$ is known, and looks as sketched in Fig. 20-3. Although $x$ and $dx/dt$ are as yet unknown functions of $t$, they satisfy a relation indicated by the curve in

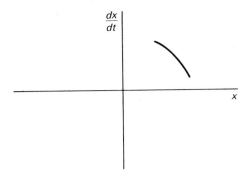

Figure 20-3.

the phase plane. This curve is quite significant because we can determine certain qualitative features of the solution directly from it. For example for the curve in Fig. 20-3, since the solution is in the *upper half plane*, $dx/dt > 0$, it follows that $x$ increases as $t$ increases. Arrows are added to the phase plane diagram to indicate the direction the solution changes with time. In the phase plane shown in Fig. 20-4, since $x$ increases, the solution $x(t)$ moves to the right as time increases. As another example, suppose that the curve shown in Fig. 20-5 corresponds to the solution in the phase plane. Again in the upper half plane $dx/dt > 0$ (and hence $x$ increases). However, in the lower half plane, $x$ decreases.

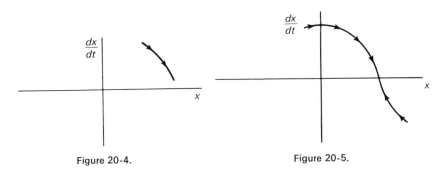

Figure 20-4.                                     Figure 20-5.

Although the explicit solution of nonlinear equations only occasionally is easily interpreted, the solution in the phase plane often quickly suggests the qualitative behavior.

# 21. Phase Plane
## of a Linear Oscillator

As a simple example of the analysis of a problem using a phase plane, consider the linear spring-mass system

$$m\frac{d^2x}{dt^2} = -kx. \qquad (21.1)$$

Although we already know the explicit solution (including the solution of the initial value problem), let us ignore it. Instead, let us suppose that we do not know the solution nor any of its properties. We will show how the energy integral determines the qualitative features of the solution.

The energy integral is formed by multiplying the above equation by $dx/dt$ and then integrating:

$$\frac{m}{2}\left(\frac{dx}{dt}\right)^2 + k\frac{x^2}{2} = E, \qquad (21.2)$$

where the constant $E$ can be determined by the initial conditions of the mass. Thus,

$$E = \frac{m}{2}v_0^2 + \frac{k}{2}x_0^2. \qquad (21.3)$$

As a check, differentiating equation 21.2 yields equation 21.1.

The potential energy is $kx^2/2$. Since the kinetic energy is positive, only the region, such as that shown in Fig. 21-1, where $E - kx^2/2$ is positive corresponds to a real solution, namely

$$|x| < \left(\frac{2E}{k}\right)^{1/2}.$$

The mass cannot have potential energy greater than the total energy.

The energy equation relates $x$ and $dx/dt$. A typical curve, defined by equation 21.2 corresponding to one value of $E$, $E = E_0$, is an ellipse in the phase plane shown in Fig. 21-2 with intercepts at $x = \pm\sqrt{2E_0/k}$ and at $dx/dt = \pm\sqrt{2E_0/m}$.

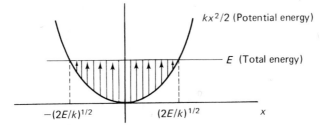

Figure 21-1 Potential energy of a spring-mass system.

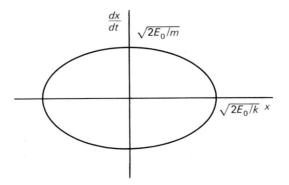

Figure 21-2 Elliptical trajectory in the phase plane.

How does this solution behave in time? Recall, in the upper half plane $x$ increases, while in the lower half plane $x$ decreases. Thus we have Fig. 21-3. The solution goes around and around (clockwise) in the phase plane. After one circuit in the phase plane, no matter where it starts, the solution returns to the same position with the same velocity. It then repeats the same trajectory in the same length of time. This process continues and thus the solution is periodic. Or is it? How do we know the solution in the phase plane doesn't continually move in the direction of the arrow but never reaches a certain point? Suppose that, as in Fig. 21-4, the solution only approaches a point. As illustrated, $dx/dt$ and $x$ tend to constants as $t \longrightarrow \infty$. Can $x$ steadily tend to a

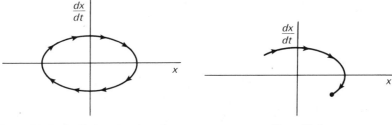

Figure 21-3 Oscillation in the phase plane.

Figure 21-4.

constant, and $dx/dt$ tend to a constant? It can, only if $dx/dt \rightarrow 0$. Thus Fig. 21-5 appears possible:

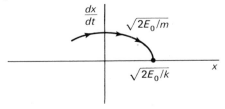

Figure 21-5.

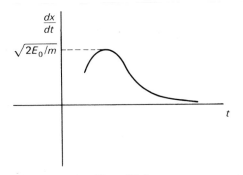

Figure 21-6.

However, if $x \rightarrow \sqrt{2E_0/k}$ as $t \rightarrow \infty$, then the above trajectory implies that $dx/dt$ must depend on time as shown in Fig. 21-6. As illustrated $dx/dt$ approaches 0 but does *not* reach that point in a *finite* amount of time. Clearly, $d^2x/dt^2 \rightarrow 0$. The differential equation, $d^2x/dt^2 = -(k/m)x$, then implies that $x \rightarrow 0$, i.e., $x \nrightarrow \sqrt{2E_0/k}$ as $t \rightarrow \infty$. Consequently, the solution never "stops." It oscillates between a maximum value of $x$, $x = +\sqrt{2E_0/k}$, and a minimum value, $x = -\sqrt{2E_0/k}$. (Note that at the maximum and minimum values, the velocity, $dx/dt$ equals zero.) Since the solution oscillates, perhaps as shown in Fig. 21-7, the solution is periodic in time. Many of the qualitative features of the solution in the phase plane agree with the exact results.

Furthermore an expression for the period, that is the time to go once completely around the closed curve in the phase plane, can be obtained with-

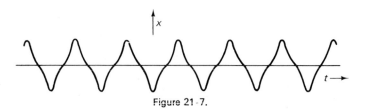

Figure 21-7.

out the explicit solution. The velocity $v$ is determined from equation 21.2 as a function of $x$,

$$v = \pm\sqrt{\frac{2E}{m} - \frac{k}{m}x^2}. \tag{21.4}$$

Since $v = dx/dt$, it follows that

$$dt = \frac{dx}{v}, \tag{21.5}$$

which can be used to determine the period. If we integrate equation 21.5 over an entire period $T$, then the result is

$$T = \oint \frac{dx}{v}, \tag{21.6}$$

where $\oint$ represents the integral of $dx/v$ as the displacement $x$ traverses a complete cycle (the plus sign in equation 21.4 must be used in equation 21.6 if $v$ is positive and vice versa). This calculation is rather awkward. Instead, the time it takes the moving spring-mass system to go from the equilibrium position ($x = 0$) to the maximum displacement ($x = \sqrt{2E_0/k}$) is, by symmetry, exactly one quarter of the period, as indicated by Fig. 21-8. Integrating equation 21.5 in this manner yields

$$\frac{T}{4} = \int_0^{\sqrt{2E_0/k}} \frac{dx}{\sqrt{\dfrac{2E_0}{m} - \dfrac{k}{m}x^2}}, \tag{21.7}$$

since in this case the sign of $v$ is always positive. The integral in equation 21.7 can be calculated (by trigonometric substitution or by using a table of integrals), yielding the result

$$T = 2\pi\sqrt{\frac{m}{k}}$$

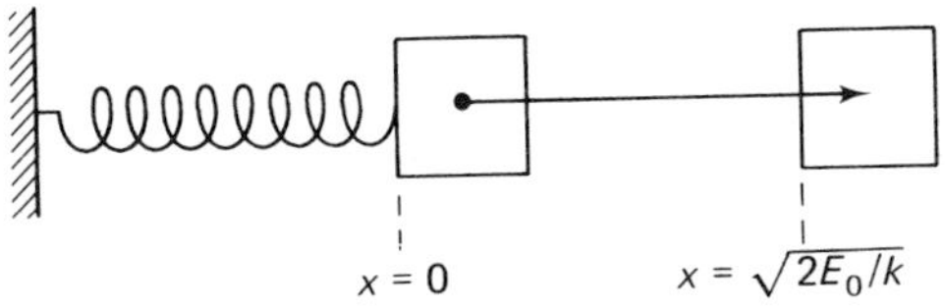

$$x = 0 \qquad\qquad x = \sqrt{2E_0/k}$$

Figure 21-8   Maximum displacement of a spring-mass system.

which agrees with the result obtained from the explicit solution. Interestingly enough the period does not depend on the energy (i.e., the period does not depend on the amplitude of the oscillation). This is a general property of linear systems. Can you give a simple mathematical explanation of why for linear problems the period cannot depend on the amplitude? [Answer: For a linear (homogeneous) differential equation, if $x(t)$ is a solution, then $Ax(t)$ is also a solution for any constant $A$. Thus if $x(t)$ is periodic with period $T$, $Ax(t)$ is also periodic with the same period. The period does not depend on the amplitude parameter $A$.] However, it will be shown that for a nonlinear system the period can depend on the amplitude.

The only information not determined from the phase plane curve is that the solution is exactly sinusoidal (rather than some other periodic function). Appropriate integration of equation 21.5 shows the solution to be sinusoidal. Instead let us briefly show that the ellipses in the phase plane also follow from the knowledge that the solution is sinusoidal. Since $x(t) = A \sin (\omega t + \phi_0)$, where $\omega = \sqrt{k/m}$, it follows that $dx/dt = A\omega \cos (\omega t + \phi_0)$. The phase plane is a curve relating $x$ and $dx/dt$, but not depending on $t$. Thus, $t$ must be eliminated from these two equations. This is accomplished as follows:

$$\left(\frac{x}{A}\right)^2 + \left(\frac{\frac{dx}{dt}}{A\omega}\right)^2 = 1,$$

or equivalently

$$\frac{m}{2}\left(\frac{dx}{dt}\right)^2 + \frac{k}{2}x^2 = \frac{k}{2}A^2.$$

In exercise 21.5, it is verified that

$$\frac{k}{2}A^2 = E = \frac{m}{2}v_0^2 + \frac{k}{2}x_0^2.$$

Actually only one closed curve in the phase plane has been illustrated. A few more curves corresponding to other values of the energy $E$ are sketched in Fig. 21-9 to indicate the phase plane for the linear oscillator:

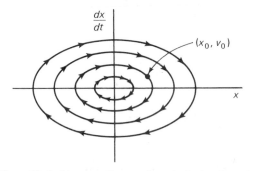

Figure 21-9   Linear oscillator: trajectories in the phase plane.

The initial value problem,

$$x(t_0) = x_0$$

$$\frac{dx}{dt}(t_0) = v_0,$$

is satisfied as follows. First the initial values $(x_0, v_0)$ are located in the phase plane. Then the curve (see Fig. 21-9) which goes through it is determined (note that $E = (m/2)v_0^2 + (k/2)x_0^2$), representing how $x$ changes periodically in time.

In summary, for equation 21.1 the energy curves determined the trajectories in the phase plane. Those energy curves are closed curves implying that the solution oscillates periodically. The amplitude of oscillation is obtained from the initial conditions. Thus the entire qualitative behavior of the solution can be determined by analyzing the phase plane.

# EXERCISES

**21.1.** Suppose the motion of a mass $m$ was described by the nonlinear differential equation $m(d^2x/dt^2) = -\beta x^3$, where $\beta > 0$.
   (a)   What is the dimensions of the constant $\beta$?
   (b)   What are the equilibrium positions?
   (c)   Derive an expression for conservation of energy.
   (d)   Using a phase plane analysis, show that the position $x$ oscillates around its equilibrium position.
   (e)   If at $t = t_0$, $x = x_0$ and $dx/dt = v_0$, then what is the maximum displacement from equilibrium? Also, what velocity is the mass moving at when it is at $x = 0$?

**21.2.** Suppose that the motion of a mass $m$ were governed by $m\,d^2x/dt^2 = kx$, where $k > 0$. Show that the phase plane indicates the equilibrium position ($x = 0$) is unstable.

**21.3.** Assume that a mass $m$ satisfies $m(d^2x/dt^2) = -x^2$.
   (a)   What are the equilibrium positions?
   (b)   Derive an expression for conservation of energy.
   (c)   Using a phase plane analysis, show that for most initial conditions the mass eventually tends towards $-\infty$. Is that reasonable? However, show that for certain initial conditions the mass tends towards its equilibrium position.
   (d)   How long does it take that solution to approach the equilibrium position?
   (e)   Would you say the equilibrium solution is stable or unstable?

**21.4.** Show that the test for the stability of an equilibrium solution by the linearized stability analysis of Sec. 18 is inconclusive for exercises 21.1 and 21.3. Can you suggest a generalization to the criteria developed in Sec. 18?

**21.5.** The motion of a frictionless spring-mass system with a linear restoring force is described by

$$x(t) = A \sin (\omega t + \phi_0),$$

where $\omega = \sqrt{k/m}$. Show that the total energy $E$ satisfies

$$E = \frac{k}{2} A^2 = \frac{m}{2} v_0^2 + \frac{k}{2} x_0^2,$$

where $x_0$ is the initial position and $v_0$ the initial velocity of the mass.

**21.6.** The phase plane equation for a linear oscillator can be used to directly obtain the solution.

(a)   Show that

$$dt = \frac{dx}{\pm \sqrt{\dfrac{2E}{m} - \dfrac{k}{m} x^2}}.$$

(b)   Assume $x = x_0$ at $t = 0$. (Why is $E \geq (k/2)x_0^2$?) Integrate the above expression to obtain $t$ as a function of $x$. Now solve for $x$ as a function of $t$. Is your answer reasonable?

**21.7.** Evaluate the following integral to determine the period $T$:

$$\frac{T}{4} = \int_0^{\sqrt{2E/k}} \frac{dx}{\sqrt{\dfrac{2E}{m} - \dfrac{k}{m} x^2}}.$$

Show that the period does *not* depend on the amplitude of oscillation.

**21.8.** Consider the linear spring-mass system, equation 21.1. Show that the average value of the kinetic energy equals the average value of the potential energy, and both equal one-half of the total energy.

# 22.  Phase Plane
# of a Nonlinear Pendulum

The energy integral sketched in the phase plane can be used to determine the qualitative behavior of nonlinear oscillators. As an example consider the differential equation of a nonlinear pendulum,

$$L\frac{d^2\theta}{dt^2} = -g \sin \theta. \qquad (22.1)$$

Multiplying each side of equation 22.1 by $d\theta/dt$ and integrating, yields

$$\frac{L}{2} \left(\frac{d\theta}{dt}\right)^2 = g(\cos \theta - 1) + E. \qquad (22.2)$$

Here the potential energy has been calculated relative to the natural position of the pendulum $\theta = 0$:

$$\int_0^\theta g \sin \bar{\theta} \, d\bar{\theta} = g(1 - \cos \theta).$$

At $\theta = 0$, the "energy"* $E$ consists only of kinetic energy. Again as a check, differentiate equation 22.2 with respect to $t$ yielding equation 22.1. The energy $E$ is constant and determined from the initial conditions,

$$E = \frac{L}{2}\Omega_0^2 + g(1 - \cos \theta_0),$$

where $\Omega_0 = d\theta/dt(t_0)$ and $\theta_0 = \theta(t_0)$.

To sketch the trajectories in the phase plane ($d\theta/dt$ as a function of $\theta$), equation 22.2 must be analyzed. Unfortunately equation 22.2 does not represent an easily recognizable type of curve (for the linear oscillator in Sec. 21, we immediately noticed equation 21.2 implied that the trajectories were ellipses). Instead, the energy integral equation 22.2 is used as the basis for sketching the trajectories. First, we sketch in Fig. 22-1 the potential energy $g(1 - \cos \theta)$ as a function of $\theta$:

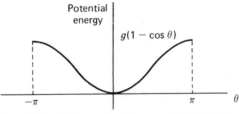

Figure 22-1    Nonlinear pendulum: potential energy.

Drawing vertical lines whose length equals the difference between the total energy $E$ and the potential energy, as in Fig. 22-2 yields an expression for $L/2(d\theta/dt)^2$, the kinetic energy, which must be positive. Figure 22-2 gives a graphical representation of $L/2(d\theta/dt)^2$ dependence on $\theta$, which is easily related to $d\theta/dt$ dependence on $\theta$.

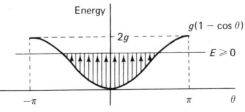

Figure 22-2    Nonlinear pendulum: kinetic energy.

---

*$E$ here does not have the units of energy. Instead multiplying equation 22.2 by $mL$ yields an expression for energy. Thus $mLE$ is actually the constant energy.

The solution curve corresponding to $E = 0$ is trivial (see Fig. 22-2). $d\theta/dt = 0$ and hence $\cos \theta = 1$, as marked on Fig. 22-3. These isolated points are the only stable equilibrium positions of a pendulum. If the initial energy is zero, then the pendulum must be at its stable equilibrium position. The pendulum will not move from that position.

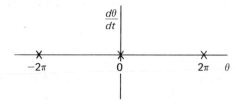

Figure 22-3  Positions of zero energy.

To sketch the remaining curves, it helps to notice that the curves must be even in $d\theta/dt$ (i.e., replacing $d\theta/dt$ by $-d\theta/dt$ does not change eq. 22.2). Also the curves are even in $\theta$. Furthermore, curves in the phase plane are periodic in $\theta$, with period $2\pi$. Thus the curves are sketched only for $d\theta/dt > 0$ and $0 < \theta < \pi$.

For $2g > E > 0$, all values of $\theta$ do not occur. Only angles such that $E \geq g(1 - \cos \theta)$ or equivalently $\cos \theta \geq 1 - E/g$ are valid. From Fig. 22-2, where as sketched $0 < E < 2g$, it is observed that $\cos \theta \geq 1 - E/g$ is equivalent to

$$|\theta| \leq \cos^{-1}(1 - E/g)$$

as long as $-\pi \leq \theta \leq \pi$. The solution can only correspond to these angles. Our sketch of the phase plane is improved by noting that the magnitude of $d\theta/dt$ is larger in regions where the difference between the total energy $E$ and the potential energy is the greatest. Thus, for each fixed energy level such that $0 < E < 2g$, $L/2(d\theta/dt)^2 = g(\cos \theta - 1) + E$ yields Fig. 22-4, where we have used the fact that $(d\theta/dt)^2 = 2E/L$ when $\theta = 0$. The calculation of the slope of the curve sketched in Fig. 22-4 is outlined in exercise 22.2. We have included an arrow to indicate changes in the solution as $t$ increases. The evenness in $\theta$

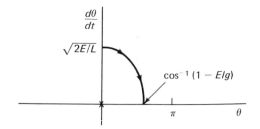

Figure 22-4  Trajectory in the phase plane.

and $d\theta/dt$ yields solutions which as before must be periodic in time, as shown in Fig. 22-5. The periodic solution oscillates around the stable equilibrium position. For each fixed $E$ in this range, the largest angle is called $\theta_{\max}$ (see Fig. 22-6):

$$\boxed{\theta_{\max} = \cos^{-1}(1 - E/g).}$$

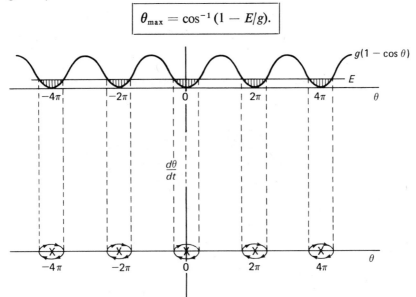

Figure 22-5   Potential energy, kinetic energy, and energy curves.

Figure 22-6   Oscillation of a pendulum.

For small energy, the solution is nearly the periodic solution of the linearized pendulum. As $E$ increases away from zero, the motion represents a periodic solution (though not sinusoidal) with larger and larger amplitudes. Sketching the phase plane for other values of $E$ such that $2g > E > 0$, yields Fig. 22-7.

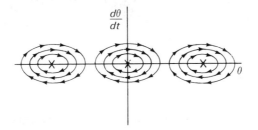

Figure 22-7   Nonlinear pendulum: trajectories in the phase plane (for sufficiently small energy).

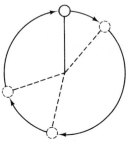

Figure 22-8.

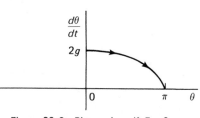

Figure 22-9   Phase plane if $E = 2g$.

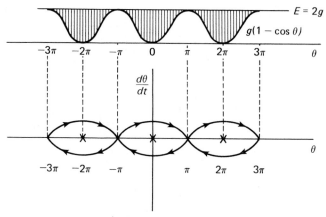

Figure 22-10   Energy curve, $E = 2g$.

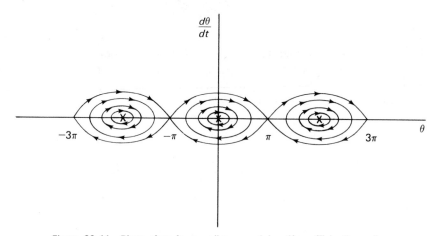

Figure 22-11   Phase plane for a nonlinear pendulum (for sufficiently small energies including critical energy).

If $E = 2g$, the energy is at the level necessary for all angles to be possible as illustrated in Fig. 22-8. In the phase plane, the curve corresponding to $E = 2g$ is that shown in Fig. 22-9. Thus, we have Fig. 22-10. Using this last result, the still incomplete phase plane is sketched in Fig. 22-11.

The energy integral enables us to sketch the trajectories in the phase plane. Note the key steps:

1. Sketch the potential energy as a function of $\theta$.
2. For a representative value of the total energy $E$, diagram the kinetic energy (the difference between the total energy and the potential energy).
3. From the kinetic energy, sketch the angular velocity $d\theta/dt$ as a function of $\theta$.

## EXERCISES

**22.1.** Suppose a spring-mass system is on a table retarded by a Coulomb frictional force (equation 10.3):

$$m\frac{d^2x}{dt^2} + kx = F_f, \quad \text{where } F_f = \begin{cases} \gamma & \text{if } \dfrac{dx}{dt} < 0 \\[2mm] -\gamma & \text{if } \dfrac{dx}{dt} > 0. \end{cases}$$

(a) If $dx/dt > 0$, determine the energy equation. Sketch the resulting phase plane curves. [Hint: By completing the square show that the phase plane curves are ellipses centered at $v = 0$, $x = -\gamma/k$; *not* centered at $x = 0$.]

(b) If $dx/dt < 0$, repeat the calculation of part (a). [Hint: The ellipses now are centered at $v = 0$, $x = \gamma/k$.]

(c) Using the results of (a) and (b), sketch the solution in the phase plane. Show that the mass stops in a finite time!!!

(d) Consider a problem in which the mass is initially at $x = 0$ with velocity $v_0$. Determine how many times the mass passes $x = 0$ as a function of $v_0$.

**22.2.** Consider the phase plane determined by equation 22.2.

(a) Show that $d/d\theta\,(d\theta/dt) = 0$ at $\theta = 0$ (if $E \neq 0$), which has been used in the figures of this section.

(b) Verify $d/d\theta\,(d\theta/dt) = \infty$ at $d\theta/dt = 0$ (if $E \neq 0$ and if $E \neq 2g$) as also assumed in the figures.

(c) If $E = 2g$, calculate $(d/d\theta)\,(d\theta/dt)$, and briefly explain how that information is used in the last three sketches of Sec. 22.

**22.3.** Consider a nonlinear pendulum. Show that the sum of the potential energy ($mgy$, where $y$ is the *vertical* distance of the pendulum above its natural position) and the kinetic energy ($\frac{1}{2}mv^2$, where $v$ is the speed of the mass) is a constant. [Hint: See exercise 19.6.]

# 23.  Can a Pendulum Stop?

The phase plane, Fig. 22-10, for the limiting energy curve $E = 2g$ shows that the pendulum tends towards the inverted position (either $\theta = -\pi$ or $\theta = \pi$). For example, $E = 2g$ corresponds to initially starting a pendulum at $\theta = \pi/2$ with just the right velocity such that the pendulum approaches the top with zero velocity, as shown in Fig. 23-1. It appears to reach that position with zero

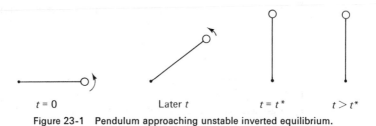

| $t = 0$ | Later $t$ | $t = t^*$ | $t > t^*$ |

Figure 23-1    Pendulum approaching unstable inverted equilibrium.

angular velocity $(d\theta/dt = 0)$. There is some theoretical difficulty with this solution as the uniqueness theorem† for ordinary differential equations implies that if the pendulum ever reaches the top with exactly zero velocity, then it would have to stay there (both in positive and negative time), since that point is an equilibrium position. How do we remedy this nonuniqueness difficulty‡? It will be shown that *the pendulum never reaches the top*; instead it only approaches the top, taking an infinite amount of time to reach the top. We will show this in two ways. Thus our phase plane picture is correct (but slightly misleading).

The first technique will involve an approximation. We would like to know what happens as $\theta \to \pi$. How long does it take the pendulum to get there if it is initially close to $\theta = \pi$ with exactly the critical energy? From equation 22.2, since $E = 2g$,

$$L\left(\frac{d\theta}{dt}\right)^2 = 2g(\cos\theta + 1). \qquad (23.1)$$

Expanding the above energy equation in a Taylor series around $\theta = \pi$, yields

$$L\left(\frac{d\theta}{dt}\right)^2 = 2g\left[1 + \cos\pi - (\theta - \pi)\sin\pi - \frac{(\theta - \pi)^2}{2!}\cos\pi + \cdots\right].$$

---

†The theorem states that for equation 22.1 there is a unique solution (for all time) satisfying any given initial conditions.

‡The difficulty is that there *appears* to be more than one solution corresponding to the initial condition at $t = t^*$ that $\theta = \pi$ and $d\theta/dt = 0$. One solution is $\theta = \pi$ for all time and another solution is one in which $\theta \neq \pi$ (at least for $t < t^*$).

We neglect all terms of the Taylor series beyond the first nonzero one. In that manner the following is a reasonable *approximation*:

$$L\left(\frac{d\theta}{dt}\right)^2 = g(\theta - \pi)^2 \quad \text{or equivalently} \quad \frac{d\theta}{dt} = \pm(\theta - \pi)\sqrt{\frac{g}{L}}.$$

The $\pm$ sign indicates a pendulum can be swinging clockwise or counter-clockwise either towards or away from the equilibrium position, $\theta = \pi$. For the case we are investigating in which the pendulum swings towards the equilibrium position,

$$\frac{d\theta}{dt} = -(\theta - \pi)\sqrt{\frac{g}{L}} \qquad (23.2)$$

(if $\theta < \pi$, then $d\theta/dt > 0$ and if $\theta > \pi$, then $d\theta/dt < 0$). This first-order constant coefficient differential equation is easily solved (especially if $\theta - \pi$, rather than $\theta$, is considered as the dependent variable). Thus $\theta - \pi = Ae^{-(t-t_0)\sqrt{g/L}}$. This equation implies that if $\theta$ is initially (at $t = t_0$) near $\pi$, then it takes an infinite amount of time for $\theta$ to reach $\pi$, (i.e., it never reaches $\pi$). Furthermore, equation 23.2 shows that the trajectories (for $E = 2g$) can be approximated near $\theta = \pi$ by two straight lines with slopes in the phase plane equal to $\pm\sqrt{g/L}$ (as sketched in Figs. 22-10 and 22-11).

A more rigorous derivation of this result is now briefly discussed. If $E = 2g$, then from equation 23.1

$$\frac{d\theta}{dt} = +\sqrt{\frac{2g}{L}}\sqrt{\cos\theta + 1},$$

where the positive sign is again chosen to ensure that $\theta$ increases (assuming $\theta < \pi$ initially). Since

$$\frac{d\theta}{\sqrt{\frac{2g}{L}}\sqrt{\cos\theta + 1}} = dt,$$

if $\theta = \theta_0$ at $t = 0$, then the time $t^*$ at which $\theta = \pi$ is given by

$$\frac{1}{\sqrt{\frac{2g}{L}}}\int_{\theta_0}^{\pi}\frac{d\theta}{\sqrt{\cos\theta + 1}} = t^*.$$

This integral is divergent as $\theta \to \pi$. Hence $t^* = \infty$.

## EXERCISES

**23.1.**  Assume that a nonlinear pendulum is initially at its stable equilibrium position.

(a)  How large an initial angular velocity is necessary for the pendulum to go completely around?

(b)    At what initial angular velocity will the pendulum never pass its equilibrium position again?

**23.2.**    If a pendulum is initially at its unstable equilibrium position, then how large an initial angular velocity is necessary for the pendulum to go completely around?

**23.3.**    Consider $d^2x/dt^2 = -f(x)$, with $x = x_0$ a linearly unstable equilibrium position.

(a)    Show that

$$\frac{1}{2}\left(\frac{dx}{dt}\right)^2 + \int_{x_0}^{x} f(\bar{x})\, d\bar{x} = E = \text{constant}.$$

(b)    For what value of the constant $E$ is it possible that the solution approaches this unstable equilibrium point, but approaches it in a manner such that the velocity approaches zero.

(c)    Show that if $E$ is the value obtained in part (b), and if $x$ is near $x_0$, then it will take an infinite amount of time for $x$ to reach $x = x_0$.

**23.4.**    Using a computer, numerically integrate differential equation 22.1 with initial conditions $\theta(0) = 0$, $d\theta/dt(0) = \Omega_0$. [Hint: Recall Sec. 16]. Estimate the value of $\Omega_0$ for which the pendulum first goes all away around. Compare your answer to the exact answer.

# 24.  What Happens If a Pendulum Is Pushed Too Hard?

If $E > 2g$, then there is more initial energy than is needed for the pendulum to almost go around. We thus expect the pendulum to complete one cycle around (see for example Fig. 24-1) and (since there is no friction) continue revolving indefinitely. If $E > 2g$, then Fig. 24-2 shows that all angles occur. Thus in the phase plane we have Fig. 24-3, since $E = L/2(d\theta/dt)^2 + g(1 - \cos\theta)$. Using this result, the sketch of the phase plane for the pendulum is completed in Fig. 24-4. For $E > 2g$, $|\theta|$ keeps increasing (and $\rightarrow \infty$). As expected, the pendulum rotates around and around (clockwise or counterclockwise in real space depending on whether $\theta$ is increasing or decreasing). The entire qualita-

Figure 24-1    Rotating pendulum.

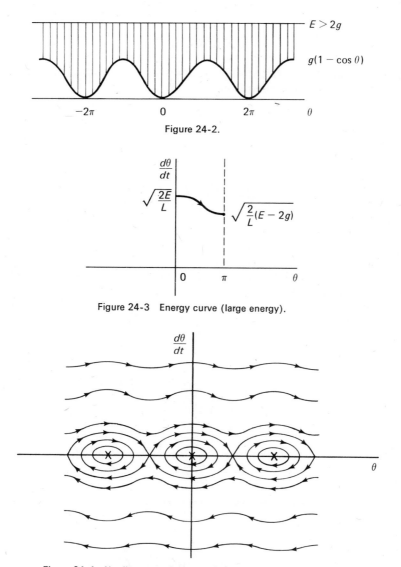

Figure 24-2.

Figure 24-3   Energy curve (large energy).

Figure 24-4   Nonlinear pendulum: trajectories in the phase plane.

tive behavior of the nonlinear pendulum has been determined using the energy curves in the phase plane.

Note that the curve in the phase plane for which $E = 2g$ separates the phase plane into two distinct regions of entirely different qualitative behavior. Such a curve is called a **separatrix**, in this case

$$L(d\theta/dt)^2 = 2g(1 + \cos \theta).$$

# EXERCISES

**24.1.** Assume that the forces acting on a mass are such that the potential energy is the function of $x$ shown in Fig. 24-5:

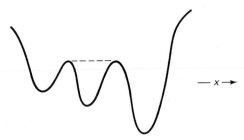

—$x$→

Figure 24-5.

Sketch the solutions in the phase plane. Describe the different kinds of motion that can occur.

**24.2.** Repeat exercise 24.1 for the potential shown in Fig. 24-6.

—$x$→

Figure 24-6.

**24.3.** Repeat exercise 24.1 for the potential shown in Fig. 24-7.

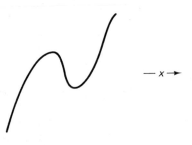

—$x$→

Figure 24-7.

**24.4.** Assume that the following equation describes a spring-mass system:

$$m\frac{d^2x}{dt^2} = -kx - \alpha x^3,$$

where $\alpha > 0$. Sketch the solution in the phase plane. Interpret the solution (see exercise 18.4).

**24.5.**  Suppose that a spring-mass system satisfies $m(d^2x/dt^2) = -kx + \alpha x^3$, where $\alpha > 0$. Sketch the solution in the phase plane. Interpret the solution (see exercise 18.5).

**24.6.**  Suppose that the potential energy is known. Referring to Fig. 24-8:

Figure 24-8.

(a)  Locate all equilibrium positions.
(b)  Sketch the force as a function of $x$ [Hint: Your answer should be consistent with part (a).]
(c)  Sketch the solutions in the phase plane.
(d)  Explain how part (c) illustrates which of the equilibrium positions are stable and which unstable.

**24.7.**  Suppose $m(d^2x/dt^2) = -ke^{2\alpha x}$ where $\alpha > 0$ and $k > 0$.
(a)  Determine all (if any) equilibrium positions.
(b)  Formulate conservation of energy.
(c)  Sketch the solution in the phase plane.
(d)  Suppose that a mass starts at $x = -1$. For what initial velocities will the mass reach $x = 0$?

# 25. Period of a Nonlinear Pendulum

Using the energy integral,

$$\frac{L}{2}\left(\frac{d\theta}{dt}\right)^2 = g(\cos\theta - 1) + E,$$

the qualitative behavior of the nonlinear pendulum,

$$L\frac{d^2\theta}{dt^2} = -g\sin\theta,$$

was obtained in Secs. 22–24. For infinitesimally small amplitudes the period of oscillation is $2\pi\sqrt{L/g}$.

Is the period unaltered as the amplitude becomes larger? Using the energy integral, an expression for the period is obtained (see Sec. 21),

$$T = 4\int_0^{\theta_{max}} \frac{d\theta}{\sqrt{\frac{2}{L}}\sqrt{g(\cos\theta - 1) + E}}, \qquad (25.1)$$

where $g(\cos \theta_{max} - 1) + E = 0$. (Recall, $\theta_{max}$ is the largest angle of oscillation.) This expression is valid when the pendulum oscillates back and forth as in Fig. 25-1 (that is, if $E < 2g$):

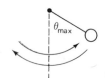

Figure 25-1.

This integral is not easily evaluated. It even causes trouble numerically (rectangles, trapezoids, Simpson's rule, etc.) as the denominator of the integrand $\longrightarrow 0$ at the endpoint $\theta = \theta_{max}$.

In order to determine the manner in which the period $T$ depends on the energy $E$ (or $\theta_{max}$), a change of variables is employed. Let

$$u = 1 - \frac{g}{E}(1 - \cos \theta).$$

Under this transformation, the limits of the integral do not depend on $E$,

$$T(E) = 2\sqrt{\frac{L}{g}} \int_0^1 \frac{du}{u^{1/2}(1 - u)^{1/2}\left[1 - \frac{E(1 - u)}{2g}\right]^{1/2}}. \qquad (25.2)$$

Although this is still difficult to evaluate analytically or numerically, it can be approximated for small values of $E$. For $E = 0$,

$$T(0) = 2\sqrt{\frac{L}{g}} \int_0^1 \frac{du}{u^{1/2}(1 - u)^{1/2}},$$

corresponding to the period of an infinitesimal amplitude. Since $1 - u \geq 0$, it is seen that for $E > 0$ the denominator of the integrand in (25.2) is smaller than that which occurs when $E = 0$:

$$1 - \frac{E(1 - u)}{2g} < 1 \quad \text{for } E > 0 \text{ and } 0 \leq u < 1.$$

Thus

$$T(E) > T(0), \quad \text{for } E > 0,$$

showing that the *period of a nonlinear pendulum is larger than that corresponding to an infinitesimal amplitude.* Evaluating $T(0)$ involves methods of integration. Let

$$w = u^{1/2} \qquad \left(dw = \frac{du}{2u^{1/2}}\right), \qquad (25.3)$$

in which case, as expected, $T(0)$ equals the period of a linearized pendulum,

$$T(0) = 4\sqrt{\frac{L}{g}} \int_0^1 \frac{dw}{(1-w^2)^{1/2}} = 4\sqrt{\frac{L}{g}} \sin^{-1} w \Big|_0^1 = 2\pi \sqrt{\frac{L}{g}}.$$

Let us attempt to calculate the first effects of the nonlinearity. The period is given by equation 25.2. $E$ is small and thus

$$\frac{E(1-u)}{2g} < 1.$$

For $E$ very small, this quantity is much smaller than 1. Consequently, the first few terms of a Taylor expansion of the integrand (around $E = 0$) will yield a good approximation

$$\left[1 - \frac{E(1-u)}{2g}\right]^{-1/2} = 1 + \frac{E}{4g}(1-u) + \cdots$$

Only the desire to keep the amount of calculations to a minimum, prevents us from developing additional terms in this approximation. The use of the binomial expansion facilitates the above calculation.* Thus

$$T(E) = 2\sqrt{\frac{L}{g}} \int_0^1 \frac{1}{u^{1/2}(1-u)^{1/2}}\left[1 + \frac{E}{4g}(1-u) + \cdots\right] du$$

or, equivalently,

$$T(E) = T(0) + \frac{E}{2g}\sqrt{\frac{L}{g}} \int_0^1 \left(\frac{1-u}{u}\right)^{1/2} du + \cdots$$

To evaluate this additional term, the transformation given by equation 25.3 is again made. Using it yields

$$\int_0^1 \left(\frac{1-u}{u}\right)^{1/2} du = 2\int_0^1 (1-w^2)^{1/2}\,dw.$$

This last integral can be evaluated using trigonometric substitutions, integration-by-parts, or integral tables (for the lazy ones among us). In that manner

$$2\int_0^1 (1-w^2)^{1/2}\,dw = w(1-w^2)^{1/2} + \sin^{-1} w \Big|_0^1 = \frac{\pi}{2}.$$

---

*The binomial expansion

$$(1+a)^n = 1 + na + \frac{n(n-1)}{2}a^2 + \frac{n(n-1)(n-2)}{3!}a^3 + \cdots$$

is an example of a Taylor series. It is valid for all $n$ (including negative and noninteger $n$) as long as $|a| < 1$. Many approximations requiring a Taylor series need only an application of a binomial expansion, saving the tedious effort of actually calculating a Taylor series via its definition.

Thus, for $E$ small, an expression for the increased period is obtained,

$$T(E) = \sqrt{\frac{L}{g}} \left(2\pi + \frac{\pi}{4}\frac{E}{g} + \cdots \right).$$

The dependence of the period on the energy has been determined for small energies. For larger values of $E$ (corresponding to a larger maximum angle), the period may be obtained by numerically evaluating either equation 25.1 or equation 25.2.

# EXERCISES

**25.1.** (a) If the initial energy is sufficiently large, determine an expression for the time it takes a pendulum to go completely around.
  (b) Estimate this time if the energy is very large ($E \gg 2g$). Give a physical interpretation of this answer.

**25.2.** Consider formula 25.1.
  (a) Using a computer, numerically evaluate the period of a nonlinear pendulum as a function of the energy $E$.
  (b) Also determine the period as a function of $\theta_{max}$.

**25.3.** Consider the differential equation of a nonlinear pendulum, equation 22.1. Numerically integrate (using a computer) this equation. Evaluate the period as a function of the energy $E$ and of $\theta_{max}$. [Hint: Assume initially $\theta = \theta_0$ and $d\theta/dt = 0$].

**25.4.** Compare the results of exercise 25.3 to exercise 25.2.

**25.5.** (a) From equation 25.2, show that a nonlinear pendulum has a longer period than the linearized pendulum.
  (b) Show that $dT/dE > 0$. Briefly describe a physical interpretation of this result.

**25.6.** If $\theta_{max} = 5°$, approximately what percentage has the period of oscillation increased from that corresponding to a linearized pendulum?

**25.7.** The transformation $w = u^{1/2}$ has been used in Sec. 25.
  (a) Relate the new variable $w$ directly to $\theta$. [Hint: You will need the trigonometric identity $\cos 2\theta = 1 - 2\sin^2 \theta$.]
  (b) The integrations performed in Sec. 25 can be analyzed by the trigonometric substitution suggested by the triangle in Fig. 25-2.

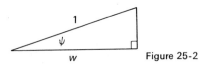

Figure 25-2

Show that, as defined in Fig. 25-2,

$$\sin \psi = \frac{\sin \theta/2}{\sin k/2},$$

where $\cos k = 1 - E/g$.

(c)   Using $\psi$ as the new integration variable, directly transform equation 25.2. Approximate the period for $E$ small, i.e., for $\sin k/2$ small.

# 26.  Nonlinear Oscillations with Damping

In the last few sections, we have analyzed the behavior of nonlinear oscillators neglecting frictional forces. We have found that the properties of nonlinear oscillators are quite similar to those of linear oscillators with the major differences being:

1. For nonlinear oscillators the period (of a periodic solution) depends on the amplitude of oscillation.
2. More than one equilibrium solution is possible.

Since even in linear problems we know that friction cannot be completely neglected, we proceed to investigate systems in which the frictional and restoring-type forces interact in a rather arbitrary way,

$$m\frac{d^2x}{dt^2} = h\left(x, \frac{dx}{dt}\right). \tag{26.1}$$

The forces depend only on the position and velocity of the mass.

In order to understand how to analyze this type of equation, recall that with no friction (but allowing a nonlinear restoring force) a significant amount of information was obtained by considering the energy integral as it related to the solution in the phase plane. However, with a frictional force, energy is not expected to be conserved.

As an example, reconsider the linear oscillator with linear damping,

$$m\frac{d^2x}{dt^2} = -kx - c\frac{dx}{dt}. \tag{26.2}$$

Let us attempt to form an energy integral by multiplying both sides of this equation by $dx/dt$ and then integrating:

$$\frac{m}{2}\left(\frac{dx}{dt}\right)^2 + \frac{k}{2}x^2 = E_0 - c\int_0^t \left(\frac{dx}{dt}\right)^2 dt, \tag{26.3}$$

where $E_0$ is the initial energy, i.e., the energy at $t = 0$,

$$E_0 = \frac{m}{2} v_0^2 + \frac{k}{2} x_0^2.$$

Explicitly we see that the energy depends on time,

$$E(t) = \frac{m}{2} \left(\frac{dx}{dt}\right)^2 + \frac{k}{2} x^2;$$

it is not constant. It decreases in time (see equation 26.3) and is said to dissipate. Thus, if we sketched ellipses in the phase plane (corresponding to the
conservation of energy), then the solutions would continually remain inside
smaller and smaller ellipses, *perhaps* as illustrated in Fig. 26-1. Thus the solution cannot be periodic. However, the energy equation is not convenient for a
more detailed understanding of the solution. We are unable to sketch the
phase plane from this equation, as in equation 26.3 $dx/dt$ does not depend
only on $x$. We will return to this example in a later exercise.

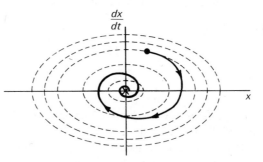

Figure 26-1    Energy dissipation in the phase plane.

A slightly different technique can be used to obtain information about the
solution. Reconsider the *general* form of Newton's law allowing restoring and
frictional forces,

$$\frac{d^2x}{dt^2} = f\left(x, \frac{dx}{dt}\right).$$

Here we have incorporated the mass $m$ into the function $f$. This is *not* the most
general form of a second-order differential equation. The most general form
is

$$\frac{d^2x}{dt^2} = g\left(x, \frac{dx}{dt}, t\right).$$

In the equation representing Newton's law, there is no explicit dependence on *t*. Such an equation is called **autonomous**. The simplest property of an autonomous equation is that translating the time origin does not change the equation (see exercise 26.10). Autonomous equations are quite important since in many physical phenomena translation in time is insignificant, and in this text we restrict attention to such equations.

Qualitative features of the solution of autonomous systems can be obtained by considering the equation in the phase plane. An energy integral will not always exist, but it will be shown that an autonomous equation can be interpreted as a relationship between *dx/dt* and *x*. Let

$$v = \frac{dx}{dt}.$$

A simple use of the chain rule shows that

$$\frac{d^2x}{dt^2} = \frac{dv}{dt} = \frac{dv}{dx}\frac{dx}{dt} = v\frac{dv}{dx}. \qquad \textbf{(26.4)}$$

In this way, the general autonomous equation,

$$\frac{d^2x}{dt^2} = f\left(x, \frac{dx}{dt}\right), \quad \text{becomes} \quad v\frac{dv}{dx} = f(x, v).$$

Using *v* and *x* as variables, a first order differential equation is derived,

$$\frac{dv}{dx} = \frac{f(x, v)}{v}. \qquad \textbf{(26.5)}$$

If an energy integral had existed, then this first order differential equation could be directly integrated yielding solution curves as before. Here we are not necessarily as fortunate since first order differential equations cannot always be solved explicitly. However, the solution of first-order differential equations can always be sketched in the following way. Suppose that

$$\frac{dv}{dx} = g(x, v).$$

At each value of *x*, the differential equation prescribes the slope of the solution *dv/dx* (if *v* is known). Through each point in a *v*–*x* plane, a short straight line is drawn with slope equal to *g*(*x*, *v*) as illustrated in Fig. 26-2.

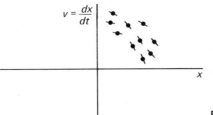

$$v = \frac{dx}{dt}$$

$x$

Figure 26-2   Direction field.

This graph is called the **direction field** of the differential equation. At each point the solution must be parallel to these "dashes." By roughly connecting these line segments, the solution in the phase plane ($v$ as a function of $x$) can be sketched (given $x$ and $v$ initially). To facilitate sketching of the direction field, *curves along which the slope of the solution is a constant* sometimes can be calculated. These curves are called **isoclines*** (Be careful to distinguish between isoclines and solution curves. Sometimes to confuse matters they are the same, but usually they are quite distinct from each other.) From equation 26.5, isoclines are curves along which $f(x, v)/v$ is constant. One isocline is immediately obtainable, namely when $v = 0$, $dv/dx = \infty$. As a review of the method of isoclines, the solution to equation 26.5 is sketched by noting that along the $x$-axis ($v = 0$) any solution must have an infinite slope. To indicate this small dashes are drawn with infinite slope on Fig. 26-3. $v = 0$ is an isocline. Solution curves which cross the $x$-axis must be parallel to these dashes.

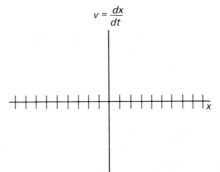

$$v = \frac{dx}{dt}$$

$x$

Figure 26-3.

Let us consider a specific example. For a spring-mass system with a linear restoring force but without friction,

$$m\frac{d^2x}{dt^2} = -kx.$$

---

*__Iso__ meaning equal as in *iso*tope or *iso*bar; *cline* meaning slope as in in*cline*.

Although we can solve this problem explicitly or solve it by sketching the solution in the phase plane using the energy integral, we will illustrate the method of isoclines to sketch the solution in the phase plane. Letting $v = dx/dt$ and using the chain rule $(d^2x/dt^2) = v(dv/dx)$ yields the first order differential equation

$$\frac{dv}{dx} = -\frac{kx}{mv}. \tag{26.6}$$

(Explicitly integrating this equation is equivalent to the energy integral.) We sketch the solution by first drawing the isoclines, curves along which the slope of the solution is constant. As above along $v = 0$, $dv/dx = \infty$. The isocline is the straight line $v = 0$, along which the slope of the solution is always infinite, indicated by the vertical slashes. Furthermore $x = 0$ is another isocline, as along $x = 0$, $dv/dx = 0$ (a constant). Other isoclines, for example, are $v = (k/m)x$ along which $dv/dx = -1$, and $v = -(k/m)x$ along which $dv/dx = +1$. These isoclines are sketched in Fig. 26-4. To locate the

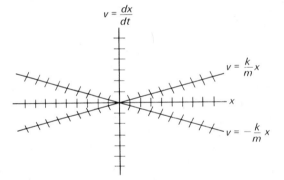

Figure 26-4    Isoclines for $md^2\,x/dt^2 = -kx$.

most general isocline, we look for the curve along which the slope of the solution is the constant $\lambda$, $dv/dx = \lambda$. From equation 26.6,

$$-\frac{k}{m}\frac{x}{v} = \lambda.$$

Solving for $v$, we see these isoclines are $v = -(k/m\lambda)x$. *For this example* all the isoclines are straight lines (in general isoclines need *not* be straight lines). We indicate in Fig. 26-5 some of these other isoclines. Any solution must be tangent to the slashes. In this manner a solution in the phase plane can be sketched (as indicated by the darkened curve in Fig. 26-5). In particular, note the difference between the solution curves (ellipses) and the isoclines (straight lines). Actually a *rough* sketch might not guarantee solutions are the ellipses which our previous analysis tells us they must be.

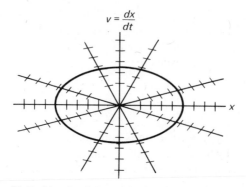

Figure 26-5   Direction field sketched by the method of isoclines.

What happens as time increases? As before when considering energy curves in the phase plane, arrows are used to indicate the direction of changes in time. We note (returning to the general time-dependent equations),

$$\frac{dx}{dt} = v$$

$$\frac{dv}{dt} = \frac{d^2x}{dt^2} = f(x, v).$$

(Note that dividing one of these equations by the other yields equation 26.5.) From $dx/dt = v$, it follows that in the upper half plane ($v > 0$) $x$ increases (arrows point to the right) and in the lower half plane ($v < 0$) $x$ decreases (arrows point to the left); see Fig. 26-6. Along the line $v = 0$, the direction in time is determined by considering the other time-dependent equation, $dv/dt = f(x, v)$. Along $v = 0$, $dv/dt = f(x, 0)$. Recall that $f(x, 0)$ is the "force" assuming no friction. *If* this force is restoring (which in general it does *not* have to be),

$$\frac{dv}{dt} = \frac{d^2x}{dt^2} = f\left(x, \frac{dx}{dt}\right),$$

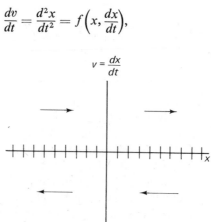

Figure 26-6.

then it is concluded that for $x > 0$, $f(x, 0) < 0$ (and vice versa). Hence $dv/dt > 0$ for $x < 0$ at $v = 0$, and thus $v$ increases in the left half plane. Similarly for $x > 0$ at $v = 0$, $v$ decreases in the right half plane. These results yield (if the force is always restoring) Fig. 26-7.

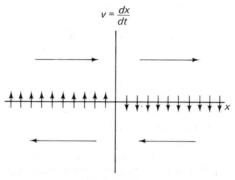

Figure 26-7.

For the example $m(d^2x/dt^2) = -kx$, arrows can be added to the phase plane yielding Fig. 26-8, the same result as previously sketched in Sec. 21.

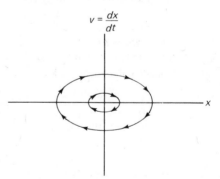

Figure 26-8 Phase plane for a linear spring-mass system.

# EXERCISES

**26.1.** Consider $dv/dx = (cx + dv)/(ax + bv)$. Curves along which the slope $(dv/dx)$ is constant are called **isoclines**. Thus the method of isoclines implies

$$\frac{dv}{dx} = \lambda \quad \text{when } \lambda = \frac{cx + dv}{ax + bv}.$$

(a) For this problem, show that the isoclines are all straight lines.

(b)   What is the slope of each isocline? (Be careful to distinguish between the slope of the solution and the slope of an isocline.)

(c)   Is it possible for the slope of an isocline to be the same as the slope of the solution? In this case show that the isocline itself is a solution curve.

**26.2.**   Consider a linear oscillator with linear friction:

$$m\frac{d^2x}{dt^2} + c\frac{dx}{dt} + kx = 0.$$

(a)   Show that $E \equiv m/2 \, (dx/dt)^2 + (k/2) \, x^2$ is a decreasing function of time.

(b)   Let $v = dx/dt$ and show that $dv/dx = (-cv - kx)/mv$.

(c)   Show that if $c^2 < 4mk$, then $v = \lambda x$ is not a solution in the phase plane.

(d)   If $m = 1, c = 1, k = 1$, then roughly sketch the solution in the phase plane. (Use known information about the time-dependent solution to improve your sketch.)

(e)   Show that if $c^2 > 4mk$, then $v = \lambda x$ is a solution in the phase plane for two different values of $\lambda$. Show that both values of $\lambda$ are negative.

(f)   If $m = 1, c = 3, k = 1$, then roughly sketch the solution in the phase plane. [Hint: Use the results of part (e)].

(g)   Explain the qualitative differences between parts (d) and (f).

**26.3.**   Reconsider exercise 26.2 if friction is negative, $c < 0$.

(a)   Show that the energy is an increasing function of time.

(b)   If $m = 1, c = -1, k = 1$, then roughly sketch the solution in the phase plane.

(c)   Repeat part (b) if $m = 1, c = -3, k = 1$.

(d)   Explain the qualitative differences between parts (b) and (c).

**26.4.**   Consider the linear oscillator without friction:

$$m\frac{d^2x}{dt^2} = -kx.$$

(a)   *Without* forming an energy integral, let $v = dx/dt$ and show that

$$\frac{dv}{dx} = \frac{-kx}{mv}.$$

(b)   Sketch the solution in the phase plane.

(c)   Interpret the solution.

**26.5.**   Briefly explain why only one solution curve goes through each point in the phase plane except for an equilibrium point in which case there may be more than one.

**26.6.**   Suppose that $dv/dx = v^2 - x$.

(a)   Show that the isoclines are not straight lines.

(b)   Sketch the solution.

**26.7.**   Consider a spring-mass system with cubic friction

$$m\frac{d^2x}{dt^2} + \sigma\left(\frac{dx}{dt}\right)^3 + kx = 0, \qquad \sigma > 0.$$

Show that $E \equiv m/2(dx/dt)^2 + k/2 \, x^2$ is a decreasing function of time.

**26.8.**  Consider

$$m\frac{d^2x}{dt^2} = -kx - \alpha x^3 - \sigma\left(\frac{dx}{dt}\right)^3.$$

Assume $k > 0$, $m > 0$, $\alpha > 0$, and $\sigma > 0$. Show that as $t \to \infty$, $x \to 0$. [Hint: Form an energy integral and show $dE/dt \le 0$. Since $E \ge 0$ (why?), show that Fig. 26-9 implies that $E \to 0$:

Figure 26.9  Energy decay.

Why can't $E \to E_0 > 0$ as $t \to \infty$?]

**26.9.**  Reconsider exercise 26.8 if $\alpha < 0$. Show that the conclusion of the problem may no longer be valid.

**26.10.**  Consider the general second-order autonomous equation:

$$\frac{d^2x}{dt^2} = f\left(x, \frac{dx}{dt}\right).$$

Show that if $x = g(t)$ is a solution, then $x = g(t - t_0)$ is another solution for any $t_0$.

**26.11.**  Assume

$$m\frac{d^2x}{dt^2} + c\frac{dx}{dt} + f(x) = 0,$$

with $c > 0$ and $f(0) = 0$.
(a)  Give a physical interpretation of this problem.
(b)  By considering the energy, show that there are no periodic solutions (other than $x(t) \equiv 0$).

**26.12.**  Show that if a solution in the phase plane is a straight line, it corresponds to $x$ growing or decaying exponentially in time.

**26.13.**  Consider

$$m\frac{d^2x}{dt^2} = \alpha(e^{\beta x} - 1) - c\frac{dx}{dt}.$$

(a)  What first-order differential equation determines the solution curves in the phase plane?
(b)  What curves are isoclines?

**26.14.**  Suppose that $m\, d^2x/dt^2 = kx$ with $m > 0$ and $k > 0$.
(a)  Briefly explain why $x = 0$ is an unstable equilibrium position.
(b)  Using the method of isoclines sketch the solution in the phase plane (for ease of computation, let $m = 1$ and $k = 1$). [Hint: At least sketch the isoclines corresponding to the slope of the solution being 0, $\infty$, $\pm 1$.]
(c)  Explain how part (b) illustrates part (a).

# 27. Equilibrium Positions and Linearized Stability

The general autonomous system,

$$\frac{d^2x}{dt^2} = f\left(x, \frac{dx}{dt}\right),$$

yields a first-order differential equation for the phase plane

$$\frac{dv}{dx} = \frac{f(x, v)}{v} \qquad (27.1)$$

where $v = dx/dt$ (see Sec. 26). The slope of the solution in the phase plane is uniquely determined everywhere. Well, not quite: at any point where both the numerator and denominator is zero, $dv/dx$ is not uniquely determined since $dv/dx = 0/0$ (it depends on how you approach that point). Such points are called singular points of the phase plane equation 27.1. Singular points occur whenever

$$\begin{aligned} v &= 0 \\ f(x, 0) &= 0. \end{aligned} \qquad (27.2)$$

In other words, the velocity is zero, $v = 0$, and there are no forces at any such singular point. These singular points thus represent **equilibrium positions**, values of $x$ for which the forces cancel if there is no motion. For example, such points were encountered in the discussion of a nonlinear pendulum without friction. As in that problem we are quite interested in determining which such equilibrium points are stable.

As has been shown in Sec. 18, stability can be investigated most easily by considering a **linearized stability analysis**. The analysis here differs from the previous one only by certain mathematical details now necessitated by the possible velocity dependence of the force. Suppose that $x = x_E$ is an equilibrium time-independent solution of the equation of motion,

$$\frac{d^2x}{dt^2} = f\left(x, \frac{dx}{dt}\right). \qquad (27.3)$$

If $x$ is initially near $x_E$ with a small velocity, then it is reasonable to expand

$f(x, dx/dt)$ in a Taylor series of a function of two variables*:

$$f\left(x, \frac{dx}{dt}\right) = f(x_E, 0) + (x - x_E)\frac{\partial f}{\partial x}\bigg|_{x_E, 0} + \frac{dx}{dt}\frac{\partial f}{\partial\left(\frac{dx}{dt}\right)}\bigg|_{x_E, 0} + \cdots$$

Since $f(x_E, 0) = 0$ ($x_E$ is an equilibrium solution),

$$\frac{d^2x}{dt^2} = (x - x_E)\frac{\partial f}{\partial x}\bigg|_{x_E, 0} + \frac{dx}{dt}\frac{\partial f}{\partial\left(\frac{dx}{dt}\right)}\bigg|_{x_E, 0},$$

where higher-order terms in the Taylor series have been neglected since $x$ is near $x_E$ and $dx/dt$ is small. Again introducing the displacement from equilibrium, $z$,

$$z = x - x_E,$$

it follows that

$$\boxed{\frac{d^2z}{dt^2} = -kz - c\frac{dz}{dt},}$$   (27.4)

where

$$\boxed{-k = \frac{\partial f}{\partial x}\bigg|_{x_E, 0}}$$

$$\boxed{-c = \frac{\partial f}{\partial\left(\frac{dx}{dt}\right)}\bigg|_{x_E, 0}.}$$

The notation used has taken advantage of the analogy of equation 27.4 to a spring-mass system with friction. However, here it is *not* necessary that $k$ and $c$ be positive!

   This equation is a constant coefficient second-order homogeneous ordinary differential equation; exactly the kind analyzed earlier. Solutions are exponentials $e^{rt}$, where

$$\boxed{r = \frac{-c \pm \sqrt{c^2 - 4k}}{2}}$$

---

*The formula for the Taylor series of a function of two variables is

$$f(x_0 + h, y_0 + k) = f(x_0, y_0) + h\frac{\partial f}{\partial x}\bigg|_{x_0, y_0} + k\frac{\partial f}{\partial y}\bigg|_{x_0, y_0} + \cdots$$

or equivalently

$$f(x, y) = f(x_0, y_0) + (x - x_0)\frac{\partial f}{\partial x}\bigg|_{x_0, y_0} + (y - y_0)\frac{\partial f}{\partial y}\bigg|_{x_0, y_0} + \cdots$$

(except if $c^2 = 4k$, in which case the solutions are $e^{-ct/2}$ and $te^{-ct/2}$). The equilibrium solution is said to be linearly stable if, for all initial conditions near $x = x_E$ and $v = 0$, the displacement from equilibrium does not grow. The following table indicates the behavior of the equilibrium solution:

$c^2 - 4k > 0$
$\begin{cases} \text{Unstable if } c \leq 0. \\ \text{Also unstable if } c > 0 \text{ but } k < 0. \\ \text{Otherwise stable (i.e., } c > 0 \text{ and } k \geq 0). \end{cases}$

$c^2 - 4k = 0$
$\begin{cases} \text{Stable if } c > 0. \\ \text{Unstable if } c \leq 0. \end{cases}$

$c^2 - 4k < 0$
$\begin{cases} \text{Unstable if } c < 0. \\ \text{Stable if } c \geq 0 \text{ (sometimes said to be} \\ \textit{neutrally stable*} \text{ if } c = 0 \text{ since the solu-} \\ \text{tion purely oscillates if } c = 0). \end{cases}$

This information can also be communicated using a stability diagram in $c$–$k$ parameter space, Fig. 27-1. The equilibrium position is stable only if the linearized displacement $z$ satisfies a differential equation corresponding to a linear spring-mass system $k \geq 0$ with damping $c \geq 0$ (except if $c = k = 0$).

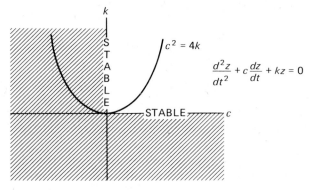

Figure 27-1   Stability diagram (the hatched region is *unstable*).

As an example, suppose that

$$\frac{d^2x}{dt^2} = -(x - 4) + x^3 \frac{dx}{dt}.$$

We see that $x = 4$ is the only equilibrium position ($dx/dt = 0$ and $d^2x/dt^2 = 0$). Letting $f(x, dx/dt) = -(x - 4) + x^3(dx/dt)$, we can determine the stability of $x = 4$ by simply calculating the partial derivatives of $f(x, dx/dt)$:

*See page 58.

$$\frac{\partial f}{\partial x} = -1 + 3x^2 \frac{dx}{dt} \qquad \frac{\partial f}{\partial x}\bigg|_{4,0} = -1 = -k$$

$$\frac{\partial f}{\partial(dx/dt)} = x^3 \qquad \frac{\partial f}{\partial(dx/dt)}\bigg|_{4,0} = 64 = -c.$$

From the table or the diagram above, we see $x = 4$ is an unstable equilibrium position.

This determines what happens near the equilibrium position. The non-linear terms in the neighborhood of the equilibrium position have been neglected. Are we justified in doing so? A complete answer to that question is postponed, but will be analyzed in later sections on population dynamics. For the moment, let us just say that in "most" cases the results of a linearized stability analysis explains the behavior of the solution in the immediate vicinity of the equilibrium position.

In the case in which the linearized stability analysis predicts the equilibrium solution is unstable, the displacement grows (usually exponentially). Eventually the solution is perturbed so far from the equilibrium that neglecting the nonlinear terms is no longer a valid approximation. When this occurs we can not rely on the results of a linear stability analysis. The solution may or may not continue to depart from the equilibrium position. To analyze this situation, the solution can be discussed in the phase plane.

# EXERCISES

**27.1.** Suppose that

$$\frac{d^2z}{dt^2} + c\frac{dz}{dt} + kz = 0,$$

where $c$ and $k$ are parameters which can be negative, positive or zero.
   (a)   Under what circumstances does $z$ oscillate with an amplitude staying constant? growing? decaying?
   (b)   For what values of $c$ and $k$ do there exist initial conditions such that $z$ exponentially grows? decays?

**27.2.** Assume that for a spring-mass system the restoring force does not depend on the velocity and the friction force does not depend on the displacement. Thus

$$m\frac{d^2x}{dt^2} = -f(x) - g\left(\frac{dx}{dt}\right).$$

If $x = 0$ is an equilibrium point, then what can be said about $f(x)$ and $g(dx/dt)$? Analyze the linear stability of the equilibrium solution $x = 0$.

**27.3.** Where in the phase plane is it possible for trajectories to cross?

**27.4.** Analyze equation 27.4 if $c = 0$ with $k > 0$, $k = 0$, and $k < 0$.

# 28.  Nonlinear Pendulum with Damping

As an example of an autonomous system, let us consider a nonlinear pendulum with a damping force. If the frictional force is proportional to the velocity of the mass with frictional coefficient $c$, then

$$L\frac{d^2\theta}{dt^2} = -g\sin\theta - k\frac{d\theta}{dt},\qquad\qquad\text{(28.1)}$$

where $k = cL/m$ is positive, $k > 0$. Can you envision a situation in which damping occurs in this manner?

We recall the phase plane for the nonlinear pendulum without friction sketched in Fig. 24-4. In particular we are now interested in determining effects due to friction. Before this problem is mathematically solved, can you describe what you expect to occur

1. If a small angle with small velocity is initially prescribed?
2. If an extremely large initial velocity is prescribed?

Hopefully your intuition is good and the mathematics will verify your predictions.

Since an energy integral does not exist for equation 28.1, we must again introduce the phase plane variable, the angular velocity,

$$v = d\theta/dt.$$

$d^2\theta/dt^2 = dv/dt = (d\theta/dt)(dv/d\theta) = v\,dv/d\theta$ and hence equation 28.1 becomes a first-order differential equation,

$$Lv\frac{dv}{d\theta} = -g\sin\theta - kv,$$

or equivalently

$$\frac{dv}{d\theta} = \frac{-g\sin\theta - kv}{Lv}.\qquad\qquad\text{(28.2)}$$

Unlike the frictionless pendulum, we cannot integrate this immediately to obtain energy curves. Instead, the phase plane is sketched. Along $v = 0$, $dv/d\theta = \infty$. There the direction field is vertical. We also recall, for example, that in the upper half plane $\theta$ increases since $v = d\theta/dt > 0$ (and arrows thus point to the right as in Fig. 28-1):

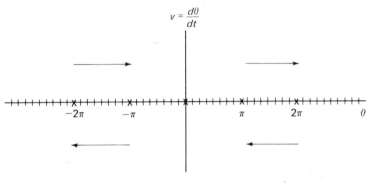

Figure 28-1.

The equilibrium positions are marked with an 'x'. They occur where $dv/d\theta = 0/0$ (see Sec. 27). Note again that $\theta = 0$ is expected to be stable, and that $\theta = \pi$ is expected to be an unstable equilibrium position. This can be verified in a straightforward manner by doing a linearized stability analysis in the neighborhood of the equilibrium positions, as suggested in Sec. 27. For example, near $\theta = 0$, $\sin \theta$ is approximated by $\theta$ and hence

$$L\frac{d^2\theta}{dt^2} = -g\theta - k\frac{d\theta}{dt}. \tag{28.3}$$

This equation is mathematically analogous to the equation describing a linear spring-mass system with friction (see Secs. 10–13). $\theta = 0$ is a stable equilibrium position. The angle $\theta$ is damped; it is underdamped if $k^2 < 4Lg$ (sufficiently small friction) and overdamped if $k^2 > 4Lg$.

Along the isocline $v = 0$, the solutions in the phase plane must have vertical tangents. However, at $v = 0$ is $v$ increasing or decreasing? In other words, should arrows be introduced on the vertical slashes pointing upwards or downwards? The sign of $dv/dt$ at $v = 0$ determines whether $v$ is increasing or decreasing there. It cannot be determined from the phase plane differential equation, equation 28.2. Instead the time-dependent equation must be analyzed. From equation 28.1, $dv/dt = -g \sin \theta$ at $v = 0$. Thus at $v = 0$, $dv/dt$ is positive where $\sin \theta$ is negative (for example, $-\pi < \theta < 0$) and vice versa. (Can you give a physical interpretation of this result?) Consequently we have Fig. 28-2.

Other than the isocline along which $dv/d\theta = \infty$ (namely $v = 0$), the next most important isocline (and also usually an easy one to determine) is the one along which $dv/d\theta = 0$. From equation 28.2, the curve along which $dv/d\theta = 0$ is

$$v = -\frac{g}{k} \sin \theta.$$

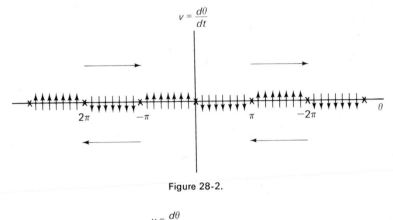

Figure 28-2.

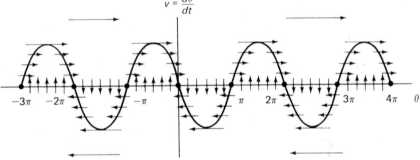

Figure 28-3   Nonlinear pendulum with damping: direction field corresponding to $dv/d\theta$ equal 0 and $\infty$.

Sketching this curve, the direction field, and the corresponding arrows yields Fig. 28-3.

Before we attempt to make sketches of the solution, the sign of $dv/dt$ should be calculated from

$$\frac{dv}{dt} = -g\frac{\sin\theta}{L} - \frac{kv}{L}.$$

If $dv/dt = h(v, \theta)$, then we know that the sign of $dv/dt$ usually changes at $h(v, \theta) = 0$, in this example the sinuous isocline that has been drawn in Fig. 28-3. As this curve is crossed, the sign of $dv/dt$ changes (if the zero is a simple zero, which it is in this case). On one side of this curve $dv/dt$ is positive, and on the other side $dv/dt$ is negative. For example if $v > -g/k \sin\theta$, then $dv/dt < 0$. Thus trajectories go downward (as indicated by ↓) above the sinuous sketched curve and vice versa. An alternate method to calculate the sign of $dv/dt$ is to analyze the sign for very large $v$ (both positive and negative). Then, since

$$\frac{dv}{dt} \approx -\frac{k}{L}v,$$

$v$ must decrease if $v$ is sufficiently large and positive. (How large is sufficiently large?) This yields the same result.

In every region of the phase plane, it has been determined whether both $v$ and $\theta$ are increasing or decreasing with time. Let us use arrows in the following way to suggest the general direction of the trajectories: for example, if $\theta$ decreases in time $\leftarrow$ and $v$ increases in time $\uparrow$, then the symbol $\nwarrow$ is introduced in the corresponding region of the phase plane. Our results for the nonlinear pendulum with friction are shown in Fig. 28-4.

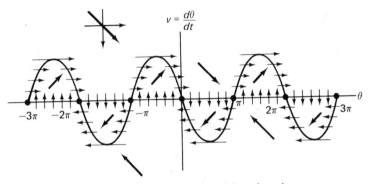

Figure 28-4   General direction of the trajectories.

To determine the accurate behavior of the trajectories, we may further use the method of isoclines. Before doing so, however, we note that often the qualitative behavior can be more easily obtained by first analyzing the phase plane in the neighborhood of the equilibrium positions. Eventually in the context of population dynamics (see Sec. 47), we will discuss a wide range of possible phase planes in the vicinity of equilibrium points. In the meantime, let us discuss the two specific equilibrium positions that occur for a nonlinear pendulum with friction.

Near the "natural" position of the pendulum, $\theta = 0$, the phase plane is as shown in Fig. 28-5. The curve along which $dv/d\theta = 0$, $v = -g/k \sin \theta$, is

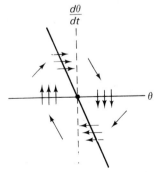

Figure 28-5   Damped pendulum: qualitative behavior of the trajectories in the neighborhood of the natural equilibrium position.

approximated near $\theta = 0$ by the straight line $v = -(g/k)\theta$. The linearized stability analysis in the vicinity of $\theta = 0$ (see equation 28.3) helps to determine the approximate behavior in the neighborhood of $\theta = 0$ of the phase plane. Without the linearized stability analysis, the above diagram suggests the motion may be one of the four types sketched in Fig. 28-6. Note that all four sketches satisfy the qualitative behavior suggested by the arrows in Fig. 28.5. In the vicinity of the equilibrium position, the trajectories (a) spiral

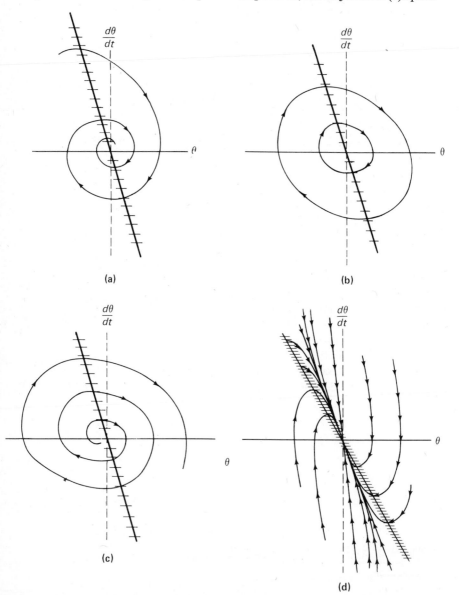

Figure 28-6  Some different types of trajectories in the neighborhood of an equilibrium position (not necessarily for a pendulum).

in towards the equilibrium position, in which case we would say the equilibrium position is stable; or (b) the trajectories could "circle" around the
equilibrium position (that is, the trajectories would be closed curves), in
which case we say the equilibrium position is neutrally stable; or (c) the
trajectories could spiral out from the equilibrium position, in which case we
would say the equilibrium position is unstable; or (d) the trajectories tend
directly towards the equilibrium position without oscillating around it, a
different kind of equilibrium position (details of this last case, called a stable
node, are given in Sec. 47).

As we have suggested, the type of equilibrium position is easily determined from the linearized analysis valid in the vicinity of the equilibrium
position. From equation 28.3, we see that if there is sufficiently small friction
(i.e., *if $k^2 < 4Lg$*), since the solution is an underdamped oscillation, the
trajectories must be as illustrated in (a) and spiral inwards. Alternatively, the
decay of the energy implies that either (a) or (d) is the correct case (see
Fig. 26.1). If $k^2 < 4Lg$, the effect of friction (even the slightest amount of
friction, $k > 0$, no matter how small) is to transform the trajectories from
closed curves ($k = 0$) to spirals. This is not surprising because we observed in
exercise 26.2d the same phenomena when comparing a damped linear oscillator to an undamped one. If $k^2 > 4Lg$, the trajectories will be different.
Exercise 28.2 discusses this latter case.

Can a similar analysis be done near $\theta = \pi$? See Fig. 28-7. The trajectories
seem to tend towards the equilibrium position if they are in certain regions in

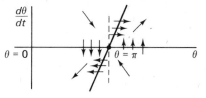

Figure 28-7   Phase plane of a damped pendulum: qualitative behavior near the inverted
equilibrium position.

the phase plane, while in other regions the trajectories move away. Clearly
this indicates that $\theta = \pi$ is an unstable equilibrium position of the pendulum
(as we already suspect on physical grounds and can verify using the linearized
analysis of Sec. 27). Let us roughly sketch in Fig. 28-8 some trajectories in the
neighborhood of $\theta = \pi$:

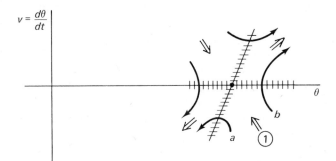

Figure 28-8.

Consider trajectories near the area marked ① in the figure. Some trajectories on the left must cross the isocline along which $dv/d\theta = 0$ and then curve downward as illustrated by curve *a*. Others, more to the right, must turn towards the right as illustrated by curve *b*. Thus there must be a trajectory (in between) which "enters" the unstable equilibrium position. In a similar manner we can easily see that there are four trajectories which enter this unstable equilibrium position (two enter backwards in time) as illustrated in Fig. 28-9. In Sec. 47B we will call such an equilibrium position a **saddle point**. In the neighborhood of the equilibrium, the trajectories that enter a saddle point can be shown to be approximated by *two* straight lines as sketched (see exercise 26.2 and the further developments of exercise 28.1).

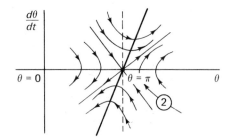

Figure 28-9   Trajectories for a damped pendulum in the vicinity of the unstable equilibrium position.

Some thought questions (not intended to be difficult) follow:

1. Two of the trajectories seem to be tending towards the unstable equilibrium position. What might this correspond to physically? Do you expect that it ever gets there?
2. In Fig. 28-9 consider the trajectory marked ②. Can you explain what is happening? What do you expect will eventually happen to that solution?

Determining the phase plane in the neighborhood of the equilibrium position is not sufficient to completely understand the behavior of the nonlinear pendulum with damping. We can easily imagine an initial condition near $\theta = 0$ with a large angular velocity such that the pendulum does not remain near $\theta = 0$. For this case additional analysis would be necessary. The motion would not be restricted to the area near $\theta = 0$. Furthermore, since $\theta = \pi$ is unstable, we will rarely be interested in trajectories that remain near $\theta = \pi$. To investigate solutions for which the angle is at some time far away from an equilibrium, in the phase plane we can roughly connect the solution curves that are valid in the neighborhood of $\theta = 0$ and $\theta = \pi$ as illustrated in Fig. 28-10 (assuming that $k^2 < 4Lg$). Energy considerations, for example, show that the trajectory emanating from $\theta = -\theta_0$ $(0 < \theta_0 < \pi)$ with

$v = d\theta/dt = 0$ must fall short of $\theta = \theta_0$, when again $v = 0$. The maximum displacement of a pendulum diminishes after each oscillation due to the small friction (as illustrated in Fig. 28-10).

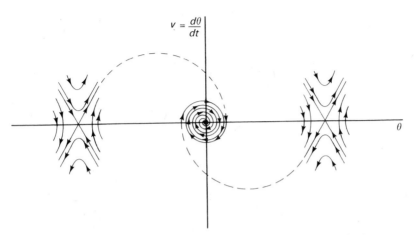

Figure 28-10   Phase plane if $k^2 < 4Lg$: sketch illustrating trajectories in the neighborhood of both equilibrium positions.

To improve this rough sketch, and, in particular, to sketch the phase plane for large velocities, the method of isoclines should be systematically employed. Along the curve

$$v = g\frac{\sin \theta}{k}, \qquad \frac{dv}{d\theta} = \frac{-2k}{L}.$$

More generally along the curves

$$v = \frac{\lambda g \sin \theta}{k}, \qquad \frac{dv}{d\theta} = \frac{-(1 + \lambda)k}{\lambda L}.$$

Using these isoclines we obtain an improved sketch of the phase plane in Fig. 28-11 (if $k^2 < 4Lg$). The sketch of the trajectories of the slightly damped nonlinear pendulum shows that we can understand the solution of a complicated mathematical problem without obtaining an explicit solution. Under certain determinable circumstances, the pendulum oscillates with smaller and smaller amplitude. If a sufficiently large initial angular velocity is given, the pendulum will go around a finite number of times (this contrasts with the frictionless nonlinear pendulum in which the pendulum continually goes around and around). The pendulum will be continually slowing down and eventually it will not be able to go completely around. Then the pendulum will oscillate around its natural position with decreasing amplitude (except in the very special cases in which the pendulum approaches the inverted position with zero velocity, but never gets there).

Exercise 28.2 modifies the above discussion when $k^2 > 4Lg$.

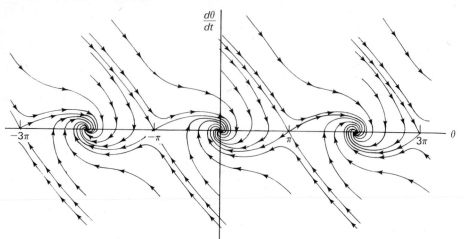

Figure 28-11    Trajectories of a pendulum with damping (if $k^2 < 4Lg$).

# EXERCISES

**28.1.** Consider equation 28.1.

(a) Approximate $\sin \theta$ in the neighborhood of the unstable equilibrium position.

(b) Show that the resulting approximation of the phase plane equation can be put into the form

$$\frac{dv}{d\theta^*} = \frac{c\theta^* + dv}{a\theta^* + bv},$$

where $\theta^* = \theta - \pi$.

(c) Show that two solution curves are straight lines going through the origin $(v = 0, \theta^* = 0)$. [Hint: See exercise 26.2]. Show that one straight line has positive slope and the other negative.

**28.2.** For the nonlinear pendulum with friction, equation 28.1, sketch the solution in the phase plane if friction is sufficiently large, $k^2 > 4Lg$. Pay special attention to the phase plane in the neighborhood of $\theta = 0$ and $\theta = \pi$. Show that there are straight line solutions in the neighborhood of both $\theta = 0$ and $\theta = \pi$. For sketching purposes, you may assume that $L = 1$, $g = 1$, $k = 3$. [Hint: See exercises 26.2 and 28.1.]

**28.3.** If a spring-mass system has a friction force proportional to the cube of the velocity, then

$$m\frac{d^2x}{dt^2} + \sigma\left(\frac{dx}{dt}\right)^3 + kx = 0.$$

(a) Derive a first-order differential equation describing the phase plane $(dx/dt$ as a function of $x)$.

(b)   Sketch the solution in the phase plane.

**28.4.**   Consider the spring-mass system of exercise 28.3 without a restoring force (i.e., $k = 0$).
(a)   How do you expect the solution to behave?
(b)   Let $v = dx/dt$ and sketch the solution in the phase plane.
(c)   Let $v = dx/dt$ and solve the problem exactly.
(d)   Show that the solutions of parts (b) and (c) verify part (a).

**28.5.**   Consider a linear pendulum with linearized friction

$$L\frac{d^2\theta}{dt^2} = -g\theta - k\frac{d\theta}{dt}.$$

Under what condition does the pendulum continually oscillate back and forth with decreasing amplitude?

**28.6.**   Consider a nonlinear pendulum with Newtonian damping (see exercise 10.6):

$$L\frac{d^2\theta}{dt^2} = -g\sin\theta - \beta\frac{d\theta}{dt}\left|\frac{d\theta}{dt}\right|,$$

where $\beta > 0$.
(a)   Show that an energy integral does not exist.
(b)   By introducing the phase plane variable $v = d\theta/dt$, show that

$$\frac{dv}{d\theta} = \frac{-g\sin\theta - \beta v|v|}{Lv}.$$

(c)   Instead of sketching the isoclines, show that

$$L\frac{d}{d\theta}(v^2) \pm \beta v^2 = -g\sin\theta.$$

(d)   Under what conditions does the $+$ or $-$ sign apply?
(e)   This is a linear differential equation for $v^2$. Solve this equation.
(f)   Using this solution, roughly sketch the phase plane.
(g)   What qualitative differences do you expect to occur between this problem and the one discussed in Sec. 28?

**28.7.**   The Van der Pol oscillator is described by the following nonlinear differential equation:

$$\frac{d^2x}{dt^2} - \epsilon\frac{dx}{dt}(1 - x^2) + \omega^2 x = 0,$$

where $\epsilon \geq 0$.
(a)   Briefly describe the physical effect of each term.
(b)   If $\epsilon = 0$, what happens?
(c)   Is the equilibrium position $x = 0$, linearly stable or unstable?
(d)   If displacements are large, what do you expect happens?
(e)   Sketch the trajectories in the phase plane if $\omega = 1$ and $\epsilon = \frac{1}{10}$. Describe any interesting features of the solution.

**28.8.**  Reconsider the Van der Pol oscillator of exercise 28.7.

  (a)  Numerically integrate the differential equation with $\omega = 1$ and $\epsilon = \frac{1}{10}$.

  (b)  Can the scaling of time justify letting $\omega = 1$ always?

  (c)  Compare your numerical results to the sketch in the phase plane (exercise 28.7e).

**28.9.**  Rescale equation 28.1 to determine the important dimensionless parameters.

**28.10.**  Consider equation 28.1. Assume $k^2 < 4Lg$. (Let $k = 1, L = 1, g = 1$). Using a computer, solve the initial value problem:

$$\theta(0) = 0, \qquad \frac{d\theta}{dt}(0) = \Omega_0.$$

Determine how many times the pendulum goes completely around as a function of $\Omega_0$.

**28.11.**  Using a linearized stability analysis, show that $\theta = \pi$ is an unstable equilibrium position of a nonlinear pendulum with friction.

# 29.  Further Readings in Mechanical Vibrations

In the preceding sections, only some of the simplest models of mechanical vibrations have been introduced. We progressed from linear undamped oscillators to nonlinear ones with frictional forces. The behavior of the nonlinear systems we have analyzed seem qualitatively similar to linear ones. However, we have *not* made a complete mathematical analysis of all possible problems. By including other types of nonlinear and frictional forces (for example, as occur in certain electrical devices), we could find behavior not suggested by linear problems especially if external periodic forces are included. However, our goal is only to *introduce* the concepts of applied mathematics, and thus we may end our preliminary investigation of mechanical vibrations at this point. For further studies, I refer the interested reader to the following excellent books:

ANDRONOW, A. A., CHAIKIN, C. E., and WITT, A. A., *Theory of Oscillations*. Princeton, N.J.: Princeton University Press, 1949. (This includes a good discussion of the theory of the clock!)

STOKER, J. J., *Nonlinear Vibrations*. New York: Interscience, 1950.

Other interesting problems involving the coupling of two or more spring-mass systems and/or pendulums as well as problems involving rigid bodies in two and three dimensions can be found in a wide variety of texts, whose titles often contain "mechanics" or "dynamics." In particular, two well-known ones are:

GOLDSTEIN, H., *Classical Mechanics*. Reading, Mass.: Addison-Wesley, 1950.

LANDAU, L. D. and LIFSHITZ, E. M., *Mechanics*. Readings Mass.: Addison-Wesley, 1960.

# Population Dynamics— Mathematical Ecology

# 30.  Introduction to Mathematical Models in Biology

In the past, mathematics has not been as successful a tool in the biological sciences as it has been in the physical sciences. There are probably many reasons for this. Plants and animals are complex, made up of many components, the simplest of which man is just learning to comprehend. There seems to be no fundamental biological law analogous to Newton's law. Thus the scientific community is a long way from understanding cause-effect relationships in the biological world to the same degree that such laws exist for spring-mass systems. In addition, many animals possess an ability to choose courses of action, an ability that cannot be attributed to a spring-mass system nor a pendulum.

In the following sections we will develop mathematical models describing one aspect of the biological world, the mutual relationships among plants, animals, and their environment, a field of study known as **ecology**. As a means of quantifying this science, the number of individuals of different species is investigated. We will analyze the fluctuations of these populations, hence the other part of the title of this chapter, **population dynamics**. The mathematical models that are developed are frequently crude ones. Observations of population changes are limited. Furthermore, it is not always apparent what factors account for observed population variations. We cannot expect simple models of the biological world to accurately predict population growth. However, we should not hesitate to discuss simple models, for it is reasonable to expect that such models may be as significant in the biological sciences as spring-mass systems are in contemporary quantum, atomic, and nuclear physics.

We will formulate models based on observed population data of various species, such as human population in specified areas or the population of fish and algae in a lake. We might want to try to understand the complex ecosystem of a lake, involving the interaction of many species of plant and animal life. Another example might be to study the growth of a forest. On the most grandiose scale, we might model the entire world's plant and animal populations (consisting of many smaller ecosystems). Surely it is reasonable to proceed by asking simpler questions. Here we will attempt to mathematically model processes involving a few species. As in the modeling of any problem, many assumptions will be made.

**119**

We start our study of mathematical ecology by briefly discussing some basic assumptions of the population models utilized in this text (Sec. 31). Our first models involve the simplest birth and death processes of one-species ecosystems (Secs. 32–36), which must be modified to model more realistic environmental influences (Secs. 37–39). Experiments suggest that these models are also at times inadequate, motivating our investigation of population growth with time delays (Secs. 40–42). Then we begin to model more complex ecosystems involving the interaction of two species (Secs. 43–44), pausing to discuss some necessary mathematics (Secs. 45–47). Specific predator-prey and competing two-species models accounts for the concluding parts of our discussion of population dynamics (Secs. 48–54).

Throughout our study we focus our attention on the modeling process, qualitative behavior, explicit solutions, and the resulting ecological interpretations. Fundamental concepts (as with mechanical vibrations) involve equilibriums and their stability.

# 31.  Population Models

We begin the study of ecosystems, by considering the population of one species in a specified region, whether it is the number of people in the world, the number of pine trees in a forest, or the number of bacteria in an experiment. We ignore any differences in the individuals comprising the group (i.e., male-female differences, age differences). What kinds of data might be observed? Perhaps the number of monkeys in a laboratory as a function of time would be as shown in Fig. 31-1. This curve is discontinuous since changes in the monkey population occur in integral units ($+1$ for single births, $-1$ for deaths, $+2$ for twins, and so on). Furthermore, the number of monkeys, $N(t)$, can only be an integer. In many situations involving a *large number* of a species, it is reasonable to approximate $N(t)$ as a continuous function of time, perhaps by fitting a smooth curve through the data. In this manner, it is frequently possible to use continuous functions of time to represent populations.

The previous population data were observed continuously in time. However, some populations are normally measured periodically. For example, the bear population in a forest might be estimated only once a year. Thus data might be $N(t_i)$, where each $t_i$ represents the time at which a measurement was made. Although this could be modeled as a continuous function of time (by again fitting a smooth curve through the data points), the limitations of the observed data suggest that it might be only necessary to model the population at certain discrete times.

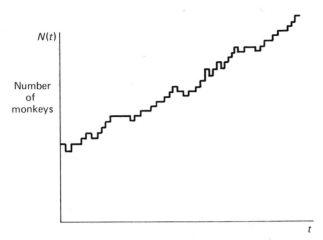

Figure 31-1   Discontinuous population growth.

An additional difficulty occurs, for example, when considering the population of the United States as a function of time. Data is gathered through a census taken every ten years. However, the accuracy of these census figures have been questioned. The data to which a mathematical model is compared may be inaccurate. Here, we will not pursue the question of how to analyze data with inaccuracies, a field of study in itself.

In formulating a model of the population growth of a species, we must decide what factors affect that population. Clearly in some cases it depends on many quantities. For example: the population of sharks in the Adriatic Sea will depend on the number of fish available for the sharks to consume (if there are none, sharks would become extinct). In addition, the presence of a harmful bacteria will affect a number of sharks. It would be incorrect to assume that the population of sharks is affected only by other species. We should not be surprised if, for example, the water temperature and salinity (salt content) are important in determining the shark population. Other factors may also be significant. We will model the population of sharks later.

Now we will study a simpler species, one not affected by any others. Such a species might be observed in a laboratory experiment of well-fed animals. Suppose we perform such an experiment starting with $N_0$ animals and model population as a continuous function of time $N(t)$. We might observe the graph in Fig. 31-2. Before attempting to analyze this situation, let us rerun the hypothetical experiment, trying to make no variation in the initial population nor in the laboratory environment. We might observe the second graph in Fig. 31-2. We would be quite surprised if we got identical results. What caused the differences?

It seems impossible to exactly repeat a given experimental result. Thus, we do not have complete control of the experiment. (Is this also true for a

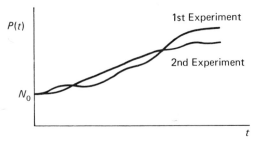

Figure 31-2   Experimental variability.

spring-mass system?) To account for this (perhaps caused by an indeterminateness of some environmental factors), we might introduce some random quantities into the mathematical model. This randomness in the model would predict different results in each experiment. However, in this text, there will not be much discussion of such probabilistic models. Instead, we will almost exclusively pursue deterministic models, because of the author's own orientation and because a complete discussion of probabilistic models requires a previous course in probability (a prerequisite the author did not want for this text). However, in many ways the best agreements with experiments occur with probabilistic models.

To account for the observed variability from experiment to experiment, we will model some type of average in many experiments, rather than attempting to model each specific experiment. Thus, if a later experiment or observation does not correspond precisely to a prediction of a mathematical model, then it may be the result of some randomness rather than some other inherent failure of the model.

# 32.  *A Discrete One-Species Model*

In this section, one of the simplest models of population growth of a species is developed. Typical data on the variations of the population of a species in a specified region might be as represented in Fig. 32-1, where measurements might have been taken over an interval of time $\Delta t$. The **rate of change of the population** as measured over the time interval $\Delta t$ would be

$$\frac{\Delta N}{\Delta t} = \frac{N(t + \Delta t) - N(t)}{\Delta t}.$$

This indicates the absolute rate of increase of the population. A quantity which will prove to be quite important is the rate of change of the population per individual, $R(t)$. This is called the **growth rate per unit time** (for example,

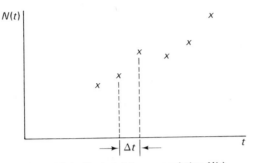

Figure 32-1   Typical data on population $N(t)$.

per year) as measured over the time interval $\Delta t$:

$$R(t) = \frac{N(t + \Delta t) - N(t)}{\Delta t N(t)}. \tag{32.1}$$

The percentage change in the population is $100 \, \Delta N/N(t) = 100 \, R(t) \, \Delta t$. Thus one hundred times the growth rate $R(t)$ is the **percentage change in the population per unit time**. For example, if in one-half year the population increases by 20%, then $R(t) = \frac{2}{5}$ and the growth rate is 40% per year (as measured for one-half year). Equation 32.1 cannot be used to determine the population at future times since it is just the definition of $R(t)$. However, if the growth rate and the initial population were known, then the population at later times could be calculated:

$$N(t + \Delta t) = N(t) + \Delta t R(t) N(t). \tag{32.2}$$

We assume that the population of the species only changes due to births and deaths. No outside experimenter slips some extra species into the system. There is no migration into or out of the region. Thus

$$N(t + \Delta t) = N(t) + (\# \text{ of births}) - (\# \text{ of deaths}).$$

The **reproductive (birth) rate $b$ per unit time** measured over the time interval $\Delta t$ and the **death rate $d$** are defined as

$$b = \frac{\# \text{ of births}}{\Delta t N(t)} \quad \text{and} \quad d = \frac{\# \text{ of deaths}}{\Delta t N(t)}.$$

Consequently, the population at a time $\Delta t$ later, $N(t + \Delta t)$, is

$$N(t + \Delta t) = N(t) + \Delta t (b - d) N(t).$$

The *growth rate $R$,*

$$R = b - d, \tag{32.3}$$

is the birth rate minus the death rate. In recent years, the world human population growth rate approximately equals .019. This means that the growth rate (the birth rate minus the death rate) is 1.9 percent per year. This figure gives no other information concerning the birth and death rates.

Since we focus our attention on the *total population* in a region, the birth and death rates are averages, averaged over this entire population. We are not distinguishing between older or younger individuals. In discussing human population growth, actuaries and demographers would be upset with our approach. They realize that accurate predictions of future growth depend on a thorough knowledge of the age distribution within the population. Two populations are likely to grow quite differently if one has significantly more senior citizens than the other. Thus the mathematical model we are developing can be improved to allow for an age distribution in the population. This will be briefly discussed in a later section (Sec. 35). We now proceed to discuss the total population of a species, assuming the effects of a possibly changing age distribution can be neglected.

As a first step in the mathematical modeling of population growth, we assume that the number of births and the number of deaths are simply proportional to the total population. Thus the growth rate $R$ is a constant, $R = R_0$; it is assumed not to change in time. A twofold increase in the population yields twice as many births and deaths. Without arguing the merits of such an assumption, let us pursue its consequences. If the growth rate is constant, then for any $t$

$$N(t + \Delta t) - N(t) = R_0 \Delta t N(t).$$

This can be expressed as a **difference equation** for the population

$$N(t + \Delta t) = (1 + R_0 \Delta t) N(t). \tag{32.4}$$

The population at a time $\Delta t$ later is a fixed percentage of the previous population. We will show this difference equation can be solved as an initial value problem, that is given an initial population at $t = t_0$,

$$N(t_0) = N_0,$$

the future population can be easily computed.

A difference equation has certain similarities to a differential equation. However, for the initial value problem of this type of difference equation, the unique solution can always be directly calculated. None of the "tricks" of differential equations are necessary. For a constant birth rate,

$$N(t_0 + \Delta t) = (1 + R_0\Delta t)N_0$$
$$N(t_0 + 2\Delta t) = (1 + R_0\Delta t)N(t_0 + \Delta t) = (1 + R_0\Delta t)^2 N_0$$
$$N(t_0 + 3\Delta t) = (1 + R_0\Delta t)N(t_0 + 2\Delta t) = (1 + R_0\Delta t)^3 N_0.$$

Although this method gives a satisfactory answer for all times, it is clear that a general formula exists. At $m$ units of $\Delta t$ later, $t \equiv t_0 + m\Delta t$,

$$\boxed{N(t) = N(t_0 + m\Delta t) = (1 + R_0\Delta t)^m N_0,} \qquad \text{(32.5)}$$

or equivalently,

$$N(t) = (1 + R_0\Delta t)^{t - t_0/\Delta t} N_0.$$

If the birth rate is greater than the death rate (i.e., if $R_0 > 0$), the population grows. A sketch of the solution is easily accomplished by noting

$$(1 + R_0\Delta t)^m = e^{\alpha m},$$

where $\alpha$ is a constant, $\alpha = \ln(1 + R_0\Delta t)$. Thus, if $R_0 > 0$ we have Fig. 32-2. Growth occurs over each **discrete** time interval of length $\Delta t$. In each interval of time $\Delta t$ the population increases by the same rate, but not by the same

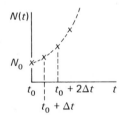

Figure 32-2    Constant growth rate.

amount, rather an increasing amount. Around 1800, the British economist Malthus used this type of population growth model to make the pessimistic prediction that human population would frequently outgrow its food supply. Malthus did not foresee the vast technological achievements in food production.

The assumption that the growth rate is constant frequently does not approximate observed populations. We illustrate some environmental factors which have caused human growth rates to vary:

1. The failure of the potato harvest (due to blight) in Ireland in 1845 resulted in widespread famine. Not only did the death rate dramatically increase, but immigration to the United States (and elsewhere) was so large that during the years that followed the population of Ireland

significantly *decreased*. Population estimates for Ireland speak for themselves:

Estimated Population of Ireland
(Including Northern Ireland)

| *Year* | *Population in millions* |
|--------|--------------------------|
| 1800 | 4.5 |
| 1845 | 8.5 |
| 1851 | 6.5 |
| 1891 | 6.7 |
| 1951 | 4.3 |
| 1971 | 4.5 |

2. A famous long power blackout in 1965 in the northeast United States resulted in an increased growth rate nine months later. This effect also occurred, for example, as the result of curfew laws in Chile in 1973.
3. The pill and other birth control measures have contributed to decreases in the 1960s and 1970s in the growth rate in the United States.
4. The average number of desired children seems to depend on economic and other factors. During the depression in the 1930s, birth rates in the United States were lower than they were both before and after.

Examples (2)–(4) vividly illustrate the difference between fertility (the ability to reproduce, the reproductive capacity) and fecundity (the actual rate of reproduction).


# EXERCISES

**32.1.** Assume that the growth rate of a certain species is constant, but negative. Sketch the population if at $t = 0$, $N = N_0$. What happens as $t \longrightarrow \infty$? Is your answer expected?

**32.2.** Suppose that the birth rate of a species is 221 per 1000 (per year), and the death rate is 215 per 1000 (per year). What is the predicted population as a function of time if the species numbers 2000 in 1950?

**32.3.** Suppose, in addition to births and deaths (with constant rates $b$ and $d$ respectively), that there is an increase in the population of a certain species due to the migration of 1000 individuals in each $\Delta t$ interval of time.
(a) Formulate the equation describing the change in the population.
(b) Explicitly solve the resulting equation. Assume that the initial population is $N_0$.
(c) Verify that if $b = d$, your answer reduces to the correct one.

**32.4.** Assume that a savings bank gives $I$ percent interest (on a yearly basis) and compounds the interest $n$ times a year. If $N_0$ dollars is deposited initially, then show that

$$N(t_0 + m\Delta t) = \left(1 + \frac{I}{n}\right)^m N_0,$$

where $t_0$ is the time of the initial deposit. [Hint: First show that $\Delta t = 1/n$ and $N(t + \Delta t) = N(t)(1 + I/n)$.]

**32.5.** Referring to exercise 32.4, show that after one year the total interest paid is

$$[(1 + I/n)^n - 1]N_0.$$

The **yield** is defined as the total interest at the end of the year divided by the money on deposit at the beginning of the year.
(a) What is the yield?
(b) Evaluate the yield if $n = 1$ or $n = 2$.

**32.6.** The yield (derived in exercise 32.5) can be difficult to evaluate if $n$ is large. For example, some banks compound interest daily, and for that reason we may wish to evaluate the yield if $n = 365$. We describe in this problem how to approximate the yield if $I/n$ is small (this occurs often as either $n$ is large or the interest rate $I$ is small). To analyze $(1 + I/n)^n$ for $I/n$ small, let

$$C \equiv (1 + I/n)^n,$$

and hence $\ln C = n \ln (1 + I/n)$. We now will approximate $\ln (1 + I/n)$ for $I/n$ small.
(a) Determine the Taylor series of $\ln (1 + x)$ around $x = 0$ by term-by-term integration of the Taylor series for $1/(1 + x)$. [Hint: The sum of an infinite geometric series implies that (if $|x| < 1$)

$$\frac{1}{1 + x} = 1 - x + x^2 - x^3 + x^4 - x^5 + \ldots]$$

(b) Thus show that $\ln C = I - I^2/2n + \ldots$, or equivalently that $C = e^{I - I^2/2n + \ldots}$.
(c) For a typical interest rate of 5 percent, compare the yield of daily compounding ($n = 365$) to the yield of continual compounding (the limit as $n \to \infty$). [Hint: For $y$ small, $e^y = 1 + y + \ldots$]
(d) If \$100 is the initial deposit, approximately how much more money is made in a year in a bank compounding every day at 5 percent than one compounding every month at 5 percent? The hint of part (c) may again by helpful.

**32.7.** Assume that a savings bank gives 6 percent interest (on a yearly basis) and compounds the interest 4 times a year. If you deposit \$100, how much money is in your account after one year?

**32.8.** Suppose that the bank described in exercise 32.7 is in competition with a bank which offers the same interest rate, but only compounds 3 times a year. In the first year, how much more money would you save in the bank that compounds 4 times a year?

**32.9.** Most banks advertise their interest rate (on a yearly basis) and also advertise their method of compounding. For one of your local banks, taking their advertised information, compute their annual yield. Show that your calculation agrees with their advertised yield! [Warning: If they do not agree, check your work carefully. However, state and federal banking laws can be tricky, and you may actually receive a higher yield than you should mathematically. If this is the case, ask your bank for the explanation. Some banks call 360 days a year, in which case you benefit from 5 or 6 extra days of interest!]

**32.10.**   At 5 percent interest compounded 4 times a year, in how many years does your money double?

**32.11.**   Suppose that each time a savings bank compounds the interest, you make an additional deposit $D(t)$. Show that

$$N(t + \Delta t) = N(t)\left(1 + \frac{I}{n}\right) + D(t),$$

(if $D(t)$ is negative, this is a withdrawal). If an initial deposit is made and $50 is withdrawn every month (with $I$ percent interest compounded every month), then how much money must be initially deposited such that the $50 can be withdrawn every month FOREVER!

**32.12.**   Suppose that you borrow $P_0$ dollars (called the principal) from a bank at $I$ percent yearly interest and repay the amount in equal monthly install-ments of $M$ dollars.

(a)   If $P(t)$ is the money owed at time $t$, show that $P(0) = P_0$ and

$$P(t + \Delta t) = P(t)\left(1 + \frac{I}{n}\right) - M.$$

What is $\Delta t$ and $n$?

(b)   For example, part of the first payment consists of $P_0 \, I/n$ interest. How much of your first payment goes towards reducing the amount owed?

(c)   Solve the equation for $P(t + i\Delta t)$.

(d)   How much should your monthly payments be if the money is to be completely repaid to the bank in $N$ years?

(e)   What is the total amount of money paid to the bank?

(f)   If you borrow $3000 for a car and pay it back monthly in 4 years at 12.5 percent yearly interest, then how much money have you paid in total for the car?

**32.13.**   In this problem, we wish to prove

$$\frac{\ln (1 + R_0\Delta t)}{\Delta t} < R_0 \quad (\text{if } R_0\Delta t \neq 0).$$

(a)   If you have not already done so, do exercise 32.6a.

(b)   Show how part (a) suggests the desired result.

(c)   Show that

$$\frac{1}{1 + x} = 1 - \frac{x}{1 + x}.$$

(d)   By integrating the result of part (c), show that

$$\ln(1 + x) = x - \int_0^x \frac{\bar{x}}{1 + \bar{x}} d\bar{x}.$$

(e)   Using the result of part (d), prove that if $x > 0$, then

$$\ln (1 + x) < x.$$

**32.14.**   Use the Taylor series with remainder of $\ln (1 + x)$ around $x = 0$ to prove the result of exercise 32.13.

**32.15.**   A species has a growth rate (measured over one year) of $\alpha$ percent. If the initial population is $N_0$, in how many years will the population double?


# 33. Constant Coefficient First-Order Difference Equations

When discussing a population at various discrete times, it is convenient to introduce the following notation:

$$N_0 = N(t_0)$$
$$N_1 = N(t_0 + \Delta t)$$
$$N_2 = N(t_0 + 2\Delta t)$$
$$\cdots$$

Thus the population at the *mth* time is

$$N_m = N(t_0 + m\Delta t). \tag{33.1}$$

For a constant growth rate $R_0$, the population at the $m + 1st$ time is determined from the previous population

$$N_{m+1} = \alpha N_m, \tag{33.2}$$

where

$$\alpha = 1 + R_0 \Delta t,$$

as derived in Sec. 32. Equation 33.2 is called a linear difference equation of the first order with constant coefficients. It is called first order since equation 33.2 involves one difference in time, i.e., $t + \Delta t$ and $t$. An example of a difference equation without constant coefficients (but still linear) is

$$N_{m+1} = \alpha(m)N_m, \quad \text{while } N_{m+1} = \alpha N_m^2$$

is an example of a nonlinear difference equation.

The solution of the linear first order difference equation with constant coefficients, equation 33.2, was constructed earlier:

$$N_m = \alpha^m N_0. \tag{33.3}$$

A *general technique* to solve constant coefficient difference equations (as will later be shown for a higher order difference equation) is to try a solution to the difference equation in the form:

$$N_m = r^m,$$

an unknown number raised to the *mth* power. Substituting this expression into the difference equation 33.2, yields

$$r^{m+1} = \alpha r^m.$$

Dividing both sides by $r^m$, determines $r$,

$$r = \alpha.$$

Thus $N_m = \alpha^m$ is a solution. The linearity property implies that any multiple of that solution,

$$N_m = C\alpha^m,$$

is also a solution. Since at $m = 0$ (corresponding to $t = t_0$) the population is known, the arbitrary constant is determined

$$N_0 = C.$$

Thus equation 33.3 is valid, derived by a general technique for constant coefficient difference equations. This method is quite similar to the technique of substituting an unknown exponential into a constant coefficient differential equation.

# EXERCISES

**33.1.**   Suppose that the growth of a population is described by

$$N_{m+1} = (1 + R_0 \Delta t) N_m,$$

where $R_0 < 0$.
(a)   Determine the population at later times, if initially the population is $N_0$.
(b)   Sketch the solution if $-1 < R_0 \Delta t < 0$.
(c)   Sketch the solution if $-2 < R_0 \Delta t < -1$. The result is called a convergent oscillation.
(d)   Sketch the solution if $R_0 \Delta t < -2$. The result is called a divergent oscillation.

(e)   Why are parts (c) and (d) *not* reasonable ecological growth models, while part (b) is? What ecological assumption of the model caused parts (c) and (d) to yield unreasonable results?

**33.2.**   Consider $N_{m+1} = \alpha N_m$. Instead of substituting $N_m = r^m$, substitute an exponential ($N_m = e^{sm}$). Show that the result is the same.

**33.3.**   Consider a species of animal which only breeds during the spring. Suppose that all adults die before the next breeding season. However, assume that every female produces (on the average) $R$ female offspring which survive to breed in the next year. Determine the female population as a function of time.

# 34.  Exponential Growth

The definition of the growth rate is

$$R(t) = \frac{N(t + \Delta t) - N(t)}{\Delta t N(t)}.$$

In general, this growth rate can depend on time. It is calculated over a time interval of length $\Delta t$. By this definition, the growth rate also depends on the measuring time interval. More likely of interest is the **instantaneous growth rate** (which we will now refer to as the growth rate),

$$R(t) \equiv \lim_{\Delta t \to 0} \frac{N(t + \Delta t) - N(t)}{\Delta t N(t)} = \frac{1}{N}\frac{dN}{dt}. \qquad (34.1)$$

For this to be meaningful, the population must be approximated as a continuous function of time, which is assumed to be differentiable. This approximation is most reasonable for *large* populations. The growth rate is the rate of change in the population per individual. Alternatively, the rate of change of the population, $dN/dt$, equals the growth rate $R$ times the population $N$.

As a first model, we again assume the growth rate is a constant. If this growth rate is a constant $R_0$, then the population growth is described by the solution to the first order linear differential equation with constant coefficients

$$\frac{dN}{dt} = R_0 N, \qquad (34.2)$$

which satisfies the initial condition

$$N(t_0) = N_0.$$

The solution exhibits exponential behavior

$$N(t) = N_0 e^{R_0(t-t_0)}, \tag{34.3}$$

as sketched in Fig. 34-1 for $R_0 > 0$. *A population grows exponentially if the growth rate is a positive constant.* Similarly, a population decays exponentially if its growth rate is a negative constant as shown in Fig. 34-2. (It is often convenient to let the initial time $t_0 = 0$.)

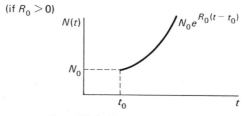

Figure 34-1   Exponential growth.

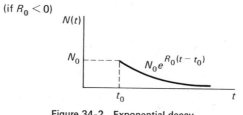

Figure 34-2   Exponential decay.

Of interest is the time necessary for a population to double if the growth rate is a positive constant. The length of time, $t_1 - t_0$, such that the population doubles, $N(t_1) = 2N(t_0)$, is obtained from the expression

$$2N_0 = N_0 e^{R_0(t_1-t_0)}.$$

$N_0$ cancels. Hence, the time it takes to double does not depend on the initial population. In particular,

$$t_1 - t_0 = \frac{\ln 2}{R_0}, \tag{34.4}$$

where, from a table of natural logarithms, $\ln 2 \approx .69315$. This result can be applied to the following problem. If a population grows continually at the instantaneous rate of 2 percent a year ($R_0 = .02$), then in how long will the population double? The required time is

$$t_1 - t_0 \approx \frac{.69315}{.02} \approx 35.$$

Thus, the population doubles in approximately 35 years. An accurate rule of thumb (very useful as described in the exercises for savings bank interest rates, inflation rates, and so on) is to note that if $R_0$ *is the instantaneous rate of growth per year measured as a percentage, then the number of years to double is approximately* $70/R_0$ *years.*\* How many years would it take the population to quadruple?

$R_0$ is the instantaneous growth rate per year. In one year, the population will have grown from $N_0$ to $N_0 e^{R_0}$. The **measured growth rate** over that one year is

$$\frac{1}{N_0} \frac{\Delta N}{\Delta t} = \frac{N_0 e^{R_0} - N_0}{N_0} = e^{R_0} - 1.$$

Since the Taylor series of $e^{R_0}$ is

$$e^{R_0} = 1 + R_0 + \frac{R_0^2}{2!} + \frac{R_0^3}{3!} + \cdots,$$

there is a small difference between the instantaneous growth rate and the resulting growth rate measured over one year *only if $R_0$ is small.* If a population grows continually at the rate of 2 percent a year ($R_0 = .02$), then after one year an original population of 1,000,000 grows to 1,020,201.3 rather than 1,020,000, since

$$e^{.02} = 1 + .02 + \frac{(.02)^2}{2!} + \frac{(.02)^3}{3!} + \cdots.$$

Biologists frequently speak of the **mean generation time**, that is the time necessary for a population to reproduce itself, which we have called the doubling time. If $t_d$ is the mean generation time, then from equation 34.4

$$\boxed{t_d = \frac{\ln 2}{R_0}.} \qquad (34.5)$$

In terms of this parameter, the exponential growth equation 34.3, becomes

$$N(t) = N_0 e^{(\ln 2/t_d)(t-t_0)},$$

---

\*This is one of the more practical formulas we offer in this text. (Memorize it; not for an exam, but for your everyday experiences.)

which, using properties of logarithms and exponentials, becomes

$$N(t) = N_0(e^{(\ln 2)})^{t - t_0/t_d}$$

or finally

$$N(t) = 2^{(t - t_0/t_d)} N_0,$$

an equivalent formula which is often easy to evaluate. In this latter form growth is measured in intervals of the doubling time.

We now compare the population growths predicted by the discrete and continuous models. For a *continuous* growth model (with growth rate $R_0$),

$$N_c(t) = N_0 e^{R_0(t - t_0)},$$

while for population growth (with growth rate $R_0$) occurring over each *discrete* $\Delta t$ time interval,

$$N_d(t) = N_0(1 + R_0 \Delta t)^{(t - t_0/\Delta t)}.$$

An equivalent expression for the discrete case is

$$N_d(t) = N_0 e^{(\ln(1 + R_0 \Delta t)/\Delta t)(t - t_0)}.$$

For both models, the population grows exponentially. The exponential coefficient for a population increasing every $\Delta t$ time is $\ln(1 + R_0 \Delta t)/\Delta t$ as compared to $R_0$ for continual growth. The discrete growth process causes a slower population growth as expected since

$$\frac{\ln(1 + R_0 \Delta t)}{\Delta t} < R_0 \quad (\text{if } R_0 \Delta t > 0),$$

as is shown in exercises 32.13 or 32.14. These two models should give the same result in the limit as $\Delta t \to 0$. We verify this using L'Hôpital's rule,

$$\lim_{\Delta t \to 0} \frac{\ln(1 + R_0 \Delta t)}{\Delta t} = \lim_{\Delta t \to 0} \frac{\dfrac{R_0}{1 + R_0 \Delta t}}{1} = R_0.$$

Alternatively, this can be shown using the Taylor series of $\ln(1 + R_0 \Delta t)$.

In a problem, we might wish to assume a constant growth rate $R_0$, but not know what value to take for it. Thus, the population would be

$$N = N_0 e^{R_0 t},$$

where $N_0$ is the known initial population at $t = 0$. Another condition is necessary to determine the growth rate. Suppose at a later time, $t = t_1$, the population is also known $N(t_1) = N_1$. Let us use this information to determine $R_0$:

$$N_1 = N_0 e^{R_0 t_1}.$$

Although we can directly solve for $R_0$,

$$R_0 = \frac{1}{t_1} \ln\left(\frac{N_1}{N_0}\right),$$

a simpler approach is to note $e^{R_0} = (N_1/N_0)^{1/t_1}$, and hence

$$N = N_0 \left(\frac{N_1}{N_0}\right)^{t/t_1}.$$

This gives the expression for the population at all times if it is $N_0$ initially and $N_1$ at time $t_1$ (assuming a constant growth rate). If additional data is known, then the problem may be over determined. However, as this is frequently the case, we might want to know the exponential curve that best fits the data. This can be done using the method of least squares as is discussed in the exercises.

# EXERCISES

**34.1.** A certain bacteria is observed to double in number in 8 hours. What is its growth rate?

**34.2.** A population of bacteria is initially $N_0$ and grows at a constant rate $R_0$. Suppose $\tau$ hours later the bacteria is put into a different culture such that it now grows at the constant rate $R_1$. Determine the population of bacteria for all time.

**34.3.** The growth rate of a certain strain of bacteria is unknown, but assumed to be constant. When an experiment started, it was estimated that there were about 1500 bacteria, and an hour later 2000. How many bacteria would you predict there are four hours after the experiment started?

**34.4.** Suppose the growth rate of a certain species is not constant, but depends in a known way on the temperature of its environment. If the temperature is known as a function of time, derive an expression for the future population (which is initially $N_0$). Show that the population grows or decays with an exponential growth coefficient, $(R_E(t)$, where $N(t) \propto e^{R_E(t)t})$, equal to the average of the time-dependent growth rate.

**34.5.** In this problem we study the effect of any time-dependent migration, $f(t)$. Consider both the resulting discrete and continuous growth models:

$$N_{m+1} - N_m = R_0 \Delta t N_m + \Delta t f_m \qquad \text{(i)}$$

$$\frac{dN}{dt} = R_0 N + f(t) \qquad \text{(ii)}$$

(a) If the growth rate is zero ($R_0 = 0$), show that the solution of the discrete growth model is analogous to integration.

(b) If the growth rate is nonzero, show that

$$N_{m+1} = \alpha N_m + f_m \Delta t \qquad \text{(iii)}$$

where $\alpha = 1 + R_0 \Delta t$. By explicit calculation of $N_1, N_2, N_3, \ldots$, determine $N_m$, if $N_0$ is known.

(c)   For the differential equation (ii), calculate the solution using the integrating factor $e^{-R_0 t}$.

(d)   In this part of the problem, we wish to develop a technique to solve difference equation (i), analogous to the integrating factor method used in part (c). By dividing equation (iii) by $\alpha^{m+1}$, show that

$$Q_{m+1} - Q_m = \frac{f_m}{\alpha^{m+1}} \Delta t \qquad \text{(iv)},$$

where $Q_m = N_m/\alpha^m$. Using the result of part (a), solve equation (iv), and thus determine $N_m$. Show that your answer agrees with part (b), and show how your answer is analogous to the results of part (c).

**34.6.**   For small growth rates, estimate the difference between the measured growth rate over one year and the instantaneous growth rate per year.

**34.7.**   Consider a species which is modeled as growing at an instantaneous rate of 3 percent per year. Another species grows at 3 percent per year when measured every year. Compare the time it takes both species to double.

**34.8.**   Suppose that a species is described by equation 32.4 with $R_0 > 0$. How long does it take the population to double?

**34.9.**   Suppose that one species has an instantaneous growth rate of $\alpha$ percent per year while another species grows in discrete units of time at the annual rate of $\beta$ percent per year. Suppose the second species has four growth periods a year. What relationship exists between $\alpha$ and $\beta$ if both species (starting with the same number) have the same number 5 years later?

**34.10.**   The cost of a large bottle of soda was 32¢ each. One year later the cost had increased to 37¢ each. If this rate of increase continued, approximately when would soda be 50¢ each.

**34.11.**   The G.N.P. (Gross National Product) of a certain country increased by 6.4 percent. If it continued at that rate, approximately how many years would it take the G.N.P. to double?

**34.12.**   One year food prices increased at a yearly rate of 15 percent. At that rate, in approximately how many years would food prices double.

**34.13.**   If the cost of living rose from $10,000 to $11,000 in one year (a 10 percent net increase), what is the instantaneous rate of increase of the cost of living in that year?

**34.14.**   The parameters of a theoretical population growth curve are often estimated making the best fit of this curve to some data. If discrete population data is known (not necessarily measured at equal time intervals), $N_d(t_m)$, then the mean-square deviation between the data and a theoretical curve, $N(t)$, is

$$\sum_m [N(t_m) - N_d(t_m)]^2,$$

the sum of the squared differences. The "best" fit is often defined as those values which minimize the above mean-square deviation.

(a)   Assume that the initial population is known with complete certainty, so that we insist that the theoretical population curve initially agree exactly. Assume the theoretical curve exhibits exponential growth. By minimizing the above mean-square deviation, obtain an equation for the best estimate of the growth rate. Show that this is a transcendental equation.

(b)  One way to bypass the difficulty in part (a) is to fit the natural logarithm of the data to the natural logarithm of the theoretical curve. In this way the mean-square deviation is

$$\sum_m [\ln N_0 + R_0 t_m - \ln N_d(t_m)]^2.$$

Show that this method now is the least squares fit of a straight line to data. If $N_0$ is known ($N_0 = N_d(t_0)$), determine the best estimate of the growth rate using this criteria.

(c)  Redo part (b) assuming that a best estimate of the initial population is also desired (i.e., minimize the mean-square deviation with respect to both $N_0$ and $R_0$).

**34.15.**  Suppose an experimentally determined growth *curve* $N_d(t)$ was known. Using the ideas presented in exercise 34.14b and c, determine a best estimate of the initial population and the exponential growth rate of the population.

**34.16.**  The growth rate of a certain bacteria is unknown. Suppose that the following data were obtained:

| time | 0 | 1 | 2 |
|------|------|------|------|
| number | 100 | 120 | 160 |

Using the ideas of exercise 34.14b and c, estimate the best fitted exponential growth curve. Predict the population at $t = 4$.

**34.17.**  In this section it was shown that the difference equation of discrete growth becomes a differential equation in the limit as $\Delta t \to 0$. If a differential equation is known, for example,

$$\frac{dN(t)}{dt} = R_0 N(t),$$

we will show how to calculate a difference equation which corresponds to it. This idea is useful for obtaining numerical solutions on the computer of differential equations. If a Taylor series is used, then

$$N(t + \Delta t) = N(t) + \Delta t \frac{dN}{dt} + O((\Delta t)^2).$$

Thus, if higher order terms are neglected:

(a)  Show that

$$\frac{dN}{dt} = \frac{N(t + \Delta t) - N(t)}{\Delta t} + O(\Delta t).$$

Replacing the derivative by this difference is known as **Euler's method** to numerically solve ordinary differential equations.

(b)  Show that the resulting difference equation (called the **discretization** of the differential equation) is itself a discrete model of population growth.

(c)   At the very least, for this to be a reasonable procedure, the first neglected term in the Taylor series $(\Delta t)^2\, d^2N/dt^2/2$ must be much less than $\Delta t(dN/dt)$. Using the differential equation, are there thus any restrictions on the **discretization time** $\Delta t$ for this problem?

# 35.  Discrete One-Species Models with an Age Distribution

For accurate predictions of the future population of species with variable age distributions, it is necessary to discuss the birth and death rates for different age groups. We formulate this problem using the discrete population changes as measured every year, i.e., $\Delta t = 1$ year (for many species this measuring interval is too long). Instead of the total population, we must know the population in each age group. Let

$N_0(t) =$ number of individuals less than one year old

$N_1(t) =$ number of individuals one year old

$N_2(t) =$ number of individuals two years old

.
.
.

$N_m(t) =$ number of individuals $m$ years old, where $m$ terminates at $N$, the oldest age at which there is an appreciable population.

Furthermore let $b_m$ be the birth rate of the population $m$ years old and $d_m$ its death rate. The difference equations describing the populations (assuming there is no migration) are

$$N_0(t + \Delta t) = b_0 N_0(t) + b_1 N_1(t) + \cdots + b_N N_N(t) \qquad (35.0)$$
$$N_1(t + \Delta t) = (1 - d_0)N_0(t) \qquad (35.1)$$
$$N_2(t + \Delta t) = (1 - d_1)N_1(t) \qquad (35.2)$$

.
.
.

$$N_m(t + \Delta t) = (1 - d_{m-1})N_{m-1}(t) \qquad (35.m)$$

.
.
.

$$N_N(t + \Delta t) = (1 - d_{N-1})N_{N-1}(t) \qquad (35.N)$$

Equation 35.0 states that the number of individuals less than one year old at the time $t + \Delta t$ (i.e., one year after the time $t$, since $\Delta t = 1$) equals the sum (over all age groups) of the individuals born during the preceeding year (who survived until the time $t + \Delta t$). For example, the number of individuals born to 25 year olds during the year is the number of 25 year olds, $N_{25}(t)$, times the birth rate for 25 year olds, $b_{25}$. The birth rate as used in this section is a slight modification from that discussed in other sections. Instead of the average number of births per individual between $t$ and $t + \Delta t$, it is the average number of births between $t$ and $t + \Delta t$ *who survive until $t + \Delta t$*.

Equation 35.1 states that the number of one year old individuals at time $t + \Delta t$ (now) equals the number whose age is less than one year at time $t$ (one year ago) times the survivorship rate for those less than one year old, since one minus the death rate $(1 - d_0)$ is the survivorship rate. Equations 35.2–35.N are derived using the same principles as equation 35.1. Knowing all the birth and death rates and the initial population in every age group is sufficient to predict the future population. For large $N$ such problems are ideally suited for computer calculations.

Matrix methods were introduced by Leslie in 1945 to simplify these types of calculations. Consider the $n$-dimensional population vector $(n = N + 1)$

$$\vec{N}(t) = \begin{pmatrix} N_0(t) \\ N_1(t) \\ \cdot \\ \cdot \\ \cdot \\ N_N(t) \end{pmatrix}.$$

Then equations 35.0–35.N become

$$\boxed{\vec{N}(t + \Delta t) = \mathbf{A}\vec{N}(t),}$$

where the $n \times n$ matrix $\mathbf{A}$ is given by

$$\mathbf{A} = \begin{bmatrix} b_0 & b_1 & b_2 & \cdots & b_N \\ 1 - d_0 & 0 & 0 & \cdots & 0 \\ 0 & 1 - d_1 & 0 & \cdots & 0 \\ 0 & 0 & 1 - d_2 & \cdots & 0 \\ & & \cdots & & \\ 0 & 0 & 0 & \cdots & 1 - d_{N-1} & 0 \end{bmatrix}$$

In exercise 35.2 we explain how to solve this linear system of difference equations using the matrix notation if the birth and death rates do not change with time.

A simplified model with age distributions is sometimes desired. Instead of separating the population into each age division, the population is divided up into larger groups. As a *very rough* model of human population growth suppose we divide the population into three age groups (group 1 aged 0–14, group 2 of child-bearing age 15–39, and group 3 aged 40 and older). We assume we know the average birth and death rates for each age group ($b_1$, $b_2$, $b_3$ and $d_1$, $d_2$, $d_3$). Can we predict the future population if we know the present age distribution? The number in group 1 consists of the number born (and surviving a year) plus the number who have survived from group 1 but not "advanced" into group 2. The number born is $b_1 N_1(t) + b_2 N_2(t) + b_3 N_3(t)$. However, the total number from group 1 who survived is $(1 - d_1)N_1(t)$. Some of these advance age groups. We estimate the number that did not advance in a very rough way. We assume that in each population group the ages are evenly distributed within the group (this is not entirely accurate). Thus since the first group has 15 different years, approximately $\frac{14}{15}$ remain after one year ($\Delta t = 1$). Consequently,

$$N_1(t + \Delta t) = b_1 N_1(t) + b_2 N_2(t) + b_3 N_3(t) + \frac{14}{15}(1 - d_1)N_1(t)$$

$$N_2(t + \Delta t) = \frac{1}{15}(1 - d_1)N_1(t) + \frac{24}{25}(1 - d_2)N_2(t)$$

$$N_3(t + \Delta t) = \frac{1}{25}(1 - d_2)N_2(t) + (1 - d_3)N_3(t).$$

Since both $b_1$ and $b_3$ are much less than $b_2$, in this example as an additional approximation $b_1$ and $b_3$ can be set equal to zero.

Using these types of models we can compare the growths of two similar populations which differ only in their age distribution. We could calculate how much faster a population predominantly of child-bearing age would double. Besides predicting more accurately the growth of the total population, these techniques can be used to estimate the future population in each age group. These types of models of age-dependent population growth thus enable demographers to predict the future need of resources ranging from elementary schools to old-age facilities.

# EXERCISES

**35.1.** If $A$ is a constant matrix, show that $\vec{N}(t + m\Delta t) = A^m \vec{N}(t)$.

**35.2.** (This problem requires a knowledge of elementary linear algebra.) If $A$ is a constant matrix, then

$$\vec{N}(t + \Delta t) = A\vec{N}(t)$$

is a linear system of constant coefficient first order difference equations. The solution can be obtained by a method similar to that developed in Sec. 33.

(a)  Use the notation $\vec{N}_m \equiv \vec{N}(m\Delta t)$, and hence $\vec{N}_{m+1} = A\vec{N}_m$. Try a solution to this system of difference equations in the form $\vec{N}_m = r^m\vec{C}$, where $\vec{C}$ is a constant vector and where $r$ will be determined. Show that

$$(A - rI)\vec{C} = \vec{0},$$

where $I$ is the identity matrix. From linear algebra, we know that for nontrivial solutions (i.e., $\vec{C} \neq 0$), $r$ can be only certain values called **eigenvalues** of the matrix $A$, obtained by insisting $A - rI$ has a zero determinant,

$$|A - rI| = 0.$$

If $A$ is an $n \times n$ matrix, then there will be $n$ eigenvalues (call them $r_i$, $i = 1, \ldots, n$). We assume (for mathematical simplicity) that the eigenvalues of $A$ are all distinct. Corresponding to each eigenvalue $r_i$, there is a vector $\vec{C}_i$ satisfying $(A - r_i I)\vec{C}_i = \vec{0}$, which we call an **eigenvector**.

(b)  The general solution of the system of difference equations is an arbitrary linear combination of the solutions obtained in part (a). Thus show that

$$\vec{N}_m = \sum_{i=1}^{n} a_i r_i^m \vec{C}_i \quad \text{or} \quad \vec{N}(t) = \sum_{i=1}^{n} a_i r_i^t \vec{C}_i,$$

since $t = m\Delta t$ and $\Delta t = 1$. The population in each age group grows or decays depending on the eigenvalues $r_i$. In fact if any of the eigenvalues are complex, then the populations can also oscillate (the mathematics necessary to analyze this case is discussed in Sec. 41).

(c)  We say the populations represented for example by

$$\begin{bmatrix} 1 \\ 3 \\ 8 \end{bmatrix} \quad \text{and} \quad \begin{bmatrix} 4 \\ 12 \\ 32 \end{bmatrix}$$

have the same age distribution. Show that in general the age distribution derived in part (b) changes with time.

(d)  A stable age distribution exists if the populations approach, as time increases, an age distribution independent of time. Show that *if* there exists a real positive eigenvalue (call it $r_1$) which is greater than the absolute value of the real part of all the other eigenvalues, then a stable age distribution exists. Show that a stable age distribution is $\vec{C}_1$, where $\vec{C}_1$ is an eigenvector corresponding to the eigenvalue $r_1$. Note that such a stable age distribution is independent of the initial age distribution; it only depends on the birth and death rates of each age grouping!

(e)  If a stable age distribution exists, show that the total population grows like $e^{\sigma t}$, where $\sigma = \ln r_1$. Thus show that the population exponentially grows if $r_1 > 1$, exponentially decays if $r_1 < 1$, and approaches a constant if $r_1 = 1$.

**35.3.** Consider a species in which both no individuals live to three years old and only one-year olds reproduce.
  (a)  Show that $b_0 = 0, b_2 = 0, d_2 = 1$ satisfy both conditions.
  (b)  Let $b_1 = b$. What is the **A** matrix?
  (c)  Determine (a computer is *not* necessary) the time development of a population initially consisting of $N_0 = 100, N_1 = 100, N_2 = 100$. Explicitly calculate the following three cases of birth and death rates:

$$1. \ b = 1, d_0 = \tfrac{1}{2}, d_1 = \tfrac{1}{2}$$
$$2. \ b = 2, d_0 = \tfrac{1}{2}, d_1 = \tfrac{1}{2}$$
$$3. \ b = 3, d_0 = \tfrac{1}{2}, d_1 = \tfrac{1}{2}$$

  (d)  Compare your results in part (c) to that predicted by the theoretical considerations of exercise 35.2a–b.

**35.4.** For a species that lives at most four years (i.e., only four age groups), show that the eigenvalues $r$ of the matrix **A** satisfy:

$$0 = r^4 - b_0 r^3 - b_1(1 - d_0)r^2 - b_2(1 - d_0)(1 - d_1)r$$
$$- b_3(1 - d_0)(1 - d_1)(1 - d_2)$$

**35.5.** Consider the growth of a human population split into the three age groups discussed in Sec. 35. Assume:

| | |
|---|---|
| $b_1 = 0$ | $d_1 = .005$ |
| $b_2 = .04$ | $d_2 = .010$ |
| $b_3 = 0$ | $d_3 = .015$ |

Using a computer, qualitatively and quantitatively compare the growth of the following three initial populations (measured in thousands).

| Case | $N_1$ | $N_2$ | $N_3$ | Total |
|------|-------|-------|-------|-------|
| (1) | 200 | 400 | 400 | 1000 |
| (2) | 400 | 300 | 300 | 1000 |
| (3) | 200 | 500 | 300 | 1000 |

How long does it take each total population to double once?

**35.6.** Reconsider exercise 35.5. Assume new medical advances cut each death

rate in half, but at the same time people's attitudes change reducing the birth rate by 25 percent.
(a)  Analyze the three cases of that exercise.
(b)  How long does it take each to double?
(c)  Compare the results of this problem to exercise 35.5.

**35.7.**  Collect human population data in the United States, including the present population and the birth and death rates, for every yearly age group. Using a computer, predict the population for the next 25 years ignoring migration. Are there any significant changes in the age distribution?

**35.8.**  Collect human population data in the United States, including the present population and the birth and death rates, for every yearly age group. Do not predict the change in number of each age group. Instead, pick more convenient age groupings to do a computer calculation, and predict the population for the next 25 years ignoring migration. Are there any significant changes in the age distribution?

**35.9.**  Compare exercise 35.7 to exercise 35.8.

**35.10.**  Redo exercise 35.7 without ignoring migration.

**35.11.**  Redo exercise 35.8 without ignoring migration.

# 36. Stochastic Birth Processes

The previous approximations considered birth and death processes to be deterministic. In contrast to that, in this section we formulate a simple model of a stochastic (probabilistic) process. In order to facilitate the analysis, we will assume that there are no deaths or that the deaths have a negligible effect as compared to births. This is a reasonable approximation for bacteria and other species which grow by cell division. In many circumstances this model may need to be replaced by other stochastic growth models (usually more difficult to analyze).

Suppose we *cannot* say with certainty that there will be a population increase of exactly $R\Delta t$ percent in time $\Delta t$ (later in the analysis $\Delta t$ will be infinitesimally small). Instead we assume the birth process is random. A birth associated with an individual might randomly occur at any time with equal probability.

Suppose an "x" represents the hatching of a baby chick from one hen as in Fig. 36-1. In a sufficiently small time interval $\Delta t$, we assume the probability of one birth is proportional to $\Delta t$, let it be

$$\lambda \Delta t.$$

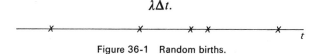

Figure 36-1   Random births.

The probability of two or more births in a time interval $\Delta t$ is considered to be negligible if $\Delta t$ is small enough. (We are assuming there are no multiple births). The probability of it not giving birth in time $\Delta t$ is thus $1 - \lambda \Delta t$, since a fundamental law of probability states that the sum of all the probabilities must be one. In this case either a birth occurs or it does not; there are no other possibilities.

In $\Delta t$ time, if the probability of one birth from one hen is $\lambda \Delta t$, then we "expect" if there are a *large* number of hens $N_0$, then there would be $N_0 \lambda \Delta t$ births. This shows that the birth rate $(\Delta N/(N_0 \Delta t)$, since there are no deaths in this model and hence the birth rate equals the growth rate) is $\lambda$. Thus not only is $\lambda$ the **probability of a birth per unit time**, but $\lambda$ is also the birth rate (if growth occurs in a deterministic manner). In the exercises, it will be shown that $\lambda$ is the *expected* growth rate for this stochastic birth process. Consequently, if $\lambda$ is unknown, we estimate $\lambda \Delta t$ be dividing the total number of births in $\Delta t$ time by the total population (if the time $\Delta t$ is small enough such that the number of births is a small percentage of the total population). For example, if in one hour 20 hatchings occur from a population of 600, then the birth rate is estimated as $\frac{1}{30}$ per hour and also the probability of a birth is estimated as $\frac{1}{30}$ per hour, i.e., $\lambda = \frac{1}{30}$ per hour.

We cannot calculate the exact population at a given time. We can only discuss probabilities. Let $P_N(t)$ be the probability that at time $t$ the population is $N$. At time $t + \Delta t$, what is the probability of the population being $N$? We will discuss the answer first, and then formulate an equation describing it. How is it possible to have $N$ of the species at time $t + \Delta t$? A population $N$ can come about in two ways: either the population was $N - 1$ at the previous time and a birth occurs in time interval $\Delta t$, or the population was $N$ at time $t$ and no births occur during $\Delta t$. We have ignored the possibility of two or more births from different individuals (in exercise 36.2, it is shown that this assumption is a good approximation if $\Delta t$ is small enough). Thus

$$P_N(t + \Delta t) = \sigma_{N-1} P_{N-1}(t) + v_N P_N(t), \qquad (36.1)$$

where $\sigma_{N-1}$ is the probability that exactly one birth occurs among the $N - 1$ individuals, and where $v_N$ is the probability that no births occur among the $N$ individuals.*

Let us calculate these probabilities. If the probability of one individual not giving birth is $1 - \lambda \Delta t$, then the probability of no births among $N$

---

*This can occur in two different ways; it is the sum of the probabilities of the two compound events. The probability of one compound event is the product of the individual probabilities (if the events are independent).

independent individuals is $(1 - \lambda \Delta t)^N$, that is

$$\boxed{v_N = (1 - \lambda \Delta t)^N.}$$

The probability of at least one birth occuring among $N$ individuals is then

$$1 - v_N = 1 - (1 - \lambda \Delta t)^N,$$

(one minus the probability of no births). If $\Delta t$ is small enough so that the probability of two or more births even from $N$ individuals is negligible, then the probability of exactly one birth is approximately the same as the probability of at least one birth. Thus,

$$\sigma_{N-1} \approx 1 - (1 - \lambda \Delta t)^{N-1}*$$

For this last expression to be valid $\Delta t$ must be extremely small. Let us consider these probabilities if $\Delta t$ is that small. Then (from the binomial expansion)

$$v_N \approx 1 - \lambda N \Delta t.$$

In a similar manner,

$$\sigma_{N-1} \approx \lambda(N - 1)\Delta t.$$

That is, for $\Delta t$ small, the probability of exactly one birth among $m$ individuals is approximately $m$ times the probability of an individual giving birth. Also the probability of no births is approximately 1 minus the probability of exactly one birth (since in the limit of a small time interval two or more births are virtually impossible). Thus, from equation 36.1

$$P_N(t + \Delta t) \approx \lambda(N - 1)\Delta t P_{N-1}(t) + (1 - \lambda N \Delta t)P_N(t).$$

This equation becomes more accurate as $\Delta t$ becomes smaller. Using a Taylor expansion of the left hand side of this equation, yields

$$P_N(t) + \Delta t \frac{dP_N(t)}{dt} + \cdots = P_N(t) + \Delta t[\lambda(N - 1)P_{N-1}(t) - \lambda N P_N(t)].$$

---

*We can be more precise in this calculation. The probability of exactly one birth among $m$ individuals is calculated in the following way. Exactly one birth can occur in $m$ different equally likely ways. One way is for an individual (numbered) 1 to have a birth and the other $m - 1$ individuals not to. The probability of this is

$$\lambda \Delta t(1 - \lambda \Delta t)^{m-1}.$$

Thus the probability of exactly one birth among $m$ individuals is

$$\sigma_m = m\lambda \Delta t(1 - \lambda \Delta t)^{m-1}.$$

For $N - 1$ individuals,

$$\boxed{\sigma_{N-1} = (N - 1)\lambda \Delta t(1 - \lambda \Delta t)^{N-2}.}$$

After canceling $P_N(t)$, dividing by $\Delta t$ and taking the limit as $\Delta t \to 0$, a system of ordinary differential equations result:

$$\frac{dP_N}{dt} = \lambda(N - 1)P_{N-1} - \lambda N P_N. \qquad (36.2)$$

This equation describes how the probability of a population of $N$ changes in time due to a random birth process.

To solve this system, initial conditions are necessary. These are the initial probabilities. The problem we will solve is one in which the initial population ($t = 0$) is known with certainty, being some value $N_0$. In that case all the initial probabilities are also known,

$$P_N(0) = \begin{cases} 0 & N \neq N_0 \\ 1 & N = N_0. \end{cases}$$

With these initial conditions we will show that the system of differential equations can be successively solved.

In the form,

$$\frac{dP_N}{dt} + \lambda N P_N = \lambda(N - 1)P_{N-1}, \qquad (36.3)$$

the procedure to solve the system of differential equations is clearer. First determine $P_{N-1}(t)$, and then use it to determine $P_N(t)$. Since there are no deaths, we are interested only in populations greater than or equal to the initial population $N_0$. For example, the probability of $N_0$ individuals is given by

$$\frac{dP_{N_0}}{dt} + \lambda N_0 P_{N_0} = \lambda(N_0 - 1)P_{N_0-1}.$$

But $P_{N_0-1}(t) = 0$ since it is impossible for the population to be less than $N_0$. Upon solving the resulting constant coefficient differential equation,

$$P_{N_0}(t) = P_{N_0}(0)e^{-\lambda N_0 t},$$

where the initial condition implies $P_{N_0}(0) = 1$. Thus

$$P_{N_0}(t) = e^{-\lambda N_0 t} \qquad (36.4)$$

which is sketched in Fig. 36-2. The probability of the population being $N_0$ decreases in time. As time goes on, the likelihood of the population remaining the same diminishes, since there are births but no deaths! $P_{N_0}(t)$ is always a

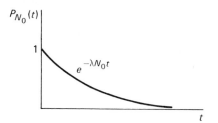

Figure 36-2  Probability of population remaining the same.

probability function, namely it never is greater than 1 and is always non-negative.

For example, if the probability of a birth is 2 percent in a year (i.e., $\lambda = .02$), then for an initial population of 10, the probability that the population will remain 10 one year later is $P_{10}(1) = e^{-.2} \approx 82$ percent. It is unlikely that a population of 10 will change in one year since the likelihood of a birth is only 2 per 100. However, if the initial population had been 1000, then the probability of it remaining 1000 is as we expect extremely small, $P_{1000}(1) = e^{-20} \approx 2 \times 10^{-9} = 2 \times 10^{-7}$ percent.

The probability of the population being $N_0 + 1$ is determined from equation 36.3, where $N = N_0 + 1$ and where $P_{N_0}(t)$ is eliminated using equation 36.4:

$$\frac{dP_{N_0+1}(t)}{dt} + \lambda(N_0 + 1)P_{N_0+1}(t) = \lambda N_0 e^{-\lambda N_0 t}.$$

This is a nonhomogeneous constant coefficient first order differential equation, which can be solved by the method of undetermined coefficients, yielding

$$P_{N_0+1}(t) = A_{N_0+1}e^{-\lambda(N_0+1)t} + N_0 e^{-\lambda N_0 t}.$$

The homogeneous solution is multiplied by the arbitrary constant $A_{N_0+1}$, determined from the initial condition that $P_{N_0+1}(0) = 0$. Thus,

$$P_{N_0+1}(t) = N_0 e^{-\lambda N_0 t}(1 - e^{-\lambda t}), \tag{36.5}$$

sketched in Fig. 36-3. The probability of $N_0 + 1$ individuals initially increases (from zero), but eventually diminishes to zero. You should be able to explain, based on the birth process, why this is so. At what time is it most likely that

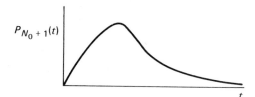

Figure 36-3  Probability of population increasing by one.

there are $N_0 + 1$ individuals? [Answer: The time at which $N_0 + 1$ individuals is most likely occurs at the maximum of $P_{N_0+1}(t)$. Thus

$$0 = \frac{dP_{N_0+1}(t)}{dt} = N_0 e^{-\lambda N_0 t}[-\lambda N_0(1 - e^{-\lambda t}) + \lambda e^{-\lambda t}].$$

After some algebra

$$e^{-\lambda t} = \frac{\lambda N_0}{\lambda(N_0 + 1)} = \frac{N_0}{N_0 + 1} \quad \text{or} \quad t = \frac{1}{\lambda} \ln\left(\frac{N_0 + 1}{N_0}\right).$$

Note that $e^{\lambda t} = (N_0 + 1)/N_0$. If a population grew in a deterministic manner with an instantaneous growth rate of $\lambda$, then at this time an original population of $N_0$ would have become $N_0 + 1$ since $N_0 e^{\lambda t} = N_0(N_0 + 1)/N_0 = N_0 + 1$. Thus the most likely time the population will be $N_0 + 1$ is the same time that a population growing via a deterministic model would exactly equal $N_0 + 1$.]

Let us continue the calculation to determine $P_{N_0+2}(t)$. The differential equation 36.2 with $N = N_0 + 2$, after using equation 36.5, becomes

$$\frac{dP_{N_0+2}(t)}{dt} + \lambda(N_0 + 2)P_{N_0+2}(t) = \lambda N_0(N_0 + 1)[e^{-\lambda N_0 t} - e^{-\lambda(N_0+1)t}].$$

Solving this we obtain (with a little bit of algebra, which is good practice in obtaining particular solutions by the method of undetermined coefficients),

$$P_{N_0+2}(t) = A_{N_0+2}e^{-\lambda(N_0+2)t} + \frac{N_0(N_0 + 1)}{2}e^{-\lambda N_0 t} - N_0(N_0 + 1)e^{-\lambda(N_0+1)t}.$$

The initial condition is again $P_{N_0+2}(0) = 0$ and thus a few additional algebraic manipulations show that

$$\boxed{P_{N_0+2}(t) = \frac{N_0(N_0 + 1)}{2}e^{-\lambda N_0 t}(1 - e^{-\lambda t})^2.} \qquad (36.6)$$

We have determined the probabilities of the first three possible populations. In order to determine the probabilities for all cases we could continue this type of calculation. However, "a little bit" of insight* suggests that the solution for all $j$ might just be (for $j \geq 1$)

$$\boxed{P_{N_0+j}(t) = \frac{N_0(N_0 + 1) \cdots (N_0 + j - 1)}{j!}e^{-\lambda N_0 t}(1 - e^{-\lambda t})^j.} \qquad (36.7)$$

At this point this is only a hypothesis. Let us prove it using **induction**. As a review, we outline the concepts behind a mathematical proof by induction.

---

*A considerable amount of insight is probably required!

We would like to prove the validity of a statement for all integers $j$. A proof by induction involves three steps:

1. Explicitly prove the statement is true for the first value of $j$, usually $j = 0$ or $j = 1$. (Sometimes it is advantageous to prove the statement for the first few values of $j$.)
2. Then assume it holds for all $j$ (less than or equal to any value $j_0$).
3. Using the assumption *prove* it holds for the next value, $j_0 + 1$ (using ordinary proof techniques).

If steps (1), (2), and (3) have been followed, why have we proved that the statement is valid for all finite values of $j$?

Let us prove our proposed formula, equation 36.7, by induction. We have already verified this is valid for $j = 1, 2$. Let us assume it is valid for all $j \leq j_0$. If we know all of these probabilities, let us determine the next one, $P_{N_0+j_0+1}(t)$, *from the differential equation* 36.3 with $N = N_0 + j_0 + 1$. Using the formula for $P_{N_0+j_0}(t)$, which is valid by the induction assumption, we have

$$\frac{dP_{N_0+j_0+1}(t)}{dt} + \lambda(N_0 + j_0 + 1)P_{N_0+j_0+1}(t)$$

$$= \frac{N_0(N_0 + 1) \cdots (N_0 + j_0)}{j_0!}\lambda e^{-\lambda N_0 t}(1 - e^{-\lambda t})^{j_0}.$$

To solve this differential equation by undetermined coefficients is difficult (Why?). Instead, note that a simple integrating factor exists, $e^{\lambda(N_0+j_0+1)t}$. Multiplying both sides of the above equation by this factor, yields

$$\frac{d}{dt}[e^{\lambda(N_0+j_0+1)t}P_{N_0+j_0+1}(t)]$$

$$= \frac{N_0(N_0 + 1) \cdots (N_0 + j_0)}{j_0!}\lambda e^{\lambda(j_0+1)t}(1 - e^{-\lambda t})^{j_0}.$$

Then by integrating,

$$e^{\lambda(N_0+j_0+1)t}P_{N_0+j_0+1}(t)$$

$$= \frac{N_0(N_0 + 1) \cdots (N_0 + j_0)}{j_0!}\lambda \int e^{\lambda(j_0+1)t}(1 - e^{-\lambda t})^{j_0}\, dt,$$

where the integral is easily calculated, since

$$e^{\lambda(j_0+1)t}(1 - e^{-\lambda t})^{j_0} = e^{\lambda t}e^{\lambda j_0 t}(1 - e^{-\lambda t})^{j_0}$$

$$= e^{\lambda t}[e^{\lambda t}(1 - e^{-\lambda t})]^{j_0}$$

$$= e^{\lambda t}(e^{\lambda t} - 1)^{j_0}$$

and

$$\int e^{\lambda t}(e^{\lambda t} - 1)^{j_0} \, dt = \frac{(e^{\lambda t} - 1)^{j_0+1}}{\lambda(j_0 + 1)} + c,$$

(which can be verified by differentiating or by making a change of variables). Thus,

$$e^{\lambda(N_0+j_0+1)t}P_{N_0+j_0+1}(t) = \frac{N_0(N_0 + 1) \cdots (N_0 + j_0)}{(j_0 + 1)!}(e^{\lambda t} - 1)^{j_0+1},$$

where the constant has been chosen such that $P_{N_0+j_0+1}(0) = 0$. Thus

$$P_{N_0+j_0+1}(t) = \frac{N_0(N_0 + 1) \cdots (N_0 + j_0)}{(j_0 + 1)!}e^{-\lambda N_0 t}(e^{-\lambda t})^{j_0+1}(e^{\lambda t} - 1)^{j_0+1},$$

which is the proposed formula for $N_0 + j_0 + 1$. Equation 36.7 has been derived for $N_0 + j_0 + 1$ assuming it is valid for $N_0 + j_0$. Thus by induction equation 36.7 is the probability distribution for a population initially $N_0$ with births occurring randomly with probability $\lambda \Delta t$ (for a short time $\Delta t$).

In the exercises, further analysis of this stochastic birth model is undertaken. Suggestions are made relating this model to the deterministic model of exponential growth. Additional probability concepts imply that the deterministic model is a better and better approximation to the stochastic model as the size of the initial population increases!

This model of stochastic births shows one manner in which uncertainty can be introduced in a mathematical model. Let us just mention another way without pursuing its consequences. We have assumed that each individual randomly gives birth with certain known probabilities. We could also assume the growth rate $R$, itself, is a random variable, fluctuating in time over different values, perhaps due to uncontrollable changes in the environment. This ends the discussion of stochastic models in this text. Those interested in additional knowledge in this area can consult the books referred to in Sec. 55.

# EXERCISES

**36.1.** Formulate a stochastic model for population growth including births and deaths (i.e., what system of differential equations determines $P_N(t)$?) What mathematical difficulty is presented by this system?

**36.2.** Modify equation 36.1 to take into account the possibility of *exactly* two births occurring among $N - 2$ individuals in time $\Delta t$. Show that equation 36.2 still remains valid.

**36.3.** (a) Based on probabilistic ideas, why should

$$\sum_{j=0}^{\infty} P_{N_0+j}(t) = 1?$$

(b) Using the known expression for $P_{N_0+j}(t)$, equation 36.7, verify that part (a) is valid. [Hint: Explicitly calculate the first few terms of the summation; compare this to the binomial expansion (Sec. 25)].

**36.4.** The expected population at time $t$, $E(t)$, is obtained from the formula

$$E(t) = \sum_{j=0}^{\infty} (N_0 + j)P_{N_0+j}(t).$$

(a) Can you explain why this is valid using probabilistic ideas?
(b) Show that $E(t) = N_0 e^{\lambda t}$. [Hint: Explicitly calculate the first few terms of the summation; compare this to the derivative of the binomial expansion (Sec. 25)].
(c) Explain the significance of part (b).

**36.5.** In this problem we will derive the results of exercise 36.4 by an alternative method.

(a) If you have not already done so, do exercise 36.4a.
(b) Using the differential equation for $P_{N_0+j}(t)$, show that

$$\frac{dE}{dt} = \lambda E.$$

(c) What is $E(0)$?
(d) Derive the result of exercise 36.4b, and explain its significance.

**36.6.** Consider equation 36.7. Assume $N_0 = 10,000$. Estimate $\lambda$, if it is observed that a total of 4500 births occur in 20 days. [Hint: See exercise 36.4.]

**36.7.** If $\lambda = .09$ and initially $N = 10$, what is the probability that $N = 12$ one year later? What is the probability that $N = 12$ two years later?

# 37. Density-Dependent Growth

The fundamental prediction of the constant growth rate population model,

$$\frac{dN}{dt} = R_0 N,$$

is that the population exponentially grows without limits (if $R_0 > 0$). Although this model may accurately reflect experiments *in the initial stages*, we realize that no population will grow exponentially indefinitely. A more complex population growth model is needed. The growth rate cannot remain constant. What might prevent a population from growing without a bound? Essentially we suspect that once a population grows sufficiently large it will begin to interact in a different way with its environment or with other species. Laboratory experiments have shown that the lack of food (nutrients) to sustain an indefinitely large population can limit the population growth. Even if the food supply is sufficiently increased, experiments have indicated that the growth rate still diminishes as the population density* increases. In some manner, still being investigated by researchers, the increase in density causes the birth rate to decrease, the death rate to increase, or both. At some population, the birth rate equals the death rate and the resulting growth rate is zero. Thus, crowding may have the same effect as limiting the food supply. Space can be considered necessary to sustain life for certain species.

Let us attempt to mathematically model this process. In general, the growth rate $(1/N)\,dN/dt$ may not be constant, but might depend on the population:

$$\boxed{\frac{1}{N}\frac{dN}{dt} = R(N)} \quad \text{or} \quad \boxed{\frac{dN}{dt} = NR(N).} \qquad (37.1)$$

What mathematical properties might the function $R(N)$ have? We must remember that we have already assumed that the population is large enough so that we may model $N(t)$ as a continuous function of time. Thus we are not particularly interested in $R(N)$ for $N$ extremely small. For moderate size populations, growth occurs with only slight limitations from the species' total environment; as $N$ diminishes $R(N)$ should approach the growth rate without environmental influences. As the population increases, we still expect it to grow, but at a smaller rate due to the limitation on growth caused by the increased population density. Thus $R(N)$ decreases as $N$ increases. For a much larger population, experiments show the growth rate to be negative (more deaths than births). If we assume that the growth rate is continuous, then we know there is a population at which the growth rate is zero as sketched in Fig. 37-1:

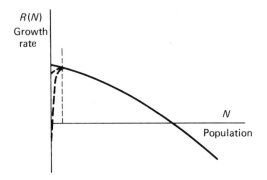

Figure 37-1    Possible density-dependent growth rates, $R(N)$.

---

*Population density is proportional to the total population since the region is assumed fixed and since the population is also assumed uniformly distributed throughout the region. If instead the population density significantly varies in the region, then it may be necessary to introduce a more complex mathematical model than the ones developed in this text.

In particular, note that we have not attempted as yet to give a specific model of the growth rate for extremely small populations. However, *for simplicity* we now model the growth rate for very small populations in the same manner (solid curve). We cannot expect this model to always make accurate predictions if the population ever gets sufficiently small. The *simplest* function with this property is the straight line,

$$R(N) = a - bN,$$

sketched in Fig. 37-2, yielding the nonlinear first order differential equation known as the **logistic equation,**

$$\frac{dN}{dt} = N(a - bN). \tag{37.2}$$

$a$ is the growth rate without environmental influences, and $b$ represents the effect of increased population density. Note that $a$ and $b$ are positive constants. This model was first investigated by Verhulst in the late 1830s and later "rediscovered" by Pearl and Reed in the 1920s.

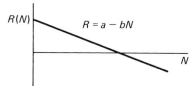

Figure 37-2   Logistic growth rate.

Before solving this equation let us indicate a more specific model from which it may arise. If growth was limited by the supply of food, then another variable can be introduced equal to some measure of the yearly available food, $F_a$. Perhaps the growth rate is proportional to the difference between the available food and the food necessary for a subsistence level of food consumption, $F_c$. Under these assumptions,

$$\frac{1}{N}\frac{dN}{dt} = \alpha(F_a - F_c).$$

Suppose that the available food per year $F_a$ is fixed. The subsistence level of food consumption can be assumed to be proportional to the population,

$$F_c = \beta N.$$

This again yields the logistic equation

$$\frac{dN}{dt} = N(\alpha F_a - \alpha \beta N).$$

The population at which the growth rate is zero is an **equilibrium popula-tion** in the sense that if the population was initially at that value it would stay there. That is, the number of births would exactly offset the number of deaths. Using the logistic model, equation 37.2, the equilibrium populations are

$$N = 0 \quad \text{and} \quad N = \frac{a}{b}.$$

Zero population is certainly an equilibrium population. However, the major interest is in the case in which $N = a/b$. This is the largest population which the environment can sustain without loss, the so-called **carrying capacity** of the environment. This theory predicts that the population $N = a/b$ would correspond to Z.P.G. (zero population growth). A question we will answer in the next section is whether this equilibrium population is stable or un-stable. That is, if there were more than the equilibrium number, then would the population eventually decrease and approach this equilibrium figure? Also, if there were initially less than this "crowded" population, then would the population this time increase towards the equilibrium population?

# EXERCISES

**37.1.** Let us modify our derivation of the logistic equation. Suppose the growth rate is a *function* of the difference between the available food, $f_a$, and a sub-sistence level of yearly food consumption, $f_c$. Again assume $f_c = \beta N$. What equation describes this situation? What properties do we suspect are valid for this functional relationship? Is there an equilibrium population?

**37.2.** F. E. Smith suggested a different simple model of the population growth of a species limited by the food supply based on experiments on a type of water bug. As in the logistic model, the growth rate is proportional to the difference between the available food $f_a$ and the subsistence level of food consumption $f_c$:

$$\frac{1}{N}\frac{dN}{dt} = \alpha(f_a - f_c).$$

However, previously $f_c$ was assumed proportional to the number of individ-uals of the species. Smith instead assumed that more food is necessary for survival during the growing phase of a population. Consequently a simple model would be

$$f_c = \beta N + \gamma\frac{dN}{dt}$$

with $\gamma > 0$. What differential equation describes this model? What are the equilibrium populations?

**37.3.** Consider the following models of population growth:
(1) $dN/dt = -aN + bN^2$
(2) $dN/dt = -aN - bN^2$
(3) $dN/dt = aN + bN^2$
(4) $dN/dt = aN - bN^2$,
with $a > 0$ and $b > 0$. For each case, describe possible birth and death mechanisms.

**37.4.** Which of the following are reasonable models of the spread of a disease among a finite number of people:
(1) $dN/dt = \alpha N$
(2) $dN/dt = \alpha(N_T - N)$
(3) $dN/dt = \alpha(N - N_T)$,
where $N$ is the number of infected individuals and $N_T$ is the total population.

**37.5.** A certain species has an instantaneous growth rate of 27 percent per year when not affected by crowding. Experimentally, for each 1000 of the species the birth rate drops by 12 per 1000 per year, and the death rate increases by 50 per 1000 per year. Determine the parameters of a logistic equation which models this species. What is the expected nonzero equilibrium population?

**37.6.** Suppose we are considering the growth as measured over a time $\Delta t$. The growth rate is defined by equation 32.1. What nonlinear difference equation models population growth of a species if the basic idea behind the logistic equation is applied to the discrete model?

# 38.  Phase Plane Solution
# of the Logistic Equation

The logistic equation,

$$\frac{dN}{dt} = N(a - bN), \qquad (38.1)$$

describes the environmentally limited growth of a population. In the next section, we will explicitly solve this equation. However, before doing so, let us determine from the differential equation the qualitative features of the solution. The logistic equation is a first-order differential equation that does not explicitly depend on time—i.e., it is autonomous. The solution of first-order autonomous equations can be understood using a phase plane analysis having certain similarities to the approach which we developed concerning vibrating mechanical systems. As in that case, we will be able to determine the qualitative behavior of the solution quite quickly.

Graphing $dN/dt$ as a function of $N$, yields Fig. 38-1:

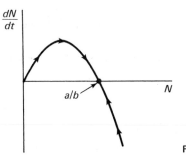

Figure 38-1    Phase plane of the logistic equation.

(Hopefully only the right half plane is necessary since $N$ represents the number of the species and must be non-negative.) Only points on the sketched curve correspond to a possible solution. Again arrows are introduced, designating how the solution changes in time. $N$ increases if $dN/dt > 0$ and vice versa. Not surprisingly, this diagram indicates that the model has the desired qualitative behavior. For populations less than the equilibrium population, $N = a/b$, the population increases, and for populations more than the equilibrium, the population decreases. If initially less than the equilibrium population, the population continually grows, but we will show it never reaches the equilibrium population. If initially greater than the equilibrium population, the population continually diminishes towards the equilibrium population, as shown in Fig. 38-2:

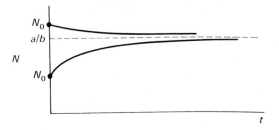

Figure 38-2    Logistic growth model: approach to equilibrium.

The population level $a/b$ is sometimes called the saturation level, since for larger populations there are more deaths than births.

The equilibrium population is clearly stable. This can be further mathematically demonstrated in two equivalent ways:

1. We wish to analyze the solution in the neighborhood of the equilibrium population. If we approximate the phase plane curve in the vicinity of

Figure 38-3  Population growth near equilibrium.

the equilibrium population by a straight line as in Fig. 38-3 (the first two terms of a Taylor series), then we derive the following first-order linear differential equation with constant coefficients:

$$\frac{dN}{dt} = \alpha\left(N - \frac{a}{b}\right),$$

where $\alpha$ is negative (the negative slope of the curve). It can be more easily solved than the logistic equation, yielding the behavior of the population in the neighborhood of the equilibrium,

$$N - \frac{a}{b} = (N_0 - a/b)e^{\alpha t},$$

where $N_0$ is the initial population (close to equilibrium and either less than or greater than the equilibrium population). Explicitly as $t \to \infty$, (since $\alpha < 0$), $N \to a/b$, but never reaches it in a finite time. For any initial population (near equilibrium) the displacement tends to zero. The equilibrium population is thus *stable*!

2. Equivalent to this method, we use a linear stability analysis as developed in the discussions of nonlinear vibrations. The equilibrium population is $N = a/b$. Using the perturbation method, let

$$N = \frac{a}{b} + \epsilon N_1.$$

$\epsilon N_1$ is the displacement from equilibrium and must be small, $|\epsilon N_1| \ll a/b$, (where $\epsilon$ is a small parameter). Substituting this into the logistic equation yields

$$\epsilon\frac{dN_1}{dt} = \left(\frac{a}{b} + \epsilon N_1\right)(a - a - \epsilon b N_1),$$

or equivalently

$$\frac{dN_1}{dt} = -bN_1\left(\frac{a}{b} + \epsilon N_1\right).$$

Since $\epsilon N_1$ is small, we neglect the nonlinear term (corresponding to the linearization done geometrically in (1)). Thus

$$\frac{dN_1}{dt} = -aN_1.$$

The solution of this differential equation,

$$N_1 = ce^{-at},$$

again shows that the equilibrium population is stable. The exponential decay constant is $a$. Using the geometric argument, the decay constant was $-\alpha$. However, these values are the same since $\alpha$ is the slope of the phase plane curve at $N = a/b$,

$$\alpha = \frac{d}{dN}[N(a - bN)]\Big|_{N=a/b} = -bN\Big|_{N=a/b} = -a.$$

# EXERCISES

**38.1.** In an experiment on fruit flies, the initial number doubled in approximately 2 hours, but at both 12 and 24 hours after the beginning of the experiment there were only approximately 8 times as many as there were initially. Model this phenomena using a logistic equation (i.e. estimate the parameters).

**38.2.** Suppose the *growth rate* of a species is as sketched in Fig. 38-4:

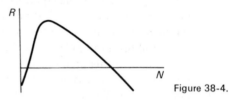

Figure 38-4.

Show that there are 3 equilibrium populations. Which (if any) are stable? Show how the eventual population of the species depends on its initial population.

**38.3.** Consider Smith's model of population growth (see exercise 37.2)

$$\frac{dN}{dt} = \frac{\alpha N(f_a - \beta N)}{1 + \alpha \gamma N}.$$

Are the equilibrium populations stable?

**38.4.** Show that the solution of the logistic equation has an inflection point at a population equal to $\frac{1}{2}$ the saturation level. Explain why the sketches in Fig. 38-2 do not have inflection points.

**38.5.** Using Taylor series methods, show that the nonzero equilibrium population of the logistic equation is stable. Show that if the initial population is near (but not at) this equilibrium population, the population nevertheless does not ever attain the equilibrium population.

**38.6.** Consider the logistic equation. Sketch $N$ as a function of $t$ using the direction field and the method of isoclines. How does this differ from the first order differential equations analyzed in the sections on mechanical vibrations?

# 39. Explicit Solution of the Logistic Equation

Although the logistic equation,

$$\frac{dN}{dt} = N(a - bN), \qquad (39.1)$$

was qualitatively analyzed in the previous section, more precise quantitative behavior may at times be desired. An explicit solution to the logistic equation can be obtained since the equation is separable:

$$\frac{dN}{N(a - bN)} = dt.$$

The method of partial fractions will be successful in integrating this equation. Since

$$\frac{1}{N(a - bN)} = \frac{1/a}{N} + \frac{b/a}{a - bN},$$

integration yields

$$\frac{1}{a}\ln|N| - \frac{1}{a}\ln|a - bN| = t + c,$$

where the absolute values in the resulting logarithms can be very important! The arbitrary constant $c$ enables the initial value problem, $N(0) = N_0$, to be solved. Eliminating $c$ in that way yields

$$\frac{1}{a}\ln|N| - \frac{1}{a}\ln|a - bN| = t + \frac{1}{a}\ln|N_0| - \frac{1}{a}\ln|a - bN_0|.$$

Since both $N$ and $N_0$ must be positive,

$$\frac{1}{a}\ln\frac{N}{N_0} + \frac{1}{a}\ln\left|\frac{a - bN_0}{a - bN}\right| = t. \qquad (39.2)$$

This equation gives $t$ as a function of $N$, not a desirable form. Multiplying by $a$ and exponentiating, yields

$$\frac{N}{N_0}\left|\frac{a - bN_0}{a - bN}\right| = e^{at}.$$

$a - bN$ and $a - bN_0$ have the same sign* and hence,

$$\frac{N}{N_0}\left(\frac{a - bN_0}{a - bN}\right) = e^{at},$$

or equivalently

$$N(a - bN_0) = (a - bN)N_0 e^{at}.$$

This equation can be solved for $N$

$$N = \frac{aN_0 e^{at}}{a - bN_0 + bN_0 e^{at}},$$

or

$$N = \frac{a/b}{1 + \left(\dfrac{a - bN_0}{bN_0}\right)e^{-at}}. \qquad (39.3)$$

As an exercise (see exercise 39.2) show how this solution verifies the qualitative results obtained from the phase plane. Specific logistic curves depend on the three parameters $a$, $b$, and $N_0$. One example is sketched in Fig. 39-1:

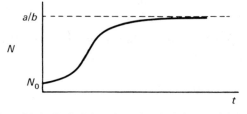

Figure 39-1 Typical time-dependent logistic growth curve.

Laboratory experiments, for examples, on the growth of yeast in a culture and on the growth of paramecium, have indicated good quantitative agreement to logistic curves.

# EXERCISES

**39.1.** Consider $dN/dt = \alpha N^2 - \beta N$ (with $\alpha > 0$, $\beta > 0$).
   (a)  How does the growth rate depend on the population?
   (b)  Sketch the solution in the phase plane.

---

*Initially $a - bN_0$ and $a - bN$ have the same sign. The sign of $(a - bN_0)/(a - bN)$ can change only if there is a finite value of $t$, such that $a - bN = 0$; that is, if the equilibrium population is reached in a finite time. As we know, this cannot occur. Specifically, if $a - bN = 0$, then equation 39.2 shows $t = +\infty$. Thus the sign of $(a - bN_0)/(a - bN)$ remains positive for all time.

(c)   Obtain the exact solution.

(d)   Show how both parts (b) and (c) illustrate the following behavior:

     (i) If $N_0 > \beta/\alpha$, then $N \rightarrow \infty$. (At what time does $N \rightarrow \infty$?)

     (ii) If $N_0 < \beta/\alpha$, then $N \rightarrow 0$.

     (iii) What happens if $N_0 = \beta/\alpha$?

**39.2.**   The general solution of the logistic equation, equation 39.1, has been shown to be equation 39.3. Show that this exact solution has the following properties:

(1) It is defined for all $t \geq 0$.

(2) As $t \rightarrow \infty$, $N \rightarrow a/b$ for all initial conditions except $N_0 = 0$. (Note: It takes an infinite amount of time to reach the equilibrium population.)

**39.3.**   The logistic curve, equation 39.3, is sometimes referred to as an S-curve for the reasons to be described.

(a)   Show that

$$N = \alpha + \beta \frac{e^{(a/2)(t-t_0)} - e^{-(a/2)(t-t_0)}}{e^{(a/2)(t-t_0)} + e^{-(a/2)(t-t_0)}}.$$

What is $\alpha$, $\beta$, and $t_0$? [Hint: Put the above expression over a common denominator. Multiply numerator and denominator by $e^{-(a/2)(t-t_0)}$.]

(b)   Recall that the *hyperbolic* functions are defined as follows:

$$\sinh x = \frac{e^x - e^{-x}}{2}$$

$$\cosh x = \frac{e^x + e^{-x}}{2}$$

$$\tanh x = \frac{\sinh x}{\cosh x}.$$

Thus show that

$$N = \alpha + \beta \tanh \frac{a}{2}(t - t_0).$$

(c)   Sketch $\tanh x$ as a function of $x$. Show that it might be called "S-shaped". Hints:

     (i) Show that $\tanh 0 = 0$.

     (ii) Show that $\tanh x$ is an odd function (i.e., $\tanh(-x) = -\tanh x$).

     (iii) Show that $\lim_{x \to \infty} \tanh x = 1$, and thus what is $\lim_{x \to -\infty} \tanh x$?

(d)   Now sketch the logistic curve.

(e)   Show that $\alpha + \beta = a/b$ and $\alpha - \beta = 0$.

**39.4.**   Consider the following growth model:

$$\frac{dN}{dt} = aN + bN^2 \quad \text{with } a > 0, b > 0.$$

(a)   How does the growth rate depend on $N$?

(b)   What would you expect happens to the population?

(c)   By using the phase plane, show that the population tends towards infinity.

(d)   By considering the exact solution, show that the population reaches infinity in a *finite* time; what might be called a population explosion.

# 40. Growth Models with Time Delays

Although some experiments on environmentally limited population growth have shown good qualitative and quantitative agreement with the logistic growth model, other experiments have shown that the carrying capacity of the environment is not always reached monotonically. Instead, some of these experiments show the types of behavior sketched in Fig. 40-1:

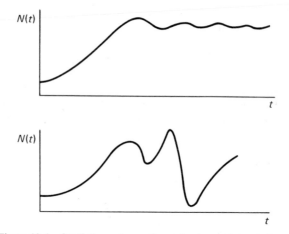

Figure 40-1   Oscillations of experimentally observed populations.

In Fig. 40-1a the population oscillates around its carrying capacity in a manner similar to the decaying oscillation of a spring-mass system with friction. Other experiments show wild oscillation as in Fig. 40-1b.

The preceding types of experiments motivate us to develop other models of population growth of one species. Consider

$$\frac{1}{N}\frac{dN}{dt} = R(N) \quad \text{or} \quad \frac{dN}{dt} = f(N), \qquad (40.1)$$

a model in which the rate of change of the population depends only on the present size of the population in an otherwise arbitrary way. Of most importance for any specific model is knowing the possible equilibrium populations as well as which (if any) are stable. Of secondary interest is the explicit solution, especially since in many cases it is so complicated as to disguise the frequently simple qualitative behavior of the solution. However, we can verify using the phase plane analysis of Sec. 38 that for any population growth model of the above form, a stable equilibrium population will be approached monotonically. It is impossible for a population to vary in an oscillatory manner around a stable equilibrium population. Other types of models will be introduced which may allow oscillations of the observed type.

Let us describe one situation in which a population may oscillate about its carrying capacity. Perhaps the understanding of one such ecosystem will suggest to us ways to modify the general one-species deterministic continuous growth models, equation 40.1. Consider the growth of a small forest composed of one species of trees. This is a reasonable ecosystem to investigate since we expect the population to exponentially grow when the forest is sparse, and since we know that due to limited nutrients (sunlight, water, etc.) the population will not grow forever. However, the population could oscillate around its carrying capacity in a manner that we now explain.

Suppose that at a given time the population of trees was slightly less than its carrying capacity. Having sufficient nutrients the trees would produce a large number of seeds, yielding a few years later, a large number of young trees. Before these young trees mature, the older trees would not feel their presence, and hence would continue for a few years to produce large numbers of newer trees. The total tree population might easily be larger than the environment could sustain. Only in a few years would the mature trees notice the effects of their earlier overproduction. Then the death rate of trees might surpass the birth rate, finally causing the tree population to tend back towards the carrying capacity. The delayed response of the tree population to its environment could cause the population to go beyond its saturation level. The carrying capacity is not necessarily reached monotonically.

Furthermore, the overcrowded ecosystem would prevent large number of seeds from being produced as well as developing into young trees for a number of years. Even as the number of seeds produced was decreased, the trees might not immediately feel any noticable improvement. More deaths than births could occur until the tree population diminished *below* the saturation level. Again the delay in the trees response to its environment might prevent the population from monotonically approaching its equilibrium. Although the situation described above might not happen under all circumstances, we have indicated a possible cause of oscillations.

To mathematically model this phenomena, we note that the basic idea is that the population does not respond immediately to its environment. Instead there is a delay. The rate of change of the population is not a function of the present population $N(t)$, but a past population $N(t - t_d)$, where $t_d$ is the delay time. Two slightly different models of this situation are:

$$\frac{dN(t)}{dt} = f(N(t - t_d)), \tag{40.2a}$$

$$\frac{1}{N(t)} \frac{dN(t)}{dt} = R(N(t - t_d)). \tag{40.2b}$$

For animals, the delay time may be the time it takes an egg to develop into a fertile adult. Equations 40.2a and 40.2b are called **delay-differential equations**. For example, suppose the growth rate is a constant $R_0$, but occurs with a delay $t_d$. Then

$$\frac{dN(t)}{dt} = R_0 N(t - t_d), \qquad (40.3)$$

a linear delay-differential equation. If we apply the ideas behind logistic growth to the delay mechanism, then population growth is modeled by

$$\frac{dN(t)}{dt} = N(t)[a - bN(t - t_d)]. \qquad (40.4)$$

We will attempt to illustrate how a delay can cause the population to oscillate around an equilibrium population. Suppose a species grows in the logistic manner without a delay; for populations less than equilibrium, the population grows, and vice versa. If there were a delay mechanism, described for example by equation 40.4, then the species would grow at a rate determined by the population at a previous time. At a time when the population has almost reached equilibrium (indicated in Fig. 40-2 with a star), the population would continue to grow at the rate for a population not near equilibrium

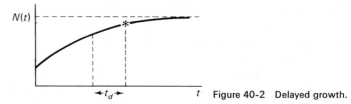

Figure 40-2  Delayed growth.

(if $t_d$ is sufficiently large). In this way, the population *could* go beyond its equilibrium value. Furthermore if the delay is sufficiently large the population *might* oscillate around its equilibrium population as illustrated by Fig. 40-1a, or perhaps the delay would destabilize the equilibrium population as illustrated by Fig. 40-1b.

In general, delay-differential equations are considerably more difficult to solve than ordinary differential equations. We will not discuss their solution in this text. However, see exercise 40.1 for a simple example of the solution of a delay-differential equation, 40.3. In order to simplify our calculations we will return to the discrete time formulation.

If we measure population growth over a time interval $\Delta t$, then a general model of discrete population growth without a delay is

$$\frac{N(t + \Delta t) - N(t)}{\Delta t N(t)} = R(N(t)),$$

where the growth rate measured over the time $\Delta t$ may depend on the population, $N(t)$. $\Delta t$ is sometimes called the discretization time, i.e., the discrete time over which changes are measured. For example, as discussed previously the constant growth model (using discrete time) is

$$N(t + \Delta t) - N(t) = R_0 \Delta t N(t); \qquad (40.5)$$

the growth rate is proportional to the population. However, if nutrients are limited, the growth rate may decrease as the population increases, in which case this situation may be modeled by the **discrete logistic equation**:

$$N(t + \Delta t) - N(t) = \Delta t N(t)[a - bN(t)]. \tag{40.6}$$

These equations automatically take into account a "delay" $\Delta t$. The change in population depends on the population $\Delta t$ time ago.

The discrete formalism is especially appropriate for perennial plants and animals which breed only during a specific time of the year. In these cases, the change in population from one year to the next clearly depends not on the present population but only on the past population. We have assumed the change in population only depends on the previous year's population. In particular, the change does not depend explicitly on the population two years previous. The solution to the discrete logistic equation is pursued in exercise 40.3. Here, we would like to consider a slightly more complicated problem.

Suppose that we employ a discrete formulation of population growth, but in addition growth occurs with a delay of $t_d$ units of time. A **discrete constant growth model with delay time** $t_d$ is

$$N(t + \Delta t) - N(t) = R_0 \Delta t N(t - t_d), \tag{40.7}$$

while a **discrete logistic growth model with delay time** $t_d$ is

$$N(t + \Delta t) - N(t) = \Delta t N(t)[a - bN(t - t_d)]. \tag{40.8}$$

Since measurements are made every $\Delta t$ time, the time delay $t_d$ in this model must be an integral multiple of $\Delta t$.

For a specific example, consider a deer population, $N(t)$, measured every year ($\Delta t = 1$). The increase of deer over a year in a given area depends on the vegetation, which in turn depends on how much vegetation was left uneaten by the deer during the previous year. In this way, the delay in the growth mechanism is also a year ($t_d = \Delta t = 1$). A much oversimplified model for this process is the discrete logistic equation with a time delay,

$$N(t + \Delta t) - N(t) = \Delta t N(t)[a - bN(t - \Delta t)]. \tag{40.9}$$

Equation 40.9 involves three levels of time, $t + \Delta t$, $t$, and $t - \Delta t$. It is called a **second-order difference equation** since the times involved differ in integral units of $\Delta t$ by at most two units of $\Delta t$.

We can directly solve this equation by explicit numerical calculations. An example of this will be given. The notation

$$t \equiv m\Delta t$$

and

$$N(t) = N(m\Delta t) \equiv N_m$$

is perhaps more convenient. Using this notation the discrete logistic equation with a delay, equation 40.9, becomes

$$N_{m+1} - N_m = N_m(\alpha - \beta N_{m-1}), \qquad \textbf{(40.10)}$$

where $\alpha = a\Delta t$ and $\beta = b\Delta t$. Note that since 3 levels of time are involved, the appropriate conditions to initiate a calculation are the population at two successive years. For example, knowing only an initial population is not sufficient to be able to use this equation for calculations!

Suppose, as an example, that the growth rate without environmental influences is 20 percent per year ($a = \frac{1}{5}$), but as the population increases the growth rate decreases proportionally such that $b = \frac{1}{400}$ (for every 4 individuals, the growth rate is reduced 1 percent per year). The initial population is known to be ten ($N_0 = 10$). Let us calculate the population changes if equation 40.10 is appropriate with a delay in the growth process of 1 year ($\Delta t = 1$). To solve the difference equation 40.10 with $\Delta t = 1$, the population is also needed one year later, which we assume to be given as fifteen ($N_1 = 15$). In summary

$$\alpha = a\Delta t = \frac{1}{5}$$

$$\beta = b\Delta t = \frac{1}{400}$$

$$N_0 = 10$$
$$N_1 = 15$$

Then equation 40.10 becomes

$$N_{m+1} = N_m(\alpha + 1 - \beta N_{m-1}) = N_m(1.2 - .0025N_{m-1}).$$

Calculating the population for the following year, yields

$$N_2 = N_1(1.2 - .0025N_0) = 15(1.175) = 17.625$$

Additional results have been calculated from the difference equation using a computer

| | | | |
|---|---|---|---|
| $N_0 = 10.0$ | $N_8 = 39.4$ | $N_{16} = 70.0$ | $N_{24} = 79.0$ |
| $N_1 = 15.0$ | $N_9 = 43.9$ | $N_{17} = 72.2$ | $N_{25} = 79.3$ |
| $N_2 = 17.6$ | $N_{10} = 48.3$ | $N_{18} = 74.0$ | $N_{26} = 79.5$ |
| $N_3 = 20.5$ | $N_{11} = 52.7$ | $N_{19} = 75.5$ | $N_{27} = 79.6$ |
| $N_4 = 23.1$ | $N_{12} = 56.8$ | $N_{20} = 76.6$ | $N_{28} = 79.7$ |
| $N_5 = 27.2$ | $N_{13} = 60.7$ | $N_{21} = 77.5$ | $N_{29} = 79.8$ |
| $N_6 = 31.0$ | $N_{14} = 64.2$ | $N_{22} = 78.1$ | $N_{30} = 79.8$ |
| $N_7 = 35.1$ | $N_{15} = 67.3$ | $N_{23} = 78.6$ | $N_{31} = 79.9$ |

and sketched in Fig. 40-3.

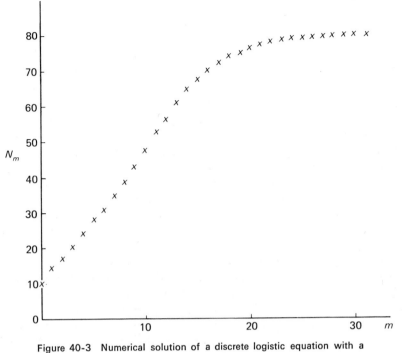

Figure 40-3 Numerical solution of a discrete logistic equation with a delay.

In the previous calculation, the population seems to be tending to 80. This is not surprising as we note that there exists an equilibrium population $N_E$ ($N_m = N_E$ for all $m$) if

$$0 = N_E(\alpha - \beta N_E).$$

A nonzero equilibrium population is

$$N_E = \frac{\alpha}{\beta} = \frac{a\Delta t}{b\Delta t} \equiv \frac{a}{b},$$

the same equilibrium population as in the case without a delay mechanism (see the logistic equation, Secs. 37–39). For this example, $\alpha = \frac{1}{5}$ and $\beta = \frac{1}{400}$, and consequently there is an equilibrium population of $N_E = \frac{400}{5} = 80$.

In this case the behavior of the discrete logistic equation with a delay is quite analogous to the continuous logistic equation. However, we introduced the discrete model with a delay in order to show an oscillation around the carrying capacity. At first, we might conclude that a different type of mathematical model is necessary. We have just illustrated a disadvantage of explicit numerical calculations because actually we are *not* justified in assuming this same type of behavior occurs for all other delayed growth problems described by equation 40.10. Perhaps (as we will show) oscillation occurs in other cases. In fact, we do not even know if the equilibrium population will always be stable!

Recall without a delay a population satisfying the logistic *differential* equation will approach the environment's carrying capacity without going beyond it; that is the population increases if it is less than the carrying capacity and decreases if it is greater than the carrying capacity. The discrete logistic equation with a delay, equation 40.10, may sometimes have this property, as illustrated by the numerical example. However, we will show that an oscillation can occur. Note that the population increases (i.e., $N_{m+1} - N_m > 0$) if $N_{m-1} < \alpha/\beta$. Thus if the population one interval of time earlier is less than the carrying capacity, then the population increases. It is *perhaps* possible that $N_m$ might be greater than the carrying capacity but $N_{m-1}$ less than the carrying capacity. Then equation 40.10 predicts that although the population has grown beyond the carrying capacity, it is still growing (that is, $N_{m+1} - N_m > 0$ if $N_m > \alpha/\beta$ and $N_{m-1} < \alpha/\beta$). The population *must* decrease at the next interval since $N_{m+2} - N_{m+1} = N_{m+1}(\alpha - \beta N_m)$. Introducing a discrete time enables the population, although always tending towards the equilibrium, to go beyond the equilibrium. However, it is the delay that allows the population once past equilibrium to continue to grow away from equilibrium (but this latter effect occurs only for the length of the delay). The population decreases to either less than or greater than the carrying capacity, as shown in Fig. 40-4. In a similar manner one can try to understand how the population may decrease even when it is less than the carrying capacity. It is the above ideas that form the basis for oscillations to be possible for solutions to the discrete logistic equation with a delay.

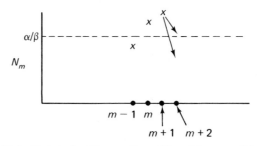

Figure 40-4   Discrete logistic equation with a delay: possible growth beyond the environment's carrying capacity.

In the previous paragraph we have described a plausible circumstance. We will now try to determine under what conditions this occurs. To more accurately analyze the population satisfying a discrete logistic equation with a delay, we must linearize the nonlinear difference equation in the neighborhood of the equilibrium population, $\alpha/\beta$. The linearization can be accomplished by Taylor series methods as outlined in exercise 40.6. Here we will do the linearization using the perturbation procedure. This analysis will not only show that oscillations are possible, but will also determine the conditions under which the equilibrium population is stable. Let

$$N(t) = \frac{\alpha}{\beta} + \epsilon N_1(t) \qquad \textbf{(40.11a)}$$

or equivalently

$$N_m = \frac{\alpha}{\beta} + \epsilon y_m, \qquad \textbf{(40.11b)}$$

where the displacement from equilibrium, $\epsilon N_1(t) = \epsilon y_m$, will be assumed to be much smaller than the equilibrium population:

$$|\epsilon y_m| \ll \frac{\alpha}{\beta}.$$

Substituting equation 40.11b into the nonlinear difference equation, equation 40.10, yields

$$\frac{\alpha}{\beta} + \epsilon y_{m+1} - \frac{\alpha}{\beta} - \epsilon y_m = \left( \frac{\alpha}{\beta} + \epsilon y_m \right)(\alpha - \alpha - \epsilon \beta y_{m-1}),$$

which when simplified becomes

$$y_{m+1} - y_m = -\beta y_{m-1} \left( \frac{\alpha}{\beta} + \epsilon y_m \right).$$

The nonlinear term, $-\beta y_{m-1}(\epsilon y_m)$, can be neglected (analogous to the linearization of a nonlinear continuous growth differential equation) since the population displacement is much less than the equilibrium, $|\epsilon y_m| \ll \alpha/\beta$. Thus as a good approximation

$$y_{m+1} - y_m = -\alpha y_{m-1}. \qquad \textbf{(40.12)}$$

As we could have suspected, small displacements from an equilibrium population satisfy a linear constant coefficient difference equation. However only $\alpha = a\Delta t$ and not $\beta = b\Delta t$ determines the behavior of the population near the equilibrium.

Thus, in order to judge the effects of a delay, in the next section we will analyze linear constant coefficient (second-order) difference equations. After doing so, we will be able to determine the behavior of a population near equilibrium with a delay present in the discrete growth mechanism.

# EXERCISES

**40.1.** Assume the growth of a population is described by equation 40.3, a **linear delay-differential equation.**

    (a)   Explain (both ecologically and mathematically) why in order to solve this equation one needs to know not just the population at one time, but the population for an interval of time of length $t_d$.

    (b)   Suppose that the population $N(t)$ is a constant $N_0$ for $-t_d \leq t < 0$. Determine the population for $0 \leq t < t_d$. Can you determine the population for $m t_d \leq t < (m + 1)t_d$?

**40.2.** Suppose

$$\frac{dN}{dt} = N(t - t_d)[a - bN(t - t_d)].$$

Determine a nonzero equilibrium population. What linear delay-differential equation determines the stability of that equilibrium population?

**40.3.** (a)   Briefly explain why

$$N(t + \Delta t) - N(t) = \Delta t N(t)[a - bN(t)]$$

    is called a discrete logistic model. ($\Delta t$ may be called a delay).

    (b)   Using the discrete variable $t = m\Delta t + t_0$, show that

$$N_{m+1} = N_m + \Delta t N_m (a - bN_m),$$

    a nonlinear difference equation.

    (c)   Show that an equilibrium solution is $N_m = a/b$, the same as for the continuous logistic model.

    (d)   Is $N_m = a/b$ a stable equilibrium population? [Hint: Let $N_m = a/b + \epsilon y_m$ and neglect terms of $O(\epsilon^2)$. Show that $y_m$ satisfies a linear difference equation, and solve it.]

    (e)   Explain the differences between the solutions of the continuous and discrete logistic equations. How small must $\Delta t$ be such that solutions of the discrete logistic equation have a behavior similar to solutions of the continuous logistic model?

**40.4.** Leslie proposed the following discrete growth process:

$$N(t + \Delta t) = \frac{R_0 \Delta t N(t)}{1 + \sigma N(t)}.$$

What are the equilibrium populations? Compare this model to those discussed in Sec. 40.

**40.5.** Consider the following three general models for population growth with a delay:

(1) $dN/dt = N(t - t_d)R[N(t - t_d)]$
(2) $dN/dt = N(t)R[N(t - t_d)]$
(3) $dN/dt = N(t - t_d)R[N(t)]$

Briefly discuss the differences in the models.

**40.6.** Suppose that $N_{m+1} - N_m = f(N_m, N_{m-1})$.
  (a)  How would you determine all possible equilibrium populations, $N_E$?
  (b)  Using Taylor series methods, obtain the linear difference equation which determines the stability of an equilibrium population, $N_E$.
  (c)  If $f(N_m, N_{m-1}) = N_m(\alpha - \beta N_{m-1})$, as it did in Sec. 40 (see equation 40.10), show that equation 40.12 follows using the result of part (b).

**40.7.** Suppose that $dN/dt = NR(N)$ with $R(N)$ a steadily decreasing function ($R'(N) < 0$). Assume $R(0) > 0$ and $R(N_0) = 0$ with $N_0 > 0$. Without using the phase plane, show that $N = N_0$ is a stable equilibrium solution.

# 41. Linear Constant Coefficient Difference Equations

The stability of an equilibrium solution of a *nonlinear autonomous* second order difference equation is determined from its linearization, a *constant coefficient* difference equation. An equation of this kind can be put in the form

$$\boxed{y_{m+1} + py_m + qy_{m-1} = 0.}$$    **(41.1)**

We claim that the solution to this equation is quite analogous to the solution of constant coefficient second-order differential equations. Two initial conditions, for example the first two values, $y_0$ and $y_1$, are necessary for a unique solution. For a constant coefficient differential equation, the solution usually exists in the form of exponentials, while for linear constant coefficient difference equations, the solution almost always is in the form of algebraic powers. We look for solutions to equation 41.1 in the form,

$$\boxed{y_m = r^m,}$$

just as we did for first-order constant coefficient difference equations (see Sec. 33). Again value(s) for $r$ are determined by substitution:

$$r^{m+1} + pr^m + qr^{m-1} = 0.$$

Dividing by $r^{m-1}$ yields a quadratic equation for $r$

$$r^2 + pr + q = 0,$$

whose two roots,

$$\boxed{r = \frac{-p \pm \sqrt{p^2 - 4q}}{2},}$$    **(41.2)**

we call $r_1$ and $r_2$. The general solution should contain two arbitrary constants. It is obtained by taking an arbitrary linear combination of the two solutions,

$$y_m = c_1 r_1^m + c_2 r_2^m. \tag{41.3}$$

This result has assumed the two roots are distinct, $p^2 \neq 4q$.

The arbitrary constants are uniquely determined from the initial conditions:

$$y_0 = c_1 + c_2$$
$$y_1 = c_1 r_1 + c_2 r_2.$$

Since $r_1 \neq r_2$, these two equations can be uniquely solved for $c_1$ and $c_2$ in terms of $y_0$ and $y_1$ (see exercise 41.1).

If the roots are equal, this solution must be modified, just as a similar modification was necessary for constant coefficient differential equations. This case will only be discussed in exercise 41.2.

Thus we have a complete description of the solution. However, suppose the roots are complex, that is $p^2 - 4q < 0$, $r = -p/2 \pm i\sqrt{4q - p^2}/2$. How is $r^m$ interpreted (for integer $m$) when $r$ is complex? Since $m$ is an integer, it is possible to directly calculate powers of a complex number $r = x + iy$. For example,

$$(x + iy)^2 = x^2 - y^2 + 2ixy.$$

However, for large integers this becomes unmanageable, and thus the polar form of a complex number is often much more convenient. The complex number is represented as a vector in Fig. 41-1. Introducing polar coordinates, we see

$$\theta = \tan^{-1} y/x$$
$$|r| = (x^2 + y^2)^{1/2}$$
$$x = |r| \cos \theta$$
$$y = |r| \sin \theta.$$

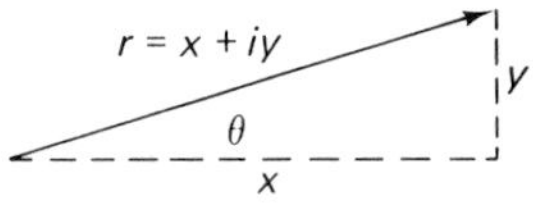

Figure 41-1    Polar representation of a complex number.

Finally we arrive at the polar form of a complex number

$$r = x + iy = |r|(\cos \theta + i \sin \theta) = |r| e^{i\theta}.$$

Thus

$$r^m = |r|^m e^{im\theta} = |r|^m (\cos m\theta + i \sin m\theta)$$

or

$$(\cos \theta + i \sin \theta)^m = \cos m\theta + i \sin m\theta,$$

the latter result known as De Moivre's theorem.

In our case of complex roots,

$$r_1 = \frac{-p}{2} + \frac{i\sqrt{4q - p^2}}{2}$$

$$r_2 = \frac{-p}{2} - \frac{i\sqrt{4q - p^2}}{2};$$

one root is the complex conjugate of the other. Since $|r_1| = |r_2|$ and $\theta_1 = -\theta_2$ (as illustrated in Fig. 41-2), it follows that the solution of the difference equation is

$$y_m = |r_1|^m(c_1 e^{im\theta_1} + c_2 e^{-im\theta_1}).$$

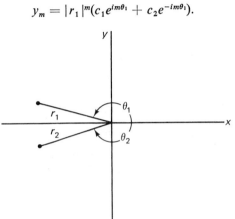

Figure 41-2   Complex conjugate roots.

Earlier in our study of differential equations arising for mechanical vibrations, a linear combination of imaginary exponentials was encountered. There it was shown that an arbitrary linear combination of these functions is equivalent to an arbitrary linear combination of sines and cosines. Thus in the case of complex roots

$$\boxed{y_m = |r_1|^m(c_3 \cos m\theta_1 + c_4 \sin m\theta_1),} \qquad (41.4)$$

where

$$\theta_1 = \tan^{-1}\frac{y}{x}$$

$$r_1 = x + iy$$

$$x = \frac{-p}{2}$$

$$y = \frac{\sqrt{4q - p^2}}{2}.$$

Consequently,

$$|r_1| = (x^2 + y^2)^{1/2} = q^{1/2}.$$

The solution "oscillates" with an approximate period given by

$$m = \frac{2\pi}{\tan^{-1}(y/x)}.$$

The amplitude of oscillation, defined as $\sqrt{c_3^2 + c_4^2}\,|r_1|^m$ (see Secs. 5 and 12), grows if $|r_1| > 1$ (i.e., $q > 1$) and decays if $|r_1| < 1$ (i.e., $q < 1$). [Note that we have defined the amplitude of oscillation initially (i.e., at $m = 0$) to be $\sqrt{c_3^2 + c_4^2}$, while $y_0 = c_3$ from equation 41.4.] If the amplitude of oscillation grows, let us compute the number of intervals $m_d$ it takes for the amplitude to double:

$$|r_1|^{m_d} = 2.$$

Thus, the amplitude has doubled when

$$m_d = \ln 2 / \ln |r_1|$$

An alternate expression for the amplitude of oscillation is $A 2^{m/m_d}$, where $A = \sqrt{c_3^2 + c_4^2}$, since $|r_1| = 2^{1/m_d}$.

As an example, let us analyze the difference equation

$$y_{m+1} + 2y_m + 2y_{m-1} = 0. \tag{41.5}$$

Solutions exist in the form $y_m = r^m$, where by substitution the roots $r$ satisfy

$$r^2 + 2r + 2 = 0$$

and thus are

$$r = \frac{-2 \pm \sqrt{4 - 8}}{2} = -1 \pm i.$$

We see, as sketched in Fig. 41-3, that $|r_1| = \sqrt{2}$ and $\theta_1 = 3\pi/4$:

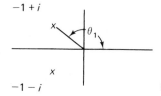

$-1 + i$

$-1 - i$

Figure 41-3.

Consequently, the general solution of this difference equation is (see equation 41.4)

$$y_m = 2^{m/2}\left(c_3 \cos \frac{3\pi m}{4} + c_4 \sin \frac{3\pi m}{4}\right).$$

It is a growing oscillation with period $m = 8/3$. The amplitude of oscillation is $2^{m/2}\sqrt{c_3^2 + c_4^2}$; the doubling interval of the amplitude of oscillation is $m = 2$ (slightly less than the period). Suppose that we wish to solve equation 41.5 subject to the initial conditions

$$y_0 = 2, \qquad y_1 = 1. \tag{41.6}$$

We already know the basic behavior of the solution; all that is unknown are the constants $c_3$ and $c_4$ (now determinable from equation 41.6):

$$2 = c_3$$

$$1 = 2^{1/2}\left(c_3 \cos \frac{3\pi}{4} + c_4 \sin \frac{3\pi}{4}\right).$$

Using the trigonometric formulas,

$$\cos \frac{3\pi}{4} = \frac{-\sqrt{2}}{2} \quad \text{and} \quad \sin \frac{3\pi}{4} = \frac{\sqrt{2}}{2},$$

it follows that

$$c_3 = 2 \quad \text{and} \quad c_4 = 3.$$

The solution to the initial value problem is

$$y_m = 2^{m/2}\left(2 \cos \frac{3\pi m}{4} + 3 \sin \frac{3\pi m}{4}\right). \tag{41.7}$$

Although we may sketch a smooth curve from equation 41.7, it is a meaningful solution of equation 41.5 only at integral values of $m$. For example, $y_2 = 2(2 \cos (3\pi/2) + 3 \sin (3\pi/2)) = -6$. However, if we were only interested in the first few explicit values of $y_m$, we could have more easily obtained them directly from the difference equation 41.5. Thus $y_2 = -2(y_0 + y_1) = -6$ and similarly:

| $m$ | 0 | 1 | 2 | 3 | 4 | 5 | 6 | 7 | 8 | 9 | 10 |
|-----|---|---|----|----|----|----|----|-----|----|----|-----|
| $y_m$ | 2 | 1 | $-6$ | 10 | $-8$ | $-4$ | 24 | $-40$ | 32 | 16 | $-96$ |

Let us show that these first few computed values, when sketched, indicate the correct general behavior of the solution. The sketch also can be used to *estimate* the period of oscillation and *estimate* the doubling time of the amplitude of oscillation. The tabulated values are sketched in Fig. 41-4. We *observe* maximums at $m = 3$ and 6. These are not necessarily positions of the maximum of the oscillation since the "crests" may occur at nonintegral values of $m$. Thus from the sketch we can only roughly *estimate* the period as being equal to $m = 3$ ($6 - 3 = 3$), not far different from the exact result, $m = \frac{8}{3}$. By sketching a smoothly growing oscillatory function from the data, we can improve our estimate of the position of the crests, and thus improve our estimate of the period. To estimate the doubling time, we let the geometrically-doubling amplitude of oscillation curve go through our estimated maximum points rather than the actual maximum points (unknown from only the numerical values). The theoretical amplitude is $A2^{m/m_d}$ where $A$ is an unknown constant and $m_d$ the unknown doubling interval. Using the two points $m = 3$ and 6 at which $y_m = 10$ and 24 respectively, we obtain

$$10 = A2^{3/m_d} \quad \text{and} \quad 24 = A2^{6/m_d}.$$

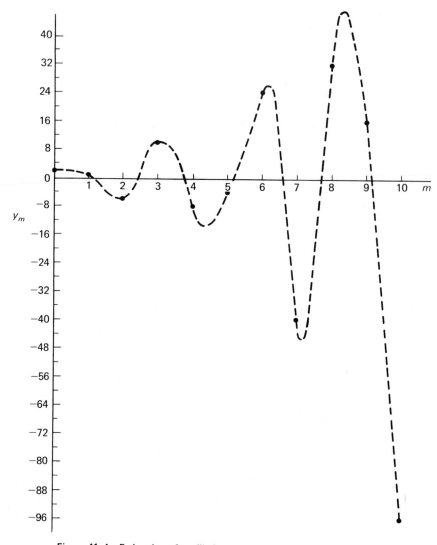

Figure 41-4   Estimation of oscillation properties from data numerically obtained.

Eliminating $A$ (by dividing the two equations) we determine that $2.4 = 2^{3/m_d}$ and thus roughly estimate $m_d$ as $\ln 2.4 = 3/m_d \ln 2$ or

$$m_d = 3\,\frac{\ln 2}{\ln 2.4} \approx 3\frac{.69315}{.87547} \approx 2.38,$$

not far from the exact value of $m_d = 2$.

In the next section we will apply the results of this section in order to investigate populations which are near the carrying capacity of the discrete logistic model with a delay.

# EXERCISES

**41.1.** The general solution of the difference equation 41.1 is given by equation 41.3. Show that the constants $c_1$ and $c_2$ can be uniquely determined in terms of $y_0$ and $y_1$.

**41.2.** Consider equation 41.1 in the case in which $p^2 = 4q$.

(a) Show that $x_m = r^m$ satisfies

$$x_{m+1} + px_m + qx_{m-1} = r^{m-1}\left(r + \frac{p}{2}\right)^2. \tag{*}$$

The right-hand side of (*) is zero only if $r = -p/2$. Thus one solution is $y_m = (-p/2)^m$.

(b) In order to obtain a second solution, take the derivative of (*) with respect to $r$ and show that

$$\frac{\partial x_{m+1}}{\partial r} + p\frac{\partial x_m}{\partial r} + q\frac{\partial x_{m-1}}{\partial r} = (m-1)r^{m-2}\left(r + \frac{p}{2}\right)^2 + 2r^{m-1}\left(r + \frac{p}{2}\right).$$

Thus show that

$$y_m = \frac{\partial x_m}{\partial r}\bigg|_{r=-p/2}$$

is a second solution of equation 41.1.

(c) Since $x_m = r^m$, using part (b) show that the general solution is

$$y_m = c_1\left(\frac{-p}{2}\right)^m + c_2 m\left(\frac{-p}{2}\right)^m.$$

(d) Verify the second solution by direct substitution.

**41.3.** If $r = x + iy$, we have shown

$$r^m = |r|^m e^{im\theta},$$

where $x = r\cos\theta$ and $y = r\sin\theta$. For real $r$ we know that

$$r^m = e^{m\ln r}$$

For complex $r$, let us define $\ln r$ such that $r^m = e^{m\ln r}$. Thus solve for $\ln r$ for $r$ complex.

**41.4.** Simple harmonic motion can be represented (as is discussed in Sec. 5) by the formula

$$x = ae^{i\omega t} + be^{-i\omega t},$$

where $a$ and $b$ are arbitrary constants. Assume that $b$ is the complex conjugate of $a$ (see exercise 5.5). Use the polar representation of $a$ to derive equation 5.5.

# 42. Destabilizing Influence of Delays

In order to investigate the behavior of a population near its carrying capacity, in Sec. 40 we discussed the discrete logistic equation (equation 40.10). Populations near the equilibrium population, $N = a/b$, are governed by the following linear difference equation:

$$N_1(t + \Delta t) - N_1(t) = -\alpha N_1(t - \Delta t)$$ 

(42.1a)

or

$$y_{m+1} - y_m = -\alpha y_{m-1},$$ 

(42.1b)

where $\epsilon N_1(t) = \epsilon y_m$ is the displacement from the equilibrium and $\alpha = a\Delta t$.

The results of Sec. 41 imply that the solutions of this constant coefficient linear difference equation can be obtained in the form

$$y_m = r^m.$$

Although we could quote specific results from that section, let us instead only use the method. Substituting, we obtain the quadratic equation

$$r^2 - r + \alpha = 0,$$

whose roots are

$$r = \frac{1 \pm \sqrt{1 - 4\alpha}}{2}.$$

Thus the general solution is

$$y_m = c_1 r_1^m + c_2 r_2^m.$$ 

(42.2)

The equilibrium population is stable if this solution does not grow as $t \rightarrow \infty$ (i.e., $m \rightarrow \infty$) for any initial conditions. Recall that for the continuous logistic growth model, the equilibrium population was always stable; the population always tended monotonically to the environment's capacity. We will discuss what occurs in the discrete delay case.

If $0 < \alpha < \frac{1}{4}$, then both roots are real, positive, and less than 1, i.e., $0 < r_1 < 1$ and $0 < r_2 < 1$, where we denote $r_2$ as the larger root, $0 < r_1 < r_2 < 1$. Consequently, if $0 < \alpha < \frac{1}{4}$, then as $t \rightarrow \infty$, $y_m = N_1(t) \rightarrow 0$. The population displacement vanishes and hence the population tends to the equilibrium population. The equilibrium population is stable if $0 < \alpha < \frac{1}{4}$. Although the population tends to the carrying capacity of the environment, it may go beyond it once. This is analogous to the overdamped oscillations of a spring-mass system (see Sec. 13). We show this by analyzing the solution, equation 42.2. The initial value problem implies

$$y_0 = c_1 + c_2 \quad \text{and} \quad y_1 = c_1 r_1 + c_2 r_2$$

and hence

$$c_1 = \frac{r_2 y_0 - y_1}{r_2 - r_1} \quad \text{and} \quad c_2 = \frac{y_1 - r_1 y_0}{r_2 - r_1}.$$

If $y_0$ and $y_1$ are of the same sign, the population goes beyond the carrying capacity only if for large times (large $m$) the population has the opposite sign from its initial sign. Thus the sign of $c_2$ must differ from the sign of $y_1$. $c_2$ has the opposite sign from $y_1$ if

$$(\text{if } y_1 > 0) \qquad y_1 - r_1 y_0 < 0$$
$$(\text{if } y_1 < 0) \qquad y_1 - r_1 y_0 > 0.$$

Thus the population goes beyond the carrying capacity if

$$|y_1| < r_1 |y_0|.$$

Whether this occurs or not depends on the initial conditions. For the example of Sec. 40 in which $\alpha = \frac{1}{5}$, $\beta = \frac{1}{400}$, $N_0 = 10$ and $N_1 = 15$, we see $r_1 = (1 - \sqrt{1 - 4\alpha})/2 \approx .27$. However, $y_0$ and $y_1$ are any two initial displacements from equilibrium only when the linearization is valid. From the computation in Sec. 40 it is seen that when the *linearization is valid* $.27\, y_0 < y_1$ for any two successive populations. Thus we should not expect the population to go beyond the carrying capacity in that case.

If $\alpha > \frac{1}{4}$, then the two roots are complex conjugates. As we have shown the solution oscillates (see equation 41.4)

$$N_1(t) = |r|^{t/\Delta t} \left[ c_3 \cos\left(\frac{t\theta}{\Delta t}\right) + c_4 \sin\left(\frac{t\theta}{\Delta t}\right) \right], \qquad (42.3)$$

where

$$r = \frac{1 \pm \sqrt{1 - 4\alpha}}{2} = \frac{1 \pm i\sqrt{4\alpha - 1}}{2}$$

$$|r| = \frac{1}{2}(1 + 4\alpha - 1)^{1/2} = \alpha^{1/2} \qquad (42.4)$$

$$\theta = \tan^{-1}\frac{y}{x} = \tan^{-1}\sqrt{4\alpha - 1}.$$

The solution grows or decays as it oscillates, depending on $|r| = \alpha^{1/2}$. There are two important cases:

(1) If $\frac{1}{4} < \alpha < 1$, then the solution is a decaying oscillation (called a **convergent oscillation**), as shown in Fig. 42-1. The population oscillates around the equilibrium population. The delay enables the population

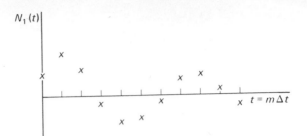

Figure 42-1 Decaying oscillation for moderate delays ($\frac{1}{4} < \alpha < 1$).

to go beyond its saturation level, but the population still tends to its equilibrium value if $\frac{1}{4} < \alpha < 1$.

(2) However, consider the case in which $\alpha > 1$. In the continuous model the equilibrium population is reached quickly. Here, the large delay causes an oscillatory growth around the equilibrium population (a **divergent oscillation**), as shown in Fig. 42-2. The population goes beyond the equilibrium population by larger and larger amounts. In other words, the delay tends to destabilize an otherwise stable population.

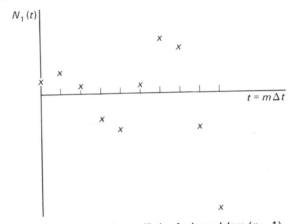

Figure 42-2 Growing oscillation for large delays ($\alpha > 1$).

Note in both cases (1) and (2), that, for example, if the displacement population is greater than 0, it can increase only until the next interval after which it must decrease (see exercise 42.16).

The special cases $\alpha = \frac{1}{4}$ and $\alpha = 1$ are only briefly discussed in the exercise 42.18. Why are these cases of no particular importance?

If $\alpha > 1$, the equilibrium population $N = a/b$ is unstable. Let us discuss what occurs in this case. The population cannot tend to its equilibrium value. On the other hand, the species does not become extinct, since for small populations this model,

$$N_{m+1} - N_m = N_m(a - bN_{m-1}), \qquad (42.5)$$

predicts growth. Thus the population must continually vary for all time due to the delays. To illustrate this, let us consider a numerical experiment with this discrete-delay logistic model. Suppose

$$\Delta t = 1$$
$$\beta = b\Delta t = 0.02$$
$$\alpha = a\Delta t = 2 > 1.$$

Thus the theoretically unstable equilibrium population is $N = a/b = 100$. We choose as initial conditions

$$N_0 = 10, \qquad N_1 = 20.$$

A straightforward computer calculation of equation 42.5 yields:

$$N_0 = 10.0$$
$$N_1 = 20.0$$
$$N_2 = 56.0$$
$$N_3 = 145.6$$
$$N_4 = 273.7$$
$$N_5 = 24.1$$
$$N_6 = -59.6 \ (?)$$

as sketched in Fig. 42-3. Note that the population *increases* beyond the carrying capacity only for one unit of time (the delay). Although the solution continues to vary for all time, at the *6th* time step, a negative population is predicted by this model. Equation 42.5 allows in this case a growth rate less than $-1$ measured in time $\Delta t$ (or a loss of over 100 percent). As this is impossible it is clear that the mathematical model itself needs to be modified. Perhaps the species being modeled should be considered to become extinct at this time. A model which never has this difficulty is briefly discussed in exercise 42.13.

In summary, consider populations described by the discrete logistic model,

$$N(t + \Delta t) - N(t) = \Delta t N(t)[a - bN(t - \Delta t)],$$

with time delay $\Delta t$. Suppose that $a$, the positive growth rate without environmental limitations, and $b$, the environmental limiting factor, are the same for all populations, but the delay time $\Delta t$ is varied. For species with extremely small delay times ($a\Delta t < \frac{1}{4}$), the equilibrium population is stable in a manner quite similar to that which occurs for the continuous logistic equation. If the delay is moderate ($\frac{1}{4} < a\Delta t < 1$), the population may exhibit convergent oscillations around the stable equilibrium population. However, for species

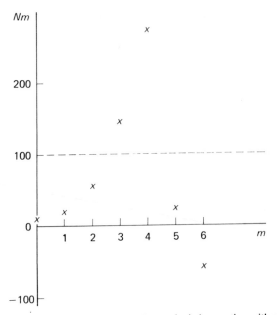

Figure 42-3    Numerical solution of a discrete logistic equation with a large delay.

with larger delays ($a\Delta t > 1$), the equilibrium population becomes unstable. Divergent oscillations occur. The delays destabilize an otherwise stable equilibrium population. To be more precise, we have shown that introducing a discrete measuring time and an equal time delay have destabilized the continuous logistic equation. The effect of a discretization alone is discussed in exercise 40.3. The effect of the delay is probed in exercise 42.3.

# EXERCISES

**42.1.** The difference equation

$$N(t + \Delta t) - N(t) = R_0 \Delta t N(t - \Delta t)$$

with $R_0$ a constant describes a pure growth process with a delay.
(a)  Show that $N_{i+1} = N_i + R_0 \Delta t N_{i-1}$.
(b)  Solve this difference equation. What is the approximate rate of growth?
(c)  Show from part (b) that as $\Delta t \longrightarrow 0$, the growth rate approaches $R_0$.

**42.2.** Consider the following model of population growth:

$$N(t + \Delta t) - N(t) = \Delta t N(t - \Delta t)[a - bN(t - \Delta t)].$$

(a)  What are the possible equilibrium populations?
(b)  Show that *small* displacements from the nonzero equilibrium popula-

tion satisfy

$$y_{m+1} - y_m = -\alpha y_{m-1}, \quad \text{where } \alpha = a\Delta t,$$

as do small displacements for the slightly different model in Sec. 42.

(c)   If $\Delta t$ is such that $a\Delta t = 1/2$, show that the population oscillates around its equilibrium population with decreasing amplitude. What is the approximate "period" of this decaying oscillation?

(d)   Show that zero population is an unstable equilibrium population. Show that small populations grow in a manner which can be approximated by $e^{at}$ if $\Delta t$ is small enough .

**42.3.**   In this problem we wish to illustrate the effect of a delay on the discrete logistic growth model. We will compare the discrete logistic equation without a delay,

(1)   $$N(t + \Delta t) - N(t) = \Delta t N(t)[a - bN(t)],$$

to the discrete logistic equation with a delay discussed in Sec. 42,

(2)   $$N(t + \Delta t) - N(t) = \Delta t N(t)[a - bN(t - \Delta t)].$$

Show that the nonzero equilibrium population of (1) is stable if $a\Delta t < 2$ and unstable if $a\Delta t > 2$. Also show the population "oscillates" around its equilibrium value if $1 < a\Delta t < 2$. Using this result, describe the effect of a delay on the discrete logistic equation. Show that it is possible for negative populations to develop.

**42.4–42.5.**   Consider the following models:

**42.4**   $$N(t + \Delta t) - N(t) = \Delta t N(t - \Delta t)[a - bN(t - \Delta t)]$$

**42.5**   $$N(t + \Delta t) - N(t) = \Delta t N(t)[a - bN(t - 2\Delta t)]$$

(a)   Determine nonzero equilibrium populations.

(b)   Analyze the stability of the equilibrium population.

(c)   Compare the model to that described in Sec. 42.

**42.6.**   Consider the following model of population growth with a large delay:

$$N(t + \Delta t) - N(t) = R_0 \Delta t N(t - 2\Delta t).$$

Approximate the general solution if $R_0 \Delta t$ is small but not zero ($0 < R_0 \Delta t \ll 1$).

**42.7.**   Consider

$$\frac{dN}{dt} = N(t)[a - bN(t - t_m)]$$

(a)   Show that small displacements from equilibrium satisfy the following linear delay-differential equation:

$$\frac{dN_1(t)}{dt} = -aN_1(t - t_m).$$

(b)   If $t_m > 0$, we will *not* find the general solution. Instead, let us look for special solutions of the form of exponentials,

$$N_1(t) = e^{rt}.$$

Show that $r = -ae^{-rt_m}$.

(c)   Show graphically there are two real solutions if the delay is small enough, but no real solutions for large delays.

**42.8.**   Consider equation 42.1. If $0 < \alpha < \frac{1}{4}$:

(a)   Show that the population may go beyond the equilibrium (at most once).

(b)   Give an example of an "initial" population that reaches equilibrium only after going beyond the equilibrium. Explicitly compute the population as a function of time.

**42.9.**   If $\alpha > 1$, what is the shortest period of oscillation that can occur?

**42.10.**   Consider equation 42.1 with $\alpha = 2$.

(a)   What is the expected behavior of the solution? What is the period and amplitude of oscillation?

(b)   If $y_0 = 0$ and $y_1 = 1$, explicitly compute $y_m$ for $m \leq 10$.

(c)   Compare periods of oscillation in parts (a) and (b).

(d)   Compare doubling times of the amplitude of oscillation.

**42.11.**   Reconsider exercise 42.10 with $\alpha = 10$.

**42.12.**   How might equation 42.5 be modified to prevent negative populations?

**42.13.**   The following equation is a discrete growth model with environmentally limited growth which never predicts a negative population:

$$N(t + \Delta t) = N(t) \exp [\Delta t(a - bN(t))].$$

(a)   Show that a negative population can never occur.

(b)   Show that this equation has the desired qualitative properties of the logistic equation.

(c)   If $\Delta t$ is very small, give an ecological interpretation of the parameters $a$ and $b$.

(d)   Analyze the solutions of this difference equation near the nonzero equilibrium population.

**42.14.**   Reconsider the population growth model described in exercise 42.13. Using a computer, do some numerical experiments for $a\Delta t > 1$.

**42.15.**   Consider the oscillations implied by equation 42.3 when $\alpha > \frac{1}{4}$.

(a)   What might be called the amplitude of oscillation.

(b)   Show the amplitude exponentially increases if $\alpha > 1$ and exponentially decreases if $\alpha < 1$.

(c)   If $\alpha < 1$, at what time has the amplitude reached $1/e$ of its initial amplitude of oscillation?

(d)   If $\alpha > 1$, how long does it take the amplitude of oscillation to double?

**42.16.**   Consider equation 42.1b.

(a)   Show that if $y_m > 0$, then the displacement population can increase only until the next interval after which the displacement population must decrease. Give an ecological interpretation of this result. Describe how Figs. 42-1 and 42-2 are consistent with this result.

(b)   Describe the result that exists which is analagous to part (a), but occurs if $y_m < 0$.

**42.17.**   Consider equation 42.1b. If $a$ is a constant, how does the condition for destabilization depend on the time delay $\Delta t$?

**42.18.** Consider equation 42.1b.
   (a)  If $\alpha = 1$, determine $y_m$. Describe the result.
   (b)  If $\alpha = \frac{1}{4}$, determine $y_m$. [Hint: See exercise 41.2]. Describe the result.

**42.19.** Consider

$$\frac{N_{m+1} - N_m}{\Delta t} = 3N_m - N_m N_{m-1} + 4.$$

   (a)  Give a brief ecological interpretation of the three terms on the right-hand side of the above difference equation.
   (b)  Show that $N_m = 4$ is the only (positive) equilibrium population.
   (c)  Linearize the difference equation for populations near $N_m = 4$. What behavior of the population is expected near $N_m = 4$?

# 43. Introduction to Two-Species Models

In the previous sections, different models of the population growth of a single species were discussed. In an attempt to understand large ecosystems, we will study situations that involve the interaction of more than one species. We have already discussed models that involve the interaction of different species. In the logistic growth model, the growth of a species is limited, perhaps by the finiteness of a nutrient which could be another species. One such example was the small ecosystem formed by deer and the vegetation they consumed. However, in that case we were able to model the growth of the deer population in terms of the deer population in previous years. In that way we were able to use a single species model. In this section (and the ones to follow), we will consider more complex ecological models in which two species interact.

Before developing mathematical models, we will describe some specific observations that have motivated ecologists to seek models of population growth. The fish population in the upper Adriatic Sea forms an interesting ecological system. To simplify our discussion of this ecological system, we assume that the fish population consists of sharks (and other voracious species), smaller fish who are eaten by the sharks, and the plentiful plankton upon which the smaller fish feed. Prior to World War I, man's massive fishing industry had resulted in the populations reaching a balance. Only small changes in populations were observed to occur from year to year. However, during World War I fishing was suspended. The fishermen's catch of small fish was not removed from the sea, resulting in more small fish than usual. However, because of the war no observations were made at that time. Soon thereafter, the population of sharks increased since they had more than the usual food available. The increased number of sharks in turn devoured so many of the fish, that when the fishermen returned after the war, very few small fish were immediately observed (*contrary to what they expected*). The growth of one population was followed by its decline. In later sections we will develop a mathematical model that discusses this type of interaction.

Another example of an interaction between two species occurs in forests which are dominated by two similar trees. We will formulate a theory modeling the competition between these trees for the limited area of sunlight.

We will limit our attention to deterministic mathematical models without time lags. Consider a small ecosystem with two species, their respective populations being $N_1$ and $N_2$. As in the mathematical models of single species ecosystems, we assume that the rates of change of each species depend only on the populations of each species, not other environmental factors. Thus

$$\frac{dN_1}{dt} = g(N_1, N_2)$$

$$\frac{dN_2}{dt} = f(N_1, N_2).$$

(43.1)

We have allowed the growth of one species to depend on the populations of both species. Shortly, some specific models will be suggested.

First we discuss the kinds of interactions that can occur between two species. What type of effect can $N_1$ have on $N_2$, and vice versa? We are not as interested in what effects $N_1$ has on itself as we have already discussed one-species problems. In general, the effect of species $N_1$ is to either increase or decrease the population of the other species. Likewise species $N_2$ can affect species $N_1$ in two different ways. Thus there are four possible types of interactions between two species, represented by the four sets of symbols $+-$, $++$, $--$, $-+$. However, by symmetry, one of these interactions is equivalent to another, namely $+-$ is equivalent to $-+$, yielding three distinct types of interactions. If both populations enhance the other $(++)$, then the biological interaction is called **mutualism** or **symbiosis**. If both populations negatively affect each other $(--)$, then we say the two species are in **competition**, the simplest example of such an interaction being when two species compete for the same food source. The interaction between sharks and the small fish they eat is an example of the third type of interaction $(+-)$ called **predator-prey**. The existence of one species, the prey, enhances the other, while the predator might threaten the very existence of the prey. Other examples of predator-prey type interactions include plant-herbivore systems and a parasite-host pair.

# 44. Phase Plane, Equilibrium, and Linearization

Before investigating any particular model or type of interaction, let us discuss the general model for the interaction of two species:

$$\frac{dN_1}{dt} = g(N_1, N_2)$$

$$\frac{dN_2}{dt} = f(N_1, N_2).$$

(44.1)

If we assume that there is no migration of either species, then

$$g(0, N_2) = 0 \quad \text{and} \quad f(N_1, 0) = 0.$$

As before many other assumptions are involved in the above formulation. The mathematical model consists of a system of two first-order (possibly nonlinear) ordinary differential equations. We wish to solve the initial value problem, that is determine the solution of equation 44.1 which satisfies any given initial values of both populations, $N_1(t_0)$ and $N_2(t_0)$.

It is interesting to note that the second-order differential equations of mechanical vibrations, discussed in the first part of this text, were also put into the form of a system of two first-order differential equations:

$$\frac{dx}{dt} = v$$

$$\frac{dv}{dt} = f(x, v).$$

To understand the solution of this system, the phase plane equation

$$\frac{dv}{dx} = \frac{f(x, v)}{v}$$

was considered. Analogous to the above equation for the two-species population models is the equation which results by eliminating the explicit dependence on $t$:

$$\frac{dN_2}{dN_1} = \frac{f(N_1, N_2)}{g(N_1, N_2)},$$

(44.2)

which we also call the phase plane equation. The two populations are called the phases of the ecosystem. The solution of the phase plane equation is said to give the trajectories of the populations. The solution of the resulting first order equation can be sketched by the method of isoclines, since neither $g(N_1, N_2)$ nor $f(N_1, N_2)$ depend explicitly on time. In other words, the population model we have formulated is an autonomous system. (This is not necessary in all biological problems, but our first task in understanding complex ecological models would seem to be to study those models for which all other environmental factors do not change in time, i.e., autonomous systems.)

To study the interactions of the two populations, either the time-dependent system of equations or the phase plane equation must be analyzed. Frequently an explicit solution by either method will be lacking. Thus we will start by considering some essential qualitative features of these types of equations. We define an **equilibrium population** as a possible population of both species such that both populations will not vary in time. The births and deaths of species $N_1$ must balance, and similarly those of $N_2$ must balance. Thus an equilibrium population, $N_1 = N_{1e}$ and $N_2 = N_{2e}$, is such that *both*

and

$$f(N_{1e}, N_{2e}) = 0$$
$$g(N_{1e}, N_{2e}) = 0,$$

(44.3)

two equations in two unknowns. The vanishing of both populations is an equilibrium population. For any equilibrium population, the slope of the phase plane diagram is undefined, $dN_2/dN_1 = 0/0$, called a singular point of the phase plane equation. Singular points of the phase plane equation are equivalent to equilibrium points of the time-dependent equation, as they were in the analysis of oscillation problems in mechanics.

For a specific two-species model, it may not be difficult to calculate possible equilibrium populations (there can be more than one set). The next question is whether a known equilibrium population is stable. This is the same question we would ask had this been a one-species population model or an equilibrium position of a nonlinear pendulum! We proceed by investigating what happens in time if both populations are near their respective equilibrium populations, a so-called linear stability analysis. Let

$$N_1(t) = N_{1e} + \epsilon N_{11}(t)$$
$$N_2(t) = N_{2e} + \epsilon N_{21}(t),$$

(44.4)

where $\epsilon$ is a small number $0 < |\epsilon| \ll 1$ and where $N_{1e}$ and $N_{2e}$ are an equilibrium population (satisfying equation 44.3). $\epsilon N_{11}$ and $\epsilon N_{21}$ may be interpreted as the differences between the total population and the equilibrium population (referred to again as the **population displacement from equilibrium**). Substituting this into the time dependent population equations, yields

$$\epsilon \frac{dN_{11}}{dt} = g[N_{1e} + \epsilon N_{11}(t), N_{2e} + \epsilon N_{21}(t)]$$

$$\epsilon \frac{dN_{21}}{dt} = f[N_{1e} + \epsilon N_{11}(t), N_{2e} + \epsilon N_{21}(t)].$$

We use the Taylor expansion for a function of two variables,

$$F(x_0 + h, y_0 + k) = F(x_0, y_0) + h\frac{\partial F}{\partial x}(x_0, y_0) + k\frac{\partial F}{\partial y}(x_0, y_0) + \cdots,$$

$$(44.5a)$$

or equivalently

$$F(x, y) = F(x_0, y_0) + (x - x_0)\frac{\partial F}{\partial x}(x_0, y_0) + (y - y_0)\frac{\partial F}{\partial y}(x_0, y_0) + \cdots,$$

$$(44.5b)$$

where the first three terms expressed above correspond to the linearization of the function in the neighborhood of the point $(x_0, y_0)$. In this manner,

$$\epsilon \frac{dN_{11}}{dt} = g(N_{1e}, N_{2e}) + \epsilon N_{11}\frac{\partial g}{\partial N_1}(N_{1e}, N_{2e}) + \epsilon N_{21}\frac{\partial g}{\partial N_2}(N_{1e}, N_{2e}) + O(\epsilon^2)$$

$$\epsilon \frac{dN_{21}}{dt} = f(N_{1e}, N_{2e}) + \epsilon N_{11}\frac{\partial f}{\partial N_1}(N_{1e}, N_{2e}) + \epsilon N_{21}\frac{\partial f}{\partial N_2}(N_{1e}, N_{2e}) + O(\epsilon^2).$$

If we neglect the $O(\epsilon^2)$ terms (corresponding to the nonlinear terms in the neighborhood of the equilibrium populations) and if we recall that $N_{1e}$ and $N_{2e}$ is an equilibrium population, then the following is obtained:

$$\frac{dN_{11}}{dt} = \frac{\partial g}{\partial N_1}(N_{1e}, N_{2e})N_{11} + \frac{\partial g}{\partial N_2}(N_{1e}, N_{2e})N_{21}$$

$$(44.6)$$

$$\frac{dN_{21}}{dt} = \frac{\partial f}{\partial N_1}(N_{1e}, N_{2e})N_{11} + \frac{\partial f}{\partial N_2}(N_{1e}, N_{2e})N_{21}.$$

This is a linear system of differential equations with constant coefficients. Do not forget that the coefficients of the unknowns ($N_{11}$ and $N_{21}$) on the right-hand side of this equation are evaluated at the known equilibrium population ($N_{1e}$ and $N_{2e}$). In the next section we will discuss the solutions of such a general system of two coupled first-order linear differential equations with constant coefficients. Depending on the nature of the solution, the equilibrium population will be stable or unstable.

Knowing the solution of the linearized equation will only indicate the behavior of each species in the immediate vicinity of an equilibrium population. In order to describe population growth far away from an equilibrium population, we may instead use the phase plane equation. The method of isoclines may again assist in the sketching of the solution curves. Recall in the study of mechanical vibrations that the most important features of the solution in the phase plane occurred in the vicinity of the equilibrium positions. Hence, at first we study the phase plane equation in the neighborhood of an equilibrium population. Again perturbations may be introduced. If equation 44.4 is substituted into the phase plane equation, equation 44.2, expanded via Taylor's theorem, and the nonlinear terms are neglected, then we derive

$$
\frac{dN_2}{dN_1} = \frac{\dfrac{\partial f}{\partial N_1} N_{11} + \dfrac{\partial f}{\partial N_2} N_{21}}{\dfrac{\partial g}{\partial N_1} N_{11} + \dfrac{\partial g}{\partial N_2} N_{21}}.
$$

Comparing this with equation 44.6, the slopes of the phase plane are approximated in the vicinity of an equilibrium population by the slopes of the phase plane of the linear system. Knowing and understanding the phase plane of all possible linear systems are necessary in the investigation of the phase plane corresponding to nonlinear systems. Shortly the phase plane of such linear systems will be studied. Before doing so, the linear systems of differential equations themselves must be analyzed.

For those who prefer examples before a general discussion (the author usually does), the ecological models discussed in Secs. 48–54 may be interspersed with the mathematical developments of the next sections (Secs. 45–47).

# EXERCISES

**44.1.** Show that the vanishing of both populations in a two-species model without migration is an equilibrium population.

**44.2.** Show that singular points of the phase plane diagram are equivalent to an equilibrium population.

**44.3.** Consider the following nonlinear systems:

(i) $\dfrac{dx}{dt} = e^x - 1$

$\quad\;\; \dfrac{dy}{dt} = ye^x$

(ii) $\dfrac{dx}{dt} = x^2 + y^2 - 1$

$\quad\;\; \dfrac{dy}{dt} = x + y$

(iii) $\dfrac{dx}{dt} = x^2 + y^2 - 5$                   (iv) $\dfrac{dx}{dt} = x^2 + y^2 - 1$

$\dfrac{dy}{dt} = x^2 + 2y^2 - 9$                       $\dfrac{dy}{dt} = x - 4.$

(a) Determine all real equilibrium solutions.
(b) Linearize the nonlinear system in the vicinity of *each* equilibrium solution.

**44.4.** Suppose that

$$\frac{dN_1}{dt} = N_1 g_1(N_1, N_2)$$

$$\frac{dN_1}{dt} = N_2 g_2(N_1, N_2).$$

(a) Give an ecological interpretation of the variables $g_1(N_1, N_2)$ and $g_2(N_1, N_2)$.
(b) Suppose that $N_{1e}$ and $N_{2e}$ are both *nonvanishing* equilibrium populations. What linear system of differential equations determines the behavior of populations near to this equilibrium population?

**44.5.** An equivalent method to linearize equation 44.1 in the neighborhood of an equilibrium population is to directly expand equation 44.1 via its Taylor series around the equilibrium population. Do this and show that equation 44.6 results.

# 45. System of Two Constant Coefficient First-Order Differential Equations

We will discuss the solution of a system of two coupled first-order homogeneous linear differential equations with constant coefficients,

$$\frac{dx}{dt} = ax + by \tag{45.1a}$$

$$\frac{dy}{dt} = cx + dy. \tag{45.1b}$$

Such a system is of interest in studying the stability of an equilibrium population. Here $x$ and $y$ are the displacements from an equilibrium population (see equation 44.6). Two methods to solve these equations will be discussed.

## A. METHOD OF ELIMINATION

The first method is straightforward (but has the disadvantage of frequently being cumbersome with problems involving more than two equations). If $c \neq 0*$, then $x$ can be eliminated from equation 45.1a using equation 45.1b

$$x = \frac{1}{c}\frac{dy}{dt} - \frac{d}{c}y.$$

For this reason this method is called elimination. The system of equations is reduced to one second-order differential equation,

$$\frac{1}{c}\frac{d^2y}{dt^2} - \frac{d}{c}\frac{dy}{dt} = \frac{a}{c}\frac{dy}{dt} - \frac{ad}{c}y + by,$$

or after some algebra

$$\frac{d^2y}{dt^2} - (a+d)\frac{dy}{dt} + (ad - bc)y = 0.$$

This equation is easily solved since it has constant coefficients. Seeking solutions in the form $e^{rt}$, yields the characteristic polynomial

$$r^2 - (a+d)r + (ad - bc) = 0,$$

the two roots being

$$r = \frac{a + d \pm \sqrt{(a+d)^2 - 4(ad - bc)}}{2}. \qquad (45.2)$$

Thus

$$y = c_1 e^{r_1 t} + c_2 e^{r_2 t}$$

$$x = c_1\frac{r_1 - d}{c}e^{r_1 t} + c_2\frac{r_2 - d}{c}e^{r_2 t}. \qquad (45.3)$$

This solution will be discussed in Secs. 46 and 47.

---

*If $c = 0$, then equation 45.1b is directly solvable for $y$, $y = Be^{dt}$. Thus $x$ can be solved from equation 45.1a:

$$x = Ae^{at} + \frac{bB}{d - a}e^{dt} \qquad \text{if } d \neq a$$

$$x = Ae^{at} + bBte^{at} \qquad \text{if } d = a.$$

## B. SYSTEMS METHOD (USING MATRIX THEORY)

An alternative to the method of elimination is to solve the linear system, equations 45.1a and 45.1b, using the matrix and vector notation:

$$\frac{d}{dt}\begin{bmatrix} x \\ y \end{bmatrix} = \begin{bmatrix} a & b \\ c & d \end{bmatrix}\begin{bmatrix} x \\ y \end{bmatrix}$$

or

$$\frac{d\vec{v}}{dt} = A\vec{v},$$

(45.4)

where

$$\vec{v} = \begin{bmatrix} x \\ y \end{bmatrix} \quad \text{and} \quad A = \begin{bmatrix} a & b \\ c & d \end{bmatrix}.$$

This method has the advantage that it is easily generalized to solve a larger number of coupled first-order equations. In what ecological circumstances might there occur a larger number of coupled first-order equations? Solutions are again sought in terms of exponentials

$$\vec{v} = \vec{v}_0 e^{rt},$$

or equivalently

$$\begin{bmatrix} x \\ y \end{bmatrix} = \begin{bmatrix} x_0 \\ y_0 \end{bmatrix} e^{rt},$$

(45.5)

where $\vec{v}_0 = \begin{bmatrix} x_0 \\ y_0 \end{bmatrix}$ is a constant vector to be determined. The substitution of equation 45.5 into equation 45.4 yields

$$A\vec{v}_0 = r\vec{v}_0,$$

or equivalently

$$\begin{bmatrix} a & b \\ c & d \end{bmatrix}\begin{bmatrix} x_0 \\ y_0 \end{bmatrix} = r\begin{bmatrix} x_0 \\ y_0 \end{bmatrix}.$$

(45.6)

Nontrivial solutions of equation 45.6 (i.e., $\vec{v}_0 \neq 0$) exist only for certain values of $r$, called the **eigenvalues** of the matrix $\mathbf{A}$. Equation 45.6 can be written as a homogeneous system (using the identity matrix $\mathbf{I}$):

$$(\mathbf{A} - r\mathbf{I})\vec{v}_0 = 0,$$

or

$$\begin{bmatrix} a - r & b \\ c & d - r \end{bmatrix} \begin{bmatrix} x_0 \\ y_0 \end{bmatrix} = 0. \tag{45.7}$$

From linear algebra, there are nontrivial solutions to a homogeneous linear system if and only if the determinant of the coefficients equals zero. Thus

$$|\mathbf{A} - r\mathbf{I}| = 0,$$

or

$$\begin{vmatrix} a - r & b \\ c & d - r \end{vmatrix} = 0. \tag{45.8}$$

Solving this determinant, we obtain

$$(a - r)(d - r) - bc = 0.$$

This yields two values for the exponent

$$r = \frac{a + d \pm \sqrt{(a + d)^2 - 4(ad - bc)}}{2}, \tag{45.9}$$

the same result as obtained by elimination.

If the roots are distinct, then the nontrivial value of $\vec{v}_0 = \begin{bmatrix} x_0 \\ y_0 \end{bmatrix}$ corresponding to each eigenvalue (called the **eigenvector** corresponding to that eigenvalue) must be determined. If an eigenvalue is designated $r_i$ and its corresponding eigenvector $\vec{v}_i = \begin{bmatrix} x_i \\ y_i \end{bmatrix}$, then the solution is given by

$$\vec{v} = \sum_{i=1}^{2} c_i \vec{v}_i e^{r_i t}, \tag{45.10a}$$

where $c_i$ are arbitrary constants or

$$\begin{bmatrix} x \\ y \end{bmatrix} = \sum_{i=1}^{2} c_i \begin{bmatrix} x_i \\ y_i \end{bmatrix} e^{r_i t}. \tag{45.10b}$$

As an example, let us solve the following system:

$$\begin{aligned} \frac{dx}{dt} &= -4x + 3y \\ \frac{dy}{dt} &= -2x + y. \end{aligned}$$

(45.11)

In the matrix notation, $d\vec{v}/dt = \mathbf{A}\vec{v}$, where

$$\vec{v} = \begin{bmatrix} x \\ y \end{bmatrix} \quad \text{and} \quad \mathbf{A} = \begin{bmatrix} -4 & 3 \\ -2 & 1 \end{bmatrix}.$$

We look for solutions of the form

$$\vec{v} = \vec{v}_0 e^{rt} \quad \text{or} \quad \begin{bmatrix} x \\ y \end{bmatrix} = \begin{bmatrix} x_0 \\ y_0 \end{bmatrix} e^{rt}.$$

By substitution we see that

$$\begin{bmatrix} -4-r & 3 \\ -2 & 1-r \end{bmatrix} \begin{bmatrix} x_0 \\ y_0 \end{bmatrix} = 0.$$

(45.12)

For nontrivial solutions of matrix equation 45.12, we know that

$$\begin{vmatrix} -4-r & 3 \\ -2 & 1-r \end{vmatrix} = 0.$$

Evaluating this determinant yields

$$r^2 + 3r + 2 = 0$$

or $(r+2)(r+1) = 0$. The two eigenvalues are $r = -1$ and $r = -2$, agreeing with the values obtained directly from equation 45.9. The eigenvector corresponding to the eigenvalue $r = -1$ is determined from equation 45.12. The two equations so implied *must* be equivalent. We write both equations as a check against a possible error in our calculation of the eigenvalue:

$$\begin{aligned} -3x_0 + 3y_0 &= 0 \\ -2x_0 + 2y_0 &= 0. \end{aligned}$$

Both equations are indeed equivalent. From either equation, $x_0 = y_0$ and thus the eigenvector is

$$\begin{bmatrix} x_0 \\ y_0 \end{bmatrix} = \begin{bmatrix} x_0 \\ x_0 \end{bmatrix} = x_0 \begin{bmatrix} 1 \\ 1 \end{bmatrix};$$

the eigenvector is *any* multiple of the constant vector $\begin{bmatrix} 1 \\ 1 \end{bmatrix}$. It is more convenient to introduce $c_1$ as the arbitrary constant associated with the eigenvalue

$r = -1$. Thus a solution of the system of equations 45.11 is

$$\begin{bmatrix} x \\ y \end{bmatrix} = c_1 \begin{bmatrix} 1 \\ 1 \end{bmatrix} e^{-t}.$$

We now do a similar calculation corresponding to the eigenvalue $r = -2$. Two equivalent equations follow from equation 45.12:

$$-2x_0 + 3y_0 = 0$$
$$-2x_0 + 3y_0 = 0.$$

The eigenvector corresponding to $r = -2$ is

$$\begin{bmatrix} x_0 \\ y_0 \end{bmatrix} = \frac{1}{3} \begin{bmatrix} 3x_0 \\ 2x_0 \end{bmatrix} = \frac{x_0}{3} \begin{bmatrix} 3 \\ 2 \end{bmatrix};$$

the eigenvector is any multiple of the constant vector $\begin{bmatrix} 3 \\ 2 \end{bmatrix}$ (it usually is easier

not to deal with fractions, which is why we prefer the eigenvector to be a

multiple of $\begin{bmatrix} 3 \\ 2 \end{bmatrix}$ rather than, for example, a multiple of $\begin{bmatrix} 1 \\ \frac{2}{3} \end{bmatrix}$ ). In this man-

ner we have obtained the general solution of equation 45.11:

$$\begin{bmatrix} x \\ y \end{bmatrix} = c_1 \begin{bmatrix} 1 \\ 1 \end{bmatrix} e^{-t} + c_2 \begin{bmatrix} 3 \\ 2 \end{bmatrix} e^{-2t},$$

or equivalently

$$x = c_1 e^{-t} + 3c_2 e^{-2t}$$
$$y = c_1 e^{-t} + 2c_2 e^{-2t},$$

where $c_1$ and $c_2$ are arbitrary constants.

The eigenvalues need not be real as in the previous example. However, if $a, b, c,$ and $d$ are real, it follows from equation 45.9 that any complex eigenvalues at least must be complex conjugates of each other. In the example to follow, we will illustrate how to obtain real solutions to the system of differential equations 45.1 when the eigenvalues are complex. The ideas are quite similar to those discussed earlier in Secs. 5 and 12, where Euler's formulas were utilized:

$$e^{i\omega t} = \cos \omega t + i \sin \omega t$$
$$e^{-i\omega t} = \cos \omega t - i \sin \omega t. \tag{45.13}$$

Consider the example

$$\frac{dx}{dt} = 4x - 5y$$

$$\frac{dy}{dt} = 2x - 2y. \tag{45.14}$$

Upon looking for solutions in the form $\begin{bmatrix} x \\ y \end{bmatrix} = \begin{bmatrix} x_0 \\ y_0 \end{bmatrix} e^{rt}$, it immediately follows that

$$\begin{bmatrix} 4-r & -5 \\ 2 & -2-r \end{bmatrix} \begin{bmatrix} x_0 \\ y_0 \end{bmatrix} = 0. \qquad (45.15)$$

Thus the eigenvalues satisfy

$$\begin{vmatrix} 4-r & -5 \\ 2 & -2-r \end{vmatrix} = 0,$$

which yields $r^2 - 2r + 2 = 0$, or

$$r = \frac{2 \pm \sqrt{4-8}}{2} = 1 \pm i;$$

the eigenvalues are complex conjugates of each other. The eigenvector corresponding to $r = 1 + i$ satisfies the two equivalent equations:

$$(3-i)x_0 - 5y_0 = 0$$
$$2x_0 + (-3-i)y_0 = 0.$$

(To show these are equivalent, note that multiplying the second equation by $(3 - i)$ yields

$$2(3-i)x_0 + (3-i)(-3-i)y_0 = 0$$

or $2(3-i)x_0 - 10y_0 = 0$, which is exactly twice the first equation.) The eigenvector may be written as

$$\begin{bmatrix} x_0 \\ y_0 \end{bmatrix} = \frac{1}{5} \begin{bmatrix} 5x_0 \\ (3-i)x_0 \end{bmatrix} = \frac{x_0}{5} \begin{bmatrix} 5 \\ 3-i \end{bmatrix};$$

an eigenvector corresponding to a complex eigenvalue often has complex entries. To find the eigenvector corresponding to $r = 1 - i$, we can do a similar calculation. However, we note from equation 45.15 that since $r = 1 + i$ is the complex conjugate of the eigenvalue already calculated, the eigenvector must also be the complex conjugate of the above computed eigenvector. Thus the eigenvector corresponding to $r = 1 - i$ may be written as

$$\begin{bmatrix} x_0 \\ y_0 \end{bmatrix} = \frac{x_0}{5} \begin{bmatrix} 5 \\ 3+i \end{bmatrix}.$$

In this manner, the solution of equation 45.14 is

$$\begin{bmatrix} x \\ y \end{bmatrix} = c_1 \begin{bmatrix} 5 \\ 3-i \end{bmatrix} e^{(1+i)t} + c_2 \begin{bmatrix} 5 \\ 3+i \end{bmatrix} e^{(1-i)t}, \qquad (45.16)$$

where $c_1$ and $c_2$ are arbitrary constants. Using Euler's formulas, equation 45.13, it follows that

$$x = 5e^t[c_1(\cos t + i \sin t) + c_2(\cos t - i \sin t)]$$
$$y = e^t[(3 - i)c_1(\cos t + i \sin t) + (3 + i)c_2(\cos t - i \sin t)].$$

Letting $\alpha = c_1 + c_2$ and $\beta = i(c_1 - c_2)$ (as we did in Sec. 5) yields a more convenient form of the general solution of equation 45.14:

$$x = 5e^t[\alpha \cos t + \beta \sin t]$$
$$y = e^t[(3\alpha - \beta) \cos t + (3\beta - \alpha) \sin t],$$

where $\alpha$ and $\beta$ are arbitrary constants. An alternate expression for the general solution can be derived if we use some knowledge of the algebra of complex variables. For $x$ and $y$ to be real, it follows from equation 45.16 that $c_2$ must be the complex conjugate of $c_1$ (see exercise 5.5). Since the sum of a quantity and its complex conjugate is twice the real part of the quantity, equation 45.16 then yields

$$\begin{bmatrix} x \\ y \end{bmatrix} = 2\, Re\, c_1 \begin{bmatrix} 5 \\ 3 - i \end{bmatrix} e^{(1+i)t}.$$

Since $c_1$ is an arbitrary complex number, we introduce its polar representation,

$$c_1 = Ae^{i\theta}$$

(see Sec. 41), where $A$ and $\theta$ are arbitrary real constants. Thus

$$\begin{bmatrix} x \\ y \end{bmatrix} = 2A\, Re \begin{bmatrix} 5 \\ 3 - i \end{bmatrix} e^t e^{i(t+\theta)}.$$

Evaluating the real part yields a relatively simple alternative form of the general solution of equation 45.14:

$$x = 10Ae^t \cos (t + \theta)$$
$$y = 2Ae^t[3 \cos (t + \theta) + \sin (t + \theta)].$$

If the roots are not distinct the heretofore mentioned technique must be modified. Although this modification is not particularly difficult for systems of two equations in two unknowns, it may be more complicated in higher-order systems. A discussion of this case will be avoided in this text. Interested readers can consult books on differential equations which contain a substantial treatment of systems and/or matrix methods.

# EXERCISES

**45.1.** Consider

$$\frac{dx}{dt} = ax + by$$

$$\frac{dy}{dt} = cx + dy,$$

for the following cases:

| | | | | |
|---|---|---|---|---|
| (a) | $a = 0$ | $b = 1$ | $c = -4$ | $d = 0$ |
| (b) | $a = 1$ | $b = 3$ | $c = 1$ | $d = -1$ |
| (c) | $a = 2$ | $b = 1$ | $c = 1$ | $d = 2$ |
| (d) | $a = -3$ | $b = -2$ | $c = 1$ | $d = -5$ |
| (e) | $a = 1$ | $b = 2$ | $c = -1$ | $d = -2$ |
| (f) | $a = 3$ | $b = -1$ | $c = 1$ | $d = 2$ |
| (g) | $a = -2$ | $b = 0$ | $c = 0$ | $d = -3$ |
| (h) | $a = 1$ | $b = 0$ | $c = 1$ | $d = -3$ |
| (i) | $a = -1$ | $b = 3$ | $c = 1$ | $d = 1$ |
| (j) | $a = 4$ | $b = -3$ | $c = 1$ | $d = 0$ |
| (k) | $a = -1$ | $b = 2$ | $c = -2$ | $d = -1$ |
| (l) | $a = 2$ | $b = -1$ | $c = 1$ | $d = 0$ |
| (m) | $a = 3$ | $b = 2$ | $c = 0$ | $d = 4$ |
| (n) | $a = 1$ | $b = 0$ | $c = 0$ | $d = -3$ |
| (o) | $a = 4$ | $b = 2$ | $c = 2$ | $d = 1$ |

Determine $x$ and $y$ as functions of time.

**45.2.** Consider

$$\frac{d}{dt}\begin{bmatrix} x \\ y \\ z \end{bmatrix} = \begin{bmatrix} 4 & -9 & 5 \\ 1 & -10 & 7 \\ 1 & -17 & 12 \end{bmatrix}\begin{bmatrix} x \\ y \\ z \end{bmatrix}.$$

Find the general solution. [Hints: Show that the eigenvalues are 1, 2, and 3.]

# 46. Stability of Two-Species Equilibrium Populations

The behavior of populations near equilibrium are governed by a system of constant coefficient differential equations, analyzed in the previous section:

$$\frac{dx}{dt} = ax + by$$

$$\frac{dy}{dt} = cx + dy. \tag{46.1}$$

It was shown that the solution consists of a linear combination of exponentials, $e^{rt}$, where

$$r = \frac{a + d \pm \sqrt{(a+d)^2 - 4(ad - bc)}}{2}$$

are the roots of the characteristic polynomial (see equation 45.2). The roots are real and unequal if $(a + d)^2 - 4(ad - bc) > 0$, the roots are real and equal if $(a + d)^2 - 4(ad - bc) = 0$, while the roots are complex conjugates of each other if $(a + d)^2 - 4(ad - bc) = 0$.

Since we are interested in these equations primarily in the context of the stability of equilibrium populations, we must discuss what happens as $t \to \infty$. This is determined by the signs of the two values of the real part of the roots (see equation 45.3). An equilibrium solution is said to be stable (see Sec. 18) if the real parts of both roots are less than zero; unstable if at least one is greater than zero; neutrally stable* if the real part of one root equals zero and the other is less than or equal to zero (except if both roots are identically zero in which case the solution is algebraically unstable). It is usual to let

$$p \equiv a + d$$

$$q \equiv ad - bc \qquad\qquad\qquad \textbf{(46.2)}$$

$$\Delta \equiv (a + d)^2 - 4(ad - bc) = p^2 - 4q.$$

Using these definitions,

| roots | condition |
|---|---|
| (1) real and unequal | $\Delta > 0$ |
| (2) real and equal | $\Delta = 0$ |
| (3) complex conjugates | $\Delta < 0$. |

The following table describes the many cases:

(1) real and unequal $\qquad\qquad \Delta > 0$
    A. same sign $\qquad\qquad\qquad q > 0$
       (a) both positive $p > 0$ $\qquad$ UNSTABLE
       (b) both negative $p < 0$ $\qquad$ STABLE
    B. different signs $\qquad\qquad q < 0$ $\quad$ UNSTABLE
    C. one root zero $\qquad\qquad\; q = 0$
       (a) other root positive $p > 0$ $\quad$ UNSTABLE
       (b) other root negative $p < 0$ $\quad$ NEUTRALLY STABLE

---

*See p. 58 and p. 102.

(2) real and equal $\qquad\Delta = 0$
   A. same sign
      (a) both positive $p > 0$ $\qquad$ UNSTABLE
      (b) both negative $p < 0$ $\qquad$ STABLE
   B. both zero $\qquad\qquad\quad p = 0$ $\quad$ ALGEBRAICALLY UNSTABLE*
(3) complex conjugates $\qquad\Delta < 0$
   A. real part has same sign
      (a) real part positive $\quad p > 0$ $\quad$ UNSTABLE
      (b) real part negative $\quad p < 0$ $\quad$ STABLE
   B. real part zero $\qquad\quad p = 0$ $\quad$ NEUTRALLY STABLE

These results are summarized in Fig. 46-1. A similar diagram appeared in Sec. 27 referring to the stability of an equilibrium position of a spring-mass system with friction. In this manner we are able to determine if a given equilibrium population is stable or not. Examples are given in the exercises and also in later sections.

If there are small errors in the measurements of the quantities $a, b, c, d$ (yielding small errors in the measurements of $p, q, \Delta$), then certain of the above cases are subject to change, namely any case which contains an equal

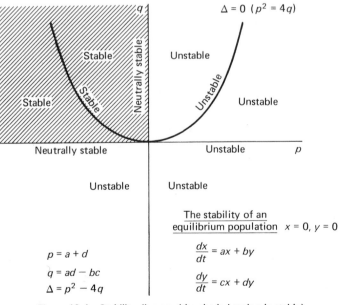

$$p = a + d$$
$$q = ad - bc$$
$$\Delta = p^2 - 4q$$

The stability of an equilibrium population $x = 0, y = 0$

$$\frac{dx}{dt} = ax + by$$
$$\frac{dy}{dt} = cx + dy$$

Figure 46-1   Stability diagram (the shaded region is stable).

*Except if $a = b = c = d = 0$, in which case we say this is NEUTRALLY STABLE (see exercise 46.3).

sign. Those cases in which small errors in measurements cannot induce changes are called the major cases, while the others are referred to as borderline cases. The major cases are (1)A, (1)B, and (3)A.

If $q = 0$ (i.e., $ad = bc$), then the linear system (46.1) has an equilibrium point not only at $x = 0$, $y = 0$ but at any point along the straight line $ax + by = 0$. In this case the equilibrium point $x = 0$, $y = 0$ is not **isolated**, since there are other equilibrium points *arbitrarily close*. In considering population models we will concern ourselves only with cases having isolated equilibrium populations. Consequently the borderline case $q = 0$ will not be considered.

Another distinguishing feature between the major and borderline cases is now described. The study of linear systems was motivated by considering the linearization of a nonlinear system. Topics which are not covered in this text show that *in the major cases the behavior of the linear system is an accurate approximation to the nonlinear system* (*at least in some immediate neighborhood of the equilibrium solution*). Furthermore, the stability of a borderline equilibrium population for a nonlinear system is the same as the stability of its linearization except for the one borderline case that divides regions of stability from instability ($p = 0$, $\Delta < 0$—case (3)B). For the stability of this latter case as well as the phase plane analysis for all borderline cases, some of the nonlinear terms neglected in the linearization process may be necessary in order to yield an accurate approximation in the vicinity of the equilibrium point. Usually only the quadratic terms from the Taylor series are then necessary, but sometimes even additional terms are needed. The phase plane analyses for the major cases are described in the next section.

# EXERCISES

**46.1.** Show that the solution $x = 0$, $y = 0$ of the linear system of equations 45.1 is stable if

$$a + d < 0 \quad \text{and} \quad ad - bc > 0.$$

**46.2.** Use the diagram in this section to determine the stability of the solution $x = 0$, $y = 0$ for the examples in exercise 45.1.

**46.3.** Consider the case (2)B in which $p = 0$ and $\Delta = 0$. The equilibrium $x = 0$, $y = 0$ of equation 46.1 is said to be **algebraically unstable** if solutions to equation 46.1 grow in some *algebraic* power of $t$, $t^\alpha$, rather than exponentially in time, $e^{rt}$. Show that in case (2)B the equilibrium is algebraically unstable except if $a = b = c = d = 0$. Show that in this latter case the equilibrium $x = 0$, $y = 0$ is neutrally stable.

**46.4.**   Consider

$$\frac{dx}{dt} = x(a - 4 + 2y) - a$$

$$\frac{dy}{dt} = y(a + 1 - x) - 2a,$$

where $a$ is a constant that may be positive or negative.
(a)   Show that $x = 1$, $y = 2$ is an equilibrium solution.
(b)   Linearize this system near this equilibrium. Show that

$$\frac{dx_1}{dt} = ax_1 + \beta y_1$$

$$\frac{dy_1}{dt} = -\beta x_1 + ay_1,$$

where $x_1$, $y_1$ are respective displacements from equilibrium. What is $\beta$?
(c)   Given that the linearization is of the form above, for what values of $a$ and $\beta$ is $x = 1$, $y = 2$ stable? [Hint: Eliminate $x_1$ or $y_1$.]

# 47.  Phase Plane of Linear Systems

## A.   GENERAL REMARKS

Not only does analysis of the linear system determine the stability or instability of an equilibrium population, but the resulting phase plane of the linear system will yield an approximation to the phase plane of the nonlinear system valid in the neighborhood of the equilibrium population (at least in the major cases as described in Sec. 46). The equation for the phase plane of the linear system is

$$\boxed{\frac{dy}{dx} = \frac{cx + dy}{ax + by}.} \tag{47.1}$$

This equation does not explicitly depend on time.

To determine how the population changes along a trajectory, arrows are introduced *via the time-dependent equations*. The phase plane equation alone cannot determine stability or instability. Reversing the role of time (replacing $t$ by $-t$) may change a stable equilibrium point into an unstable equilibrium point. Why? [Answer: A term in the solution similar, for example, to $e^{-t}$

becomes $e^{+t}$, growing exponentially.] However, the phase plane equation remains the same. As another example, consider the following two systems:

(1)  $\dfrac{dx}{dt} = x$  $\qquad\qquad\qquad$  (2)  $\dfrac{dx}{dt} = -2x$

$\qquad\ \dfrac{dy}{dt} = y$  $\qquad\qquad\qquad\qquad\ \ \dfrac{dy}{dt} = -2y.$

System (1) is unstable, while system (2) is stable. Why? [Answers: The solution of system (1) is $x = x_0 e^t$, $y = y_0 e^t$, while the solution of system (2) is $x = x_0 e^{-2t}$, $y = y_0 e^{-2t}$.] However, the phase plane differential equation for both is the same:

$$\frac{dy}{dx} = \frac{y}{x}.$$

Thus given the phase plane equation, it would be impossible to determine the stability or instability of an equilibrium population. We reiterate, to determine stability the time dependence must be considered.

If we change all the signs of $a$, $b$, $c$, $d$ (i.e., $a$ replaced by $-a$, $b$ replaced by $-b$, and so on), the phase plane equation remains unaltered. Thus since

$$p = a + d$$
$$q = ad - bc$$
$$\Delta = p^2 - 4q,$$

$p$ changes sign, but $q$ and $\Delta$ do not. Thus in discussing trajectories in the phase plane, the cases distinguished by $p > 0$ and $p < 0$ need not be considered separately. Arrows will indicate motion in opposite directions for increasing time and will be the only distinguishing feature.

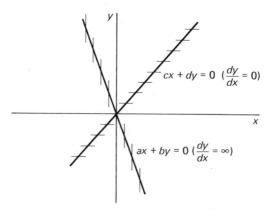

Figure 47-1   Typical isoclines corresponding to zero and infinite slopes.

We will show that to each different case there corresponds only one qualitative behavior in the phase plane. We will consider only the three major cases: (1)A ($\Delta > 0, q > 0$), (1)B ($\Delta > 0, q < 0$), and (3)A ($\Delta < 0$). The borderline cases are discussed in the exercises.

In sketching the phase plane of $dy/dx = (cx + dy)/(ax + by)$, first simple isoclines might be sketched, namely along $cx + dy = 0$, $dy/dx = 0$ and along $ax + by = 0$, $dy/dx = \infty$. For example, see Fig. 47-1. Instead of sketching additional isoclines, we propose to illustrate the general configuration for each of the three major classes.

## B. SADDLE POINTS ($\Delta > 0, q < 0$)

The case in which the roots of the characteristic polynomial are of opposite signs [(1)B ($\Delta > 0, q < 0$)] is analyzed first. Before discussing this case in general, the simplest possible example yielding roots of opposite signs will be solved. We will show that the result of this simple example is quite similar to the general case. Suppose that the differential equations were not coupled,

$$\frac{dx}{dt} = -x$$

$$\frac{dy}{dt} = 2y.$$

The "roots of the characteristic equation" are $-1$ and $+2$ (having opposite signs) as follows from the exact solution

$$x = x_0 e^{-t}$$
$$y = y_0 e^{2t}.$$

The phase plane differential equation,

$$\frac{dy}{dx} = \frac{-2y}{x},$$

is separable and can be directly solved,

$$\ln |y| = -2 \ln |x| + c,$$

yielding

$$y = \frac{k}{x^2}.$$

This equation for the trajectories can also be obtained by eliminating $t$ from the time-dependent solution. These curves are sketched in Fig. 47-2 for a few different values of $k$:

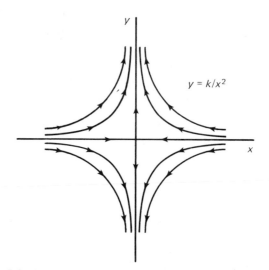

Figure 47-2  Trajectories for a system with characteristic roots of opposite signs.

Arrows in time are introduced in Fig. 47-2 from the following facts:

$$\frac{dx}{dt} > 0 \quad \text{if and only if} \quad x < 0$$

$$\frac{dx}{dt} < 0 \quad \text{if and only if} \quad x > 0$$

$$\frac{dy}{dt} > 0 \quad \text{if and only if} \quad y > 0$$

$$\frac{dy}{dt} < 0 \quad \text{if and only if} \quad y < 0.$$

The equilibrium point ($x = 0$, $y = 0$) is *unstable* as most trajectories near that point eventually tend away from the equilibrium point. The two special trajectories $y = 0$, $x > 0$ and $y = 0$, $x < 0$ tend towards the equilibrium point, but it can be shown that they take an infinite length of time to get there.

Imagine the phase plane trajectories of this example as the paths of a person moving along some hill $z = f(x, y)$ as viewed from above. If the person moves *down* the hill in some manner, then certain regions correspond to high ground and others to low ground. The resulting hill as illustrated in Fig. 47-3 resembles the shape of a saddle with the "seat" at $x = 0$, $y = 0$. For this reason this type of equilibrium point is called a **saddle point**.

We will show that whenever the two roots are of opposite signs then in the phase plane the equilibrium point is a saddle point. For this case the equilibrium is always unstable. If the roots are of opposite signs, then the solution

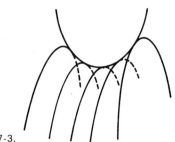

Figure 47-3.

must be a linear combination of the two exponential solutions. Referring to the time-dependent equations,

$$\frac{dx}{dt} = ax + by$$

$$\frac{dy}{dt} = cx + dy,$$

(47.2)

it was shown in Sec. 45 that if $c \neq 0$, then

$$x = c_1\frac{r_1 - d}{c}e^{r_1 t} + c_2\frac{r_2 - d}{c}e^{r_2 t}$$

$$y = c_1 e^{r_1 t} + c_2 e^{r_2 t}.$$

(47.3)

We may assume that

$$r_1 < 0 < r_2,$$

since the roots are real and of opposite signs.

To sketch the trajectories in the phase plane, $t$ must be eliminated. This is not easy in general. Instead, some specific trajectories are sketched. For example, if $c_1 = 0$, then

$$x = c_2\frac{r_2 - d}{c}e^{r_2 t}$$

$$y = c_2 e^{r_2 t},$$

and $t$ is easily eliminated:

$$\frac{x}{y} = \frac{r_2 - d}{c}.$$

This straight line represents two trajectories emanating from the origin (as $t \to -\infty$, $x \to 0$ and $y \to 0$ since $r_2 > 0$) and going toward infinity in a particular direction depending on the signs of $(r_2 - d)/c$ and $c_2$. A trajectory which starts at a finite point and goes in a straight line to infinity is called a

**ray.** These two rays are sketched in Fig. 47-4 (assuming that $(r_2 - d)/c > 0$).
Two other simple trajectories occur if $c_2 = 0$, since then

$$x = c_1 \frac{r_1 - d}{c} e^{r_1 t}$$

$$y = c_1 e^{r_1 t}.$$

Thus again, $t$ is eliminated easily:

$$\frac{x}{y} = \frac{r_1 - d}{c}.$$

Although this also represents two trajectories emanating from the origin,
these trajectories are tending to the origin as $t \to \infty$ since $r_1 < 0$ (and tend
towards infinity as $t \to -\infty$). The direction of these trajectories are determined by the sign of $c_1$ and the sign of $(r_1 - d)/c$. Thus if $(r_1 - d)/c > 0$ and
$(r_2 - d)/c > 0$, then we have Fig. 47-4, one of many different orientations
of the four simple trajectories.

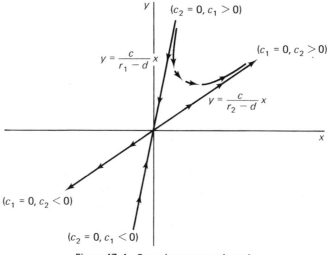

**Figure 47-4**   Some important trajectories.

We will show that the other trajectories ($c_1 \neq 0$ and $c_2 \neq 0$) do not go
through the origin. If they intersected the origin (the equilibrium point) at a
finite time, it would violate a uniqueness theorem for the initial value problem.
Of more significance to the phase plane sketch is to notice that these curves do
not tend towards the origin as $t \to \pm\infty$. As $t \to +\infty$, since $r_2 > 0$ and
$r_1 < 0$,

$$x \longrightarrow c_2 \frac{r_2 - d}{c} e^{r_2 t}$$

$$y \longrightarrow c_2 e^{r_2 t}.$$

Thus all trajectories ($c_2 \neq 0$) tend towards infinity as $t \longrightarrow +\infty$, in the direction

$$\frac{x}{y} \longrightarrow \frac{r_2 - d}{c},$$

i.e., tending towards being parallel to the outward going ray. Similarly as $t \longrightarrow -\infty$,

$$x \longrightarrow c_1 \frac{r_1 - d}{c} e^{r_1 t}$$

$$y \longrightarrow c_1 e^{r_1 t}.$$

If $c_1 \neq 0$, these trajectories also tend towards infinity as $t \longrightarrow -\infty$, in the direction $x/y \longrightarrow (r_1 - d)/c$; this time parallel to the inward going ray. The trajectory corresponding to one value of $c_1$ and $c_2$ (in addition, assuming $c_1 > 0$ and $c_2 > 0$) is sketched in Fig. 47-4 in partially dotted lines (other cases will be sketched in an analogous fashion). The curve is dotted, indicating the general behavior the curve must have for values of $t$ which are not either large and positive or large and negative.

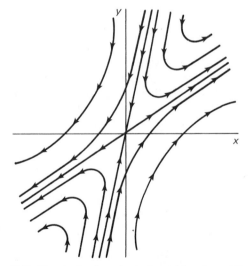

Figure 47-5   Sketch of trajectories in the vicinity of a saddle point.

In this manner we can sketch the phase plane of a saddle point, an unstable equilibrium point corresponding to one positive and one negative root, as shown in Fig. 47-5. Note that the phase plane has the "similar" general shape as that previously sketched for the example of a simple system with a saddle point (see Fig. 47-2).

In order to sketch the phase plane quickly the important curves are the straight line trajectories, the only trajectories that intersect the equilibrium

point. In some of the other cases a straight line trajectory is also of importance. An easy method to determine all straight line trajectories (assuming a
book with the answer is not readily available) is to substitute the assumed
form of a straight line trajectory into the phase plane equation,

$$\frac{dy}{dx} = \frac{cx + dy}{ax + by}.$$

Since the straight line goes through the equilibrium point,

$$y = mx,$$

which yields an equation to evaluate the slope

$$m = \frac{c + dm}{a + bm}.$$

Solving for $m$,

$$bm^2 + (a - d)m - c = 0,$$

gives two values

$$m = \frac{d - a \pm \sqrt{(a - d)^2 + 4bc}}{2b}. \tag{47.4}$$

It can easily be shown that these slopes are the same as obtained before, that
is the above formula is equivalent to $y/x = c/(r - d)$.

Knowing the straight line trajectories and the simple isoclines (along
which $dy/dx = 0$ and $dy/dx = \infty$) is sufficient to *quickly* give a *rough* sketch
of the phase plane when a saddle point occurs. As an example, consider

$$\frac{dx}{dt} = x - y$$

$$\frac{dy}{dt} = -2x - 2y,$$

which is in the form of equation 45.1 with $a = 1, b = -1, c = -2, d = -2$.
Hence from equation 46.1 $p = -1, q = -4, \Delta = 5$. As just discussed this
will be a saddle point (since $\Delta > 0$ and $q < 0$). The phase plane equation

$$\frac{dy}{dx} = -2\frac{x + y}{x - y}$$

is sketched in Fig. 47-6 by first noting the isoclines,

$$x + y = 0 \quad \text{along which} \quad \frac{dy}{dx} = 0$$

$$x - y = 0 \quad \text{along which} \quad \frac{dy}{dx} = \infty,$$

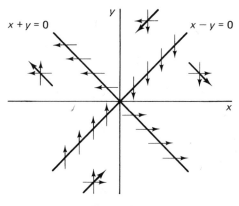

Figure 47-6.

where arrows are introduced from the time dependent equation. Straight line trajectories, $y = mx$, satisfy $m = -2[(1 + m)/(1 - m)]$ or equivalently $m^2 - 3m - 2 = 0$, and thus finally

$$m = \frac{3 \pm \sqrt{9 + 8}}{2} \approx 3.56, \, -.56.$$

Therefore we immediately have the reasonably accurate sketch shown in Fig. 47-7.

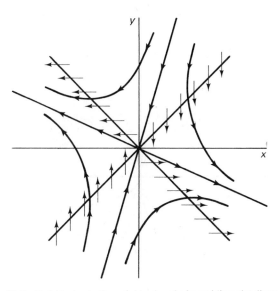

Figure 47-7   Trajectories in the neighborhood of a saddle point (based on simple isoclines and straight line trajectories).

## C.  NODES ($\Delta > 0, q > 0$)

To analyze the case in which both roots have the same sign, it is again convenient to first discuss a simple example,

$$\frac{dx}{dt} = 2x$$

$$\frac{dy}{dt} = y.$$

The exact solution is

$$x = x_0 e^{2t}$$

$$y = y_0 e^{t}.$$

The trajectories are obtained by eliminating $t$ from the above differential equations ($dy/dx = y/2x$) or by eliminating $t$ directly from the solution. In either way

$$x = ky^2.$$

Sketching these parabolas yields Fig. 47-8, where the arrows are easily added since $x = 0$, $y = 0$ is an unstable equilibrium point. This is a case in which both roots are positive. If both roots are negative, for example, if

$$\frac{dx}{dt} = -2x$$

$$\frac{dy}{dt} = -y,$$

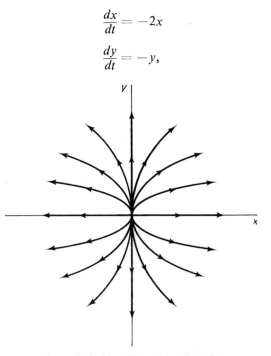

Figure 47-8   Unstable node: trajectories.

then the trajectories are identical, only the direction of the arrows is different. The equilibrium point is then stable. Examples can be constructed in which the trajectories near the equilibrium are not parabolas. Consider

$$\frac{dx}{dt} = -2x$$

$$\frac{dy}{dt} = -3y.$$

The trajectories of this equation are given by the formula

$$x = ky^{2/3}.$$

They appear similar to parabolas (as sketched in Fig. 47-9):

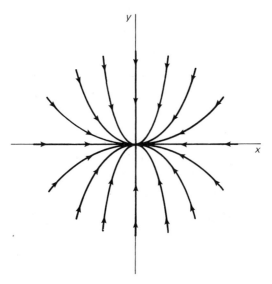

Figure 47-9 Stable node: trajectories.

In these examples all trajectories enter the equilibrium point. This type of equilibrium point is called a **node**; a **stable node** or **unstable node**, depending on whether both roots are negative or positive respectively.

In general, the solution (if $c \neq 0$) is

$$x = c_1 \frac{r_1 - d}{c} e^{r_1 t} + c_2 \frac{r_2 - d}{c} e^{r_2 t}$$

$$y = c_1 e^{r_1 t} + c_2 e^{r_2 t}.$$

(47.5)

Both roots are now considered to have the same sign, either

$$r_2 > r_1 > 0$$

or

$$0 > r_2 > r_1.$$

We will show a **node** always results. Simple trajectories are again determined by considering those with $c_1 = 0$ and those with $c_2 = 0$. Once more these trajectories are straight lines with the same slopes as in the saddle point case:

$$\frac{x}{y} = \frac{r_2 - d}{c} \quad \text{and} \quad \frac{x}{y} = \frac{r_1 - d}{c},$$

sketched in Fig. 47-10 assuming both slopes are positive:

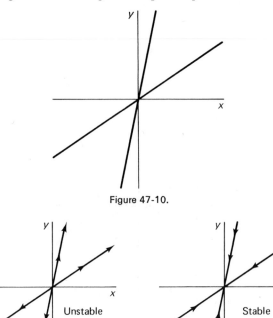

Figure 47-10.

Unstable                    Stable

Figure 47-11.

The time-dependent equations indicate that the arrows on these trajectories either all emanate from the origin (unstable, both roots positive and distinct) or all tend towards the origin (stable, both roots negative and distinct) as shown in Fig. 47-11. As in the case of a saddle point, the asymptotic behavior of the solution as $t \to \pm\infty$ helps to sketch the complete trajectories. Since $r_2 > r_1$, as $t \to +\infty$

$$x \longrightarrow c_2 \frac{r_2 - d}{c} e^{r_2 t} \longrightarrow \begin{cases} \pm\infty & \text{if both roots positive} \\ 0 & \text{if both roots negative} \end{cases}$$

$$y \longrightarrow c_2 e^{r_2 t} \longrightarrow \begin{cases} \pm\infty & \text{if both roots positive} \\ 0 & \text{if both roots negative.} \end{cases}$$

Similarly as $t \longrightarrow -\infty$ the opposite occurs, namely

$$x \longrightarrow c_1 \frac{r_1 - d}{c} e^{r_1 t} \longrightarrow \begin{cases} 0 & \text{if both roots positive} \\ \pm\infty & \text{if both roots negative} \end{cases}$$

$$y \longrightarrow c_1 e^{r_1 t} \longrightarrow \begin{cases} 0 & \text{if both roots positive} \\ \pm\infty & \text{if both roots negative.} \end{cases}$$

As both $x$ and $y$ tend towards infinity, the trajectories tend parallel to one of the special straight line trajectories,

$$\frac{x}{y} \longrightarrow \frac{r_2 - d}{c} \quad \text{if both roots positive}$$

$$\frac{x}{y} \longrightarrow \frac{r_1 - d}{c} \quad \text{if both roots negative.}$$

Furthermore, as the trajectories approach the origin, they do so *tangent* to the other special straight line trajectory,

$$\frac{x}{y} \longrightarrow \frac{r_2 - d}{c} \quad \text{if both roots negative}$$

$$\frac{x}{y} \longrightarrow \frac{r_1 - d}{c} \quad \text{if both roots positive.}$$

Thus, the trajectories always have the *type* of sketch shown in Fig. 47-12. This configuration is referred to as a **stable node** or an **unstable node**. For example, if both roots are positive, then it is an unstable node and arrows are introduced emanating from the origin. The simple isoclines along which $dy/dx = 0$ and $dy/dx = \infty$ can again be helpful in improving the accuracy of the sketch.

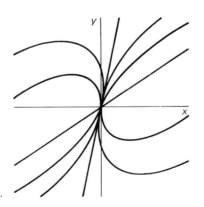

Figure 47-12   Node: typical trajectories.

## D.  SPIRALS ($\Delta < 0, p \neq 0$)

When the two roots of the characteristic equation are complex conjugates of each other, the analysis is more complicated than in the other cases. If the roots are purely imaginary (excluded by us as being a borderline case), then the solution exhibits a pure oscillation. A simple example of equation 47.2 corresponding to imaginary roots is the equations of a spring-mass system without friction,

$$\frac{dx}{dt} = v$$

$$\frac{dv}{dt} = -\frac{k}{m}x.$$

The phase plane for this example consists of closed curves (in general ellipses) encircling the equilibrium point called a **center**. However, if the roots have both nonzero real and imaginary parts, then we would expect an oscillation with the amplitude either growing or decaying. In the phase plane we should not be surprised that the resulting trajectories are spirals, as we proceed to show.

A simple example of a system of equations whose roots are complex numbers is

$$\frac{dx}{dt} = +ax + by$$

$$\frac{dy}{dt} = -bx + ay.$$

**(47.6)**

The roots of the characteristic polynomial are determined by

$$\begin{vmatrix} a - r & +b \\ -b & a - r \end{vmatrix} = 0,$$

yielding

$$(a - r)^2 + b^2 = 0,$$

or equivalently the complex conjugate pair

$$r = a \pm ib.$$

The trajectories in the phase plane can be obtained from

$$\frac{dy}{dx} = \frac{-bx + ay}{ax + by}.$$

This first-order differential equation is *not* separable. Although the solution can be sketched using the method of isoclines, the alternate form (obtained by dividing the numerator and denominator by $x$),

$$\frac{dy}{dx} = \frac{-b + a\frac{y}{x}}{a + b\frac{y}{x}},$$

suggests that the change of variables,

$$\frac{y}{x} = v \quad \text{or} \quad y = xv,$$

will enable its explicit integration.* Since $dy/dx = x(dv/dx) + v$ it follows that

$$x\frac{dv}{dx} = -v + \frac{-b + av}{a + bv}.$$

The equation is now separable; after some algebra

$$\frac{(a + bv)\,dv}{-b(1 + v^2)} = \frac{dx}{x}.$$

Integration yields

$$-\frac{a}{b}\tan^{-1} v - \frac{1}{2}\ln(1 + v^2) = \ln|x| + c,$$

where $c$ is the constant of integration. Returning to the $x$, $y$ variables ($v = y/x$) yields

$$-\frac{a}{b}\tan^{-1}\frac{y}{x} = \ln|x| + \frac{1}{2}\ln\left(1 + \frac{y^2}{x^2}\right) + c$$

or

$$-\frac{a}{b}\tan^{-1}\frac{y}{x} = \ln(x^2 + y^2)^{1/2} + c.$$

This form suggests the introduction of polar coordinates,

$$\theta = \tan^{-1}\frac{y}{x}$$

$$r = (x^2 + y^2)^{1/2}$$

in which case we see after exponentiating that

$$r = r_0 e^{-(a/b)\theta}.$$

Such curves are called **exponential spirals** (if $a \neq 0$). What happens if $a = 0$ and why? [Answer: If $a = 0$, the curves become the closed curves $r = r_0$, i.e., circles. This is not surprising for if $a = 0$, the roots are purely imaginary, $\pm ib$. Each component of the solution ($x$ or $y$) exhibits simple harmonic motion

---

*In fact this method works in all cases (see equation 47.1).

with circular frequency $b$. The trajectories are circles, perhaps most easily seen by the following calculation:

$$\frac{1}{2}\frac{d}{dt}(x^2 + y^2) = x\frac{dx}{dt} + y\frac{dy}{dt} = bxy - bxy = 0.\Bigg]$$

If $a/b < 0$, then as $\theta$ increases, $r$ increases; see Fig. 47-13. If $a/b > 0$, then as $\theta$ increases, $r$ decreases as shown in Fig. 47-14. The time-dependent equations determine the temporal evolution of the solution. For example at $x = 0$, $dx/dt = +by$. Thus at $x = 0$, $x$ decreases if $by < 0$ and $x$ increases if $by > 0$. Thus one trajectory is as shown in Fig. 47-15 (assuming $b < 0$). Similar curves can be sketched if $b > 0$ (see the exercises). For $b < 0$, as $t$ increases, there is an **unstable spiral** if $a > 0$ and a **stable spiral** if $a < 0$. These types of trajectories are also referred to as an **unstable focus** and **stable focus** respectively. The stability or instability also follow from the exponential term $e^{rt}$, where $r = a \pm ib$.

In the general case of complex conjugate roots, it is also convenient to introduce the polar angle $\theta$

$$\theta = \tan^{-1}\frac{y}{x}.$$

Thus

$$\frac{d\theta}{dt} = \frac{x\frac{dy}{dt} - y\frac{dx}{dt}}{x^2 + y^2}.$$

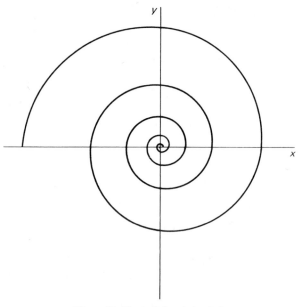

Figure 47-13   Left-handed spiral

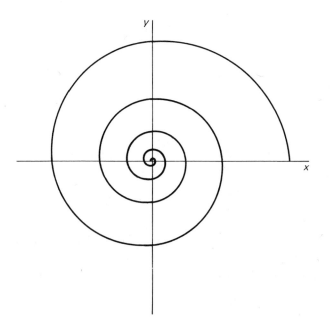

Figure 47-14   Right-handed spiral.

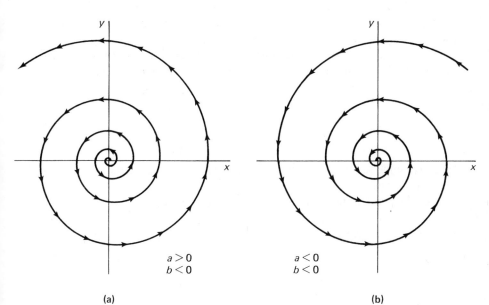

$a > 0$
$b < 0$

$a < 0$
$b < 0$

(a)

(b)

Figure 47-15   Spiral trajectories.

Eliminating $dx/dt$ and $dy/dt$ from the differential equations,

$$\frac{dx}{dt} = ax + by$$

$$\frac{dy}{dt} = cx + dy,$$

yields

$$\frac{d\theta}{dt} = \frac{cx^2 + xy(d - a) - by^2}{x^2 + y^2}.$$

We show that $d\theta/dt \neq 0$; the angle continually either increases or decreases. Suppose $d\theta/dt = 0$. Then, by dividing by $y^2$,

$$c\left(\frac{x}{y}\right)^2 + \frac{x}{y}(d - a) - b = 0$$

or

$$\frac{x}{y} = \frac{a - d \pm \sqrt{(d - a)^2 + 4bc}}{2c}.$$

However, the criteria for complex conjugate roots is

$$(a + d)^2 - 4(ad - bc) < 0,$$

or equivalently

$$(a - d)^2 + 4bc < 0.$$

Thus there are no values of $x$ and $y$ for which $d\theta/dt = 0$. Therefore $d\theta/dt$ is always of one sign (the sign of $c$, for example, or the sign of $-b$, which must be the same (why?)). The solution either spirals into the origin or spirals out from the origin.

Knowing that $\theta$ increases in time (or decreases) is not sufficient to accurately sketch the trajectories. However, recall the simple isoclines, that is

$$cx + dy = 0 \quad \text{is equivalent to} \quad \frac{dy}{dx} = 0$$

and

$$ax + by = 0 \quad \text{is equivalent to} \quad \frac{dy}{dx} = \infty.$$

In the example to follow, we show how these isoclines enable the sketching of the phase plane.

For the roots to be complex, $\Delta < 0$ or equivalently

$$(a + d)^2 - 4(ad - bc) < 0.$$

For example, consider

$$\frac{dx}{dt} = x + y \qquad \begin{aligned} a &= 1 \\ b &= 1 \end{aligned}$$

$$\frac{dy}{dt} = -4x + y \qquad \begin{aligned} c &= -4 \\ d &= 1 \end{aligned}$$

Along $x + y = 0$, $dy/dx = \infty$, and along $-4x + y = 0$, $dy/dx = 0$; see Fig. 47-16. Since $c$ is negative, $d\theta/dt < 0$. Thus $\theta$ decreases in time, yielding either Fig. 47-17a or b. The characteristic roots are determined as follows:

$$\begin{vmatrix} 1 - r & 1 \\ -4 & 1 - r \end{vmatrix} = 0.$$

Thus $(1 - r)^2 + 4 = 0$, or equivalently $1 - r = \mp 2i$. Since $r = 1 \pm 2i$, the equilibrium point is unstable. Thus the trajectories must be left-handed unstable spirals. An improved sketch is made in Fig. 47-18 using the known simple isoclines.

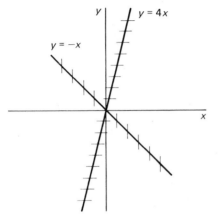

Figure 47-16.

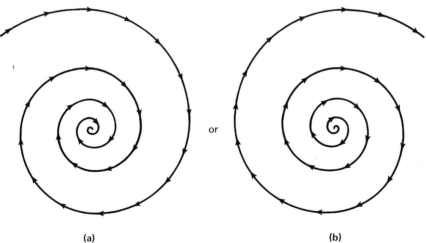

Figure 47-17.

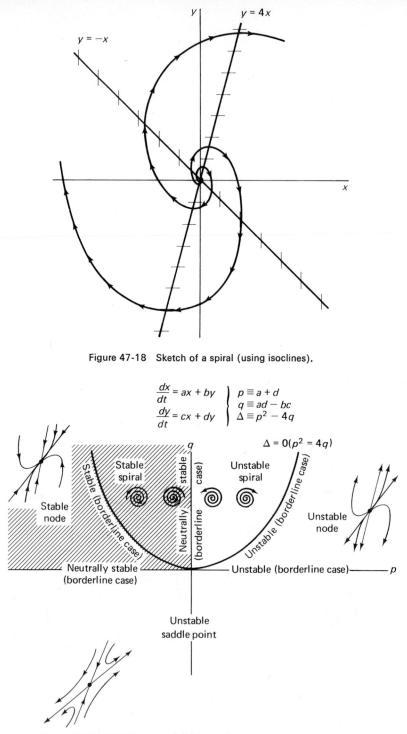

Figure 47-18   Sketch of a spiral (using isoclines).

$$\frac{dx}{dt} = ax + by$$
$$\frac{dy}{dt} = cx + dy$$

$p \equiv a + d$
$q \equiv ad - bc$
$\Delta \equiv p^2 - 4q$

$\Delta = 0(p^2 = 4q)$

Stable node

Stable spiral

Neutrally stable (borderline case)

Unstable spiral

Unstable node

Stable (borderline case)

Unstable (borderline case)

Neutrally stable (borderline case)

Unstable (borderline case) ———— $p$

Unstable saddle point

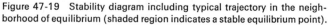

Figure 47-19   Stability diagram including typical trajectory in the neighborhood of equilibrium (shaded region indicates a stable equilibrium point).

## E. SUMMARY

The results of this section and the previous one are summarized in Fig. 47-19.

# EXERCISES

**47.1.** Consider the systems

(1) $\dfrac{dx}{dt} = 2x$

$\dfrac{dy}{dt} = x - 3y$

(2) $\dfrac{dx}{dt} = 4x$

$\dfrac{dy}{dt} = 2x - 6y.$

Show that the phase plane analysis of both problems are the same although their solutions are entirely different.

**47.2.** Reconsider exercise 45.1.
   (a)   Determine the stability of the equilibrium solution $x = 0$, $y = 0$.
   (b)   Sketch the solution in the phase plane.
   (c)   If this system was the linearization of a nonlinear population model, then what would you conclude concerning the equilibrium population and the phase plane in its vicinity?

**47.3.** Consider the linear system

$$\frac{dx}{dt} = ax + by$$

$$\frac{dy}{dt} = -bx + ay.$$

Suppose that it has been shown that

$$r = r_0 e^{-(a/b)\theta}.$$

   (a)   Sketch the trajectories in the phase plane if $a = 1$ and $b = 2$.
   (b)   Redo part (a) with $a = -1$ and $b = 2$.

**47.4.** Consider equation 28.1, describing the nonlinear pendulum. Sketch the solution in the phase plane ($d\theta/dt$ as a function of $\theta$):
   (a)   in the neighborhood of $\theta = \pi$.
   (b)   in the neighborhood of $\theta = 0$, if $k^2 < 4Lg$.
   (c)   in the neighborhood of $\theta = 0$, if $k^2 > 4Lg$.

**47.5.** Consider equation 21.1, describing a linear spring-mass system. Sketch the solution in the phase plane ($dx/dt$ as a function of $x$). Show that this linear system is a borderline case.

# 48. Predator-Prey Models

One of the first two-species ecosystems which has been mathematically modeled involves a predator and its prey. We will study the interaction in the sea between sharks and the small fish consumed by the sharks. (Another predator-prey situation, frequently investigated in mathematics texts, describes the ecosystem of foxes and rabbits.) Let

$$F = \begin{cases} \text{number of a certain species of} \\ \text{fish (eaten by sharks) in a specific} \\ \text{region of the sea} \end{cases}$$

$$S = \quad \text{number of sharks in the same area.}$$

The area is assumed bounded in a way such that migration across the boundary is, if not impossible, at least unlikely to be a major factor. Many other assumptions are involved in stating that

$$\frac{dF}{dt} = g(F, S)$$

$$\frac{dS}{dt} = h(F, S).$$

Before formulating a specific model, let us again describe the effects we would like to model. If the fishermen refrained from fishing for the small plankton-eating fish for a couple of years (as occurred during World War I), then these fish might be expected to increase in number. Once having increased, the sharks would have enough food to sustain a larger population of sharks. Thus the population of sharks would increase, and in a short time pose a severe threat to the small fish. Eventually the population of the plankton-eating fish would diminish. Once the small fish have diminished in number, the sharks can no longer sustain their enlarged population and must decrease in number. This in turn allows the small fish to return towards their original population. It is possible that this process continues on indefinitely, in which case the ecosystem would consist of periodic population variations. Although this may seem somewhat unreasonable, certain observations (see Sec. 43) indicate oscillatory fluctuations, close to what has just been described.

This description of shark-fish interaction applies to other predator-prey situations. Thus the model to be developed may have validity to other ecosystems besides the one involving sharks and fish. For another example of two-species interactions, consider the lynx (a type of wildcat) and hare populations in Canada. Observational data of these populations have been available for many years. The Hudson Bay Company trapped both the lynx and its primary food the hare, keeping yearly records of the numbers caught (presumably reflecting the total populations of lynx and hare). The data reveals remarkably periodic fluctuations of the populations of lynx and hare as illustrated in Fig. 48-1.

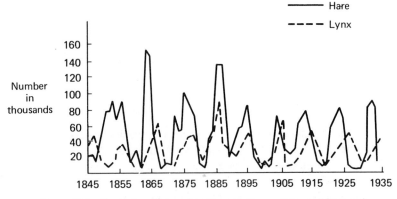

Figure 48-1    Oscillation observed in Canada of populations of lynx and hare (*data from* E. P. Odum, *Fundamentals of Ecology*, Philadelphia: W. B. Saunders, 1953).

# 49. Derivation of the Lotka-Volterra Equations

In developing a model of an ecosystem representing the interaction of its two species, it is advantageous to first model the population growths ignoring the interactions between the species. Thus we ask what equation should the population of sharks satisfy if there were no fish and vice versa.

In considering the fish without sharks, the assumptions concerning the birth and death processes of the fish must be delineated. Since the fish eat plankton which are presumed to be very abundant, it is suspected that the growth rate of the fish (without sharks) is constant,

$$\frac{dF}{dt} = aF.$$

The birth rate is larger than the death rate, yielding an exponential growth. This assumes that the plankton is unlimited. On the other hand, if the population growth of the fish ceases at some large population, then a logistic growth model might be proposed,

$$\frac{dF}{dt} = aF - bF^2.$$

Thus, the rate of population change of the fish, $dF/dt = g(F, S)$, is such that $g(F, 0)$ is given by either $g(F, 0) = aF$ or $g(F, 0) = aF - bF^2$. The latter equation incorporates the first. If $b \neq 0$, then there exists an equilibrium population of fish, $F = a/b$, if there are no sharks.

The sharks behave in an entirely different manner. If there are no fish, then the food source of the sharks is nonexistent. In this case, the death rate of the sharks is expected to exceed the birth rate. Hence in the absence of fish we assume that

$$\frac{dS}{dt} = -kS.$$

With no fish, the sharks would be an endangered species eventually vanishing. Thus we have determined $dS/dt = h(F, S)$, where $h(0, S) = -kS$.

We now will model the complex interaction between fish and sharks. The existence of fish enhances the shark population; thus fish will cause an increase in the growth rate of the sharks. For the simplest mathematical model of this process, we assume that the growth rate of sharks is increased proportional to the number of fish. The growth rate of the sharks, which was $-k$ without fish, is modeled as $-k + \lambda F$ with fish, where $\lambda$ is the positive proportionality constant. Thus

$$\frac{dS}{dt} = S(-k + \lambda F).$$

To model the growth of fish, we use similar ideas. However, in this case the existence of sharks will decrease the growth rate of fish. We again assume this interaction effect on the growth rate is proportional to the population. Consequently the growth rate of the fish, which was $a - bF$ without sharks, becomes $a - bF - cS$ with sharks, where $c$ is this positive proportionality constant. Thus we have described the background to the set of differential equations developed independently by Lotka and Volterra in the 1920s,

$$
\begin{array}{|c|}
\hline
\dfrac{dF}{dt} = F(a - bF - cS) \\
\hline
\dfrac{dS}{dt} = S(-k + \lambda F), \\
\hline
\end{array}
$$

where the constants $a, b, c, \lambda, k$ describing the different processes are all positive (except for $b$ which may $= 0$ if an unlimited amount of plankton is permitted). (You should be able to quickly explain what effect each term in these equations represents.) This is *not* the only possible model of a predator-prey ecosystem, but it is one of the simplest. Other models are suggested in the exercises in later sections. The question you should now be asking is: Does the qualitative behavior of solutions of this nonlinear system of differential equations seem consistent with the observed oscillatory behavior?

# EXERCISES

**49.1.** Consider the following three-species ecosystem:

$$\frac{dF}{dt} = F(a - cS)$$

$$\frac{dS}{dt} = S(-k + \lambda F - mG)$$

$$\frac{dG}{dt} = G(-e + \sigma S).$$

Assume that the coefficients are positive constants. Describe the role each species plays in this ecological system.

**49.2.** A two-species ecological system is described by the equations

$$\frac{\bar{x}_{m+1} - \bar{x}_m}{\bar{x}_m \, \Delta t} = 2 - \bar{y}_m$$

$$\frac{\bar{y}_{m+1} - \bar{y}_m}{\bar{y}_m \, \Delta t} = -3 + \bar{x}_m,$$

where $\bar{x}_m$ and $\bar{y}_m$ are the populations at time $m\Delta t$.
(a) Briefly describe the interaction.
(b) Find all equilibrium populations.
(c) Show that small perturbations to the equilibrium population $\bar{x}_m = 3$, $\bar{y}_m = 2$ satisfy the system of linear difference equations

$$x_{m+1} - x_m = -3\Delta t y_m$$
$$y_{m+1} - y_m = 2\Delta t x_m.$$

(d) If $x_m$ is eliminated from this system, show that

$$y_{m+2} - 2y_{m+1} + [1 + 6(\Delta t)^2]y_m = 0.$$

(e) Solve this difference equation and determine the behavior of the solution as time increases.

# 50. Qualitative Solution of
## the Lotka-Volterra Equations

Is the model proposed for the population changes of a predator-prey system,

$$\frac{dF}{dt} = F(a - bF - cS)$$

$$\frac{dS}{dt} = S(-k + \lambda F),$$

(50.1)

reasonable? Solutions must be calculated and compared to observations.

We will discuss the case in which the food source (plankton) is unlimited. Then the sea environment can sustain an infinite population of prey (fish) if there were no predators (sharks). This is equivalent to assuming that $b = 0$, in which case the ecosystem is governed by the following system of coupled nonlinear ordinary differential equations:

$$\frac{dF}{dt} = F(a - cS)$$

$$\frac{dS}{dt} = S(\lambda F - k).$$

(50.2)

The case in which $b \neq 0$ is posed as an exercise.

These equations imply that for a sufficiently large population of sharks ($S > a/c$) the fish population diminishes. If at some time the sharks number exactly $S = a/c$, then at that time the fish population does not vary. This level of sharks depends on $a$, the growth rate of the fish in the absence of sharks and $c$, the inhibiting effect of the sharks on the fish. If the growth rate of fish increases, then this level of sharks increases. Similarly if $c$ is increased, this level of sharks decreases. Equivalently if the sharks become more effective in attacking the fish (larger $c$), then less sharks are necessary to prevent the fish from growing. The equation describing the growth of the shark population can be analyzed in a similar manner.

Before attempting to solve this equation, let us briefly explain how the sharks limit the growth of the fish. Suppose initially that there are very few sharks. From the differential equations it is clear that the fish will grow in number. As the number of fish increases, the number of sharks must increase. Eventually the number of sharks will become so large that the growth rate of fish will become negative. At that time, the number of fish will cease to increase. We could continue the qualitative description of what should happen based on the differential equations.

Instead let us investigate mathematical properties of the special case of the Lotka-Volterra equations, equation 50.2. No simple explicit solution to these equations in terms of elementary functions has been obtained. Hence in order to understand at least the qualitative behavior of the solution (and also certain quantitative behavior), the trajectories of the solution in the phase plane will be sketched:

$$\frac{dF}{dS} = \frac{F(a - cS)}{S(\lambda F - k)}. \tag{50.3}$$

Unlike the phase plane of mechanical systems, only the first quadrant is necessary since both the populations $F$ and $S$ must be positive. We should first verify that the model does *not* have the indignity of predicting negative populations. We note that if $F = 0$, then $dF/dS = 0$ and if $S = 0$, then $dF/dS = \infty$. Thus the lines $F = 0$ and $S = 0$ are both isoclines as well as solution curves. Consequently, a solution once positive can never become negative, since to do so it must cross either axis, which is an impossibility. Other simple isoclines are:

$$S = \frac{a}{c} \quad \text{on which} \quad \frac{dF}{dS} = 0$$

and

$$F = \frac{k}{\lambda} \quad \text{on which} \quad \frac{dF}{dS} = \infty.$$

These isoclines are not solution curves, unlike the axes, as shown in Fig. 50-1. Intersections of isoclines corresponding to *different* slopes of the solution must be singular points. There are only two possible singular points, which also must be **equilibrium populations**, namely

(1) $\quad F = \dfrac{k}{\lambda} \quad \text{and} \quad S = \dfrac{a}{c}$

(2) $\quad F = 0 \quad \text{and} \quad S = 0.$

The case of zero population (2) is not as important, though knowing the

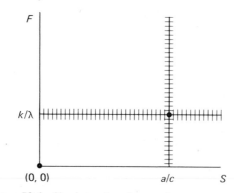

Figure 50-1    Simple isoclines for a predator-prey ecosystem.

solution curves in the neighborhood of this equilibrium population assists in
the sketching of the phase plane.

If $F = k/\lambda$ and $S = a/c$, then the predator-prey ecosystem has reached a
dynamic balance. We will show that such an equilibrium population is stable.
The equilibrium populations depend on all four parameters, but only the
appropriate two ratios are significant. The following paradoxical behavior of
this system is only understood with some care. If the growth rate of fish, $a$, is
increased, then the equilibrium population of fish remains unchanged; only
the sharks are affected. An increased number of sharks is necessary to balance
the growth of the fish. In other words increasing the egg-laying capacity of the
fish (i.e., increasing $a$) results in more fish being hatched, giving the sharks
more food. Hence, the sharks grow in number, but their increased number
consumes more fish exactly offsetting the increased birth of fish.

On the other hand, if the death rate of the sharks, $k$, is decreased, then not
only does this *not* effect the equilibrium population of sharks but more
unusually the equilibrium number of fish is actually decreased. The explanation of this last phenomena is that it takes fewer fish to balance a hardier shark
population. The efficiencies of the interactions, $\lambda$ and $c$, also behave in
seemingly surprising ways. Increasing $\lambda$ corresponds to the fish containing
additional nutrients for the sharks. This results not in increasing the sharks,
but in decreasing the fish. An increased efficiency of the predator results in
the decrease of the equilibrium number of prey. Similarly increasing $c$, corresponding to improving the sharks' ability to kill fish, results in a decrease
in sharks. Can you explain this last phenomena?

If the populations are not at equilibrium, then the phase plane is employed
to determine temporal population changes. If $S = 0$, then $dF/dt = aF$, that
is $F$ always increases. (Ecologically, if there are no sharks then the fish will

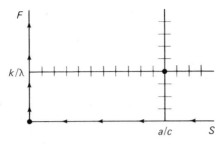

Figure 50-2   Single species trajectories.

grow.) Similarly, if $F = 0$, then $dS/dt = -kS$ and $S$ decreases (the sharks tend towards extinction). These results determine the population trajectories if either species initially is not present, as shown in Fig. 50-2.

If the fish are at the number necessary to balance the growth of sharks, $F = k/\lambda$, then $dF/dt = k/\lambda\,(a - cS)$. The fish increase from that value if the number of sharks is less than its equilibrium value ($S < a/c$). Why is this reasonable? Also the fish decrease if the number of sharks is greater than its equilibrium value ($S > a/c$). A similar analysis can be done near the equilibrium shark population, $S = a/c$. The resulting variation in shark population yields Fig. 50-3. In fact for all population of fish, the fish are increasing in number if the sharks are fewer than their equilibrium population and vice versa. Mathematically,

$$\text{if } S < \frac{a}{c}, \quad \text{then} \quad \frac{dF}{dt} > 0$$

and

$$\text{if } S > \frac{a}{c}, \quad \text{then} \quad \frac{dF}{dt} < 0$$

follow from equation 50.2. Furthermore, a similar statement about sharks is

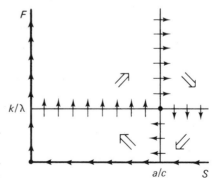

Figure 50-3   Qualitative behavior of predator-prey trajectories.

valid regardless what the population of sharks is. This explains the additional arrows ($\nearrow$, $\searrow$, etc.) that appear in the phase plane diagram, Fig. 50-3. The isoclines along which $dF/dS = 0$ or $\infty$ are seen to be quite useful as these curves separate regions for which a species is increasing from regions for which the same species is decreasing.

The phase plane diagram indicates in general a clockwise pattern. If the solution curves are sketched, then it is apparent that the populations may oscillate around the equilibrium values of the respective populations. As in mechanics, there are at least three possible kinds of "orbits" of the phase plane, as shown in Fig. 50-4. For example, suppose that the trajectories are as shown in Fig. 50-5. As drawn, part of one solution curve is spiralling inwards (as though the populations of fish and sharks after an oscillation approach closer to their equilibrium values), and also part of another solution curve is spiralling outwards (as though the fish and sharks increase in numbers after some time). If this is valid, then a "little common sense" would suggest that

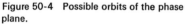

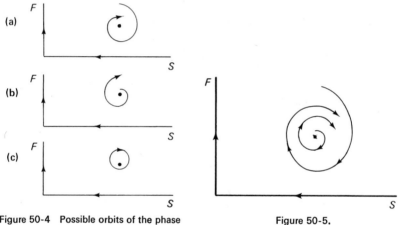

Figure 50-4   Possible orbits of the phase plane.

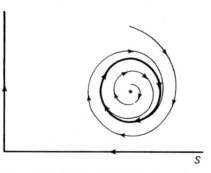

Figure 50-5.

Figure 50-6   Limit cycle (darkened curve).

there exists a solution curve "in between" the two drawn, such that for that solution the population returns to the same value, yielding a periodic oscillation of the population, called a **limit cycle** as sketched in Fig. 50-6. We will show that this phenomena as sketched in Fig. 50-6 does *not* occur for equation 50.2. However, it can occur in other population models. To elucidate the behavior of this fish-shark predator-prey ecosystem, we should investigate both species when they are near their respective equilibrium values, $F = k/\lambda$ and $S = a/c$. We do this by employing a linearized analysis as suggested in Sec. 44.

The differential equations 50.2 may be linearized in the neighborhood of the equilibrium population by using perturbation methods as follows:

$$F = \frac{k}{\lambda} + \epsilon F_1$$

$$S = \frac{a}{c} + \epsilon S_1,$$

(50.4)

where $\epsilon F_1$ and $\epsilon S_1$ represent population differences from the equilibrium population. Substituting this into the differential equations 50.2 yields

$$\epsilon \frac{dF_1}{dt} = \left(\frac{k}{\lambda} + \epsilon F_1\right)(-c\epsilon S_1)$$

$$\epsilon \frac{dS_1}{dt} = \left(\frac{a}{c} + \epsilon S_1\right)(\lambda \epsilon F_1).$$

Neglecting the nonlinear terms results in

$$\frac{dF_1}{dt} = -\frac{ck}{\lambda} S_1$$

(50.5)

$$\frac{dS_1}{dt} = \frac{a\lambda}{c} F_1.$$

(50.6)

This system of linear differential equations can be most easily solved by elimination; for example, eliminating $F_1$ from equation 50.6 yields

$$\frac{c}{a\lambda} \frac{d^2 S_1}{dt^2} = -\frac{ck}{\lambda} S_1,$$

or equivalently

$$\frac{d^2 S_1}{dt^2} = -ak S_1.$$

(50.7)

Thus, the number of sharks oscillates around its equilibrium population,

$$S_1 = S_{10} \cos \omega t + Q \sin \omega t,$$

where the circular frequency $\omega = (ak)^{1/2}$. Note that $S_{10}$ is the displacement from equilibrium population of sharks at $t = 0$. The fish also oscillate, since from equation 50.6,

$$F_1 = \frac{c}{a\lambda}(-\omega S_{10} \sin \omega t + \omega Q \cos \omega t).$$

If at $t = 0$, $F_1 = F_{10}$, then $F_{10} = (c/a\lambda)\omega Q$. In other words,

$$S_1 = S_{10} \cos \omega t + \frac{a\lambda}{c\omega} F_{10} \sin \omega t$$

$$F_1 = F_{10} \cos \omega t - \frac{c\omega}{a\lambda} S_{10} \sin \omega t.$$

The period of oscillation,

$$T = \frac{2\pi}{\omega} = 2\pi(ak)^{-1/2},$$

depends only on the growth rates $a$ and $k$. This period is only valid for small oscillations around the equilibrium population.

In the vicinity of the equilibrium population, there is a "constant of motion," an "energy" integral,

$$\left(\frac{dS_1}{dt}\right)^2 + akS_1^2 = \text{constant},$$

readily determined from the analogy between equation 50.7 and a spring-mass system or a linearized pendulum. In terms of $S_1$ and $F_1$

$$\frac{a^2\lambda^2}{c^2}F_1^2 + akS_1^2 = \text{constant},$$

which is an ellipse in the phase plane. This result can also be obtained from the phase plane differential equation,

$$\frac{dF_1}{dS_1} = -\frac{c^2k}{a\lambda^2}\frac{S_1}{F_1},$$

by separation and integration. Thus we know what is demonstrated in Fig. 50-7.

The results of a linearized analysis predict that populations oscillate with constant amplitude in the neighborhood of the equilibrium population. The equilibrium population appears to be stable. However, this conclusion is not always justified. The small nonlinear terms (neglected in the linearization) probably will make only a small change. But we must be exceedingly careful because this small change may affect the entire qualitative behavior of the solution. As the solution completes a "cycle" in the phase plane, instead of its

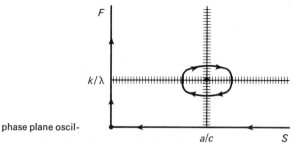

Figure 50-7    Predator-prey phase plane oscillation.

coming back exactly where it started (yielding a periodic solution), perhaps the nonlinear terms may cause it to oscillate with smaller and smaller amplitude. In this case the nonlinear terms may make the equilibrium solution more stable than predicted by the linearized stability analysis. If this occurs, our original prediction of stability is unaltered. However, the opposite can occur. It is possible for the neglected nonlinear terms to cause the solution to oscillate with increasing amplitude. In this case the equilibrium population would be unstable even though the linearized stability analysis predicted stability.

In summary, as discussed at the end of Sec. 47, the stability of an equilibrium population is always determined by a linearized stability analysis *except* when the linearized stability analysis predicts the equilibrium population is on the borderline between being stable and being unstable. This borderline situation is characterized by the solution oscillating with constant amplitude. In this case the linearized stability analysis is *inconclusive*. The nonlinear problem for a predator and its prey must be investigated!

If you have already studied Sec. 47, let us briefly show that the same conclusion can be reached by quoting the general results for linear systems. Equations 50.5–50.6 are put into the form

$$\frac{dx}{dt} = \bar{a}x + \bar{b}y$$

$$\frac{dy}{dt} = \bar{c}x + \bar{d}y,$$

where $x = F_1$, $y = S_1$ and

$$\bar{a} = 0$$

$$\bar{b} = -\frac{ck}{\lambda}$$

$$\bar{c} = \frac{a\lambda}{c}$$

$$\bar{d} = 0.$$

Thus

$$p = \bar{a} + \bar{d} = 0$$

$$q = \bar{a}\bar{d} - \bar{b}\bar{c} = ak > 0$$

$$\Delta = p^2 - 4q = -4ak < 0.$$

Since $p = 0$, the graph and table at the end of Sec. 46 indicate that the equilibrium population is neutrally stable. A neutrally stable equilibrium population (called a **center**) is a borderline case, and hence the linear analysis does not necessarily yield the same results as that of a complete nonlinear analysis.

Before analyzing the exact nonlinear problem, we should not ignore the phase plane in the neighborhood of the other equilibrium population, $S = 0$, $F = 0$. Linearizing the differential equations 50.2 in the vicinity of $S = 0$, $F = 0$ is accomplished by just neglecting the nonlinear terms in which case

$$\frac{dF}{dt} = aF$$

$$\frac{dS}{dt} = -kS.$$

The fish exponentially grow and the sharks exponentially decrease. The equilibrium population is what we called a saddle point (see Sec. 47). In the phase plane,

$$\frac{dF}{dS} = \frac{aF}{-kS} \quad \text{or} \quad F = AS^{-a/k}.$$

Thus, using information about the population near this equilibrium population, we see Fig. 50-8.

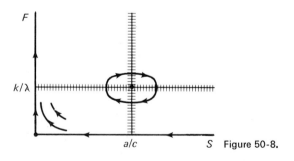

*Figure 50-8.*

Let us now reconsider the system of nonlinear differential equations describing the interaction between a predator and its prey. We will show the trajectories in the neighborhood of the equilibrium population $F = k/\lambda$ and $S = a/c$ are closed. In fact we will show that almost every solution curve is a closed curve and represents a periodic solution (see Sec. 21). To prove this, we return to the study of the phase plane, equation 50.3. This equation is separable:

$$\frac{\lambda F - k}{F} \, dF = \frac{a - cS}{S} \, dS$$

and can be directly integrated, yielding

$$\lambda F - k \ln F = a \ln S - cS + E,$$

where $E$ is a constant determined from the initial population of fish, $F(t_0) = F_0$, and the initial population of sharks, $S(t_0) = S_0$. For each value of $E$ there corresponds one solution curve. We will show all such curves are closed. To do so it is convenient to exponentiate the above equation, letting $e^E = E_0 > 0$,

$$\boxed{F^{-k} e^{\lambda F} = E_0 e^{-cS} S^a.}$$

This is an implicit equation relating the population of fish and sharks. Nevertheless we will show these equations represent closed curves. A possible difference between closed and open curves is illustrated in Fig. 50-9. For a curve which is somewhere spiral-like, there are values of $S$ for which there are more than two values of $F$.

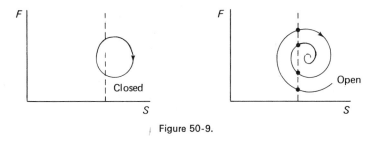

Figure 50-9.

Although we cannot easily sketch $F$ directly as a function of $S$, the functional relationship is obtained readily using an auxiliary variable $Z$. Let

$$Z = F^{-k} e^{\lambda F},$$

in which case also

$$Z = E_0 S^a e^{-cS}.$$

Let us sketch $Z$ as a function of $S$ and also as a function of $F$. For small $F$, $Z$ algebraically tends towards $+\infty$, while for large $F$, $Z$ exponentially tends towards $+\infty$. Similarly for small $S$, $Z$ tends towards 0 and for large $S$, $Z$ exponentially decays to 0. Thus roughly we obtain Fig. 50-10. We might guess the completion of both sketches (as marked in the figure in dotted lines). We can easily verify these are indeed correct by calculating the first derivatives $dZ/dF$ and $dZ/dS$ and showing each derivative is zero at only one place.

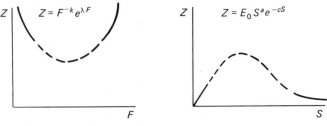

Figure 50-10.

In particular,

$$\frac{dZ}{dF} = F^{-k}e^{\lambda F}\left(\lambda - \frac{k}{F}\right)$$

$$\frac{dZ}{dS} = E_0 S^a e^{-cS}\left(-c + \frac{a}{S}\right).$$

These curves have zero slope at the respective equilibrium populations $F = k/\lambda$ and $S = a/c$. Thus we derive Fig. 50-11. Take one specific value of $S$ marked in Fig. 50-12 with ●. This determines $Z$, which yields 2 values of $F$ (also marked ●). Other values of $S$ yield either 0, 1, or 2 values of $F$ as illustrated in the figure. Specifically, for values of $S$ sufficiently small, there are no values of $F$. As $S$ is increased, there are still no values of $F$ until $S$

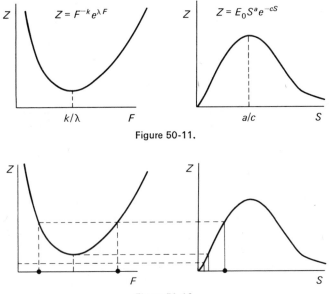

Figure 50-11.

Figure 50-12.

reaches a value at which the first intersection occurs. Then there is only one value of $F$. As $S$ is increased further, there are always exactly two values of $F$. However, as we continue to increase $S$, the process reverses itself. Thus the solution curve, $F$ as a function of $S$, is sketched in Fig. 50-13. It is a closed curve, no matter which value of $E_0$ is chosen (as long as $E_0$ is large enough to insure a solution). Thus for various values of $E_0$ we obtain Fig. 50-14. The population of fish and sharks are periodic functions of time. Can you show the period is finite? The populations fluctuate periodically around their equilibrium values in a rather complex fashion as roughly sketched in Fig. 50-15. The increase in sharks (predator) lags behind the increase in fish (prey), an oscillation similar to the one observed in nature.

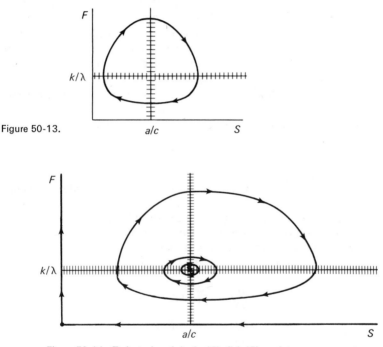

Figure 50-13.

Figure 50-14   Trajectories of sharks ($S$)- fish ($F$) predator-prey ecosystem.

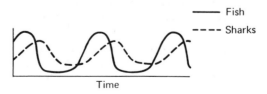

Figure 50-15   Lotka-Volterra predator-prey oscillation.

# EXERCISES

**50.1.**   Consider the predator-prey model with $b = 0$, equation 50.2. Suppose that the value of $k$ was increased.
(a)   What does increasing the value of $k$ correspond to ecologically?
(b)   How does this affect the nonzero equilibrium populations of fish and sharks?
(c)   Briefly explain this effect ecologically.

**50.2.**   Consider the predator-prey model with $b \neq 0$, equation 50.1. Calculate all possible equilibrium solutions. Compare these populations to the ones which occur if $b = 0$. Briefly explain the qualitative and quantitative differences between the two cases, $b = 0$ and $b \neq 0$.

**50.3.**   Reconsider exercise 50.2. In the phase plane, sketch the isocline(s) along which $dF/dS = 0$. Also sketch the isocline(s) along which $dF/dS = \infty$. Indicate arrows as in Fig. 50-3. Explain on your diagram where all possible equilibrium populations are. (If needed, sketch all possible cases.)

**50.4.**   Reconsider the predator-prey model of exercise 50.2 ($b \neq 0$). Determine the constant coefficient linear system of differential equations which governs the *small* displacements from the equilibrium populations,

$$F = \frac{k}{\lambda}, S = \frac{a}{c} - \frac{bk}{c\lambda} > 0.$$

Do this in two ways:
1.   Using the Taylor series for a function of two variables (equation 44.5).
2.   Using perturbation methods as described in Sec. 50.
Show that the two are equivalent. Do not attempt to solve the resulting system. [Hint: See exercise 50.5 for the answer.]

**50.5.**   Show that your answer to exercise 50.4 can be put in the form:

$$\frac{dF_1}{dt} = \frac{k}{\lambda}(-bF_1 - cS_1)$$

$$\frac{dS_1}{dt} = \left(\frac{a}{c} - \frac{bk}{c\lambda}\right)\lambda F_1,$$

where $F_1$ and $S_1$ are the displacements from the equilibrium populations of the fish and sharks respectively. Eliminate $F_1$ (from the second equation) to derive a second-order constant coefficient differential equation for $S_1$. Analyze that equation and determine the conditions under which the equilibrium population is stable.

**50.6.**   Give an ecological interpretation of the inequality in exercise 50.4,

$$\frac{a}{c} > \frac{bk}{c\lambda}$$

[Hint: Explain $a/b > k/\lambda$.]

**50.7.** Refer to exercise 50.4. Suppose that the equilibrium number of prey without predators $a/b$ is smaller than the prey necessary to sustain the predators $k/\lambda$. Sketch the solution in the phase plane. [Hint: Use the behavior of the phase plane in the neighborhood of all equilibrium populations.]

**50.8.** An alternate predator-prey model was suggested by Leslie:

$$\frac{dF}{dt} = F(a - bF - cS)$$

$$\frac{dS}{dt} = S\left(e - \lambda \frac{S}{F}\right).$$

The equation for the prey $F$ is the same. However, the predators change in a different manner. Show that if there are many predators for each prey, then the predators cannot cope with the excessive competition for their prey and die off. On the other hand if there are many prey for each predator, then the predator will find them and increase. Do you have any objections to this model? Compare this model to the Lotka-Volterra model.

**50.9.** Consider the predator-prey model, equation 50.2, with $c = 0$.
  (a) Without solving the differential equations, what do you expect to happen?
  (b) Sketch the solution curves in the phase plane.
  (c) Describe the agreement between parts (a) and (b).

**50.10.** Reconsider exercise 50.9 with $\lambda = 0$ instead of $c = 0$. Answer the same questions.

**50.11.** Reconsider exercise 49.1. What are all possible equilibrium populations?

**50.12.** Consider the following two-species population growth model:

$$\frac{dF}{dt} = F(a - bF - cS)$$

$$\frac{dS}{dt} = S(-k + \lambda F - \sigma S).$$

How does this model differ from equation 50.1. Without explicitly determining the equilibrium population, assume that one exists (with both species nonzero) and analyze its linear stability.

**50.13.** Reconsider exercise 50.12.
  (a) Sketch the phase plane in the neighborhood of the equilibrium population in which both populations are nonzero.
  (b) Sketch the phase plane in the neighborhood of $S = 0, F = a/b$. (What is the ecological significance of this population?)
  (c) Sketch the phase plane in the neighborhood of $S = 0, F = 0$.
  (d) Use the information gained from parts (a)–(c) to sketch the entire phase plane. Describe the predator-prey interaction. Sketch typical time dependence of predators and prey.

**50.14.** Sketch the phase plane for the predator-prey ecosystem described in exercise 50.2, if $a/b = k/\lambda$.

**50.15.**    Refer to exercise 50.5. Sketch the trajectories in the phase plane in the neighborhood of

$$F = \frac{k}{\lambda}, \qquad S = \frac{a}{c} - \frac{bk}{c\lambda} > 0.$$

Consider the two qualitatively different cases. [Hint: The results of Sec. 47 may be of some help.]

**50.16.**    Formulate a discrete time model (i.e., involving difference equations) for a predator-prey interaction. Determine all possible equilibrium populations. Describe the fluctuations of both species when they are near the equilibrium population in which both species are nonvanishing. Compare your results to the predictions in Sec. 50. [For a thorough discussion of this problem, see *Mathematical Ideas in Biology* by J. Maynard Smith (see p. 256 for date and publisher).]

**50.17.**    Briefly explain the mathematical reasoning you use to conclude that the natural position of the nonlinear pendulum is a stable equilibrium position.

# 51. Average Populations of Predators and Preys

For the mathematical model of predators and preys analyzed in Sec. 50, the populations of both species periodically oscillate around their equilibrium values. It is interesting to note that the average value of the populations of the predators can be easily calculated (as can the average value of the preys). Consider the time-dependent equations for the predator $S$,

$$\boxed{\frac{dS}{dt} = S(-k + \lambda F).}$$

Dividing by $S$, yields

$$\frac{1}{S}\frac{dS}{dt} = -k + \lambda F.$$

If this equation is integrated from the initial time $t_0$ to some arbitrary time, then the result is

$$\ln \frac{S(t)}{S(t_0)} = -k(t - t_0) + \lambda \int_{t_0}^{t} F(\tau)\, d\tau. \qquad (51.1)$$

Suppose we integrate over a complete period of oscillation, that is let $t = t_1$, where

$$\boxed{t_1 - t_0 = T.}$$

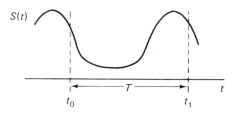

Figure 51-1    Period $T$ of oscillation of a predator $S(t)$.

The period of oscillation $T$ is indicated in Fig. 51-1. Since the population is periodic,

$$S(t_1) = S(t_0),$$

it follows by evaluating equation 51.1 at $t = t_1$ that

$$0 = -kT + \lambda \int_{t_0}^{t_1} F(\tau)\, d\tau.$$

Thus,

$$\boxed{\frac{1}{T} \int_{t_0}^{t_0+T} F(\tau)\, d\tau = \frac{k}{\lambda}.}$$    (51.2)

Note that the left-hand side is an **average value**. Consequently, the *average value of the prey population is $k/\lambda$, the same as the equilibrium population of the prey*. Similarly, it could be shown that the average population of the predator is identical with its equilibrium population, $a/c$. No matter which trajectory this ecological system traverses (i.e., independent of initial conditions), the average populations remain the same.

# EXERCISES

**51.1.**  For the ecosystem described by equation 50.2, show that the average population of the predator is the same as the equilibrium population of the predator.

**51.2.**  The notation of a bar over a quantity often denotes the average. Thus

$$\bar{F} = \frac{1}{T} \int_0^T F(t)\, dt.$$

Show that for the predator-prey system, equation 50.2,

$$\overline{FS} = \bar{F}\bar{S}.$$

# 52. Man's Influence
## on Predator-Prey Ecosystems

Suppose we observe a trajectory (see Fig. 50-7) of the predator-prey ecosystem (equation 50.2). If we consider a predator-prey ecosystem in which the prey is considered to be undesirable, then it is possible that the number of prey $F$ is so large as to upset some people (for example, if the prey were rabbits and the predator foxes, then farmers may be dissatisfied with the large number of rabbits). Can the situation be improved?

Someone suggests that introducing more predators $S$ will reduce the number of prey. Although at first that seems reasonable, let us analyze that suggestion using the mathematical model. Suppose that "$x$" marks in Fig. 52-1 the position in the fluctuation cycle at which more predators $S$ are introduced into the ecological model. The large arrow represents the instantaneous addition of more predators. As indicated, the result of this *may* be to increase the magnitude of the oscillation. In any event, the average populations of the predator and prey equal their equilibrium populations, and hence actually remain the same (see Sec. 51). No improvement has occurred.

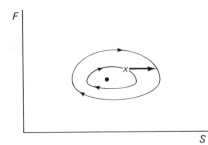

Figure 52-1   Predator-prey ecosystem: effect of instantaneously introducing additional predators.

Alternatively, it is suggested to gradually eliminate some of both the predator and prey. If this were a fox-rabbit ecosystem the suggestion might involve using animal traps. On the other hand, for two species of insects which interact as predator and prey, the use of an insecticide would have the same effect. Mathematically we can formulate this new problem by supposing that both predator and prey are eliminated in proportion to their number. Thus the new mathematical model would be

$$\frac{dF}{dt} = F(a - cS) - \sigma_1 F$$

$$\frac{dS}{dt} = S(-k + \lambda F) - \sigma_2 S,$$

where $\sigma_1$ and $\sigma_2$ represent the possibly different additional death rates because of, for example, the animal traps. It is not necessary to solve this system of equations, as it is equivalent to the original predator-prey system with slightly alterred parameters. Let

$$a' = a - \sigma_1$$
$$k' = k + \sigma_2.$$

Therefore,

$$\frac{dF}{dt} = F(a' - cS)$$

$$\frac{dS}{dt} = S(-k' + \lambda F).$$

Thus the effect, for example, of a pesticide is to *decrease* both species' interaction-free growth rates. The equivalent parameter $k$ is increased. Since the average population of the predator is $a'/c$ and the average of the prey is $k'/\lambda$, it is concluded that the predators are decreased and the preys increased. Can you explain why this happens? Thus, for example, setting traps will only yield more rabbits on the average. Try telling some farmer that! A predator-prey ecosystem illustrates the very delicate balance of nature!

# 53. Limitations of the Lotka-Volterra Equation

We have now indicated that the predator-prey model has certain qualitative features that have been observed in nature. Does this verify our model? Not really, as one should compare detailed observational data with the predictions of this predator-prey model. We have not done so here.

There are some difficulties with the previously developed predator-prey model. One objection is based on the fact that the model predicts an oscillation whose amplitude strongly depends on the initial conditions (similar to a linear problem). Thus this model predicts that an observed oscillation of many periods duration is due to some earlier event. Although this seems reasonable for the sharks and fish of the Adriatic, it is entirely unbelievable that lynx and hares should oscillate in a manner determined by events a hundred (or more) years ago. Thus a predator-prey model is sought which perhaps indicates oscillation of a type inherent to the system rather than determined by initial conditions (see a limit cycle, Fig. 50-6). A predator-prey model which results in such a feature is described in an exercise in Sec. 50. Other predator-prey models are also discussed in the exercises in which the amplitudes of oscillation decay as time goes on, as though nature seeks to restore predators and preys to an ecological balance.

There are other objections to the predator-prey models as developed here. This is best indicated by briefly mentioning some experimental results. As opposed to direct observation of nature, sometimes ecologists attempt to reproduce in the laboratory small scale ecosystems. They attempt to model situations using laboratory species in a way similar to which the mathematician models using mathematics. Predator-prey laboratory experiments usually eventually result in the predator eating all the prey. Then (of course) the predators also die out. Both species become extinct. The deterministic predator-prey population growth models do not result in any probability that one (or both) species becomes extinct. More realistic models incorporate random processes. During a wildly oscillatory predator-prey fluctuation, indicated by the trajectory in the phase plane shown in Fig. 53-1, there is a

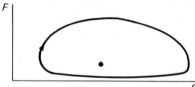

*S*   Figure 53-1   Wild predator-prey oscillation.

finite probability that when the population of prey is low, it will become extinct. Thus it is possible that the prey does not recover to dominate in numbers over the predator at some later time. Such stochastic predator-prey models will not be discussed in this text. Neither will predator-prey models which exhibit delays be discussed. More realistic mathematical models of predator-prey ecosystems involve both phenomena. The process of mathematical modeling continues as more is learned about nature.

# EXERCISES

**53.1.**   It is known that predators do not instantaneously react to an increasing or decreasing of the prey population. Formulate predator-prey equations which incorporate the above delay.

**53.2.**   If the prey become extinct, what eventually happens to the predators?

# 54.  Two Competing Species

Not all species form predator-prey relationships. In this section we will investigate a two-species ecosystem in which both species compete for the same limited source of nutrients. In deriving the governing system of ordinary differential equations, we again first specify the birth and death processes that take place for each species in the absence of the other. Since the food source (or other nutrient) is limited, a logistic growth model is proposed for each in the absence of the other,

$$\frac{dx}{dt} = ax - bx^2 \quad \text{(if } y = 0)$$

$$\frac{dy}{dt} = cy - dy^2 \quad \text{(if } x = 0),$$

where it is convenient to call one species $x$ and the other $y$.

To incorporate their competing for the same food, factors must be included which retard the growth rate of each due to the presence of the other. We assume the effect of competition is to reduce each species' growth rate by an amount proportional to the other species' population. Consequently,

$$\frac{dx}{dt} = x(a - bx - ky)$$

$$\frac{dy}{dt} = y(c - dy - \sigma x),$$

(54.1)

indicating that the respective growth rates are inhibited by both populations in a linear manner. These equations of two competing species have been derived using the same modeling techniques as we used for the predator-prey interaction. The resulting equations appear quite similar (compare equations 54.1 to 50.1, noting that only certain signs change). However, we will show that the solutions are entirely different.

In the phase plane (especially useful since the above system does not have an explicit solution involving elementary functions),

$$\frac{dy}{dx} = \frac{y(c - dy - \sigma x)}{x(a - bx - ky)}.$$

(54.2)

Unlike the predator-prey model, the phase plane differential equation is not separable. In sketching the phase plane, the axes are again both isoclines and solution curves. The other simple isoclines are

$$c - dy - \sigma x = 0 \quad \text{on which} \quad \frac{dy}{dx} = 0.$$

and

$$a - bx - ky = 0 \quad \text{on which} \quad \frac{dy}{dx} = \infty.$$

Both of these isoclines are straight lines with positive $x$ and $y$ intercepts. Geometrically, there are four types of configurations, illustrated in Fig. 54-1.

From these diagrams or directly from the time-dependent differential equations, there exist either three or four equilibrium populations (marked • on diagram), depending on the parameters in the competing-species model. In the cases sketched on top, the only equilibrium populations correspond to

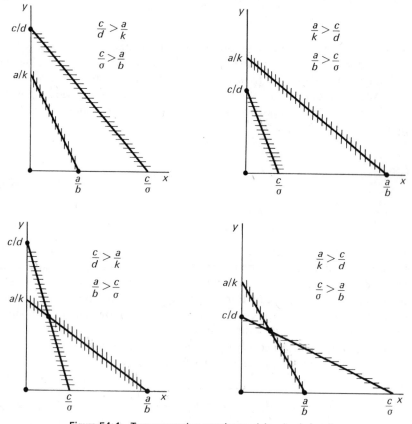

Figure 54-1   Two competing-species models: simple isoclines.

the extinction of at least one of the populations. However, in the cases sketched on the bottom, it is possible for there to be an equilibrium population in which both species coexist. In these cases it is especially important to investigate the stability of the coexistent equilibrium population in order to see if this is a viable result of two competing species. This equilibrium population is given by the intersection of the two straight lines,

$$bx_E + ky_E = a$$
$$\sigma x_E + dy_E = c,$$

where only those cases in which the equilibrium populations are both positive are pertinent. These equilibrium populations are thus

$$x_E = \frac{ck - ad}{\sigma k - bd}$$

$$y_E = \frac{a\sigma - bc}{\sigma k - bd}.$$

Note that these populations are less than the equilibrium populations that exist without any interactions. For example, $x_E < a/b$ is most easily seen geometrically.

All four cases will not be discussed. Most of the analysis of competing-species models is left to the exercises. Instead we will discuss just one case. Consider two competing species that are virtually identical. Let us assume both behave in the same manner in the absence of the other. That is the growth rates and logistic limiting factors are identical,

$$c = a \quad \text{and} \quad d = b.$$

But, we assume that one of the two species is more suited for competition. For example, if $x$ is the stronger, then $\sigma > k$ since then if $x = y$, $dx/dt > dy/dt$. Thus, the time-dependent equations are

$$\frac{dx}{dt} = x(a - bx - ky)$$

$$\frac{dy}{dt} = y(a - by - \sigma x),$$

$$(54.3)$$

and the phase plane equation is

$$\frac{dy}{dx} = \frac{y(a - by - \sigma x)}{x(a - bx - ky)}.$$

$$(54.4)$$

In addition to $x$ being the stronger, we assume that the interaction between the species is strongly competitive in the sense that the interaction terms, $-kxy$ and $-\sigma xy$, are greater (for equal populations) than the "self-interaction" terms, $-bx^2$ and $-by^2$. Thus $\sigma > b$ and $k > b$. This might occur if each species emitted a substance toxic to the other. Alternatively, it could also occur if each species psychologically affected the other adversely. Since $\sigma > k$, this problem corresponds to the inequality

$$\sigma > k > b,$$

in which case an equilibrium population can exist, as shown in Fig. 54-2.

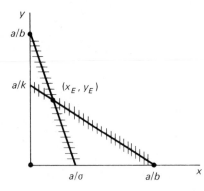

Figure 54-2   Equilibrium for the interaction of two nearly identical competing species.

Let us investigate the stability of that equilibrium population,

$$x_E = \frac{ak - ab}{\sigma k - b^2}$$

$$y_E = \frac{a\sigma - ab}{\sigma k - b^2}.$$

(54.5)

Rather than the calculations of the linearized stability, let us sketch the trajectories. Arrows are introduced to indicate changes in time. You should be able to do these calculations. As a review the steps will be outlined. From the time-dependent equation:

(1)    if $x = 0$,    $\begin{cases} \dfrac{dy}{dt} > 0 & \text{if } y < \dfrac{a}{b} \\[2mm] \dfrac{dy}{dt} < 0 & \text{if } y > \dfrac{a}{b} \end{cases}$

(2)    if $y = 0$,    $\begin{cases} \dfrac{dx}{dt} > 0 & \text{if } x < \dfrac{a}{b} \\[2mm] \dfrac{dx}{dt} < 0 & \text{if } x > \dfrac{a}{b} \end{cases}$

(3) In general,

$$\frac{dx}{dt} > 0 \quad \text{if } a - bx - ky > 0$$

$$\frac{dx}{dt} < 0 \quad \text{if } a - bx - ky < 0$$

separated by an isocline on which

$$\frac{dy}{dx} = \infty$$

$$\frac{dy}{dt} > 0 \quad \text{if } a - by - \sigma x > 0$$

$$\frac{dy}{dt} < 0 \quad \text{if } a - by - \sigma x < 0$$

separated by an isocline on which

$$\frac{dy}{dx} = 0.$$

Thus, we have Fig. 54-3, indicating that the equilibrium population involving coexistence is unstable for this problem. However, note that the two equilibrium populations corresponding to the extinction of one of the species are both stable. Thus following the arrows, one or the other of the populations will become extinct. This is an example of the **principle of competitive exclusion.**

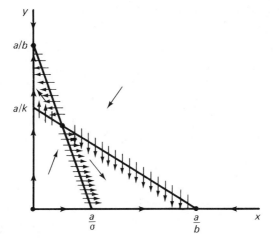

Figure 54-3    Qualitative behavior of trajectories of two competing species.

Only one species can survive. Figure 54-4 sketches solution curves that more clearly illustrate this result. Thus although species $x$ is "stronger," it is possible for it to become extinct, depending on the initial population of each species.

The sketch of the solution curves is improved by noting that the equilibrium points can be classified by the techniques of Sec. 47 as follows:

1. Coexistent equilibrium population is a saddle point (always unstable). The straight line trajectories in the neighborhood of the equilibrium population are determined in exercise 54.8.
2. A species eliminating its competitor is a stable node. In exercise 54.9 it is shown that the trajectories in the neighborhood of the node $x = a/b$, $y = 0$ can be of two different (but similar) forms depending on whether

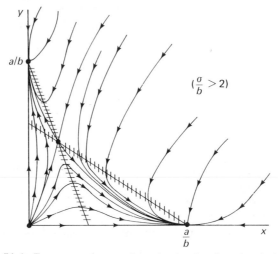

**Figure 54-4** Two competing species: sketch of trajectories (*x* is the stronger).

$\sigma/b > 2$ or $\sigma/b < 2$. Similar behavior in the neighborhood of $x = 0$, $y = a/b$ is described in exercise 54.10.

3. Zero population is an unstable node (isoclines in the neighborhood of the origin are straight lines since $a = c$—see exercise 54.1).

Furthermore we might wish to more accurately sketch the solution curves if both populations are large. In that case, as an approximation, equation 54.4 becomes

$$\frac{dy}{dx} \approx \frac{y(-by - \sigma x)}{x(-bx - ky)}.$$

It is not too difficult to see that approximate solutions (to leading order) for $x$ and $y$ large are straight lines, $y = mx + Q$. The slope is determined by substitution:

$$m = \frac{-bm^2 - \sigma m}{-b - km},$$

where in this calculation the intercept $Q$ is ignored since both $x$ and $y$ are large. It follows that

$$-bm - km^2 = -bm^2 - \sigma m \quad \text{or} \quad m = \frac{\sigma - b}{k - b}.$$

Since $\sigma > k > b$, the slope $m$ is certainly greater than 1, indicating that since $x$ is stronger, it is "more likely" that $x$ will be the surviving species.

As a specific example of the competition of two species, consider a famous experiment involving the growth of two types of yeast ($x$ and $y$) in a medium (in the absence of oxygen). Yeasts produce alcohol such that the resulting alcoholic content is approximately proportional to the total number of yeast

$(x + y)$. However, the growth rates of yeast are increasingly retarded as the content of alcohol is increased. Thus

$$\frac{dx}{dt} = x[a - b(x + y)]$$

$$\frac{dy}{dt} = y[c - d(x + y)].$$

(54.6)

This is an example of the model we have developed of competing species with $k = b$ and $\sigma = d$. Exercise 54.6 describes the competition between these two types of yeast.

# EXERCISES

**54.1.** In this problem we wish to approximate the phase plane (for the competing species model) when both species' populations are small.
   (a)   Show that for small populations

$$\frac{dx}{dt} \approx ax \quad \text{and} \quad \frac{dy}{dt} \approx cy.$$

   (b)   Without solving this simple system of differential equations, determine the phase plane differential equation. [Hint: $dy/dx = ?$]
   (c)   Solve the resulting phase plane differential equation. [Hint: It is separable.]
   (d)   Show that you can obtain the same result by solving the time-dependent differential equations of part (a), and after solving, by eliminating $t$.
   (e)   Sketch the solution in the phase plane. Show that the solution curves appear differently for the three cases:
   (1)  $a > c$
   (2)  $a = c$
   (3)  $a < c$.

**54.2.** Consider the competing species model, equation 54.1. Sketch the phase plane and the trajectories of both populations if

   (a)  $\dfrac{c}{d} > \dfrac{a}{k}$  and  $\dfrac{c}{\sigma} > \dfrac{a}{b}$    (b)  $\dfrac{a}{k} > \dfrac{c}{d}$  and  $\dfrac{a}{b} > \dfrac{c}{\sigma}$

   (c)  $\dfrac{c}{d} > \dfrac{a}{k}$  and  $\dfrac{a}{b} > \dfrac{c}{\sigma}$    (d)  $\dfrac{a}{k} > \dfrac{c}{d}$  and  $\dfrac{c}{\sigma} > \dfrac{a}{b}$

   (e)  $\dfrac{c}{d} = \dfrac{a}{k}$  and  $\dfrac{c}{\sigma} > \dfrac{a}{b}$    (f)  $\dfrac{c}{d} = \dfrac{a}{k}$  and  $\dfrac{a}{b} > \dfrac{c}{\sigma}$

   (g)  $\dfrac{a}{k} > \dfrac{c}{d}$  and  $\dfrac{a}{b} = \dfrac{c}{\sigma}$    (h)  $\dfrac{c}{d} > \dfrac{a}{k}$  and  $\dfrac{a}{b} = \dfrac{c}{\sigma}$.

Describe the interaction between the two species in each case.

**54.3.**   Consider the three-species ecosystem

$$\frac{dF}{dt} = F(-a + bR - k_1 G)$$

$$\frac{dR}{dt} = R(c - dF - k_2 G)$$

$$\frac{dG}{dt} = G(k + k_3 F - k_4 R),$$

assuming all coefficients are positive constants.
(a)   If $G = 0$, show that this represents a predator-prey situation. (Which species is the predator, and which is the prey?)
(b)   If $G \neq 0$, explain in ecological terms, the interactions of species $G$ with species $R$ and $F$.
(Do *NOT* solve any differential equations.)

**54.4.**   Consider the competing species model, equation 54.1. Suppose $b = d = 0$.
(a)   What are all possible equilibrium solutions? Show that $x = c/\sigma$, $y = a/k$ is an equilibrium population.
(b)   Show that the system of differential equations describing populations near the equilibrium $(x = c/\sigma, y = a/k)$ is

$$\frac{dx_1}{dt} = -\alpha y_1$$

$$\frac{dy_1}{dt} = -\beta x_1,$$

where $x_1$ and $y_1$ are the displacements from equilibrium. What are $\alpha$ and $\beta$? Show that $\alpha > 0$, $\beta > 0$.
(c)   By eliminating either $x_1$ or $y_1$, determine whether this equilibrium solution is stable or unstable.
(d)   Sketch the phase plane solution of equation 54.1 with $b = d = 0$. [Hint: Are there any approximately straight line solutions in the neighborhood of the equilibrium solution $x = c/\sigma, y = a/k$?]

**54.5.**   Formulate one system of differential equations describing all of the following interactions in some region between species $x$ and species $y$:
(a)   The nutrients for both species are limited.
(b)   Both species compete with each other for the same nutrients.
(c)   There is a migration (from somewhere else) of species $x$ into the region of interest at the *rate W* per unit time.

**54.6.**   Consider the competition between two types of yeast described by equation 54.6. Can you predict the outcome of the competition. If $c/d > a/b$, which yeast has the highest tolerance of alcohol?

**54.7.**   Consider equation 54.1.
(a)   Give an ecological interpretation to the quantities
(1)   $x = a/b$ and $x = c/\sigma$
(2)   $y = a/k$ and $y = c/d$.

(b)  Only using a rough phase plane analysis, show that the coexistent equilibrium population is unstable if $a/b > c/\sigma$ and $c/d > a/k$ and stable if $a/b < c/\sigma$ and $c/d < a/k$. Briefly explain this result using the terminology introduced in part (a).

**54.8.**  Consider equations 54.3 and 54.4. Show that the coexistent equilibrium population given by equation 54.5 is a saddle point in the phase plane (see Sec. 47B). Determine the straight line trajectories in the neighborhood of this equilibrium population.

**54.9.**  Consider equations 54.3 and 54.4. Show that the equilibrium population $x = a/b$, $y = 0$ is a stable node (see Sec. 47C). Show that most trajectories approach the line $y = 0$ as $t \to \infty$ if $\sigma/b > 2$. Determine what line most trajectories approach as $t \to \infty$ if $\sigma/b < 2$.

**54.10.**  Consider exercise 54.9. Without any additional calculations, describe the trajectories in the neighborhood of $x = 0$, $y = a/b$ if $k/b > 2$ and if $k/b < 2$.

**54.11.**  Consider

$$\frac{dF}{dt} = F(2 - 2F + G)$$

$$\frac{dG}{dt} = G(1 - G + F)$$

(a)  Give a brief explanation of each species' ecological behavior. (Account for each term on the right-hand side of the above differential equations.)

(b)  Determine all possible equilibrium populations.

(c)  In the phase plane, draw the isoclines corresponding to the slope of the solution being 0 and $\infty$.

(d)  Introduce arrows indicating the direction of trajectories (time changes) of this ecosystem. The qualitative time changes should be indicated everywhere ($F \geq 0$, $G \geq 0$) in the phase plane.

(e)  From the phase plane in part (d), briefly explain which (if any) of the equilibrium populations is stable and which unstable. Do *not* do a linearized stability analysis.

**54.12.**  Two species, $A$ and $B$, are in competition and are the prey of a third species $C$. What differential equations describe this ecological system?

# 55.  Further Reading
# in Mathematical Ecology

Our study of mathematical ecology and population dynamics has been limited to some relatively simple models. Problems involving more than two species, migration, stochastic fluctuations, delays, spatial dependence, and age dependence, have been treated only briefly, if at all. Comparisons of our mathematical models to experiments and observations have been essentially of a qualitative nature only. For those interested in studying further in this fascinating area, I suggest the following books:

MAY, R. M., *Stability and Complexity in Model Ecosystems.* Princeton, N.J.: Princeton University Press, 1973.

MAYNARD SMITH, J., *Mathematical Ideas in Biology.* Cambridge: Cambridge University Press, 1968.

MAYNARD SMITH, J., *Models in Ecology.* Cambridge: Cambridge University Press, 1974.

PIELOU, E. C., *An Introduction to Mathematical Ecology.* New York: John Wiley and Sons, 1969.

POOLE, R. W., *An Introduction to Quantitative Ecology.* New York: McGraw-Hill Book Company, 1974.

# Traffic Flow

# 56. Introduction to Traffic Flow

Transportation problems have plagued man long before the advent of the automobile. However, in recent years, traffic congestion has become especially acute. Traffic problems which may be amenable to a scientific analysis include: where to install traffic lights or stop signs; how long the cycle of traffic lights should be; how to develop a progressive traffic light system; whether to change a two-way street to a one-way street; where to construct entrances, exits, and overpasses; how many lanes to build for a new highway; whether to build the highway or to develop alternate forms of transportation (for example, trains or buses). In particular, the ultimate aim is to understand traffic phenomena in order to eventually make decisions which may alleviate congestion, maximize flow of traffic, eliminate accidents, minimize automobile exhaust pollution, and other desirable ends.

In this text we do not propose to formulate (no less solve) all these kinds of traffic problems. Instead we will study some simple problems which have recently received a mathematical formulation; how traffic flows along a unidirectional road. Rather than analyzing the behavior of individual cars, we will primarily study traffic situations resulting from the complex interaction of many vehicles. Statistical theories can be developed. However, here we will only formulate mathematical models that are deterministic.

We will begin our investigation of traffic problems by discussing the fundamental traffic variables: velocity, density, and flow (Secs. 57–59). We will attempt to predict these quantities if they are known initially. Conservation of cars (Sec. 60) and experimental relationships between car velocity and traffic density (Secs. 61–64) give a formulation of traffic problems in terms of a nonlinear partial differential equation (Sec. 65). Thus we will study some methods to solve partial differential equations, rather than ordinary differential equations as previously analyzed in the sections on mechanical vibrations and population dynamics. Nearly uniform traffic flow is first discussed, enabling the introduction of the concept of a traffic density wave (Secs. 66–70). The method of characteristics is developed for nonuniform traffic problems and applied to some examples (Secs. 71–75). In particular we will discuss what happens to a line of stopped traffic after a light turns green. Difficulties in this theory occur when light traffic catches up to heavy traffic, necessitating the analysis of traffic shocks, discontinuities in density, (Secs. 76–77). A number of examples with traffic shocks are described (Secs. 78–82). These include the traffic pattern formed by a uniform flow of traffic being stopped by a red light and the effect of a temporary delay of traffic caused, for example, by an accident. Then highway problems are briefly discussed which incorporate previously neglected exits and entrances (Secs. 83–85).

# 57. Automobile Velocities and a Velocity Field

Let us imagine a car moving along a highway. If the position of the car is designated $x_0(t)$, then its velocity is, of course, $dx_0(t)/dt$ and its acceleration $d^2x_0(t)/dt^2$. The position of the car might refer, for example, to the center of the car. In a highway situation with many cars each is designated by an $x_i(t)$, as shown in Fig. 57-1.

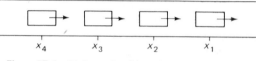

Figure 57-1    Highway (position of cars denoted by $x_i$).

There are two ways to measure velocity. The most common is to measure the velocity $u_i$ of each car, $u_i = dx_i/dt$. With $N$ cars there are $N$ different velocities, each depending on time, $u_i(t)$ $i = 1, \ldots, N$. In many situations the number of cars is so large that it is difficult to keep track of each car. Instead of recording the velocity of each individual car, we associate to each point in space (at each time) a unique velocity, $u(x, t)$, called a **velocity field**. This would be the velocity measured at time $t$ by an observer fixed at position $x$. This velocity (at $x$, at time $t$) is the velocity of a car at that place (if a car is there at that time). Expressing this statement in mathematical terms, the velocity field $u(x, t)$ at the car's position $x_i(t)$ must be the car's velocity $u_i(t)$,

$$u(x_i(t), t) = u_i(t). \qquad (57.1)$$

The existence of a velocity field $u(x, t)$ implies that at each $x$ and $t$ there is *one* velocity. Thus this model does not allow cars to pass each other (since at the point of passing there simultaneously must be two different velocities).

As an example consider two cars on a highway, labeled car 1 and car 2, as shown in Fig. 57-2. Suppose that car 1 moves at 45 m.p.h. (72 k.p.h.)* and

---

*m.p.h. = miles per hour, k.p.h. = kilometers per hour. (60 m.p.h. = 88 feet per second $\approx 96\frac{1}{2}$ k.p.h. $\approx 27$ meters per second).

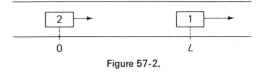

Figure 57-2.

car 2 at 30 m.p.h. (48 k.p.h.). Also assume that car 1 is at $x = L > 0$ at $t = 0$, while car 2 is at $x = 0$ at $t = 0$. Thus

$$\frac{dx_1}{dt} = 45, \quad t > 0 \qquad x_1(0) = L$$

$$\frac{dx_2}{dt} = 30, \quad t > 0 \qquad x_2(0) = 0.$$

Integrating these equations yields each car's position as a function of time;

$$x_1 = 45t + L$$

$$x_2 = 30t.$$

Sketching these motions on a space-time diagram as in Fig. 57-3 yields each car's path. In this way a velocity field can be formed; $u$ is a function of $x$ and $t$. However, on a highway with two cars, the velocity $u$ is undefined at most times at a fixed position along the highway. It is not always convenient to use a *velocity field* unless there are many cars.

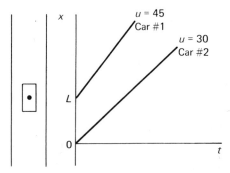

Figure 57-3 A *vertical* highway is sometimes convenient for sketches, because then the slope of a car's trajectory, $dx/dt$, is its velocity.

Suppose that a continuous velocity field defined everywhere (for $t > 0$ and $x > 0$) existed. An example of that might be

$$u(x, t) = \frac{15x + 30L}{15t + L}. \qquad (57.2)$$

(This expression is dimensionally consistent if the numbers 15 and 30 above are velocities.) Note that when $x = 30t$, then from equation 57.2 $u = 30$, and when $x = 45t + L$, then $u = 45$. This velocity field is one of many with this property. The velocity field of equation 57.2 was developed in the following manner. As a simple model, let us assume that there are an infinite number of cars (*of zero length*) each labeled with a number $\beta$. Let $\beta = 0$ correspond to the first car on the left and $\beta = 1$ correspond to the first car on the right. If the car labeled $\beta$ moves at the velocity $30 + 15\beta$, $dx/dt = 30 + 15\beta$, and starts at $t = 0$ at position $\beta L$, $x(0) = \beta L$, then the cars' velocities as $\beta$ tends from 0 to 1 range continuously (and linearly) from 30 to 45, and the initial positions range continuously (and linearly) from 0 to $L$, as illustrated in Fig. 57-4. In exercise 57.1 we show that the solution of this system of differential equations yields the velocity field given above in equation 57.2.

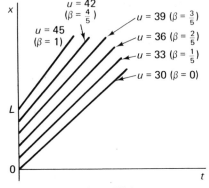

Figure 57-4.

A simpler example of a velocity field occurs if each car in a stream of traffic moves along at a constant velocity $V_0$, as indicated in Fig. 57-5. Clearly, the velocity field we use to approximate this situation is the same constant $V_0$, $u(x, t) = V_0$.

The concept of fields is common in many areas. To emphasize this concept

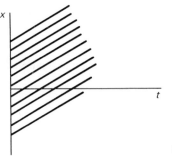

Figure 57-5    Constant velocity field.

we briefly discuss one example that is familiar to you. Temperature is often given as a function of position and time, $T(x, y, t)$. A typical weather map (with isotherms, constant values of temperature, plotted) is sketched in Fig. 57-6. It is usual to specify the temperature at fixed positions and at a fixed time, rather than to associate a temperature (possibly changing in time) with each air particle moving around in the atmosphere. We are normally interested in the temperature field since we do not move about with air particles. However, a person aboard a freely floating balloon might be more interested in the temperature at a moving position!

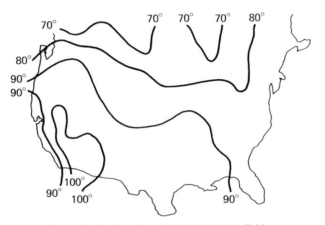

Figure 57-6   Two-dimensional temperature field.

Depending on the particular traffic application, we could be interested in either the velocity field or the velocities of individual cars. We repeat that these velocities are equal in the sense that

$$u(x_i(t), t) = u_i(t).$$

Both concepts of velocity are used in discussing traffic flow.

# EXERCISES

**57.1.** Assume that there are an *infinite* number of cars (of infinitesimal length) on a roadway each labeled with a number $\beta$ ranging from $\beta = 0$ to $\beta = 1$. (Let $\beta = 0$ correspond to the first car on the left and $\beta = 1$ to the first car on the right.) Suppose that the car labeled $\beta$ moves at the velocity $30 + 15\beta$ ($dx/dt = 30 + 15\beta$) and starts at $t = 0$ at the position $\beta L$ ($x(0) = \beta L$).

(a) Show that the cars' velocities steadily increase from 30 to 45 as $\beta$ ranges from 0 to 1.

(b) Show that the cars' initial positions range from 0 to $L$ as $\beta$ ranges from 0 to 1.

(c) Consider the car labeled $\beta$. Show that

$$x = (30 + 15\beta)t + \beta L \quad \text{and} \quad u = 30 + 15\beta.$$

(d) Eliminate $\beta$ from these two equations to "derive" the velocity field

$$u(x, t) = \frac{15x + 30L}{15t + L}.$$

**57.2.** Suppose a velocity field is given:

$$u(x, t) = \frac{30x + 30L}{15t + L}$$

(a) Determine the motion of a car which starts at $x = L/2$ at $t = 0$. [Hint: Why does $dx/dt = (30x + 30L)/(15t + L)$? Solve this differential equation. It is separable.]

(b) Show that $u(x, t)$ is constant along straight lines in the $x$–$t$ plane, but the car does not move at a constant velocity.

**57.3.** Suppose that the velocity field $u(x, t)$ is known. What mathematical problem needs to be solved in order to determine the position of a car at later times, which starts (at $t = 0$) at $x = L$?

**57.4.** Determine a velocity field satisfying all the following properties:

(a) at $x = 30t$, $u = 30$;

(b) at $x = 45t + L$, $u = 45$;

(c) the velocity field varies continuously (and steadily) from 30 to 45 as $x$ ranges from $30t$ to $45t$. [Hint: See exercise 57.1.]

(d) $u(x, t) \neq (15x + 30L)/(15t + L)$.

**57.5.** Suppose that $u(x, t) = e^{-t}$.

(a) Sketch curves in $x$–$t$ space along which $u(x, t)$ is constant.

(b) Determine the time dependence of the position of any car.

(c) In the same $x$–$t$ space used in part (a), sketch various different car paths.

**57.6.** Consider an infinite number of cars, each designated by a number $\beta$. Assume the car labeled $\beta$ starts from $x = \beta$ ($\beta > 0$) with zero velocity, and also assume it has a constant acceleration $\beta$.

(a) Determine the position and velocity of each car as a function of time.

(b) Sketch the path of a typical car.

(c) Determine the velocity field $u(x, t)$.

(d) Sketch curves along which $u(x, t)$ is a constant.

**57.7.** If the velocity field $u(x, t)$ is known, show that the trajectory of a car (the position as a function of time) can be sketched by the method of isoclines.

# 58.  Traffic Flow and Traffic Density

What traffic variables could an observer easily measure in addition to car velocities? An observer fixed at a certain position along the highway could measure the number of cars that passed in a given length of time. The observer could compute, for example, the average *number of cars passing per hour* (per lane). This quantity is called the **traffic flow**, $q$. Suppose the following measurements were taken at one place over half-hour intervals:

| Time<br>A.M. | Number of cars<br>passing | Number of cars<br>passing per hour |
|---|---|---|
| 7:00– 7:30 | 433 | 866 |
| 7:30– 8:00 | 652 | 1304 |
| 8:00– 8:30 | 594 | 1188 |
| 8:30– 9:00 | 551 | 1102 |
| 9:00– 9:30 | 280 | 560 |
| 9:30–10:00 | 141 | 282 |
| 10:00–10:30 | 167 | 334 |

In this example, the largest flow of traffic occurred during the period 7:30–8:00 in the morning. Thus the flow $q$ depends on time, $q(t)$, as shown in Fig. 58-1. At different positions along the road, the flow might be different. Thus the flow also depends on $x$, and we write $q(x, t)$.

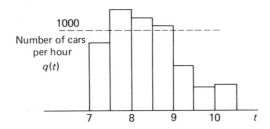

Figure 58-1   Traffic flow, $q(t)$, as a function of time (measured every half hour).

By measuring the traffic flow over half-hour intervals, we are unable to distinguish variations in the flow that occur over shorter lengths of time. For example, we cannot tell that the period from 7:45–8:00 A.M. may have had considerably "heavier" traffic than from 7:30–7:45 A.M. Measurements of traffic flow could have been taken over even shorter time intervals. However, if measurements were made on an extremely short interval of time, for example over 10-second intervals, then the following data might be observed:

| Time $\left(\begin{array}{c}\textit{in seconds}\\\textit{after 7:00}\end{array}\right)$ | Number of cars | Number of cars per hour |
|:---:|:---:|:---:|
| 0–9 | 0 | 0 |
| 10–19 | 2 | 720 |
| 20–29 | 1 | 360 |
| 30–39 | 4 | 1440 |
| 40–49 | 1 | 360 |
| 50–59 | 4 | 1440 |

In these measurements, note that the computed flow fluctuates wildly as a function of time. To remedy these difficulties, we assume that there exists a measuring interval such that

1. it is long enough so that many cars pass the observer in the measuring interval (eliminating the wild fluctuations);
2. it is short enough so that the variations in the traffic flow are not smoothed over by averaging over too long a period of time.

If such a measuring time exists, then the step-like curve for the traffic flow, Fig. 58-1, can be approximated by a continuous function of time as illustrated in Fig. 58-2.

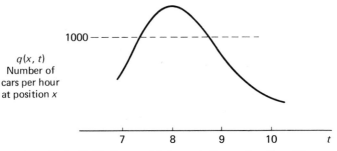

Figure 58-2   Traffic flow modeled as a continuous function of time.

Another standard traffic measurement occurs at fixed times (rather than at fixed positions as for traffic flow). The number of cars (at a fixed time)

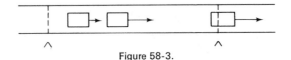

Figure 58-3.

between two positions can be counted, for example, by photography; a sketch appears in Fig. 58-3. A systematic procedure could be used to take into account cars not completely in a given region at a fixed time. Perhaps estimates of fractional cars could be used or perhaps a car is counted only if its center is in the region. These measurements yield the number of cars in a given length of roadway, which might be converted into the *number of cars per mile* (per lane), a quantity called the **density of cars** $p$. Here, all vehicles are treated the same; the word "car" is used loosely to represent any vehicle.

If **traffic density** is measured over $\frac{1}{4}$ of a mile (.4 kilometers) of roadway *at a fixed time*, then a typical measurement might be:

| Distance along road (in miles) | Number of cars | Traffic density, number of cars per mile |
|:---:|:---:|:---:|
| $1-1\frac{1}{4}$ | 23 | 92 |
| $1\frac{1}{4}-1\frac{1}{2}$ | 16 | 64 |
| $1\frac{1}{2}-1\frac{3}{4}$ | 22 | 88 |
| $1\frac{3}{4}-2$ | 8 | 32 |

As another example, imagine a situation in which cars are equally spaced. For convenience it is now assumed (as throughout the discussion of traffic flow) that all vehicles have the same length, $L$. In order to use one unit of length in traffic problems, $L$ is measured in *miles* (kilometers) rather than feet (meters). If the distance between cars is $d$ (the distance $d + L$ is called the spacing), as illustrated in Fig. 58-4, then the density, the number of cars per mile (kilometer), is

$$p = \frac{1}{L + d}. \tag{58.1}$$

(This result is most easily obtained by considering one mile (kilometer) of cars in this configuration).

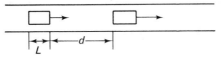

Figure 58-4   Traffic density equals the inverse of the spacing [$p = 1/(L + d)$].

As with traffic flow, there are difficulties with traffic density if measurements are made on too short an interval. Suppose the distance used in measuring density is very short ($\frac{1}{500}$ mile $\approx 10$ feet $\approx 3$ meters); then a plausible traffic situation is depicted in Fig. 58-5. The measured data (using approximate fractions of cars) would be:

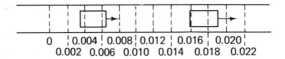

Distance (in miles)

Figure 58-5   Measuring traffic density using an extremely short interval.

| Distance | Number of cars | Numbers of cars per mile |
|---|---|---|
| 0–.002 | 0 | 0 |
| .002–.004 | $\frac{1}{6}$ | 83 |
| .004–.006 | $\frac{2}{3}$ | 333 |
| .006–.008 | $\frac{1}{6}$ | 83 |
| .008–.010 | 0 | 0 |
| .010–.012 | 0 | 0 |
| .012–.014 | 0 | 0 |
| .014–.016 | 0 | 0 |
| .016–.018 | $\frac{2}{3}$ | 333 |
| .018–.020 | $\frac{1}{3}$ | 167 |
| .020–.022 | 0 | 0 |

If the traffic density $\rho(x, t)$ is sketched as a function of position (at a fixed time), then we obtain Fig. 58-6. This measured density is an extremely discontinuous function. On the other hand, if measurements of density are taken only over large distances (for example, every 5 miles), then only average densities are computed; the real local variability of traffic density would be smoothed out.

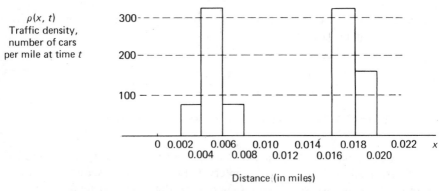

Distance (in miles)

Figure 58-6   Spatially discontinuous measurement of traffic density.

If we expect to *approximate* density as a continuous function of $x$, we obtain Fig. 58-7 and then densities must be measured over intervals of distance that are not too small nor too large. If the measuring distance is too

$\rho$

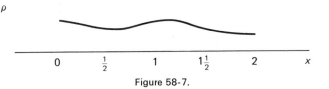

| | | | | | |
|---|---|---|---|---|---|
| 0 | $\frac{1}{2}$ | 1 | $1\frac{1}{2}$ | 2 | $x$ |

Figure 58-7.

large, then an average density is computed that does not properly take into account variations of density. On the other hand, if the measuring distance is too small, then the large variability of the traffic data disguises the desired smooth nature of density. The measuring distance must be large enough so that many cars are contained therein, but small enough so that variations in densities can be measured.

Let us illustrate by an example the significance of the measuring interval. Consider a $\frac{2}{10}$ of a mile segment of a (one-lane) highway, further subdivided into one hundred smaller intervals of equal length, with boundaries labeled from 0 to 100. Suppose a photograph was taken and from it we determined that cars were located at the following positions:

> 1.0, 3.1, 6.1, 9.4, 12.7, 14.1, 15.2, 16.9, 18.9, 20.1, 21.5, 23.5,
> 25.8, 28.9, 31.3, 34.8, 37.0, 40.1, 43.4, 44.9, 46.4, 47.9, 49.6,
> 51.6, 53.3, 54.8, 56.6, 58.3, 59.6, 60.6, 61.9, 62.9, 63.7, 65.0,
> 66.6, 69.5, 72.1, 76.3, 78.8, 81.6,84.2, 87.7, 90.8, 95.1, 99.3,

each car illustrated in Fig. 58-8 as a '•':

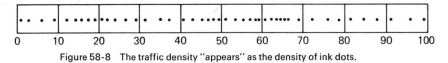

| | | | | | | | | | |
|---|---|---|---|---|---|---|---|---|---|
| 0 | 10 | 20 | 30 | 40 | 50 | 60 | 70 | 80 | 90 | 100 |

Figure 58-8   The traffic density "appears" as the density of ink dots.

From the data (or diagram) we see that near the 20 mark cars are approximately $1\frac{1}{2}$–2 intervals apart. Further along the roadway cars spread out to about 3 units apart (near the 30 mark) before again becoming close together between the 45 and 65 mark (the distances apart being about $1\frac{1}{2}$–2 units apart). We will calculate the density at the 50 mark along the highway. For simplicity, let us imagine the cars to have zero length. Cars near the 50 mark are slightly greater than $1\frac{1}{2}$ units apart and hence the traffic density is slightly less than 1 car per $1\frac{1}{2}$ units of length. Equivalently, the traffic density is slightly less than 333 cars per mile, since each mark is $\frac{1}{100}$ of $\frac{2}{10}$ of a mile (or $\frac{2}{1000}$ of a mile). To be more precise let us see how the calculation of density at the 50 mark depends on the measuring interval. If we use a length of highway of $m$ units *centered* around the 50 mark, then the density at 50 is defined to be the number of cars between $50 - m/2$ and $50 + m/2$ divided by the length $m$ (converted to cars per mile). On this basis we set up a chart recording the measured density:

| Length of interval, m | .5 | 1.0 | 1.5 | 2 | 3 | 4 | 5 | 6 | 7 | 8 | 10 | 12 | 14 | 16 | 18 | 20 | 30 | 40 | 50 | 60 | 70 | 80 | 90 | 100 |
|---|---|---|---|---|---|---|---|---|---|---|---|---|---|---|---|---|---|---|---|---|---|---|---|---|
| Interval of interest | $49\frac{3}{4}$ $50\frac{1}{4}$ | $49\frac{1}{4}$ $50\frac{1}{2}$ | $49\frac{1}{4}$ $50\frac{3}{4}$ | 49 51 | $48\frac{1}{2}$ $51\frac{1}{2}$ | 48 52 | $47\frac{1}{2}$ $52\frac{1}{2}$ | 47 53 | $46\frac{1}{2}$ $53\frac{1}{2}$ | 46 54 | 45 55 | 44 56 | 43 57 | 42 58 | 41 59 | 40 60 | 35 65 | 30 70 | 25 75 | 20 80 | 15 85 | 10 90 | 5 95 | 0 100 |
| Number of cars | 0 | 1 | 1 | 1 | 1 | 2 | 3 | 3 | 4 | 5 | 6 | 7 | 9 | 9 | 10 | 12 | 18 | 22 | 25 | 30 | 35 | 38 | 41 | 45 |
| Number of cars per interval | 0 | 1 | $\frac{2}{3}$ | $\frac{1}{2}$ | $\frac{1}{3}$ | $\frac{2}{4}$ | $\frac{3}{5}$ | $\frac{3}{6}$ | $\frac{4}{7}$ | $\frac{5}{8}$ | $\frac{6}{10}$ | $\frac{7}{12}$ | $\frac{9}{14}$ | $\frac{9}{16}$ | $\frac{10}{18}$ | $\frac{12}{20}$ | $\frac{18}{30}$ | $\frac{22}{40}$ | $\frac{25}{50}$ | $\frac{30}{60}$ | $\frac{35}{70}$ | $\frac{38}{80}$ | $\frac{41}{90}$ | $\frac{45}{100}$ |
| Traffic density: number of cars per mile (number of cars per interval × 500) | 0 | 500 | 333 | 250 | 167 | 250 | 300 | 250 | 280 | 312 | 300 | 292 | 321 | 281 | 278 | 300 | 300 | 275 | 250 | 250 | 250 | 237 | 228 | 225 |

This is more strikingly illustrated by sketching the traffic density as a function of the measuring interval, as in Fig. 58-9. For a meaningful calculation, many cars should be contained in the measuring interval, but not so many that the local average seems to be lost. Three cars is too few, but to get 9 cars requires a fairly long distance. An interval between 10 and 20 units long would seem appropriate in this problem, yielding a measured density between 275 and 325 cars per mile. For short measuring intervals, violent fluctuations occur. As $m$ is increased, eventually a car is found and the average density dramatically increases. The density then gradually decreases (as $m$ increases) again until the next car is located. The amplitude of the fluctuation decreases as the measuring interval gets longer. For extremely large measuring distances the

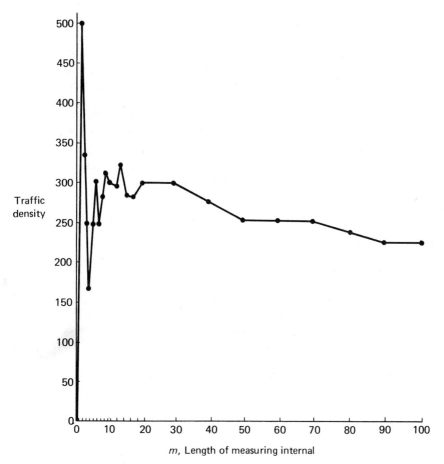

Figure 58-9   Rapid variation of density's dependence on measuring length.

average density is approaching 225 cars per mile, an amount much less than that associated with the local traffic conditions near the 50 mark.

For a reasonable *local* value of density to exist we must assume that the distance between cars stays approximately the same over a distance that includes many cars. From this example, we see this is not always entirely the case (in particular, this situation gets worse for less dense traffic conditions). However, in this text we will assume that a local traffic density is a reasonable variable.

Alternatively, especially when an appropriate measuring interval does not exist, a statistical theory may be formulated. We will limit our investigation to deterministic models.

In this text we will primarily be concerned with traffic situations involving a large number of vehicles. We will mostly be interested in the collective behavior of many vehicles (a macroscopic theory). For this reason we will be satisfied with investigating the behavior of average traffic variables (i.e., density and flow). We will assume measuring intervals exist (in space and time) such that the traffic density and traffic flow are smooth functions of position and time without the local variations being lost as a result of an extremely long measuring interval. Neglecting the possibly rapid variation from car to car of car-following distance and thus utilizing the concept of a smooth traffic density will yield a description of traffic flow problems which hopefully will be a good model. This is called the **continuum hypothesis**. (It is also used in fluid dynamics. Can you guess where the continuum hypothesis arises in investigating motions of liquids and gases?)

# EXERCISES

**58.1.** If at 10 m.p.h. (16 k.p.h.) cars are one car-length behind each other, then what is the density of traffic? [You may assume that the average length of a car is approximately 16 feet (5 meters)].

**58.2.** Assume that the probability $P$ of exactly one car being located in any fixed short segment of highway of length $\Delta x$ is approximately proportional to the length, $P = \lambda \Delta x$. Also assume that the probability of two or more cars in that segment of highway is negligible.

(a) Show that the probability of there being exactly $n$ vehicles along a high-way of length $x$, $P_n(x)$, satisfies the **Poisson distribution**,

$$P_n(x) = \frac{(\lambda x)^n e^{-\lambda x}}{n!}.$$

[Hint: Consider $P_n(x + \Delta x)$ and form a differential equation for $P_n(x)$, (see Sec. 36).]

(b) Evaluate and interpret the following quantities:
   (1) $P_n(0)$,   $n \neq 0$.

    (2) $P_0(x)$,   $x \neq 0$.
    (3) $P_1(x)$,   $x \neq 0$.
(c) Calculate the expected number of cars on a highway of length $x$. Interpret your answer.

**58.3.** Consider the example discussed in this section in which the density is calculated as a function of the measuring interval. The density has a discontinuity at distances that first include an additional car.

    (a) What is the jump in density (i.e., the magnitude of the discontinuity)?
    (b) If cars are equally spaced (100 per mile), how large must the measuring interval be such that discontinuities in density are less than 5 percent of the density? How many cars are contained in that measuring distance?
    (c) Generalize your result to a roadway with a constant density of $\rho_0$ per mile.

# 59.  Flow Equals Density Times Velocity

In the past sections we have briefly discussed the three fundamental traffic variables: velocity, density, and flow. We will show that there is a close relationship among these three. We first consider one of the simplest possible traffic situations. Suppose that on some road, traffic is moving at a constant velocity $u_0$ with a constant density $\rho_0$, as shown in Fig. 59-1. Since each car

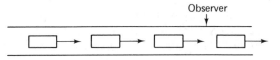

Figure 59-1    Constant flow of cars.

moves at the same speed, the distance between cars remains constant. Hence the traffic density does not change. What is the flow of cars? To answer that, consider an observer measuring the traffic flow (the number of cars per hour that pass the observer). In $\tau$ hours each car has moved $u_0\tau$ distance (moving at a constant velocity, the distance travelled equals the velocity multiplied by the time), and thus the number of cars that pass the observer in $\tau$ hours is the number of cars in $u_0\tau$ distance, see Fig. 59-2. Since $\rho_0$ is the number of cars

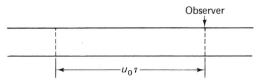

Figure 59-2    Distance a car, moving at constant velocity $u_0$, travels in $\tau$ hours.

per mile and there are $u_0\tau$ miles, then $\rho_0 u_0 \tau$ is the number of cars passing the observer in $\tau$ hours. Thus the number of cars *per hour* which we have called the traffic flow, $q$, is

$$q = \rho_0 u_0.$$

Although this has been derived from an oversimplified case, we will show that this is a fundamental law, the

> traffic flow = (traffic density)(velocity field).

If the traffic variables depend on $x$ and $t$, i.e., $q(x, t)$, $\rho(x, t)$, $u(x, t)$, then we will still show that

$$q(x, t) = \rho(x, t)u(x, t). \tag{59.1}$$

An easy way to show this is to consider the number of cars that pass $x = x_0$ in a *very small* time $\Delta t$, i.e., between $t_0$ and $t_0 + \Delta t$. In that small time the cars have not moved far and hence (if $\rho$ and $u$ are continuous functions of $x$ and $t$) $u(x, t)$ and $\rho(x, t)$ can be approximated by constants, their values at $x = x_0$ and $t = t_0$. In a small time $\Delta t$, the cars that occupy a short space, approximately $u(x, t)\Delta t$, will pass the observer, as shown in Fig. 59-3. The number of cars passing is approximately $u(x, t)\Delta t\, \rho(x, t)$. The traffic flow is given by equation 59.1. Thus the results for constant $u$ and $\rho$ do not need modification for nonuniform $u(x, t)$ and $\rho(x, t)$. Consequently, the three fundamental traffic variables, density $\rho(x, t)$, velocity $u(x, t)$ and flow $q(x, t)$, are related by equation 59.1.

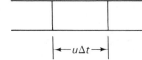

$\leftarrow u\Delta t \rightarrow$

Figure 59-3 Approximate distance a car travels in $\Delta t$ hours.

# EXERCISES

**59.1.** For traffic moving at 10 m.p.h. (16 k.p.h.) such that cars are one car length behind each other, what is the traffic flow?

**59.2.** Suppose that at position $x_0$ the traffic flow is known, $q(x_0, t)$, and varies with time. Calculate the number of cars that pass $x_0$, between $t = 0$ and $t = t_0$.

**59.3.** In an experiment the total number of cars that pass a position $x_0$ after $t = 0$, $M(x_0, t)$, is measured as a function of time. Assume this series of points has been smoothed to make a continuous curve.

(a)    Briefly explain why the curve $M(x_0, t)$ is increasing as $t$ increases.

(b)    What is the traffic flow at $t = \tau$?

# 60.  Conservation of the Number of Cars

In this section, we formulate a deterministic model for traffic flow. Suppose that the density and the velocity field are known initially for a highway of infinite length. Can we predict the densities and velocities at future times? For example, if a traffic light turns red and shortly later green, then can the pattern of traffic be predicted?

We can consider the two fundamental traffic variables to be $\rho(x, t)$ and $u(x, t)$ (since $q = \rho u$ was demonstrated in the previous section). However, suppose we knew the initial traffic density ($\rho(x, 0)$) and the traffic velocity field for all time ($u(x, t)$). Then the motion of each car satisfies the following first order differential equation:

$$\frac{dx}{dt} = u(x, t) \quad \text{with} \quad x(0) = x_0.$$

Solving this equation (which at least can be accomplished numerically using a computer) would determine the position of each car at later times. Consequently at later times, we could calculate the density (although this calculation may be difficult; it would involve deciding what measuring interval to use). Thus, the traffic density at future times can be calculated knowing the traffic velocity (and the initial density).

We want to determine how the density can be calculated easily if the velocity is known (later we will solve problems in which the velocity also isn't known). By following each car we insisted that the number of cars stays the same. However, the traffic variables density, velocity, and flow were introduced so that we wouldn't have to follow individual cars. Let us now instead try to "conserve" cars, but do so using these traffic *field* variables.

On some interval of roadway, between $x = a$ and $x = b$, as shown in Fig. 60-1, the number of cars $N$ is the integral of the traffic density:

$$\boxed{N = \int_a^b \rho(x, t)\, dx.} \tag{60.1}$$

Figure 60-1    Cars entering and leaving a segment of roadway.

If there are no entrances nor exits on this road, then the number of cars between $x = a$ and $x = b$ might still change in time. The number decreases due to cars leaving the region at $x = b$, and the number increases as a result of cars entering the region at $x = a$. Assuming that no cars are created or destroyed in between, then the changes in the number of cars result from crossings at $x = a$ and $x = b$ only. If cars are flowing at the rate of 300 cars per hour at $x = a$, but flowing at the rate of 275 cars per hour at $x = b$, then clearly the number of cars between $x = a$ and $x = b$ is increasing by 25 cars per hour. We can generalize this result to situations in which the number of cars crossing each boundary (the traffic flow $q(a, t)$ and $q(b, t)$) is not constant in time. The rate of change of the number of cars, $dN/dt$, equals the number per unit time crossing at $x = a$ (moving to the right) minus the number of cars per unit time crossing (again moving to the right) at $x = b$, or

$$\frac{dN}{dt} = q(a, t) - q(b, t), \tag{60.2}$$

since the number of cars per unit time is the flow $q(x, t)$.

Perhaps this derivation of this important result was not clear to some of you. An alternate derivation of this result follows. The difference in number of cars between times $t + \Delta t$ and $t$, $N(t + \Delta t) - N(t)$, equals the number crossing at $x = a$ between $t + \Delta t$ and $t$, which for $\Delta t$ small is approximately $q(a, t) \Delta t$, minus the number crossing at $x = b$ between $t + \Delta t$ and $t$, which for $\Delta t$ small is approximately $q(b, t)\Delta t$. Thus,

$$N(t + \Delta t) - N(t) \approx \Delta t(q(a, t) - q(b, t)).$$

Dividing by $\Delta t$ and taking the limit as $\Delta t \to 0$ again yields equation 60.2. We improve this last derivation by eliminating the need for using an approximation. Consider the difference between the number of cars in the region at $t = t_0$ and $t = t_1$ (these times do not need to be near each other). An exact expression is needed for the number of cars crossing at $x = b$ between $t = t_0$ and $t = t_1$. Since $q(b, t)$ is the number crossing at $x = b$ per unit time, then $\int_{t_0}^{t_1} q(b, t) \, dt$ is the number crossing at $x = b$ between $t = t_0$ and $t = t_1$. In the approximate derivation, $t = t_1$ was near $t = t_0$ and this integral was approximated by $\Delta t\, q(b, t_0)$. However, without an approximation

$$N(t_1) - N(t_0) = \int_{t_0}^{t_1} q(a, t)\, dt - \int_{t_0}^{t_1} q(b, t)\, dt = \int_{t_0}^{t_1} (q(a, t) - q(b, t))\, dt.$$

Divide this expression by $t_1 - t_0$ and take the limit as $t_1$ tends to $t_0$. Equivalently, (but slightly more elegantly) take the derivative with respect to $t_1$. Since $t_0$ does not depend on $t_1$ (they are two independent times), we obtain

$$\frac{dN(t_1)}{dt_1} = \frac{d}{dt_1} \int_{t_0}^{t_1} (q(a, t) - q(b, t))\, dt.$$

From the Fundamental Theorem of Calculus (the theorem that implies that the derivative of the integral of $f(x)$ is $f(x)$ itself), it follows that

$$\frac{dN(t_1)}{dt_1} = q(a, t_1) - q(b, t_1).$$

Since $t_1$ could be any arbitrary time, $t_1$ is replaced in notation by $t$, and thus the previously stated result equation 60.2 is rederived.

Combining equations 60.1 and 60.2, yields

$$\boxed{\frac{d}{dt} \int_{a}^{b} \rho(x, t)\, dx = q(a, t) - q(b, t).} \qquad (60.3)$$

This equation expresses the fact that changes in the number of cars are due only to the flow across the boundary. No cars are created or destroyed; the number of cars is conserved. This does not mean the number of cars between $x = a$ and $x = b$ is constant (if that were true then $(d/dt) \int_{a}^{b} \rho(x, t)\, dx = 0$ or $q(a, t) = q(b, t)$). Equation 60.3 is called a *conservation law in integral form* or, more concisely, an **integral conservation law**. This law expresses a property of traffic over a finite length of roadway $a \le x \le b$.

As an example, consider an extremely long highway which we model by a highway of infinite length. Let us assume that the flow of cars approaches zero as $x$ approaches both $\pm \infty$,

$$\lim_{x \to \pm\infty} q(x, t) = 0.$$

From equation 60.3, it follows that

$$\frac{d}{dt} \int_{-\infty}^{\infty} \rho(x, t)\, dx = 0.$$

Integrating this yields

$$\int_{-\infty}^{\infty} \rho(x, t)\, dx = \text{constant},$$

which states that the total number of cars is constant for all time. The constant could be evaluated if *either* the initial number of cars $N_0$ or the initial density $\rho(x, 0)$ were known:

$$\int_{-\infty}^{\infty} \rho(x, t) \, dx = N_0 = \int_{-\infty}^{\infty} \rho(x, 0) \, dx.$$

The integral conservation law, equation 60.3, will be expressed as a **local conservation law**, valid at each position of the roadway. We will do so in three *equivalent* ways.* In all three, the endpoints of the segment of the roadway, $x = a$ and $x = b$, are considered as additional independent variables. Thus, the full derivative with respect to time in equation 60.3 must be replaced by a partial derivative,

$$\frac{\partial}{\partial t} \int_a^b \rho(x, t) \, dx = q(a, t) - q(b, t), \qquad (60.4a)$$

since the derivation of equation 60.3 assumed the positions $x = a$ and $x = b$ are fixed in time. In other words, $\partial/\partial t$ means $d/dt$ holding $a$ and $b$ fixed in time. In the first derivation, we investigate a small segment of the roadway. Rough approximations are made, which yield the correct result. However, those who are not convinced by our first approximation should be patient, as we will shortly improve the derivation.

(1) Consider the integral conservation of cars over a small interval of highway from $x = a$ to $x = a + \Delta a$. Thus from equation 60.4a,

$$\frac{\partial}{\partial t} \int_a^{a+\Delta a} \rho(x, t) \, dx = q(a, t) - q(a + \Delta a, t).$$

Divide by $-\Delta a$ and take the limit as $\Delta a \rightarrow 0$:

$$\lim_{\Delta a \to 0} \frac{\partial}{\partial t} \frac{1}{-\Delta a} \int_a^{a+\Delta a} \rho(x, t) \, dx = \lim_{\Delta a \to 0} \frac{q(a, t) - q(a + \Delta a, t)}{-\Delta a}. \qquad (60.4b)$$

The right-hand side of equation 60.4b is exactly the definition of the derivative of $q(a, t)$ with respect to $a$ (properly a partial derivative should be used, since $t$ is fixed), $(\partial/\partial a)q(a, t)$. On the left-hand side of equation 60.4b the limit can be performed in two equivalent ways:

(a) The integral is the area under the curve $\rho(x, t)$ between $x = a$ and $x = a + \Delta a$. Since $\Delta a$ is small, the integral can be approximated by one rectangle; as shown in Fig. 60-2. The number of cars between $a$

---

*In these derivations we will assume $q(x, t)$, $\rho(x, t)$ and $u(x, t)$ are continuous functions of $x$ and $t$. In later sections (see Sec. 77) we will find it necessary to relax these assumptions. We will find that, although equation 60.2 is always valid, later results of this section are valid only in regions in which the traffic variables are continuous functions of $x$ and $t$.

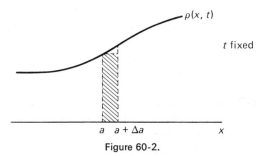

Figure 60-2.

and $a + \Delta a$ can be approximated by the length of roadway $\Delta a$ times the traffic density at $x = a$, $\rho(a, t)$. Thus,

$$-\frac{1}{\Delta a} \int_a^{a+\Delta a} \rho(x, t)\, dx \approx -\rho(a, t).$$

In a subsequent derivation, (2), we show that the error vanishes as $\Delta a \rightarrow 0$. Consequently we derive from equation 60.4b that

$$\boxed{\frac{\partial}{\partial t}\rho(a, t) + \frac{\partial}{\partial a}q(a, t) = 0.} \tag{60.5a}$$

(b) On the other hand, introduce the function $N(\bar{x}, t)$, the number of cars on the roadway between any fixed position $x_0$ and the variable position $\bar{x}$,

$$N(\bar{x}, t) \equiv \int_{x_0}^{\bar{x}} \rho(x, t)\, dx.$$

Then, the average number of cars per mile between $a$ and $a + \Delta a$ is

$$-\frac{1}{\Delta a} \int_a^{a+\Delta a} \rho(x, t)\, dx = \frac{N(a + \Delta a, t) - N(a, t)}{-\Delta a}.$$

In the limit as $\Delta a \rightarrow 0$, the right-hand side is $-\partial N(a, t)/\partial a$. Using the definition of $N(a, t)$, again from the Fundamental Theorem of Calculus,

$$\frac{\partial N(a, t)}{\partial a} = \rho(a, t).$$

Thus the left-hand side of equation 60.4b again equals $-(\partial/\partial t)\rho(a, t)$. By either method, (a) or (b), equation 60.5a follows. Since equation 60.5a holds for all values of $a$, it is more appropriate to replace $a$ by $x$, in which case

$$\boxed{\frac{\partial \rho(x, t)}{\partial t} + \frac{\partial}{\partial x}[q(x, t)] = 0,} \tag{60.5b}$$

or simply

$$\frac{\partial \rho}{\partial t} + \frac{\partial q}{\partial x} = 0. \qquad \text{(60.5c)}$$

This is a **partial differential equation** (an equation involving partial derivatives). It expresses a relationship between traffic density and traffic flow derived by assuming that the number of cars is conserved, that is, cars are not created nor destroyed. It is valid everywhere (all $x$) and for all time. It is called the equation of **conservation of cars**.

(2) The equation of conservation of cars can be derived more expeditiously. Consider the intergral conservation law, equation 60.4a, for any finite segment of highway, $a \leq x \leq b$. Now take the partial derivative with respect to $b$. (This is equivalent to letting $b = a + \Delta a$, dividing by $\Delta a$, and taking the limit as $\Delta a \longrightarrow 0$). Thus,

$$\frac{\partial \rho(b, t)}{\partial t} = -\frac{\partial}{\partial b}(q(b, t)).$$

Since $b$ represents any position on the road, again $b$ is replaced by $x$, yielding the equation of conservation of cars, equation 60.5.

(3) An alternate derivation for a roadway of finite length ($a \leq x \leq b$) is based on noting that the following relation is clearly valid for the right-hand side of equation 60.4a,

$$q(a, t) - q(b, t) = -\int_a^b \frac{\partial}{\partial x}[q(x, t)]\, dx.$$

Thus, from equation 60.4a,

$$\int_a^b \left[ \frac{\partial \rho(x, t)}{\partial t} + \frac{\partial q(x, t)}{\partial x} \right] dx = 0. \qquad \text{(60.6)}$$

Equation 60.5 immediately follows by taking the derivative with respect to $b$, as was done in derivation (2). However, let us briefly discuss a different and powerful argument. Equation 60.6 states that the definite integral of some quantity is always zero for all values of the independently varying limits of the integral. The only function whose integral is zero for *all* intervals is the zero function. Hence, again equation 60.5 follows.

By three equivalent methods, we have shown that

$$\frac{\partial \rho}{\partial t} + \frac{\partial q}{\partial x} = 0 \qquad \text{(60.7)}$$

must be valid if there are no entrances nor exits along a roadway, expressing the conservation of cars. Equation 60.7 is valid in many situations having nothing to do with traffic. In general, if $\rho$ is any local quantity that is conserved (in one spatial dimension) and if $q$ is the flow of that quantity across a boundary (often in physics called the **flux**), then it can be shown, using the same arguments we have just developed, that equation 60.7 is valid!* Sometimes experiments must be performed to determine how the flow $q$ depends on other quantities in the problem. However, for traffic problems, we know from Sec. 59 that

$$\boxed{q = \rho u,}$$

and thus conservation of cars can be written as

$$\boxed{\frac{\partial \rho}{\partial t} + \frac{\partial}{\partial x}(\rho u) = 0,} \qquad \textbf{(60.8)}$$

a partial differential equation relating the traffic density and the velocity field.

# EXERCISES

**60.1.** Consider a semi-infinite highway $0 \leq x < \infty$ (with no entrances or exits other than at $x = 0$). Show that the number of cars on the highway at time $t$ is

$$N_0 + \int_0^t q(0, \tau)\, d\tau,$$

where $N_0$ is the number of cars on the highway at $t = 0$. (You may assume that $\rho(x, t) \longrightarrow 0$ as $x \longrightarrow \infty$.)

**60.2.** Suppose that we are interested in the change in the number of cars $N(t)$ between two observers, one fixed at $x = a$ and the other moving in some prescribed manner, $x = b(t)$:

$$N(t) = \int_a^{b(t)} \rho(x, t)\, dx$$

(a)  The derivative of an integral with a variable limit is

$$\frac{dN}{dt} = \frac{db}{dt}\rho(b, t) + \int_a^{b(t)} \frac{\partial \rho}{\partial t}\, dx.$$

(Note that the integrand, $\rho(x, t)$, also depends on $t$.) Show this result

---

*In two or three dimensions using the divergence theorem equation 60.7 must be replaced by $\partial \rho / \partial t + \nabla \cdot \vec{q} = 0$, where $\vec{q}$ is the vector flow of the quantity whose density is $\rho$.

either by considering $\lim_{\Delta t \to 0} [N(t + \Delta t) - N(t)]/\Delta t$ or by using the chain rule for derivatives.

(b)  Using $\partial \rho / \partial t = -\partial / \partial x \, (\rho u)$ show that

$$\frac{dN}{dt} = -\rho(b, t)\left[u(b, t) - \frac{db}{dt}\right] + \rho(a, t)u(a, t).$$

(c)  Interpret the result of part (b) if the moving observer is in a car moving with the traffic.

**60.3.** (a)  Without using any mathematics, explain why $\int_{a(t)}^{b(t)} \rho(x, t) \, dx$ is constant if $a$ and $b$ (not equal to each other) both move with the traffic.

(b)  Using part (a), rederive equation 60.2.

(c)  Assuming $\partial \rho / \partial t = -(\partial / \partial x)(\rho u)$, verify mathematically that part (a) is valid (exercise 60.2 may be helpful).

**60.4.**  If the traffic flow is increasing as $x$ increases ($\partial q / \partial x > 0$), explain physically why the density must be decreasing in time ($\partial \rho / \partial t < 0$).

# 61.  A Velocity-Density Relationship

The two variables, traffic density and car velocity, are related by only one equation, conservation of cars,

$$\boxed{\frac{\partial \rho}{\partial t} + \frac{\partial}{\partial x}(\rho u) = 0.}$$

$\qquad\qquad$ **(61.1)**

*If the velocity field is known*, equation 61.1 reduces to a partial differential equation for the unknown traffic density. In this case, equation 61.1 can be used to predict the future traffic density if the initial traffic density is known. As an initial value problem, equation 61.1 is analogous to the ordinary differential equation for the position of a mass or the ordinary differential equations developed in population dynamics. We could pursue the solving of this partial differential equation. However, this appears senseless since *we do not know the velocity field*.

The unknown velocity field must be investigated. Considering the cars as particles, we need to know the particles' velocities. If this was a mechanical system, then we would investigate the forces in the system and use Newton's law to study the motion of the particles. However, there is no equivalent to Newton's law prescribing the manner in which cars must move. It is not forces which cause cars to move; it is the decisions of individual drivers. What factors influence individual car velocities?

A way to investigate the velocity field is to conduct experiments to understand an individual's response to traffic stimuli. Why does a particular driver drive the way he or she does? We will postpone a discussion of such experiments and the resulting mathematical models (see Sec. 64 on car-following models). Instead, let us describe some observed traffic phenomena with which you are no doubt familar. If traffic is sufficiently light, then the driver of each car has the freedom to do as he or she wishes within certain limitations (i.e., speed limits if the driver is law abiding, or certainly the technological limits of car performance). Only occasionally will each driver slow down because of the presence of other vehicles. As traffic increases to a more moderate level, encounters with slower moving vehicles are more numerous. It is still not difficult to pass slower-moving cars, and hence the drivers' average speed is not appreciably less than the desired speed. However, in heavy traffic changing lanes becomes difficult, and consequently the average speed of the traffic is lowered.

On the basis of these types of observations, we make a basic simplifying assumption that at any point along the road *the velocity of a car depends only on the density of cars*,

$$u = u(\rho).$$

$$(61.2)$$

Lighthill and Whitham* and independently Richards† in the mid-1950s proposed this type of mathematical model of traffic flow.

If there are no other cars on the highway (corresponding to very low traffic densities), then the car would travel at the maximum speed $u_{max}$,

$$u(0) = u_{max}.$$

$$(61.3)$$

$u_{max}$ is sometimes referred to as the "mean free speed" corresponding to the velocity cars would move at if they were free from interference from other cars. However, as the density increases (that is as there are more and more cars per mile) eventually the presence of the other cars would slow the car down. As the density increases further the velocities of the cars would continue to diminish, and thus

$$\frac{du}{d\rho} \equiv u'(\rho) \leq 0.$$

$$(61.4)$$

---

*LIGHTHILL, M. J. and WHITHAM, G. B., "On kinematic waves II. A theory of traffic flow on long crowded roads," *Proc. Roy. Soc. A*, *229*, 317–345 (1955).

†RICHARDS, P. I., "Shock waves on the highway," *Operations Research 4*, 42–51 (1956).

At a certain density cars stand still. This maximum density, $\rho_{\max}$, usually corresponds to what is called bumper-to-bumper traffic,

$$u(\rho_{\max}) = 0. \qquad (61.5)$$

(Cars are observed to come to a stop in dense traffic before cars touch each other. Thus $\rho_{\max} < 1/L$, where $L$ is the average length of a vehicle.) Consequently, the general type of curve shown in Fig. 61-1, $u = u(\rho)$, relating the two traffic variables (velocity and density) is reasonable. As stated earlier, the curve is steadily decreasing, that is $u'(\rho) \leq 0$.

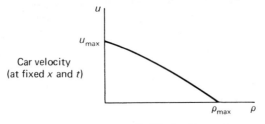

Car velocity
(at fixed $x$ and $t$)

Traffic density

Figure 61-1    Car velocity diminishes as traffic density increases.

It is not being suggested that the dependence of the velocity on the density is the same for all road conditions; a different segment of the same highway might have a different relationship (for example, because of a different road curvature and banking). Furthermore there may be time dependence in the relationship, $u(\rho, x, t)$, as a result, for examples, of the effects a police car (either moving or stationary) or weather conditions have on car velocities. If a speed limit $u_{SL}$ is obeyed, then, for example, $u_{\max} = u_{SL}$. However, the speed limit need not be constant as it might differ in various sections of the roadway. (Usually, but not always, at fixed positions along the highway, the speed limit is the same. An exception occurs when the speed limit at night differs from that during the day. Another such example is reduced speed limits near some schools during school hours.) However, we will primarily investigate a given stretch of highway with approximately constant properties (same number of lanes, no intersections, and so on). Thus we will assume $u = u(\rho)$.

There are many assumptions involved in this hypothesis. It states that every driver drives at the same velocity given the same spacing (density). This is clearly not valid, though it may *not* be a very bad approximation. We ignore the possibly erratic behavior of individual drivers. Perhaps it would be more realistic to introduce a stochastic model in which it is proposed that at a certain density some percentage of drivers drive at certain speeds and others drive at slightly different speeds. We will not discuss such stochastic models although some traffic researchers have developed mathematical models along these lines.

Some experiments have indicated that $u = u(\rho)$ is reasonable while traffic is accelerating and also reasonable while traffic is decelerating, but the velocity-density curve is different for those two circumstances.

If $u = u(\rho)$, then a high speed car as it approaches a slower line of traffic must itself slow down. This theory does not take into account that on multilane highways passing is not only permitted but is a quite frequent event. In order for this theory to be a good approximation, the effects of car passing must be small, as for examples, on one-lane roads, tunnels, or extremely crowded highways.

Another assumption is that the velocity only depends on the density, $u = u(\rho)$, not, for example, on the traffic density a few cars ahead (which may be quite different). Perhaps this is an important consideration because your own experience as a passenger or driver tells you to slow down if you observe trouble ahead; you do not wait to slow down until you actually reach the trouble. Modifications in the mathematical model to include these kinds of effects also have been attempted.

In addition $u = u(\rho, x, t)$ implies that if $\rho$ changes, then $u$ changes instantaneously. Thus the model as formulated will not take into account the finite driver reaction time nor the finite response time it takes an automobile engine to change velocity (accelerate or decelerate). These effects can also be incorporated into a more refined mathematical model.

Now that we have enumerated a number of objections to the model, let us nevertheless investigate its implications. This model represents a possible first step in the development of a mathematical theory of traffic flow.

# EXERCISES

**61.1.** Many state laws say that for each 10 m.p.h. (16 k.p.h.) of speed you should stay at least one car length behind the car in front of you. Assuming that people obey this law (i.e., *exactly one* length), determine the density of cars as a function of speed (you may assume the average length of a car is 16 feet (5 meters)). There is another law that gives a maximum speed limit (assume this is 50 m.p.h. (80 k.p.h.)). Find the flow of cars as a function of density.

**61.2.** The state laws on following distances, briefly discussed in exercise 61.1, were developed in order to prescribe spacing between cars such that rear-end collisions could be avoided.

    (a) Assume the car immediately ahead stops instantaneously. How far would the driver following at $u$ m.p.h. travel, if

(1) the driver's reaction time was $\tau$, and

(2) after then, the driver decelerated at a constant maximum deceleration $\alpha$? (Do not ignore the length of a car, $L$.)

(b)  The calculation in part (a) may seem somewhat conservative, since cars
rarely stop instantaneously. Instead, assume the first car also decelerates
at the same maximum rate $\alpha$, but the driver following still takes time $\tau$
to react. How far back does a car have to be traveling at $u$ m.p.h. in
order to prevent a rear-end collision? (Again, do not ignore the length
of a car, $L$.)

(c)  Show that the law described in exercise 61.1 corresponds to part (b) if
human reaction time is about 1 second and the length of a car is about
16 feet (5 meters).

**61.3.**  Assume that a velocity field, $u(x, t)$, exists. Show that the acceleration of an
individual car is given by

$$\frac{\partial u}{\partial t} + u\frac{\partial u}{\partial x}.$$

# 62.  Experimental Observations

In this section, we will discuss some experimental evidence which reinforces
the qualitative arguments of the previous section. The velocity is a function
of density $u = u(\rho)$, which we assume is valid on a stretch of road for which
road variables, such as the number of lanes and the smoothness of the road,
are constant.

Perhaps the best place to observe traffic flow without inhomogeneities
would be in tunnels, bridges, or highways. The following traffic data was
obtained by Greenberg.* Traffic was measured in the Lincoln Tunnel (a
heavily traveled approximately two-mile long tunnel under the Hudson River
connecting New Jersey and New York City) and also on the Merritt Parkway
(a major limited-access divided highway in Connecticut); the results are
demonstrated in table form and sketched in Fig. 62-1.

The data from the Lincoln Tunnel were obtained by two observers (with a
machine's assistance) a short distance apart, as is shown in Fig. 62-2. The
velocity of each vehicle was obtained by recording the times at which they
passed each observer ($v = d/(t_2 - t_1)$). The distance between cars was also

---

*Greenberg H., "An Analysis of Traffic Flow," *Operations Research* 7, 79–85 (1959).

| Lincoln Tunnel | | Merritt Parkway | |
|---|---|---|---|
| *Velocity* (m.p.h.) | *Density* (cars/mile) | *Velocity* (m.p.h.) | *Density* (cars/mile) |
| 32 | 34 | 38.8 | 20.4 |
| 28 | 44 | 31.5 | 27.4 |
| 25 | 53 | 10.6 | 106.2 |
| 23 | 60 | 16.1 | 80.4 |
| 20 | 74 | 7.7 | 141.3 |
| 19 | 82 | 8.3 | 130.9 |
| 17 | 88 | 8.5 | 121.7 |
| 16 | 94 | 11.1 | 106.5 |
| 15 | 94 | 8.6 | 130.5 |
| 14 | 96 | 11.1 | 101.1 |
| 13 | 103 | 9.8 | 123.9 |
| 12 | 112 | 7.8 | 144.2 |
| 11 | 108 | 31.8 | 29.5 |
| 10 | 129 | 31.6 | 30.8 |
| 9 | 132 | 34.0 | 26.5 |
| 8 | 139 | 28.9 | 35.7 |
| 7 | 160 | 28.8 | 30.0 |
| 6 | 165 | 10.5 | 106.2 |
| | | 12.3 | 97.0 |
| | | 13.2 | 90.1 |
| | | 11.4 | 106.7 |
| | | 11.2 | 99.3 |
| | | 10.3 | 107.2 |
| | | 11.4 | 109.1 |

calculated.* The data for all cars moving between 14.5 and 15.5 miles per hour was collected, for example, and the average of the distance to the preceding car was calculated. In this manner an average density for cars moving at 15 miles per hour can be calculated.

Generally the data indicates that increasing the traffic density results in lower car velocities (although there is an exception in the data). The data is recorded in a manner such that the velocity can only depend on the density. Looking at the raw data (not given here) would suggest how much variation

---

*To measure the distance between cars, note that four times are known $t_{a_1}$, $t_{a_2}$, $t_{b_1}$, $t_{b_2}$ and two velocities have been calculated $v_a$ and $v_b$ ($a$ and $b$ represent the two cars). It is assumed that the cars have maintained their speed over the distance $d$. The distance between the two cars (front of one car to the front of the next) varies from $v_b(t_{a_1} - t_{b_1})$ to $v_a(t_{a_2} - t_{b_2})$. For example, the distance between cars when the second car passes the first observer is

$$d \frac{t_{a_1} - t_{b_1}}{t_{a_2} - t_{a_1}} = v_a \, \Delta t,$$

the velocity calculated for the first car multiplied by the time interval measured by the first observer.

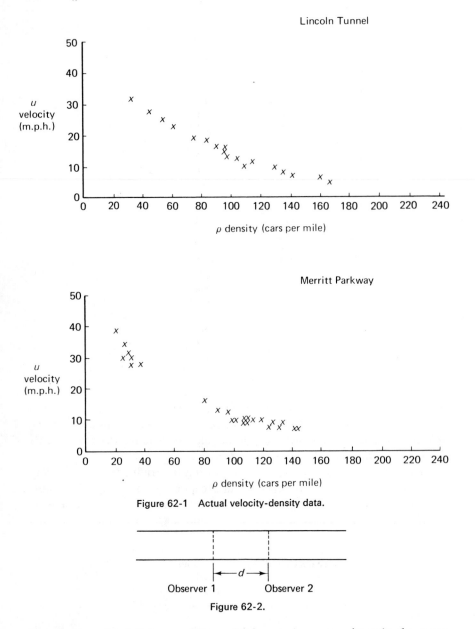

Figure 62-1   Actual velocity-density data.

Figure 62-2.

in velocity existed between drivers driving under approximately the same density conditions.

The Merritt Parkway data was accumulated in a different manner. There, velocities and densities were obtained in five-minute intervals and averaged (yielding an average velocity as a function of an average density).

In the work to follow $u(\rho)$ is assumed to be obtained by any similiar type of observation. We will postpone any attempts to explain in more detail the processes by which drivers travel. Such a theory might result in some explanations of the specific shape of the velocity-density curve.

## EXERCISES

**62.1.** (a)  Briefly explain the two different experimental methods to obtain a velocity-density curve.

      (b)  With the help of a friend, do an experiment on a road during light and heavy traffic situations. Calculate a velocity-density curve.

# 63. Traffic Flow

A traffic engineer might well request traffic-control mechanisms (traffic lights, stop signs, lane width, number of toll booths, speed limit, and so on) in order to maximize the flow on a given roadway. The largest flow $q = \rho u$ would occur if cars were bumper to bumper ($\rho = \rho_{max}$) moving at the speed limit ($u = u_{max}$). Clearly this is not safe (is that clear?), but furthermore, we have hypothesized (based on many observations) that man's driving habits are such that if $\rho = \rho_{max}$, then cars would be bumper to bumper and would not move, yielding a minimum traffic flow, namely zero.

We will assume that the road is homogeneous such that the car velocity depends on traffic density and not on the time or position along the road; see Fig. 63-1. Since the traffic flow (number of cars per hour) equals density times velocity, the flow also only depends on the density,

$$\boxed{q = \rho u(\rho).}$$                    **(63.1)**

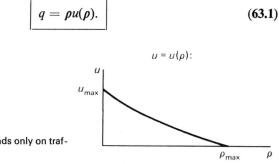

Figure 63-1   Car velocity depends only on traffic density.

The flow thus has certain general properties. The flow may be zero in two significant ways:

1. if there is no traffic ($\rho = 0$), or
2. if the traffic is not moving ($u = 0$ and thus $\rho = \rho_{max}$).

For other values of density ($0 < \rho < \rho_{max}$), the traffic flow must be positive. Thus, in general, the traffic flow's dependence on density is as illustrated in Fig. 63-2. This flow-density relationship is sometimes called the **Fundamental Diagram of Road Traffic**. This shows that a maximum of traffic flow occurs at some density (with a corresponding velocity). Traffic engineers call the maximum traffic flow the **capacity** of the road. We *assume* that the flow-density relationship is as sketched in Fig. 63-2, concave downwards, $(d^2q/d\rho^2) < 0$. In other words we *assume* that $dq/d\rho$ decreases as $\rho$ increases, as demonstrated in Fig. 63-3. The absolute maximum of the flow occurs at the only local maximum.

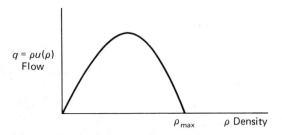

Figure 63-2   Fundamental Diagram of Road Traffic (flow-density curve).

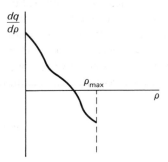

Figure 63-3.

The data from the Lincoln Tunnel indicate a maximum traffic flow of about 1600 vehicles per hour, occuring at a density of about 82 cars per mile, moving at a velocity of about 19 miles per hour. The data from the Merritt Parkway, Fig. 63-4, is inconclusive as the velocity range in which the maximum occurs was not observed.

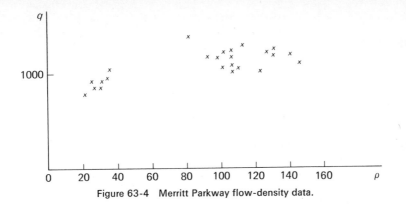
Figure 63-4  Merritt Parkway flow-density data.

If the density is almost zero, then the traffic usually travels at the maximum speed, $u_{max}$. Even as the density is somewhat increased, the cars' velocity remains nearly $u_{max}$. Thus for small densities the flow $q$ can be approximated by $u_{max}\rho$, increasing linearly with the density. Measurements in the Lincoln Tunnel and in the Holland and Queens-Midtown Tunnels (other tunnels into New York City) show nearly identical linear flow-density relationships for small traffic densities, as was suggested by the previous theoretical discussion. However, as the density increases and the flow correspondingly increases, differences among the three tunnels develop in the flow-density curves. These measurements have shown that the maximum traffic flow (the capacity) and the corresponding velocity are both lower in the older tunnels. This indicates that the newer tunnels, with greater lane width, improved lighting, and so on, permit drivers to go faster at the same traffic density.

In addition, flow-density measurements have been made in different segments of the same tunnel. These experiments have shown that the capacity of the roadway varies. There are places in which the capacity is lower than elsewhere, what might be called bottlenecks. Typically in tunnels these bottlenecks occur on the upgrade of the tunnel. Can you suggest why they occur there?

To improve traffic efficiency, traffic should somehow be forced to move at a density (and speed) corresponding to maximum traffic flow. To illustrate an application of this concept, consider a situation in which many cars are waiting to enter a tunnel. Assume that the cars, as often occurs, are moving at a speed less than that associated with maximum flow (i.e., more cars per mile than is most efficient!). A signal which literally stops traffic and then permits it to go (in intervals yielding the density corresponding to maximum flow) would result in an increased flow of cars through that tunnel. Thus, momentarily stopping traffic would actually result in an increased flow! Although we have simplified the problem somewhat, this idea resulted in increased traffic performance in the Holland Tunnel as reported in Scientific American.*

*HERMAN, R. and GARDELS, K., "Vehicular Traffic Flow," *Scientific American 209 No. 6*, December 1963, pp. 35–43.

# EXERCISES

**63.1.** (a) Briefly explain the four basic properties of a velocity-density relationship:

(1) $u(\rho_{max}) = 0$

(2) $u(0) = u_{max}$

(3) $du/d\rho \leq 0$

(4) $dq/d\rho$ decreases as $\rho$ increases (i.e., $d^2q/d\rho^2 < 0$).

(b) Assume that the velocity depends on the density in a linear way, $u(\rho) = \alpha + \beta\rho$. Show that in order for this to satisfy the properties in part (a), $\alpha = u_{max}$ and $\beta = -u_{max}/\rho_{max}$.

(c) What is the flow as a function of density? Sketch the Fundamental Diagram of Road Traffic.

(d) At what density is the flow maximum? What is the corresponding velocity? What is the maximum flow?

**63.2.** If cars obey state laws on following distances (refer to exercise 61.1), what is a road's capacity if the speed limit is 50 m.p.h. (80 k.p.h.)? At what density and velocity does this maximum flow occur? Will increasing the speed limit increase the road's capacity?

**63.3.** Some traffic data was compared to a flow-density relationship of the following from:

$$q(\rho) = \rho(\alpha - \beta\rho).$$

The best fit (in a least-squares sense) occurred for

$$\alpha = 58.6 \text{ miles/hr}; \quad \beta = .465 \text{ (miles)}^2/\text{hr}.$$

(a) What is the maximum density?

(b) What is the maximum velocity?

(c) What is the maximum flow?

(d) Guess what type of road this is.

**63.4.** Using the Lincoln Tunnel data of Sec. 62, sketch the flow as a function of density (the Fundamental Diagram of Road Traffic).

**63.5.** Show that if $u''(\rho) \leq 0$ (and $u'(\rho) \leq 0$), then the flow-density curve has only one local maximum.

**63.6.** Assume that $u = u(\rho)$. If $\alpha$ equals a car's acceleration, show that

$$\alpha = -\rho\frac{du}{d\rho}\frac{\partial u}{\partial x}.$$

Is the minus sign reasonable?

**63.7.** Consider exercise 61.3. Suppose that drivers accelerate such that

$$\frac{\partial u}{\partial t} + u\frac{\partial u}{\partial x} = -\frac{a^2}{\rho}\frac{\partial \rho}{\partial x},$$

where $a$ is a positive constant.

(a) Physically interpret this equation.

(b) If $u$ only depends on $p$ and the equation of conservation of cars is valid, show that

$$\frac{du}{dp} = -\frac{a}{p}.$$

(c) Solve the differential equation in part (b), subject to the condition that $u(p_{max}) = 0$. The resulting flow-density curve fits quite well to the Lincoln Tunnel data.

(d) Show that $a$ is the velocity which corresponds to the road's capacity.

(e) Discuss objections to this theory for small densities.

**63.8.** If $u = u_{max}(1 - p^3/p_{max}^3)$, what is the capacity of the road?

# 64. Steady-State Car-Following Models

In this section we will suggest a method for determining the specific observed velocity-density relationships. In order to explain the velocity-density curve, we can carefully analyze actual drivers making their driving decisions. The mathematical model suggested here is motivated by both its being reasonable and by the results of some experiments run for the purposes of developing such a model.

Consider the $n$th car on a highway, $x_n(t)$. As before, we assume cars cannot pass each other (frequently a rather rash assumption). We postulate that an individual car's motion only depends on the car ahead. Theories of this sort are called **car-following** models. In the simplest such model, we assume that a car's acceleration is proportional to the relative velocity,

$$\frac{d^2x_n(t)}{dt^2} = -\lambda\left(\frac{dx_n(t)}{dt} - \frac{dx_{n-1}(t)}{dt}\right). \tag{64.1}$$

If the car following is going faster than the preceding one, then the car following will slow down (and thus $\lambda > 0$). The larger the relative velocity, the more the car behind accelerates or decelerates. $\lambda$ measures the sensitivity of the two-car interaction. However, equation 64.1 suggests that acceleration or deceleration occurs instantaneously. Instead, let us allow some time delay before the driver reacts to changes in the relative velocity. This process is modeled by specifying the acceleration at a slightly later time,

$$\frac{d^2x_n(t + T)}{dt^2} = -\lambda\left(\frac{dx_n(t)}{dt} - \frac{dx_{n-1}(t)}{dt}\right), \tag{64.2}$$

where $T$ is the reaction time. Mathematically, this equation represents a system of ordinary differential equations with a delay, called a system of delay-differential equations.

Integrating equation 64.2, yields

$$\frac{dx_n(t+T)}{dt} = -\lambda(x_n(t) - x_{n-1}(t)) + d_n,$$

an equation relating the velocity of cars at a later time to the distance between cars. Imagine a **steady-state** situation in which all cars are equidistant apart, and hence moving at the same velocity. Thus

$$\frac{dx_n(t+T)}{dt} = \frac{dx_n(t)}{dt},$$

and hence letting $d_n = d$

$$\frac{dx_n(t)}{dt} = -\lambda(x_n(t) - x_{n-1}(t)) + d.$$

Since

$$x_{n-1}(t) - x_n(t) = \frac{1}{\rho} \qquad\qquad (64.3)$$

is a reasonable definition of traffic density (see equation 58.1), this car-following model yields a velocity-density relationship

$$u = \frac{\lambda}{\rho} + d.$$

We choose the one arbitrary constant $d$, such that at maximum density (bumper-to-bumper traffic) $u = 0$. In other words,

$$0 = \frac{\lambda}{\rho_{\max}} + d.$$

In this way the following velocity-density relationship is derived,

$$u = \lambda\left(\frac{1}{\rho} - \frac{1}{\rho_{\max}}\right), \qquad\qquad (64.4)$$

sketched in Fig. 64-1. How does this compare with experimental observations of velocity-density relationships? Equation 64.4 appears reasonable for large densities, i.e., near $\rho = \rho_{\max}$. However, it predicts an infinite velocity at zero

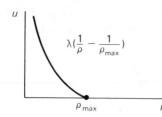

Figure 64-1   Steady-state car-following model: velocity-density relationship.

density. We can eliminate this problem, by noting that this model is not appropriate for small densities for the following reasons. At small densities, the changes in speed of a car are not due to the car in front. Instead it is more likely that the speed limit influences a car's velocity (and acceleration) at small densities. Thus we can hypothesize that equation 64.4 is valid only for large densities. For small densities, perhaps $u$ is only limited by the speed limit, $u = u_{max}$. Thus

$$u = \begin{cases} u_{max} & \rho < \rho_c \\ \lambda\left(\dfrac{1}{\rho} - \dfrac{1}{\rho_{max}}\right) & \rho > \rho_c. \end{cases}$$

We choose the critical density $\rho_c$ such that the velocity is a continuous function of density, as shown in Fig. 64-2. The flow $q = \rho u$ is thus

$$q = \begin{cases} u_{max}\rho & \rho < \rho_c \\ \lambda\left(1 - \dfrac{\rho}{\rho_{max}}\right) & \rho > \rho_c. \end{cases}$$

A comparison with the experimental data of Sec. 62 shows only a moderate agreement.

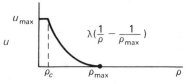

Figure 64-2  Speed limit cut-off of car-following velocity-density curve.

Let us attempt one improvement. Imagine two drivers each driving 20 m.p.h. (32 k.p.h.) faster than the car ahead, one 500 feet (160 meters) behind but the other only 25 feet (8 meters) behind. We know the drivers will decelerate quite differently. A driver's acceleration or deceleration also depends on the distance to the preceding car. The closer the driver is, the more likely the driver is to respond strongly to an observed relative velocity. The simplest way to model this is to let the sensitivity be inversely proportional to the distance

$$\lambda = \frac{c}{x_{n-1}(t) - x_n(t)}.$$

Thus the revised car-following model is

$$\frac{d^2 x_n(t + T)}{dt^2} = c\,\frac{\dfrac{dx_n(t)}{dt} - \dfrac{dx_{n-1}(t)}{dt}}{x_n(t) - x_{n-1}(t)}, \tag{64.5}$$

a nonlinear car-following model, as opposed to equation 64.2 which is linear.

Again this equation can be integrated yielding

$$\frac{dx_n(t+T)}{dt} = c \ln|x_n(t) - x_{n-1}(t)| + d_n.$$

Let us consider a steady-state situation, in which case

$$u = -c \ln \rho + d.$$

Once more the integration constant is chosen such that at maximum density, the velocity is zero. In that way

$$u = -c \ln \frac{\rho}{\rho_{max}},$$

sketched in Fig. 64-3. Difficulties as $\rho \to 0$ are again avoided by assuming

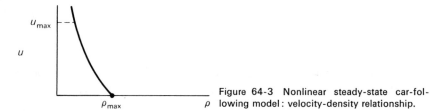

Figure 64-3  Nonlinear steady-state car-following model: velocity-density relationship.

that for low densities, $u = u_{max}$. The constant $c$ is chosen (perhaps by a least-squares fit) so that the formula agrees well with observed data on a given highway. This formula can be shown to agree quite well with the observed data. The constant $c$ has a simple interpretation, namely we will now show it is the velocity corresponding to the maximum flow:

$$q = \rho u = -c\rho \ln \frac{\rho}{\rho_{max}} \quad \text{and} \quad 0 = \frac{dq}{d\rho} = -c\left(\ln \frac{\rho}{\rho_{max}} + 1\right)$$

imply that the maximum traffic flow occurs at $\rho = \rho_{max}/e$, in which case the velocity at the maximum flow is $c$,

$$u\left(\frac{\rho_{max}}{e}\right) = c.$$

Many other types of similar car-following theories have been formulated by traffic researchers. They help to explain the relationship between the individual action of single drivers and their collective behavior described by the velocity-density curve.

# EXERCISES

**64.1.** Consider the linear car-following model, equation 64.2, with a response time $T$ (a delay).

(a) Solve for the velocity of the $n$th car, $v_n = dx_n/dt$. Show that

$$\frac{dv_n(t+T)}{dt} = -\lambda(v_n(t) - v_{n-1}(t)).$$

(b) Assume the lead driver's velocity varies periodically

$$v_0 = Re\,(1 + e^{i\omega t}).$$

Also assume the $n$th driver's velocity varies periodically

$$v_n = Re\,(1 + f_n e^{i\omega t}),$$

where $f_n$ measures the amplification or decay which occurs. Show that

$$f_n = \left(1 + \frac{i\omega}{\lambda}\,e^{i\omega T}\right)^{-n} f_0,$$

where $f_0 = 1$.

(c) Show the magnitude of the amplification factor $f_n$ decreases with $n$ if

$$\frac{\sin \omega T}{\omega} < \frac{1}{2\lambda}.$$

(d) Show that the above inequality holds for all $\omega$ only if $\lambda T < \frac{1}{2}$.

(e) Conclude that if the product of the sensitivity and the time lag is greater than $\frac{1}{2}$, it is possible for following cars to drive much more erratically than the leader. In this case we say the model predicts *instability* if $\lambda T > \frac{1}{2}$ (i.e., with a sufficiently long time lag). (This conclusion can be reached more expeditiously through the use of Laplace transforms.)

**64.2.** Consider the linear car-following model, equation 64.2, with a response time $T$ (a delay).

(a) Solve for the velocity of the $n$th car, $v_n = dx_n/dt$. Thus show that

$$\frac{dv_n(t+T)}{dt} = -\lambda(v_n(t) - v_{n-1}(t)).$$

(b) Consider two cars only, the leader and the follower. Thus

$$\frac{dv_1(t+T)}{dt} + \lambda v_1(t) = \lambda v_0(t).$$

Look for homogeneous solutions ($v_0(t) = 0$) of the form $e^{rt}$. Show that these solutions are exponentially damped if $1/e > \lambda T > 0$.

(c) For what values of $\lambda T$ do solutions exist of the form $e^{rt}$ with $r$ complex, such that the solutions are oscillatory with growing, decaying, or constant amplitude?

As with exercise 64.1, the use of Laplace transforms simplifies the above calculations.

**64.3.** General car-following models of the following form can be considered:

$$\frac{d^2 x_{n+1}(t+T)}{dt^2} = a\left(\frac{dx_{n+1}(t)}{dt}\right)^m \frac{\dfrac{dx_n}{dt}(t) - \dfrac{dx_{n+1}}{dt}(t)}{[x_n(t) - x_{n+1}(t)]^l}.$$

Note that the linear model, equation 64.2, corresponds to $m = 0$, $l = 0$ and the inverse-spacing model, equation 64.5, $m = 0$, $l = 1$.

(a)  What velocity-density curves are implied by the above general model, under the steady-state hypothesis?

(b)  Consider the case proposed by Edie, $m = 1$, $l = 2$. Show that the assumption that $u(\rho_{max}) = 0$ does not yield a reasonable velocity-density curve. Instead, assume $u(0) = u_{max}$, and briefly discuss the resulting model.

**64.4.**  Show that the two car-following models described in this section satisfy $dq/d\rho \leq 0$.

**64.5.**  Compare the two theoretical models of this section to the Lincoln Tunnel data (see Sec. 62). Which theory best fits the data? [Hint: The parameters of the model are usually chosen by making a least-squares fit to the data. However, if you wish for simplicity you may assume that $\rho_{max} = 225$ cars/mile and also assume that the theoretical curve exactly satisfies the first data point, $u = 32$ m.p.h. when $\rho = 34$ cars/mile.]

# 65. *Partial Differential Equations*

For a given segment of a highway, experiments can be run to analyze the density dependence of the velocity. *If we assume that under all circumstances the driver's velocity is a known function of $\rho$, determined by $u = u(\rho)$,* then conservation of cars (equation 60.8) implies

$$\frac{\partial \rho}{\partial t} + \frac{\partial}{\partial x}(\rho u(\rho)) = 0. \tag{65.1}$$

This is a partial differential equation in one unknown variable $\rho$.

Suppose a nonconstant initial traffic density existed, as shown in Fig. 65-1. Different cars will move at different velocities (since the spacing is nonuniform). Thus the density will change immediately, and, under our assumptions, the drivers would adjust their velocities immediately. This process would continue. If we were interested in the density of cars at a later time we would "just" need to solve the partial differential equation.

The traffic problem has been formulated in terms of one partial differential equation, equation 65.1, or equivalently

$$\frac{\partial \rho}{\partial t} + \frac{\partial}{\partial x}q(\rho) = 0, \tag{65.2}$$

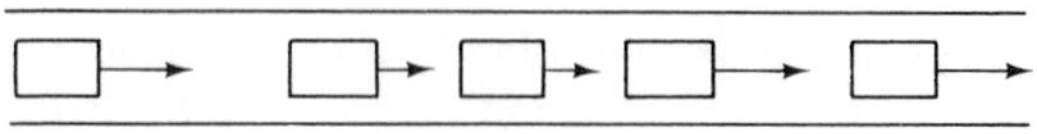

Figure 65-1    Nonuniform traffic.

since $q = \rho u$. $q$ can be considered a function of $\rho$ only. This last expression is often easier to use since by the chain rule

$$\frac{\partial}{\partial x} q(\rho) = \frac{dq}{d\rho} \frac{\partial \rho}{\partial x},$$

and thus

$$\boxed{\frac{\partial \rho}{\partial t} + \frac{dq}{d\rho} \frac{\partial \rho}{\partial x} = 0.} \qquad (65.3)$$

One appropriate condition in order to solve uniquely the partial differential equation is an initial condition. With an $n$th order ordinary differential equation, $n$ initial conditions are needed. The number of conditions are correspondingly the same for partial differential equations. Thus for equation 65.3 only one initial condition is needed since the partial differential equation only involves one *time* derivative. However, there are some major differences between ordinary and partial differential equations due to the additional independent variable.

To illustrate this difference, let us consider three extremely simple first order partial differential equations:

(1) $$\frac{\partial \rho}{\partial t} = 0$$

(2) $$\frac{\partial \rho}{\partial t} = -\rho + 2e^t$$

(3) $$\frac{\partial \rho}{\partial t} = -x\rho.$$

These are called partial differential equations because $\rho$ is assumed to depend on $x$ and $t$ (even though there is no explicit appearance of $x$ in either of the first two equations). If $\rho$ only depends on $t$, then the first two would be ordinary differential equations, the general solutions being:

(1) $$\rho = \text{constant} = c_1$$
(2) $$\rho = c_2 e^{-t} + e^t.$$

To have a unique solution, one initial condition is needed, for example, if $\rho(0) = \rho_0$, then

(1) $$\rho = \rho_0$$
(2) $$\rho = (\rho_0 - 1)e^{-t} + e^t.$$

However, now we assume (as originally proposed) that $\rho$ depends on both $x$ and $t$.

In (1), $\partial p/\partial t = 0$. The partial derivative means keeping $x$ fixed. Thus if $x$ is kept fixed, $p$ doesn't change with $t$. By integrating, $p$ is a constant *for each fixed x*. However, for different $x$'s different constants could result. The arbitrary constant now depends on $x$ in an arbitrary way. Hence the constant is an arbitrary function of $x$. In general arbitrary constants of integration become arbitrary functions when the integration is of a partial derivative. Thus

$$p = c_0(x),$$

is the general solution of $\partial p/\partial t = 0$, where $c_0(x)$ is an arbitrary function of $x$. As a check, $p = c_0(x)$ is substituted into the partial differential equation, $\partial p/\partial t = 0$, in which case we quickly can verify that $p = c_0(x)$ is the solution. To determine the arbitrary function, one initial condition is needed (corresponding to the one initial condition for the ordinary differential equation). The initial condition is the initial value of $p(x, t)$, the initial traffic density $p(x, 0)$. Can the partial differential equation be solved for any given initial condition, that is for $p(x, 0)$ being prescribed, $p(x, 0) = f(x)$? Equivalently, can the arbitrary function, $p(x, t) = c_0(x)$, be determined such that initially $p(x, 0) = f(x)$? In this case it is quite simple as $c_0(x) = f(x)$. Thus

$$p(x, t) = f(x)$$

solves the partial differential equation and simultaneously satisfies the initial condition.

We now consider example (2),

$$\frac{\partial p}{\partial t} = -p + 2e^t.$$

Again we will satisfy the initial condition $p(x, 0) = f(x)$. The partial differential equation can again be integrated yielding (for each fixed $x$)

$$p = c_1 e^{-t} + e^t.$$

As before, the constant can depend on $x$ in an arbitrary way. Hence

$$p(x, t) = c_1(x)e^{-t} + e^t.$$

The initial condition is satisfied if $f(x) = c_1(x) + 1$, and hence the solution of problem (2) satisfying the given initial condition is

$$p(x, t) = [f(x) - 1]e^{-t} + e^t.$$

For example (3),

$$\frac{\partial p}{\partial t} = -xp,$$

keeping $x$ fixed (as implied by $\partial/\partial t$) yields the solution of the ordinary differential equation,

$$p = c_3 e^{-xt}.$$

For other values of $x$ the constant may vary, and hence the solution of the partial differential equation is

$$p(x, t) = c_3(x)e^{-xt}.$$

The initial condition, $p(x, 0) = f(x)$, is satisfied if $c_3(x) = f(x)$, yielding the solution of the initial value problem,

$$p(x, t) = f(x)e^{-xt}.$$

In summary we have been able to solve partial differential equations in the case in which they can be integrated. The arbitrary constants that appear are replaced by arbitrary functions of the "other" independent variable.

## EXERCISES

**65.1.** Determine the solution of $\partial p/\partial t = (\sin x)p$ which satisfies $p(x, 0) = \cos x$.

**65.2.** Determine the solution of $\partial p/\partial t = p^2$ which satisfies $p(x, 0) = \sin x$.

**65.3.** Determine the solution of $\partial p/\partial t = p$, which satisfies $p(x, t) = 1 + \sin x$ along $x = -2t$.

**65.4.** Is there a solution of $\partial p/\partial t = -x^2 p$, such that both $p(x, 0) = \cos x$ for $x > 0$ and $p(0, t) = \cos t$ for $t > 0$?

**65.5.** Determine the solution of $\partial p/\partial t = xtp$ which satisfies $p(x, 0) = f(x)$.

# 66.   Linearization

The partial differential equation which was formulated to mathematically model traffic flow is

$$\frac{\partial p}{\partial t} + \frac{\partial}{\partial x}(pu(p)) = 0 \qquad \text{(66.1a)}$$

or equivalently

$$\frac{\partial p}{\partial t} + \frac{dq}{dp}\frac{\partial p}{\partial x} = 0. \qquad \text{(66.1b)}$$

One possible initial condition is to prescribe the initial traffic density

$$p(x, 0) = f(x).$$

We will solve this problem, that is determine the traffic density at all future times.

This partial differential equation cannot be directly integrated as could the simple examples in the previous section, since both $\partial p/\partial t$ and $\partial p/\partial x$ appear in the equation. Although we will be able to solve this partial differential equation, for now let us first discuss a simpler problem. If the initial traffic density is a constant,

$$p(x, 0) = p_0,$$

independent of $x$, then the density should remain constant (since all cars must move at the same speed). This is verified by noting that a constant density,

$$p(x, t) = p_0,$$

satisfies the partial differential equation 66.1. Any constant density is an **equilibrium**\* density. Let us imagine driving in a traffic situation in which the density is approximately constant. What does your experience tell you? What kinds of phenomena do you observe? Does the density seem to stay constant? Some of you have probably had the experience of driving at a steady speed and all of a sudden, for no apparent reason, the car in front slows down. You must slow down, then the car behind slows down, and so on. Let us investigate that situation, namely one in which the density is *nearly* constant.

If the density is nearly uniform, then there should be an approximate solution to the partial differential equation such that

$$p(x, t) = p_0 + \epsilon p_1(x, t), \qquad \text{(66.2)}$$

where $|\epsilon p_1| \ll p_0$. $\epsilon p_1(x, t)$ is called the perturbed traffic density (or the displacement from the constant density $p_0$). Assume that the initial density is a known function of $x$, nearly equaling the constant $p_0$,

$$p(x, 0) = p_0 + \epsilon f(x).$$

Thus the perturbed traffic density is also known initially, $p_1(x, 0) = f(x)$. Substituting equation 66.2 into the second form of the partial differential equation 66.1b yields

$$\not\epsilon \frac{\partial p_1}{\partial t} + \frac{dq}{dp}(p_0 + \epsilon p_1(x, t)) \not\epsilon \frac{\partial p_1}{\partial x} = 0,$$

where a power of $\epsilon$ has been cancelled. The derivative $dq/dp$ is evaluated at the total traffic density $p_0 + \epsilon p_1(x, t)$. Expanding that expression via a Taylor series, yields

$$\frac{dq}{dp}(p_0 + \epsilon p_1(x, t)) = \frac{dq}{dp}(p_0) + \epsilon p_1 \frac{d^2 q}{dp^2}(p_0) + \frac{(\epsilon p_1)^2}{2!} \frac{d^3 q}{dp^3}(p_0) + \cdots$$

Thus to leading order (that is neglecting the small terms) the following equation is obtained:

---

\*An equilibrium solution of a partial differential equation is a *solution* which does not depend on time.

$$\frac{\partial \rho_1}{\partial t} + \frac{dq}{d\rho}(\rho_0) \frac{\partial \rho_1}{\partial x} = 0.$$    (66.3)

This partial differential equation governs the perturbed traffic density. However, equation 66.3 is a *linear* partial differential equation while the exact traffic equation 66.1 is a *nonlinear* partial differential equation. The coefficient that appears in equation 66.3, $(dq/d\rho)(\rho_0)$, is a constant (the slope of the flow as a function of density evaluated at the constant density). This resulting partial differential equation is the simplest kind involving both partial derivatives,

$$\frac{\partial \rho_1}{\partial t} + c \frac{\partial \rho_1}{\partial x} = 0,$$    (66.4)

where $c = (dq/d\rho)(\rho_0)$.

## EXERCISES

**66.1.** Assume that $dq/d\rho = a + b\rho$
  (a)  What nonlinear partial differential equation describes conservation of cars?
  (b)  Describe all possible (time-independent) traffic densities $\rho(x)$ which satisfy the equation of part (a).
  (c)  Show that $\rho = \rho_0$ (any constant) is a time-independent solution.
  (d)  By substituting

$$\rho(x, t) = \rho_0 + \epsilon \rho_1(x, t)$$

into the partial differential equation of part (a) and by neglecting nonlinear terms, what equation does $\rho_1(x, t)$ satisfy? Is it the same as equation 66.3?

# 67.  A Linear Partial
#      Differential Equation

In this section, we will solve the partial differential equation corresponding to the linearization of the traffic flow problem,

$$\frac{\partial \rho_1}{\partial t} + c \frac{\partial \rho_1}{\partial x} = 0,$$    (67.1)

where $c$ is a constant, $c = (dq/dp)(p_0)$. The initial condition is that the initial *perturbed* traffic is known,

$$\rho_1(x, 0) = f(x).$$

$c$ has the dimensions of a velocity (why?). It will be shown to be a very important velocity.

Although there seems no motivation to do so, let us introduce a new spatial coordinate $x'$ moving with the constant velocity $c$. Let us assume that the two spatial coordinate systems $x$ and $x'$ have the same origin at $t = 0$: See Fig. 67-1. At a later time $t$, the moving coordinate system has moved a

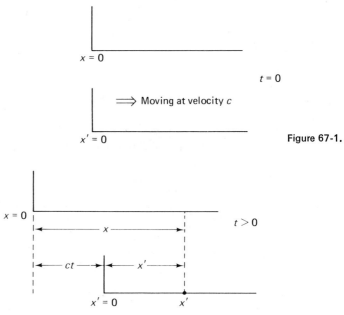

Figure 67-1.

Figure 67-2   Frame of reference $x'$ moving at velocity $c$.

distance $ct$ (since it is moving at a constant velocity $c$) as shown in Fig. 67-2. Thus, if $x' = 0$, then $x = ct$. Furthermore at $x'$, $x = ct + x'$ or

$$\boxed{x' = x - ct.}$$

We will first investigate what happens to the partial differential equation describing linearized traffic flow in this moving coordinate system. Instead of the solution depending on $x$ and $t$, it will depend on $x'$ and $t$. However, in making changes of variables involving partial derivatives, it is more convenient to introduce different notations for each set of variables. Thus for the moving coordinate system, we use the variables $x'$ and $t'$, where $t' = t$. Consequently, the change of variables we use is

$$
\begin{array}{l}
x' = x - ct \\
t' = t.
\end{array}
$$

In order to express the partial differential equation in terms of the new variables, the chain rule of partial derivatives is used:

$$\frac{\partial}{\partial x} = \frac{\partial x'}{\partial x} \frac{\partial}{\partial x'} + \frac{\partial t'}{\partial x} \frac{\partial}{\partial t'}$$

$$\frac{\partial}{\partial t} = \frac{\partial x'}{\partial t} \frac{\partial}{\partial x'} + \frac{\partial t'}{\partial t} \frac{\partial}{\partial t'},$$

and thus

$$\frac{\partial}{\partial x} = \frac{\partial}{\partial x'}$$

$$\frac{\partial}{\partial t} = -c \frac{\partial}{\partial x'} + \frac{\partial}{\partial t'}.$$

Note that even though $t' = t$, $(\partial/\partial t') \neq (\partial/\partial t)$. The reason for this is clear from the definitions of these two partial derivatives. $\partial/\partial t$ means the time derivative keeping $x$ fixed (that is, in a stationary coordinate system), while $\partial/\partial t'$ means the time derivative keeping $x'$ fixed (that is, in a coordinate system moving with velocity $c$). The changes in time may be different in the two systems. This emphasizes the importance of introducing a new time variable $t'$; it enables us to have a notational distinction between keeping $x$ fixed and keeping $x'$ fixed.

In this manner, this partial differential equation in a coordinate system moving with velocity $c$ becomes

$$-c \frac{\partial \rho_1}{\partial x'} + \frac{\partial \rho_1}{\partial t'} + c \frac{\partial \rho_1}{\partial x'} = 0,$$

which simplifies and becomes

$$\frac{\partial \rho_1}{\partial t'} = 0.$$

This partial differential equation can be directly integrated (see Sec. 65). If $x'$ is fixed, $\rho_1$ is constant; that is $\rho_1$ is constant in time in a coordinate system moving with velocity $c$. For different values of $x'$, $\rho_1$ may be a different constant; $\rho_1$ is a function of $x'$,

$$\rho_1 = g(x'),$$

where $g(x')$ is an arbitrary function of $x'$. In the original variables,

$$\boxed{\rho_1 = g(x - ct).} \tag{67.2}$$

To again verify that this really is the solution, we substitute it back into the partial differential equation 67.1. Using the chain rule

$$\frac{\partial \rho_1}{\partial x} = \frac{dg}{d(x - ct)} \frac{\partial(x - ct)}{\partial x} = \frac{dg}{d(x - ct)}$$

and

$$\frac{\partial \rho_1}{\partial t} = \frac{dg}{d(x - ct)} \frac{\partial(x - ct)}{\partial t} = -c \frac{dg}{d(x - ct)}.$$

Thus it is verified that equation 67.1 is satisfied by equation 67.2. Even though equation 67.1 involves both partial derivatives with respect to $x$ and $t$, it can be integrated (in a coordinate system moving with velocity $c$). The general solution to equation 67.1 contains an arbitrary function, just like the examples of Sec. 65. In Sec. 69 we will derive this result in an easier way; we will not find it necessary to use the change of variables formula for partial derivatives.

Can the arbitrary function be determined in order to solve the initial condition? The general solution is

$$\rho_1(x, t) = g(x - ct),$$

but initially $\rho_1(x, 0) = f(x)$. Thus $f(x) = g(x)$. Consequently, the solution of the partial differential equation satisfying the initial condition is

$$\boxed{\rho_1(x, t) = f(x - ct),} \tag{67.3}$$

or equivalently

$$\boxed{\rho(x, t) = \rho_0 + \epsilon f(x - ct).}$$

*If we move with the velocity c, the density stays the same.* The density is said to **propagate** as a **wave** (called a **density wave**) with **wave speed** $c$. Note that this velocity may be different from the velocity at which an individual car moves.

Along the curves $x - ct = $ constant, the density stays the same. These lines are called **characteristics*** of the partial differential equation,

---

*The essential property of characteristics is that along those curves the partial differential equation reduces to an ordinary differential equation. Curves along which $\rho$ is constant are not always characteristics (see Sec. 83).

$$\frac{\partial \rho_1}{\partial t} + c\frac{\partial \rho_1}{\partial x} = 0.$$

In this case the characteristics are all straight lines with velocity $c$, $dx/dt = c$. Sketching various characteristics in a space-time diagram, yields Fig. 67-3. Along each characteristic, the density equals the value it has at $t = 0$. Note that $\rho_1$ stays constant along the characteristic, but $\partial \rho_1/\partial t$ and $\partial \rho_1/\partial x$ may

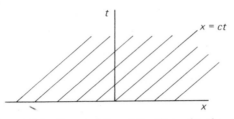

Figure 67-3   Characteristics of $\partial \rho_1/\partial t + c\,\partial \rho_1/\partial x = 0$.

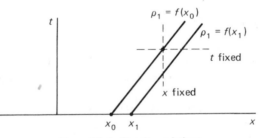

Figure 67-4   Density variations.

not be zero; see Fig. 67-4. As illustrated there $\partial \rho_1/\partial t$ may not equal zero since *keeping x fixed* $\rho_1$ may vary. Likewise $\partial \rho_1/\partial x$ is not necessarily zero since $\rho_1$ may change *keeping t fixed*. In Figs. 67-3 and 67-4 we have assumed $c > 0$. What is the sign of $c$? Recall

$$c = \frac{dq}{d\rho}(\rho_0). \qquad\qquad (67.4)$$

The Fundamental Diagram of Road Traffic is of the form shown in Fig. 67-5. Thus the slope is positive for densities less than that corresponding to the capacity of the road and the slope is negative for densities greater than that corresponding to the road capacity. The sign of the slope is significant as we have indicated that small perturbations to a uniform density move at the velocity equal to that slope (equation 67.4). The wave velocity can thus be positive or negative! In the next section we will attempt to describe what a density wave is, in particular, what it means for the velocity of a density wave to be negative!

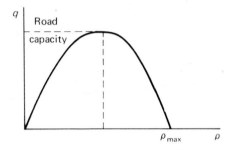

Figure 67-5   Flow-density curve: road capacity.

# EXERCISES

**67.1.** Suppose that

$$u = u_{max}\left(1 - \frac{\rho}{\rho_{max}}\right).$$

(a) What is the density wave velocity if the traffic density is nearly $\rho_0$ everywhere?

(b) Show that this density wave velocity is less than the car's velocity.

**67.2.** Suppose initially ($t = 0$) that the traffic density is

$$\rho = \begin{cases} \rho_0 & \text{if } |x| > a \\ \rho_0 + \epsilon & \text{if } |x| < a, \end{cases} \quad \text{where } |\epsilon| \ll \rho_0.$$

(a) Sketch $\rho(x)$ at $t = 0$.

(b) Sketch $\rho(x)$ at $t = 2$.

**67.3.** Suppose initially ($t = 0$) that the traffic density is $\rho = \rho_0 + \epsilon \sin x$, where $|\epsilon| \ll \rho_0$. Determine $\rho(x, t)$.

**67.4.** Consider $\partial \rho_1/\partial t + c(\partial \rho_1/\partial x) = 0$. Suppose we observe $\rho_1$ in a coordinate system moving at velocity $v$. Show that

$$\frac{\partial \rho_1}{\partial t'} + (c - v)\frac{\partial \rho_1}{\partial x'} = 0.$$

Does $\rho$ stay constant moving at the car velocity?

**67.5.** Based on a linear analysis, would you say $\rho = \rho_0$, a constant, is a stable or unstable equilibrium solution of equation 66.1?

**67.6.** Show that $c = dq/d\rho\,(\rho_0)$ has the dimensions of a velocity.

**67.7.** What is the *slope* of the straight line characteristics sketched in Fig. 67-3.

# 68. Traffic Density Waves

For convenience **heavy traffic** is defined as traffic such that the density is greater than the optimal density (corresponding to the road's capacity) and **light traffic** such that the density is less than the optimal density; see Fig. 68-1. Using these definitions and the Fundamental Diagram of Road Traffic, we conclude that in heavy traffic the perturbed densities move with a negative velocity, while in light traffic the opposite is true.

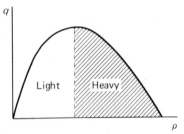

Figure 68-1   Light and heavy traffic.

Let us imagine a situation involving *heavy traffic of a nearly uniform density.* Suppose that the initial density is sketched in Fig. 68-2, where the dotted line is the approximate constant initial density, and • indicates a relative minimum or relative maximum of the density. The previous analysis has shown that the density remains constant if an observer moves with velocity $c$ which is negative. Thus density is constant along characteristics, sketched in a space-time diagram, Fig. 68-3. Positions of the relative maxima

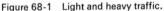

Figure 68-2   Nearly uniform heavy traffic.

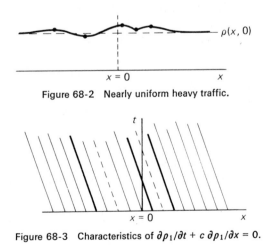

Figure 68-3   Characteristics of $\partial p_1/\partial t + c\, \partial p_1/\partial x = 0$.

are marked with heavy lines and minima in dotted lines. Let us sketch the density for different times. Initially it is as shown in Fig. 68-4. A short time $\tau$ thereafter the density has moved backwards a distance $|c\tau|$, where $c = (dq/d\rho)(\rho_0)$, as shown in Fig. 68-5. As time continues to increase the density

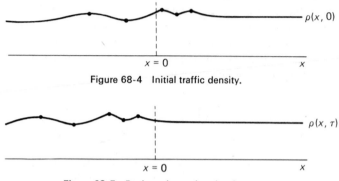

Figure 68-4   Initial traffic density.

Figure 68-5   Backwards moving density wave.

moves backwards at a constant speed $c$. This density wave travels without a change of shape. Sketching the density $\rho$ as a function of $x$ and $t$ requires a three-dimensional sketch, and hence is not always easy to draw. For this example (with $x$ horizontal, $\rho$ vertical and $t$ into the paper) we obtain Fig. 68-6. The density has been indicated as staying the same along paths with velocity $c$, ($c < 0$). The variations in the traffic density appear to be moving backwards. Of course, no car is actually moving backwards. How does this occur? The cars in a bulge of traffic have a larger density and slow down. The cars behind thus move faster than the cars in the bulge and hence it is the car's behind which will move into a region of larger density. The cars trailing an excess of traffic *may* slow down before they reach the position of the original bulge of cars due to the "chain reaction." Have you ever observed this phenomena? What happens to cars at the front of a bulge of traffic? Do they remain in the bulge?

Let us attempt to explain why for heavy traffic of nearly uniform density, the density wave moves backwards. (As an exercise, you should be able to use

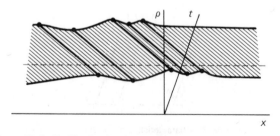

Figure 68-6   Traffic density: three-dimensional sketch $(x, t, \rho)$.

the arguments that follow to explain why the density wave moves forward for light traffic!) Consider traffic which is approximately the constant $\rho_0$ sketched in Fig. 68-7 on the Fundamental Diagram of Road Traffic:

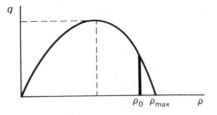

Figure 68-7   Flow-density relationship: $\rho_0$ is heavy traffic.

Consider a segment of traffic in which the density is decreasing ahead on the roadway, circled in Fig. 68-8. Since the density at $x = a$ is larger than at $x = b$, cars move slightly slower at $x = a$, than at $x = b$. At which point is the flow larger? From the Fundamental Diagram of Road Traffic, we see that for heavy traffic, the traffic flow at $x = a$ is less than at $x = b$ (in general for heavy traffic the flow decreases as the density increases). Thus the integral conservation of cars implies that the number of cars between $a$ and $b$ is decreasing. A short time later the density between $a$ and $b$ will decrease, and thus the density will be closer to that originally further ahead; the density appears to be moving backwards! A similar analysis would yield the same conclusion for regions in which the density is increasing further ahead along the roadway, as shown in Fig. 68-9.

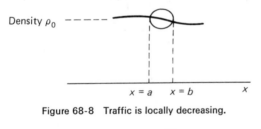

Figure 68-8   Traffic is locally decreasing.

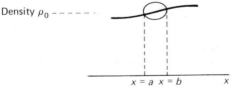

Figure 68-9   Traffic is locally increasing.

It is possible for the density waves to move backwards while all cars are moving forwards. In some sense it could be said that there is an optical illusion of backward motion. A different common example of this type of illusion is the waves present in a "jumping" rope, illustrated by Fig. 68-10.

Figure 68-10   Wave on a "jumping" rope.

When the rope is vertically moved by the person illustrated above, a "disturbance" is propagated at first to the right. A wave appears to move to the right, but we all know that the particles of the jumping rope only move up and down! For a jumping rope there are two different types of velocities, the wave velocity and the rope velocity, just as there are car velocity and density wave velocity for traffic flow problems.

In traffic flow problems, there are two important velocities: one the velocity of individual cars and the other the velocity at which a density wave travels. The slope of the Fundamental Diagram of Road Traffic ($q(\rho)$ versus $\rho$) at $\rho = \rho_0$,

$$c = \frac{dq}{d\rho}\bigg|_{\rho=\rho_0},$$

equals the density wave velocity corresponding to $\rho$ near $\rho_0$. The slope of the straight line from the origin ($q = 0$, $\rho = 0$) to the point on the flow-density curve representing the constant density $\rho_0$ is the car velocity $u$, since $u = q/\rho$. Straight lines with these two slopes are sketched in Fig. 68-11. Fig. 68-11 can be quite useful in sketching solutions to the partial differential equation

$$\frac{\partial \rho_1}{\partial t} + c\frac{\partial \rho_1}{\partial x} = 0,$$

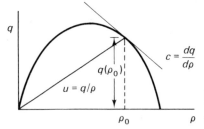

Figure 68-11   Fundamental Diagram of Road Traffic: traffic density wave velocity $c$ and car velocity $u$.

as we will show. We know $\rho_1$ is constant along curves in which $x - ct$ is constant, that is straight lines with velocity $c$. If these characteristics are sketched in a space-time diagram such that slopes have the units of velocity, then the slope of the straight line characteristics are the same as the slope of the appropriate tangent to the Fundamental Diagram of Road Traffic. Thus if the traffic density is nearly $\rho_0$, all the characteristics are straight lines *parallel* to this tangent; see Fig. 68-12. We can clearly show these lines are not the trajectories of cars because cars move at velocity $u$, and hence a car path

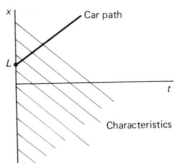

Figure 68-12   Characteristics and a car path, determined from flow-density curve.

has slope $dx/dt = u$, which equals the slope of the other straight line drawn on the Fundamental Diagram of Road Traffic. For example, the approximate path of a car moving at velocity $u(\rho_0)$ starting from $x = L$ is sketched in Fig. 68-12. The car moves forward, while the density wave moves backward. In this situation we have approximated the car's velocity as a constant because the density is approximately constant. Later we may wish to improve this approximation to take into account the effects of the variation of the traffic density.

# EXERCISES

**68.1.** Explain why a density wave moves forward for light traffic. Consider both cases in which the traffic is getting heavier down the road and lighter.

**68.2.** Suppose that $q$ as a function of $\rho$ has been experimentally determined, as illustrated in Fig. 68-13. Estimate (in m.p.h.) how fast a car moves at $\rho = \rho_{max}/2$. What is the estimated velocity of the density wave corresponding to $\rho = \rho_{max}/2$?

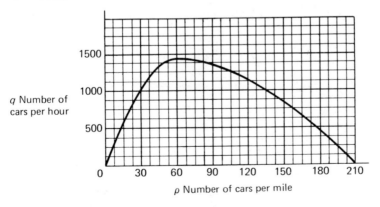

Figure 68-13.

**68.3.**    For very light traffic, we know that increased traffic density does not appreciably reduce a car's velocity. In this case, what is the velocity of a density wave?

# 69.  An Interpretation of Traffic Waves

In this section, we obtain, in an alternate way, the solution to the partial differential equation for the perturbed traffic density,

$$\frac{\partial \rho_1}{\partial t} + c \frac{\partial \rho_1}{\partial x} = 0. \tag{69.1}$$

Let us consider the traffic density measured by a moving observer (*not* necessarily in a car moving in traffic). Let the position of the observer be prescribed by $x = x(t)$. The traffic density measured by the observer depends on time, $\rho_1(x(t), t)$. The rate of change of this density depends both on the variation of the traffic and on the motion of the observer, since the chain rule of partial derivatives implies that

$$\frac{d}{dt}\rho_1(x(t), t) = \frac{\partial \rho_1}{\partial t} + \frac{dx}{dt}\frac{\partial \rho_1}{\partial x}. \tag{69.2}$$

The first term $\partial \rho_1/\partial t$ represents the change in the traffic density at the fixed position, while $(dx/dt)(\partial \rho_1/\partial x)$ represents the change due to the fact that the observer moves into a region of possibly different traffic density. Compare this expression for the change in density moving with an observer, equation 69.2, with the partial differential equation for the perturbed traffic density, equation 69.1. It is apparent that *if* the observer moves with velocity $c$, that is if

$$\frac{dx}{dt} = c, \tag{69.3a}$$

then

$$\frac{d\rho_1}{dt} = 0. \tag{69.3b}$$

Thus $\rho_1$ is constant. An observer moving with this special speed $c$ would measure no changes in density, the same conclusion we reached in Sec. 67. We will also find this concept useful in our study of the fully nonlinear traffic flow equation,

$$\frac{\partial \rho}{\partial t} + \frac{dq}{d\rho}\frac{\partial \rho}{\partial x} = 0.$$

By integrating equation 69.3, an algebraic solution is easily obtained. From equation 69.3, $\rho_1 = \beta$ along $x = ct + \alpha$, where $\alpha$ and $\beta$ are constants. However, we see that $\rho_1$ is a constant only if $x - ct$ is a constant. For a different straight line (i.e., a different constant $\alpha$), $\rho_1$ can be a different constant. Thus the constant $\beta$ depends on the constant $\alpha$, $\beta = f(\alpha)$; $\beta$ is an arbitrary function of $\alpha$, or

$$\rho_1 = f(x - ct),$$

which is identical to the result, equation 67.3, obtained by transforming the partial differential equation to a coordinate system moving with the velocity $c$.

## EXERCISES

**69.1.** Show that for an observer *moving with the traffic*, the rate of change of the measured density is

$$\frac{d\rho}{dt} = \left(u - \frac{dq}{d\rho}\right)\frac{\partial \rho}{\partial x},$$

where $u$ is the car's velocity.

**69.2.** Suppose for graphical purposes that we replace $t$ by $y$, and hence equation 69.1 becomes

$$\frac{\partial \rho_1}{\partial y} + c\frac{\partial \rho_1}{\partial x} = 0.$$

(a) For what two-dimensional vectors $\vec{g}$ does $\vec{g} \cdot \nabla \rho_1 = 0$?
(b) Briefly explain why $\vec{g}$ is perpendicular to $\nabla \rho_1$.
(c) Using part (b), explain why the curves along which $\rho_1$ is constant must be parallel to $\vec{g}$.
(d) Show that the results of part (c) are in agreement with the results of Secs. 67–69.

# 70. A Nearly Uniform
# Traffic Flow Example

In this section another type of traffic problem involving a nearly uniform traffic density will be solved. Suppose that the initial traffic density is constant for the semi-infinite expressway illustrated in Fig. 70-1. How many cars per hour would have to continually enter in order for the traffic flow to remain

Entrance

Figure 70-1    Semi-infinite highway (only entrance at $x = 0$).

uniform? The traffic flow at the entrance must be $\rho_0 u(\rho_0)$, the flow corresponding to the uniform density $\rho_0$. To prove this statement (though to many of you a mathematical proof of this should not be necessary), consider the interval of roadway between the entrance and the point $x = a$. Using the integral conservation of cars,

$$\frac{d}{dt} \int_0^a \rho(x, t) \, dx = -q(a, t) + q(0, t).$$

Since the traffic density is prescribed to be constant, the left hand side is zero. Thus the flow at $x = a$ must be the same as the flow at the entrance $q(a, t) = q(0, t)$. But the flow at $x = a$ is $\rho_0 u(\rho_0)$. Thus $q(0, t) = \rho_0 u(\rho_0)$. In other words, the flow "in" must equal the flow "out," as the number of cars in between stays the same *assuming* constant density.

However, suppose that the flow in of cars is slightly different (and varies in time) from that flow necessary for a uniform density,

$$q(0, t) = \rho_0 u(\rho_0) + \epsilon q_1(t), \tag{70.1}$$

with $q_1(t)$ known. What is the resulting traffic density? The partial differential equation is the same as before:

$$\frac{\partial \rho_1}{\partial t} + c \frac{\partial \rho_1}{\partial x} = 0,$$

being derived from

$$\rho(x, t) = \rho_0 + \epsilon \rho_1(x, t). \tag{70.2}$$

The traffic is assumed initially to be uniform, so that the initial condition is

$$\rho_1(x, 0) = 0.$$

(This could be generalized to also include initial densities that vary slightly from the uniform case.) Note that the initial condition is only valid for $x > 0$ (rather than in the previous sections in which $-\infty < x < \infty$). The initial condition must be supplemented by the flow condition, equation 70.1, called a **boundary condition** since it occurs at the boundary of the roadway, the entrance to the expressway at $x = 0$.

The general solution to the partial differential equation has already been obtained

$$\rho_1(x, t) = g(x - ct)$$

or equivalently

$$p(x, t) = p_0 + \epsilon g(x - ct). \tag{70.3}$$

Let us use the concepts of characteristics assuming *light traffic*, i.e., $c > 0$ (heavy traffic is discussed in the exercises). The characteristics are the lines $x - ct =$ constant, sketched in Fig. 70-2. The density $p_1$ is constant along

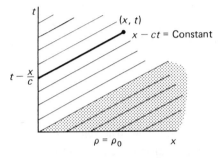

Figure 70-2   Characteristics along which the density is constant.

these lines. Hence, in the shaded region in Fig. 70-2, the density $p_1 = 0$ or the total density $p = p_0$, since $p = p_0$ at $t = 0$. The unshaded region is where on the highway it is noticed that cars are entering at a nonuniform rate. In this region the traffic density only differs slightly from a uniform density, equation 70.3. What is the density of cars if the density remains the same moving at speed $c$? From the diagram in Fig. 70-2, the traffic density at $(x, t)$ is the same as the traffic density at the entrance at a time $x/c$ earlier,

$$x - ct = 0 - c\left(t - \frac{x}{c}\right).$$

$x/c$ is the time it takes a wave to move a distance $x$ at speed $c$. Thus the density at the entrance at time $t - (x/c)$ yields the density $x$ miles along the roadway at time $t$. The traffic density at the entrance can be determined since the traffic flow is prescribed there (use equation 70.1 assuming $p$ is near $p_0$).

The traffic flow, $q(p) = q(p_0 + \epsilon g)$, may be expressed using Taylor series methods,

$$q(p) = q(p_0) + \epsilon g(x - ct)q'(p_0) + O(\epsilon^2).$$

The traffic flow is *approximated* by

$$q(p) = q(p_0) + \epsilon cg(x - ct),$$

since $c = q'(p_0)$. Thus the perturbed traffic flow is simply $c$ times the perturbed density. Since the perturbed traffic flow is known at the entrance, $q_1(t)$, then

$$q_1(t) = cg(-ct) \qquad t > 0,$$

and thus by letting $z = -ct$

$$g(z) = \frac{1}{c} q_1\left(-\frac{z}{c}\right) \qquad \text{for any } z < 0.$$

Consequently the total car density is given by equation 70.3 as

$$p(x, t) = p_0 + \epsilon \frac{q_1\left(t - \dfrac{x}{c}\right)}{c}, \qquad \text{if } x - ct < 0.$$

In summary

$$p(x, t) = \begin{cases} p_0 + \epsilon \dfrac{q_1\left(t - \dfrac{x}{c}\right)}{c} & \text{if } x - ct < 0 \\ p_0 & \text{if } x - ct > 0. \end{cases}$$

This solution clearly indicates that information (that the traffic is entering at $x = 0$) is propagated at a velocity $c$, and hence at position $x$ the information has taken time $x/c$ to travel.

# EXERCISES

**70.1.** Assume that there is nearly uniform light traffic on a semi-infinite highway. Suppose initially the traffic gradually thins out from $p = p_0 + \epsilon$ to $p = p_0$, where $0 < \epsilon \ll p_0$, in the following manner:

$$p(x, 0) = p_0 + \epsilon e^{-x/L}, \qquad x > 0.$$

Suppose that the traffic flow is prescribed at the entrance ($x = 0$),

$$q(0, t) = p_0 u(p_0) + \epsilon \alpha \sin (t/t_0), \quad t > 0.$$

Assume that $0 < \epsilon \alpha \ll p_0 u(p_0)$.
(a) What are the dimensions of $\epsilon$ and $\alpha$?
(b) Determine the traffic density at later times.

**70.2.** Assume there is nearly uniform light traffic on a semi-infinite highway. Suppose initially the traffic was exactly uniform $p(x, 0) = p_0$, but the traffic density was prescribed at the entrance, being slightly different from $p_0$,

$$p(0, t) = p_0 + \epsilon g(t), \quad t > 0,$$

where $0 < \epsilon g(t) \ll p_0$. Determine the traffic density at later times.

**70.3.** Assuming nearly uniform, but heavy traffic, show that in general it is impossible to prescribe the traffic flow at the entrance to a semi-infinite highway. In this situation what might happen to cars waiting to enter the highway?

# 71. Nonuniform Traffic—
# The Method of Characteristics

The nonlinear first-order partial differential equation derived from conservation of cars and the Fundamental Diagram of Road Traffic is

$$\frac{\partial \rho}{\partial t} + \frac{dq(\rho)}{d\rho}\frac{\partial \rho}{\partial x} = 0. \tag{71.1}$$

In the previous sections we considered approximate solutions to this equation in cases in which the density is nearly uniform. The traffic was shown to vary via density waves.

We will find the techniques of nearly uniform traffic density to be of great assistance. Again consider an observer moving in some prescribed fashion $x(t)$. The density of traffic at the observer changes in time as the observer moves about,

$$\frac{d\rho}{dt} = \frac{\partial \rho}{\partial t} + \frac{dx}{dt}\frac{\partial \rho}{\partial x}. \tag{71.2}$$

By comparing equation 71.1 to equation 71.2, it is seen that the density will remain constant from the observer's viewpoint,

$$\frac{d\rho}{dt} = 0, \tag{71.3}$$

or $\rho$ is a constant, if

$$\frac{dx}{dt} = \frac{dq(\rho)}{d\rho} \equiv q'(\rho). \tag{71.4}$$

For this to occur the observer must move at the velocity $q'(\rho)$, the velocity at which nearly uniform traffic density waves propagate. Since this velocity depends on the density (which may dramatically vary from one section of roadway to another), this velocity is called the **local wave velocity**. If the observer moves at the local wave velocity, then the traffic density will appear constant to that observer. Thus there exist certain motions for which an observer will measure a constant traffic density, as shown in Fig. 71-1. Since

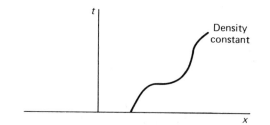

Figure 71-1    Path along which the traffic density stays the same.

equations 71.3 and 71.4 are ordinary differential equations, these curves are again called **characteristics**. Along a characteristic, $p$ is constant; the density is the same density as it is at the position at which the characteristic intersects the initial data.

In the case of nearly uniform flow,

$$\frac{dx}{dt} = c,$$

and thus all the curves (characteristics) were parallel straight lines. In nonuniform traffic flow, the observer moves at the *local* wave velocity. For each observer, the traffic density remains the same, and therefore the local wave velocity for this observer remains the same! The velocity at which each observer moves is constant! *Each observer moves at a constant velocity*, but *different observers may move at different constant velocities*, since they may start with different initial traffic densities. Each moves at its own local wave velocity. Each characteristic is thus a straight line as in the case of nearly uniform flow. However, the slopes (related to the velocities) of different characteristics may be different. The characteristics may not be parallel straight lines.

Consider the characteristic which is initially at the position $x = \alpha$ on the highway, as shown in Fig. 71-2. Along the curve $dx/dt = q'(p)$, $dp/dt = 0$ or $p$ is constant. Initially $p$ equals the value at $x = \alpha$ (i.e., at $t = 0$). Thus along this one characteristic,

$$p = p(\alpha, 0) \equiv p_\alpha,$$

which is a known constant. The local wave velocity which determines the characteristic is a constant, $dx/dt = q'(p_\alpha)$. Consequently, this characteristic

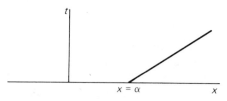

Figure 71-2    Characteristic initially at $x = \alpha$.

is a straight line,

$$x = q'(\rho_\alpha)t + k,$$

where $k$, the $x$-intercept of this characteristic, equals $\alpha$ since at $t = 0$, $x = \alpha$. Thus the equation for this one characteristic is

$$x = q'(\rho_\alpha)t + \alpha.$$

Along this straight line, the traffic density $\rho$ is a constant,

$$\rho = \rho_\alpha.$$

Similarly, for the characteristic initially emanating from $x = \beta$,

$$x = q'(\rho_\beta)t + \beta,$$

also a straight line characteristic, but with a different slope (and corresponding different velocity) if $q'(\rho_\alpha) \neq q'(\rho_\beta)$. Thus, for example, we have Fig. 71-3.

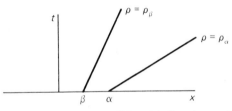

Figure 71-3   Possibly nonparallel straight line characteristics.

In this manner the density of cars at a future time can be predicted. To determine the density at some later time $t = t_*$ at a particular place $x = x_*$, the characteristic that goes through that space-time point must be obtained (see Fig. 71-4). If we are able to determine such a characteristic, then since the density is constant along the characteristic, the density of the desired point is given by the density at the appropriate $x$-intercept,

$$\rho(x_*, t_*) = \rho(\gamma, 0).$$

This technique is called the **method of characteristics**.

Figure 71-4   Using characteristics to determine the future traffic density.

The density wave velocity, $dq/d\rho$, is extremely important. At this velocity the traffic density stays the same. Let us describe some properties of this density wave velocity. We have assumed $dq/d\rho$ decreases as $\rho$ increases (see Fig. 63-3); the density wave velocity decreases as the traffic becomes denser.

Furthermore, we will now show a relationship between the two velocities, density wave velocity and car velocity. To do so the characteristic velocity is conveniently expressed in terms of the traffic velocity and density. Since we know $q = \rho u(\rho)$,

$$\frac{dq}{d\rho} = \rho \frac{du}{d\rho} + u.$$

$du/d\rho \leq 0$ by the original hypothesis that cars slow down as the traffic density increases, see Fig. 71-5. (Equality above is valid only in very light traffic when speed limits, rather than the interaction with other cars, control an auto's velocity.) Consequently, $dq/d\rho \leq u$, that is the density of automobiles (or density wave) always moves at a slower velocity than the cars themselves!

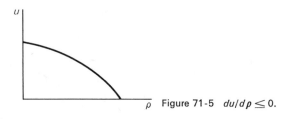

Figure 71-5  $du/d\rho \leq 0$.

# EXERCISES

**71.1.** Experiments in the Lincoln Tunnel (combined with the theoretical work discussed in exercise 63.7) suggest that the traffic flow is approximately

$$q(\rho) = a\rho \left[\ln (\rho_{max}) - \ln \rho\right]$$

(where $a$ and $\rho_{max}$ are known constants). Suppose the initial density $\rho(x, 0)$ varies linearly from bumper-to-bumper traffic (behind $x = -x_0$) to no traffic (ahead of $x = 0$) as sketched in Fig. 71-6. Two hours later, where does $\rho = \rho_{max}/2$?

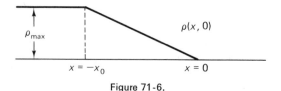

Figure 71-6.

**71.2.** Referring to the theoretical flow-density relationship of exercise 71.1, show that the density wave velocity relative to a moving car is the same constant no matter what the density.

**71.3.** Suppose that the flow-density relationship was known only as a specific sketched curve. If the initial traffic density was known, how would you determine where to look to observe the density $\rho_0$?

**71.4.** Let $c = dq/d\rho$. Show that $c_t + cc_x = 0$.

**71.5.** Let us, by a different method, determine how $x$ and $t$ should change so that the traffic density remains the same. Let us insist that

$$\rho(x + \Delta x, t + \Delta t) = \rho(x, t).$$

Using equation 71.1 and the Taylor series of two variables, rederive the fundamental result, equation 71.3.

**71.6.** Consider two observers, $x_1$ and $x_2$, moving at the same velocity $u_0$, $dx_1/dt = dx_2/dt = u_0$. Show that the rate of change of the number of cars between $x_2$ and $x_1$ equals the flow relative to the observer $x_2$ minus the flow relative to the observer at $x_1$. (Hint: See exercise 60.2).

**71.7.** Consider two moving observers (possibly far apart), both moving at the same velocity $V$, such that the number of cars the first observer passes is the same as the number passed by the second observer.
(a) Show that $V = \Delta q/\Delta \rho$.
(b) Show that the average density between the two observers stays constant.

**71.8.** In this section we have shown that if $dx/dt = dq/d\rho$, then $d\rho/dt = 0$. If $dx/dt \neq dq/d\rho$, is it possible for $d\rho/dt = 0$? Briefly explain.

**71.9.** Show that $\rho = f(x - q'(\rho)t)$ satisfies equation 71.1 for any function $f$. Note that initially $\rho = f(x)$. Briefly explain how this solution was obtained.

# 72. *After a Traffic Light Turns Green*

In the past sections the intent has been to develop in each reader a sufficient understanding of the assumptions under which we have formulated a mathematical model of traffic. The time has come to solve some problems and explain what kinds of qualitative and quantitative information the model yields. In this section we will formulate and solve one such interesting problem.

Suppose that traffic is lined up behind a red traffic light (or behind a railroad crossing, with a train stopping traffic). We call the position of the traffic light $x = 0$. Since the cars are bumper to bumper behind the traffic light, $\rho = \rho_{max}$ for $x < 0$. Assume that the cars are lined up indefinitely and, of course, are not moving. (In reality the line is finite, but could be very long. Our analysis is limited then to times and places at which the effects of a thinning of the waiting line can be ignored.) If the light stops traffic long enough, then we may also assume that there is no traffic ahead of the light, $\rho = 0$ for $x > 0$. Thus the initial traffic density distribution is as sketched in Fig. 72-1.

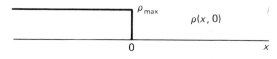

Figure 72-1    Traffic density due to an extremely long red light.

Suppose that at $t = 0$, the traffic light turns from red to green. What is the density of cars for all later times? The partial differential equation describing conservation of cars,

$$\frac{\partial \rho}{\partial t} + \frac{dq}{d\rho}\frac{\partial \rho}{\partial x} = 0,$$ (72.1)

must be solved with the initial condition

$$\rho(x, 0) = \begin{cases} \rho_{\max} & x < 0 \\ 0 & x > 0. \end{cases}$$

Note the initial condition is a discontinuous function. Before solving this problem, can we guess what happens from our own observations of this type of traffic situation? We know that as soon as the light turns green, the traffic starts to thin out, but sufficiently far behind the light, traffic hasn't started to move even after the light changes. Thus we expect the density to be as illustrated in Fig. 72-2. Traffic is less dense further ahead on the road; the density is becoming thinner or rarefied and the corresponding solution will be called a rarefactive wave.

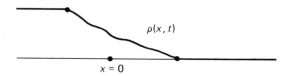

Figure 72-2    Traffic density: expected qualitative behavior after red light turns green.

We will show the solution of our mathematical model yields this type of result. Partial differential equation 72.1 may be solved by the method of characteristics as discussed in Sec. 71. As a brief review, note that if $dx/dt = dq/d\rho$, then $dp/dt = (\partial \rho/\partial t) + (dx/dt)(\partial \rho/\partial x) = 0$. Thus the traffic density $\rho(x, t)$ is constant along the characteristics, which are given by

$$\frac{dx}{dt} = \frac{dq(\rho)}{d\rho} = \rho\frac{du}{d\rho} + u.$$ (72.2)

The density propagates at the velocity $dq/dp$. Since $p$ remains constant, the density moves at a constant velocity. The characteristics are straight lines. In the $x$–$t$ plane

$$x = \frac{dq}{dp}(\rho)t + k, \tag{72.3}$$

where each characteristic may have a different integration constant $k$. Let us analyze all characteristics that intersect the initial data at $x > 0$. There $p(x, 0) = 0$. Thus $p = 0$ along all lines such that

$$\frac{dx}{dt} = \frac{dq}{dp}\bigg|_{p=0} = u(0) = u_{max},$$

where this velocity has been evaluated using equation 72.2. The characteristic velocity for zero density is always $u_{max}$, the car velocity for zero density. The characteristic curves which intersect the $x$-axis for $x > 0$ are all straight lines with velocity $u_{max}$. Hence the characteristic which emanates from $x = x_0$ ($x_0 > 0$) at $t = 0$ is given by

$$x = u_{max}t + x_0 \quad (x_0 > 0).$$

Various of these characteristics are sketched in Fig. 72-3. The first characteristic in this region starts at $x = 0$ and hence $x = u_{max}t$. Thus below in the lined region ($x > u_{max}t$), the density is zero; that is no cars have reached that region. At a fixed time if one is sufficiently far from the traffic light, then no cars have yet arrived and hence the density is zero. In fact imagine you are in the first car. As soon as the light changes you observe zero density ahead of you, and therefore in this model you accelerate instantaneously to the speed $u_{max}$. You would not reach the point $x$ until $t = x/u_{max}$, and thus there would be no cars at $x$ for $t < x/u_{max}$.

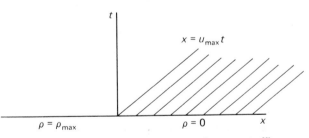

Figure 72-3  Characteristics corresponding to no traffic.

Now we analyze the characteristics that intersect the initial data for $x < 0$, where the cars are standing still being at maximum density, $p = p_{max}$. $p = p_{max}$ along these characteristics determined from equation 72.2,

$$\frac{dx}{dt} = \frac{dq}{dp}\bigg|_{p=p_{max}} = p_{max}\frac{du}{dp}\bigg|_{p=p_{max}} = p_{max} u'(p_{max}) < 0,$$

where we have used the fact that $u(\rho_{max}) = 0$. This velocity is negative since $u'(\rho_{max}) < 0$; the maximum density is certainly in the region of "heavy" traffic. Thus these characteristics are all parallel straight lines with the appropriate negative velocity that intersect the negative $x$-axis,

$$x = \rho_{max} u'(\rho_{max}) t + x_0, \quad (x_0 < 0),$$

as sketched in Fig. 72-4. The boundary of the region in which $\rho = \rho_{max}$ is the characteristic emanating from $x = 0$ (at $t = 0$). The cars are still bumper to bumper in the region indicated in Fig. 72-4 on the left,

$$x < \rho_{max} u'(\rho_{max}) t.$$

After the light changes to green the cars start moving such that it takes a finite amount of time before each car moves. (A familiar experience, wouldn't you say?)

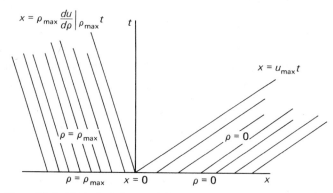

Figure 72-4    Method of characteristics: regions of no traffic and bumper-to-bumper traffic.

Consider the $n$th car in line at the light. This theory predicts that after the light changes to green, the $n$th car waits an amount of time equal to

$$t = \frac{(n-1)L}{-\rho_{max} u'(\rho_{max})},$$

where $L$ is front-to-front distance between cars. (Note $u'(\rho_{max}) < 0$.) We have ignored driver reaction and acceleration time. Hence we expect this time to be a little too short. It might be interesting to measure the waiting times at traffic lights as a function of the car's position (i.e., how far back). You can perform this experiment. Is the waiting time roughly linearly dependent on the car's position as predicted above? Use your data to compute $u'(\rho_{max})$. Does $u'(\rho_{max})$ significantly vary for different road situations?

Data roughly extrapolated from the Lincoln Tunnel experiments (see sec. 62, assuming $\rho_{max} = 225$ cars/mile) suggest that

$$u'(\rho_{max}) \approx \frac{\Delta u}{\Delta \rho} = \frac{-6 \text{ m.p.h.}}{60 \text{ cars/miles}} = -.1 \frac{\text{miles}^2}{\text{car} \cdot \text{hour}}.$$

For each car behind the light, the predicted waiting time is

$$t = \frac{L}{-\rho_{max} u'(\rho_{max})} = \frac{1}{-\rho_{max}^2 u'(\rho_{max})} = \frac{1}{.1(225)^2} \text{ hours.}$$

In seconds, the waiting time is

$$t = \frac{(60)^2}{.1(225)^2} \approx .71 \text{ seconds,}$$

or approximately $\frac{3}{4}$ second per car.

So far only the easiest part of the problem has been calculated, namely the regions of roadway in which the density is either 0 or $\rho_{max}$. We seemed to have utilized the method of characteristics to its total extent since the initial density consisted of only the two values shown in Fig. 72-1. We have predicted the density is

$$\rho = \rho_{max} \quad \text{for} \quad x < \rho_{max} u'(\rho_{max})t$$

and

$$\rho = 0 \quad \text{for} \quad x > u_{max}t,$$

as shown in Fig. 72-5. This is insufficient, as the density has not been determined in the region

$$\rho_{max} u'(\rho_{max})t < x < u_{max}t,$$

the region in which cars actually pass through the green traffic light!

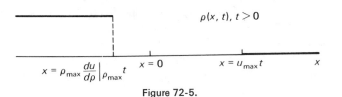

Figure 72-5.

To investigate this problem we first assume that the initial traffic density was not discontinuous, but smoothly varied between $\rho = 0$ and $\rho = \rho_{max}$ in a very small distance, $\Delta x$, near the traffic light, see Fig. 72-6. If $\Delta x$ is sufficiently small, then we expect the solution to this problem to be essentially

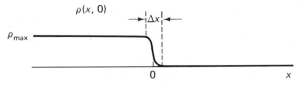

Figure 72-6   Continuous model of the initial traffic density.

equivalent to the solution in the case in which $\Delta x = 0$. If $\Delta x \neq 0$, the characteristics along which $\rho = 0$ and $\rho = \rho_{max}$ may be sketched in a space-time diagram as are demonstrated in Fig. 72-7. There must be characteristics which emanate close to the origin. $\rho$ is constant along the line

$$x = \frac{dq}{d\rho}t + x_0,$$

sketched in dotted lines in Fig. 72-7, where $x_0$ is the position of the characteristic at $t = 0$ and is very small (we might later expect that it can be ignored).

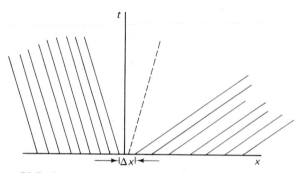

**Figure 72-7**   Space-time diagram for rapid transition from no traffic to bumper-to-bumper traffic.

Since $\rho$ ranges continuously between $\rho = 0$ and $\rho = \rho_{max}$, the velocity $dq/d\rho$ is always between its values corresponding to $\rho = 0$ and $\rho = \rho_{max}$, namely between $u_{max}$ and $\rho_{max}u'(\rho_{max})$, respectively. Where the density is smaller, the velocity $dq/d\rho$ is greater (see Fig. 72-10). As density increases, the wave velocity diminishes. There is a value at which the wave velocity is zero (recall it is a stationary wave corresponding to the road's capacity), and then for denser traffic the wave velocity is negative. A few of these characteristics are sketched in Fig. 72-8. The straight line characteristics have different slopes. Notice that the characteristics "fan out." The distance over which traffic changes from no cars to bumper to bumper increases as time increases. The traffic "spreads out" or "expands" after the light changes from red to green.

If the initial traffic density is in fact discontinuous (see Fig. 72-4), then we will obtain the density in the "unknown" region by considering the limit of the continuous initial condition problem as $\Delta x \to 0$. $\rho$ is constant along the characteristics

$$\frac{dx}{dt} = \frac{dq}{d\rho},$$

which are again straight lines (you should repeat the reasons as to why) $x = (dq/d\rho)t + x_0$. The characteristics not corresponding to $\rho = 0$ or

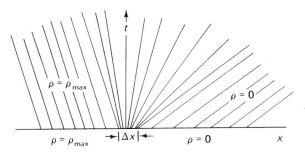

Figure 72-8   Method of characteristics: $\Delta x$ is the initial distance over which density changes from 0 to $\rho_{\max}$.

$\rho = \rho_{\max}$ go through $x = 0$ at $t = 0$ (this is the result of letting $\Delta x \rightarrow 0$). Thus $x_0 = 0$ and

$$x = \frac{dq}{d\rho} t.$$

It is as though at the discontinuity ($x = 0$) all traffic densities between $\rho = 0$ and $\rho = \rho_{\max}$ are observed. The observers (following constant density) then travel at different constant velocities $dq/d\rho$ depending on which density they initially observe at $x = 0$. The characteristics are called **fanlike** (representing an expansion wave) in the region so illustrated in Fig. 72-9. Along each

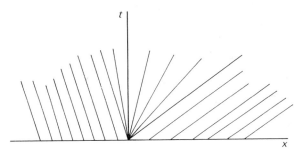

Figure 72-9   Fan-shaped characteristics due to discontinuous initial data.

characteristic, the density is constant. To obtain the density at a given $x$ and $t$, we must determine which characteristic goes through that position at that time. At the point $(x, t)$ the density wave velocity is known:

$$\boxed{\frac{dq}{d\rho} = \frac{x}{t}.} \tag{72.4}$$

Equation 72.4 must be solved for $\rho$. Since $dq/d\rho$ only depends on $\rho$, often it is possible to algebraically solve for $\rho$ as a function of $x$ and $t$ (actually, in this case, a function of $x/t$) in the region of fanlike characteristics. An explicit example of this calculation is discussed in the next section. However, sometimes only a sketch of $dq/d\rho$ may be known, as shown in Fig. 72-10. As always, we have assumed that $dq/d\rho$ decreases as $\rho$ increases. At a given position within the region of fanlike characteristics, the density may be determined graphically as follows. Given $x$ and $t$, $dq/d\rho$ is calculated via equation 72.4. $dq/d\rho$ is then located on the $dq/d\rho$ versus $\rho$ figure and the corresponding value of $\rho$ determined as illustrated in Fig. 72-10.

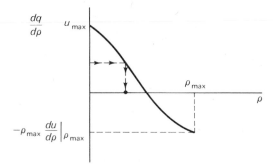

Figure 72-10    Determination of traffic density from density wave velocity.

Alternatively, the Fundamental Diagram of Road Traffic can be used to determine graphically the density at a given position on the roadway in the region of fanlike characteristics. Given $t$ and $x$, the slope of the straight line from the origin to the point $(t, x)$ in Fig. 72-11 equals $dq/d\rho$. Thus this straight line must have the same slope as the tangent to the flow-density $(q-\rho)$ curve. The traffic density can thus be estimated by finding the density on the $q-\rho$ curve whose slope is the same as $x/t$, as demonstrated in Fig. 72-11.

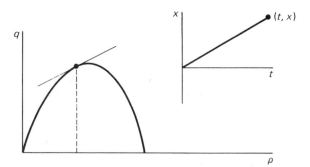

Figure 72-11    Traffic density in fan-like region of characteristics: graphical technique.

The maximum flow occurs where $dq/d\rho = 0$. Thus the density wave that is stationary (density wave velocity equals zero) indicates positions at which the flow of cars is a maximum. In the problem just discussed, as soon as the light changes from red to green, *the maximum flow occurs at the light*, $x = 0$, and stays there for all future time. This suggests a simple experiment to measure the maximum flow. Position an observer at a traffic light. Wait until the light turns red and many cars line up. Then, when the light turns green, simply measure the traffic flow at the light. If this theory is correct (that is, if $u = u(\rho)$), then this measured traffic flow of cars will be constant and equal to the maximum possible for the road (the capacity of the road).

## EXERCISES

**72.1.** Show that if $u = u(\rho)$ is determined by braking distance theory (see exercise 61.2), then the waiting time per car after a traffic light turns green is the same as the human reaction time for braking.

**72.2.** Stand at an intersection, not hampered by turns, and experimentally determine how long a car has to wait after a light turns green as a function of the number of cars it is behind the light. Compare your experimental results to the theory of this section.

**72.3.** Assume that $dq/d\rho$ is known as a function of $\rho$, as sketched in Fig. 72-10. Sketch the traffic density 10 minutes after the traffic light turns green.

**72.4.** Using the flow-density relationship of exercise 68.2, sketch the traffic density 10 minutes after the traffic light turns green.

**72.5.** Sketch $dq/d\rho$ as a function of $x$, for fixed $t > 0$ (after the light turns green).

# 73. A Linear Velocity-Density Relationship

In order to illustrate the method of characteristics as it applies to traffic problems, for educational reasons we will frequently find it convenient to choose a simple velocity-density relationship having the general desired features. Hopefully enough qualitative insight will be gained from a simple curve to justify the quantitative errors in not using an experimentally observed velocity-density curve.

If the velocity-density relationship is assumed to be linear,* then

---

*We should note that the equation expressing conservation of cars is still a *nonlinear* partial differential equation.

$$u(\rho) = \frac{u_{\max}}{\rho_{\max}}(\rho_{\max} - \rho) = u_{\max}\left(1 - \frac{\rho}{\rho_{\max}}\right), \qquad \text{(73.1)}$$

which is sketched in Fig. 73-1. This has the four desired properties:

(1) $u(\rho_{\max}) = 0$
(2) $u(0) = u_{\max}$
(3) $\dfrac{du}{d\rho} \leq 0$   (in a simple way)
(4) $dq/d\rho$ decreases as $\rho$ increases (since $d^2q/d\rho^2 < 0$, as will be shown).

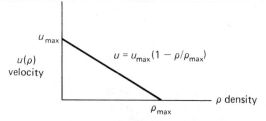

Figure 73-1   Linear velocity-density curve.

In this case the traffic flow can be easily computed,

$$q = \rho u = u_{\max}\rho\left(1 - \frac{\rho}{\rho_{\max}}\right), \qquad \text{(73.2)}$$

yielding a parabolic Fundamental Diagram of Road Traffic, which is sketched in Fig. 73-2. The density wave velocity,

$$\frac{dq}{d\rho} = u_{\max}\left(1 - \frac{2\rho}{\rho_{\max}}\right), \qquad \text{(73.3)}$$

yields both positive and negative wave velocities. The wave velocity decreases as the density increases (i.e., $d^2q/d\rho^2 < 0$). The maximum flow occurs when the density wave is stationary (density wave velocity equals zero). For this

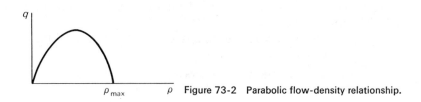

Figure 73-2   Parabolic flow-density relationship.

linear velocity-density curve, the density at which the traffic flow is maximized is exactly one-half the maximum density, $\rho = \rho_{max}/2$, and the speed is similarly one-half the maximum speed, $u(\rho_{max}/2) = u_{max}/2$. (These values should not be taken too literally for realistic situations, as they are based on the possibly inaccurate linear density-velocity curve.) Thus the maximum traffic flow is

$$q\left(\frac{\rho_{max}}{2}\right) = \frac{\rho_{max}u_{max}}{4},$$

a quarter of the traffic flow that would occur if bumper-to-bumper traffic moved at the maximum speed.

Let us suppose that the velocity is given by equation 73.1. We will solve for the traffic density after the traffic is started from a red light. That is, we will consider the initial density as before,

$$\rho(x, 0) = \begin{cases} \rho_{max} & x < 0 \\ 0 & x > 0. \end{cases}$$

The density wave velocities corresponding to $\rho = 0$ and $\rho = \rho_{max}$ are easy to calculate. From equation 73.3, $(dq/d\rho)(0) = u_{max}$ as before, and $(dq/d\rho)(\rho_{max}) = -u_{max}$. Thus the characteristics along which $\rho = 0$ and $\rho = \rho_{max}$ may be sketched on a space-time diagram, as Fig. 73-3 shows. We will explicitly

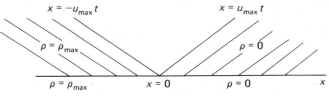

Figure 73-3  Space-time diagram for traffic light problem.

calculate the density in the fanlike region, $-u_{max}t < x < u_{max}t$. There, the characteristics are given by

$$\frac{dq}{d\rho} = \frac{x}{t},$$

since they start from $x = 0$ at $t = 0$. For the linear velocity-density relationship, the density wave velocity is given by equation 73.3 and hence

$$\frac{x}{t} = u_{max}\left(1 - \frac{2\rho}{\rho_{max}}\right).$$

Solving for $\rho$ yields

$$\rho = \frac{\rho_{max}}{2}\left(1 - \frac{x}{u_{max}t}\right). \tag{73.4}$$

For fixed time, the density is linearly dependent on $x$ (in the region of fanlike characteristics). Note at $x = 0$, $\rho = \rho_{max}/2$, the density corresponding to maximum flow (as shown in general in Sec. 72). Let us sketch in Fig. 73-4 the density at $t = 0$ and at a later time using the known positions of the boundaries of maximum and minimum traffic densities. It is seen that the density of cars spreads out.

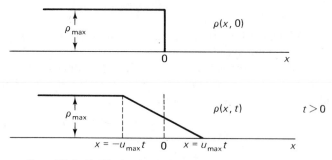

Figure 73-4    Traffic density: before and after light turns green.

The result can be seen in a different manner. We have shown the density $\rho$ stays the same moving at the density wave velocity $dq/d\rho$ given by equation 73.3. Let us follow observers staying with the constant densities $\rho_{max}$, $3\rho_{max}/4$, $\rho_{max}/2$, $\rho_{max}/4$, and 0, marked by $\bullet$ on the diagram in Fig. 73-5 representing the initial density. Each observer is moving at a different constant velocity. After some time (introducing an arrow showing how each observer must move), Fig. 73-6 shows that the linear dependence of the wave velocity on the density (equation 73.3) yields a linear density profile (as previously sketched from equation 73.4).

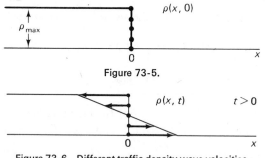

Figure 73-5.

Figure 73-6    Different traffic density wave velocities.

Let us compute the motion of an individual car starting at a distance $x_0$ in back of this light, that is $x = -x_0$ (at $t = 0$). The velocity of the car is given by the field velocity

$$\frac{dx}{dt} = u(x, t).$$

The car stays still until the wave, propagating the information of the change of the light, reaches the car, as illustrated in Fig. 73-7. After that time, $t = x_0/u_{max}$, the car moves at the velocity given in the fanlike region,

$$\frac{dx}{dt} = u(x, t) = u_{max}\left(1 - \frac{\rho}{\rho_{max}}\right).$$

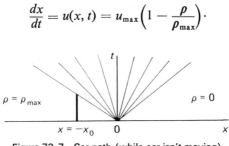

Figure 73-7   Car path (while car isn't moving).

When a car behind the light starts moving its velocity is first zero and then slowly increases. Since the density is determined from equation 73.4, it follows that the car's velocity depends on both its position and on time:

$$\frac{dx}{dt} = \frac{u_{max}}{2} + \frac{x}{2t}. \tag{73.5}$$

To determine the trajectory of each car (i.e., the position $x$ as a function of time $t$), the solution of equation 73.5, a *linear* first-order nonhomogeneous ordinary differential equation, must be obtained which satisfies the initial condition that at

$$t = \frac{x_0}{u_{max}}, \quad x = -x_0. \tag{73.6}$$

It can be solved in many ways. One method (there are others) is to note that this equation, rewritten as

$$t\frac{dx}{dt} - \frac{1}{2}x = \frac{u_{max}}{2}t,$$

is a nonhomogeneous equidimensional equation. The method to solve this equation is analogous to the method used for the second-order equidimensional equation.* The homogeneous solution is

$$x = Bt^{1/2},$$

---

*One of the simplest second-order differential equations with nonconstant coefficients is the equidimensional equation (also called the Euler or Cauchy equation):

$$t^2\frac{d^2x}{dt^2} + at\frac{dx}{dt} + bx = 0.$$

It has solutions of the form $x = t^r$.

where $B$ is an arbitrary constant (this solution is obtained either by equidimensional techniques, $x = t^r$, or by separation of variables). A particular solution is proportional to $t^r$ if the right-hand side is proportional to $t^r$ ($r \neq 1/2$). Thus $x = At$ is a particular solution if (by substitution)

$$A = \frac{u_{max}}{2} + \frac{1}{2} A.$$

Therefore the "undetermined" coefficient is $A = u_{max}$. Hence the general solution is

$$x = u_{max} t + B t^{1/2}.$$

The initial condition, equation 73.6, determines $B$

$$-x_0 = x_0 + B \left( \frac{x_0}{u_{max}} \right)^{1/2},$$

and thus

$$B = -2x_0 \left( \frac{u_{max}}{x_0} \right)^{1/2} = -2(x_0 u_{max})^{1/2}.$$

Consequently, the position of this car is determined,

$$\boxed{x = u_{max} t - 2(x_0 u_{max} t)^{1/2}.} \tag{73.7}$$

The car's velocity is

$$\frac{dx}{dt} = u_{max} - \left( \frac{x_0 u_{max}}{t} \right)^{1/2}. \tag{73.8}$$

From equation 73.6 the car starts moving with zero initial velocity; it slowly accelerates. Its velocity is always less than $u_{max}$. For very large $t$, the car approaches maximum velocity; $dx/dt \to u_{max}$ as $t \to \infty$, as shown in Fig. 73-8.

How long does it take the car to actually pass the light? That is, at what time is $x = 0$? From equation 73.7,

$$0 = u_{max} t - 2(x_0 u_{max} t)^{1/2} \quad \text{or} \quad 0 = (u_{max} t)^{1/2} - 2x_0^{1/2}.$$

Thus,

$$t = 4 \frac{x_0}{u_{max}};$$

that is 4 times longer than if the car were able to move at the maximum speed immediately.

At what speed is the car going when it passes the light? We do not need to do any calculations as at the light the traffic flow is maximum, which we have shown occurs when the velocity is $\frac{1}{2}$ the maximum velocity, $u = u_{max}/2$. Equation 73.8 agrees with this result.

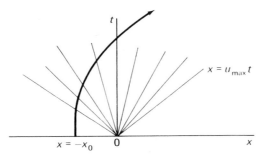

Figure 73-8   Path of a car accelerating past a traffic signal.

If the light stays green until time $T$, how many cars will pass the traffic light? We have already determined that a car starting at $-x_0$ passes the traffic light at $t = 4x_0/u_{max}$. Thus at time $T$, a car starting from $-u_{max}T/4$ will be at the light. The number of cars contained in that distance is $\rho_{max}(u_{max}T/4)$. (This result can be obtained in a simpler manner. We know the flow at the traffic light, the number of cars passing per hour, is $u_{max}\rho_{max}/4$. Thus in time $T$, $(u_{max}\rho_{max}/4)T$ cars have passed!) For a one-minute light, using $\rho_{max} = 225$ and $u_{max} = 40$ m.p.h., the number of cars is

$$\frac{225}{4} \cdot 40 \cdot \frac{1}{60} \approx 37.5 \text{ cars.}$$

The graphical technique based on the flow-density curve may also be used to determine the traffic density after the light turns green, as well as to approximate each car's path. Along characteristics, the density is constant. Since the car velocity only depends on the density, it too is constant along characteristics. Thus characteristics are isoclines for the differential equation,

$$\frac{dx}{dt} = u(x, t),$$

determining the motion of individual cars. Using an $x$–$t$ diagram such that the slopes are measured in units of velocity yields Fig. 73-9. Figure 73-9 follows from the Fundamental Diagram of Road Traffic shown in Fig. 73-10. To determine car paths, small horizontal lines (indicating no motion) are sketched wherever $\rho = \rho_{max}$. In addition, for example, we note that at $x = 0$, the density is that corresponding to the road's capacity, and a car's velocity there is marked by the dotted straight line on the Fundamental Diagram of Road Traffic. This slope is also then marked wherever the density has that value, as shown in Fig. 73-11. By connecting straight dashes (the method of isoclines, see Sec. 26), the path of a car can be estimated for this problem, as well as for those for which analytic solutions are impossible!

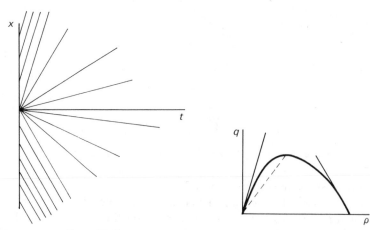

Figure 73-9.                                    Figure 73-10.

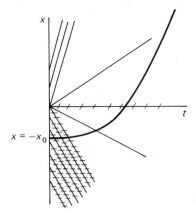

Figure 73-11    Car path: graphical sketch.

# EXERCISES

**73.1.*** Assume that the traffic density is initially

$$\rho(x, 0) = \begin{cases} \rho_{\max} & x < 0 \\ \rho_{\max}/2 & 0 < x < a \\ 0 & a < x. \end{cases}$$

Sketch the initial density. Determine and sketch the density at all later times.

---

*In exercises 73.1–73.5 assume that $u = u_{\max}(1 - \rho/\rho_{\max})$.

**73.2.\*** Calculate the maximum acceleration of a car which starts approximately one car length behind the traffic light (i.e., $x(0) = -1/\rho_{max}$).

**73.3.\*** Calculate the velocity of a car at the moment it starts moving behind a light.

**73.4.\*** Since we are assuming cars are of zero length, it is only the front of the first car that moves at the speed limit. Since the density has been determined in this section, calculate the position of the end of the first car (with length $L$) as a function of time (for sufficiently large time).

**73.5.\*** Suppose at $t = 0$ that the density is

$$\rho(x, 0) = \begin{cases} 3\rho_{max}/5 & x < 0 \\ \rho_{max}/5 & x > 0. \end{cases}$$

Sketch the initial density. Determine and sketch the density at later times.

**73.6.** Assume

$$u = u_{max}\left(1 - \frac{\rho^2}{\rho_{max}^2}\right).$$

Determine the traffic density that results after an infinite line of stopped traffic is started by a red traffic light turning green.

**73.7.** Suppose that $u \neq u_{max}(1 - \rho/\rho_{max})$. Show that a car a distance $x_0$ behind the light takes a time $x_0\rho_{max}/q_{max}$ to pass the light, where $q_{max}$ is the capacity of the road.

**73.8.** Using the flow-density relationship of exercise 68.2, sketch the trajectory of a car starting at a given distance behind the light.

**73.9.** At what velocity does the information that the traffic light changed from red to green travel?

# 74. An Example

We have shown explicitly how to use the method of characteristics to solve traffic problems which initially consist of regions of constant density. The same ideas can be utilized when the initial density varies in a prescribed way,

$$\rho(x, 0) = f(x).$$

For convenience, we again assume $u(\rho) = u_{max}(1 - \rho/\rho_{max})$, in which case the density wave velocity determines the characteristics as follows:

$$\frac{dx}{dt} = \frac{dq}{d\rho} = u_{max}\left(1 - \frac{2\rho}{\rho_{max}}\right).$$

The characteristic starting from $x = x_0$ is

$$x = u_{max}\left(1 - \frac{2\rho}{\rho_{max}}\right)t + x_0, \tag{74.1}$$

along which the density is constant, equaling its value at $t = 0$,

$$p(x, t) = p(x_0, 0) = f(x_0). \tag{74.2}$$

The characteristics are sketched in Fig. 74-1. We assume that the characteristics do *not* intersect. The more difficult case (and perhaps more interesting one) in which characteristics intersect is not discussed until Sec. 76.

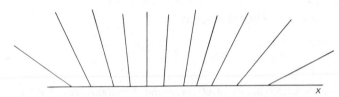

Figure 74-1    Nonparallel nonintersecting characteristics.

We use the method of characteristics in two equivalent ways to determine the traffic density as a function of $x$ and $t$:

### (1)  PARAMETERIZING THE INITIAL POSITION
### AS A FUNCTION OF $x$ AND $t$

Each characteristic is labelled by its position, $x_0$, at $t = 0$. Given $x$ and $t$, we try to find $x_0$ (i.e., which characteristic goes through the point $(x, t)$). $p$ is eliminated using equation 74.2 and thus equation 74.1 yields $x_0$ as a function of $x$ and $t$,

$$x_0 = x_0(x, t). \tag{74.3}$$

This step can not always be done explicitly as it may be impossible to solve for $x_0$. For example, if

$$p(x, 0) = \frac{p_{\max}}{1 + e^{x/L}},$$

then the characteristics are determined from equation 74.1,

$$x = u_{\max}\left(1 - \frac{2}{1 + e^{x_0/L}}\right)t + x_0,$$

from which an equation like equation 74.3 cannot be explicitly obtained. Since the density at a point only depends on $x_0$ (i.e., on which characteristic goes through it),

$$p(x, t) = p(x_0, 0) = f(x_0) = f(x_0(x, t)), \tag{74.4}$$

when equation 74.3 exists. Thus substituting equation 74.3 into equation 74.2 yields the spatial and time dependence of the traffic density, equation 74.4.

## (2) PARAMETERIZING THE INITIAL POSITION AS A FUNCTION OF THE INITIAL DENSITY

An equivalent method is to first use equation 74.2 to determine $x_0$ as a function of $\rho$,

$$x_0 = x_0(\rho). \tag{74.5}$$

Again, it is not always possible to obtain from equation 74.2 an explicit expression for $x_0$. However, when equation 74.5 is substituted into equation 74.1, an equation results involving only $x$, $t$, and $\rho$, showing $\rho$'s dependence on $x$ and $t$.

As a specific example, assume that $u(\rho) = u_{max}(1 - \rho/\rho_{max})$ and

$$\rho(x, 0) = \begin{cases} \rho_{max} & x < 0 \\ \rho_{max}\dfrac{(x - L)^2}{L^2} & 0 < x < L \\ 0 & x > L, \end{cases}$$

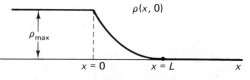

Figure 74-2   Initial traffic density.

as sketched in Fig. 74-2. If $x_0 > L$ or $x_0 < 0$, the characteristics given by equation 74.1 start from a region of constant density. Since the corresponding density wave velocities are easily calculated,

$$\left.\frac{dq}{d\rho}\right|_{\rho=0} = u_{max} \quad \text{and} \quad \left.\frac{dq}{d\rho}\right|_{\rho=\rho_{max}} = -u_{max},$$

we obtain the two regions of constant density,

$$\rho = \begin{cases} 0 & \text{for } x > u_{max}t + L \\ \rho_{max} & \text{for } x < -u_{max}t, \end{cases}$$

following from the space-time sketches of the characteristics shown in Fig. 74-3. In the region where the traffic density has not been determined as yet, let us use the method of characteristics as described by *both* equivalent procedures (1) and (2).

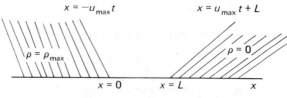

Figure 74-3   Characteristics.

### (1) $x_0(x, t)$

The characteristics which start from $0 < x_0 < L$ satisfy equation 74.1, where

$$\rho = \frac{\rho_{\max}(x_0 - L)^2}{L^2}, \tag{74.6}$$

and thus the equation for these characteristics is

$$x = u_{\max}\left(1 - \frac{2}{L^2}(x_0 - L)^2\right)t + x_0, \tag{74.7}$$

where we should remember this is valid for all $x_0$ as long as $0 < x_0 < L$. Equation 74.7 determines $x_0$ as a function of $x$ and $t$, since equation 74.7 is a quadratic equation for $x_0$ (more easily expressed in terms of $x_0 - L$ by noting $x_0 = x_0 - L + L$):

$$(x_0 - L)^2 \frac{2u_{\max}t}{L^2} - (x_0 - L) + x - L - u_{\max}t = 0.$$

The solution of this quadratic equation is

$$x_0 - L = \frac{1 \pm \sqrt{1 - \frac{8u_{\max}t}{L^2}(x - L - u_{\max}t)}}{4u_{\max}t/L^2}. \tag{74.8}$$

The negative sign must be chosen above in order for $0 < x_0 < L$ (this is seen by recalling that $-u_{\max}t < x < u_{\max}t + L$). The traffic density as a function of $x$ and $t$ in the region corresponding to $0 < x_0 < L$ follows by substituting equation 74.8 into equation 74.6:

$$\rho(x, t) = \frac{\rho_{\max}}{L^2}\frac{\left(1 - \sqrt{1 - \frac{8u_{\max}t}{L^2}(x - L - u_{\max}t)}\right)^2}{16u_{\max}^2 t^2/L^4}, \tag{74.9}$$

admittedly a rather cumbersome expression. We note that as $x$ approaches the edges of the region of varying density, the density approaches the known constants. In particular, from equation 74.9

as $x \longrightarrow u_{\max}t + L, \quad \rho \longrightarrow 0$

as $x \longrightarrow -u_{\max}t, \quad \rho \longrightarrow \dfrac{\rho_{\max}}{L^2}\dfrac{\left(1 - \sqrt{\left(1 + \dfrac{4u_{\max}t}{L}\right)^2}\right)^2}{16u_{\max}^2 t^2/L^4} = \rho_{\max}.$

Furthermore, we should verify that equation 74.9 satisfies the initial conditions. This is not obvious since as $t \rightarrow 0$, both the denominator and numerator tend to zero. To determine the limit as $t \rightarrow 0$ of equation 74.9, the simplest technique is to approximate the numerator as $t \rightarrow 0$. Since $\sqrt{1 - t} \approx 1 - \frac{1}{2}t$ as $t \rightarrow 0$, we see that as $t \rightarrow 0$

$$\rho(x, t) \longrightarrow \frac{\rho_{\max}}{L^2} \frac{\left[1 - \left(1 - \frac{4u_{\max}t}{L^2}(x - L)\right)\right]^2}{16u_{\max}^2 t^2/L^4} = \frac{\rho_{\max}(x - L)^2}{L^2},$$

as originally specified for $0 < x_0 < L$.

### (2)   $x_0(\rho)$

Alternatively, we begin by using equation 74.6 to determine $x_0$ as a function of $\rho$, $(x_0 - L)^2 = L^2 \rho/\rho_{\max}$ or $x_0 = L \pm L\sqrt{\rho/\rho_{\max}}$. However, since $0 < x_0 < L$, the minus sign must be used above:

$$x_0 = L - L\sqrt{\rho/\rho_{\max}} = L(1 - \sqrt{\rho/\rho_{\max}}). \tag{74.10}$$

Note that as $\rho$ varies between 0 and $\rho_{\max}$, $x_0$ varies between 0 and $L$. By substituting equation 74.10 into equation 74.1, an equation for the density is obtained:

$$x = u_{\max}(1 - 2\rho/\rho_{\max})t + L(1 - \sqrt{\rho/\rho_{\max}}).$$

This equation may be expressed as a quadratic equation for $\sqrt{\rho/\rho_{\max}}$:

$$(\sqrt{\rho/\rho_{\max}})^2 2u_{\max}t + L\sqrt{\rho/\rho_{\max}} + x - L - u_{\max}t = 0.$$

Thus

$$\sqrt{\rho/\rho_{\max}} = \frac{-L + \sqrt{L^2 - 8u_{\max}t(x - L - u_{\max}t)}}{4u_{\max}t},$$

where the positive sign of the square root has been chosen since $\sqrt{\rho/\rho_{\max}} > 0$. Squaring this last equation yields an expression for $\rho(x, t)$, which is identical to that derived by procedure (1), equation 74.9.

## EXERCISES

**74.1.**  Assume that $u(\rho) = u_{\max}(1 - \rho/\rho_{\max})$ and

$$\rho(x, 0) = \begin{cases} \rho_0 & x < 0 \\ \rho_0(x - L)/L & 0 < x < L \\ 0 & x > L. \end{cases}$$

Determine and sketch $\rho(x, t)$.

**74.2.** Assume $u(\rho) = u_{max}(1 - \rho^2/\rho_{max}^2)$ and

$$\rho(x, 0) = \begin{cases} \rho_{max} & x < 0 \\ \rho_{max}(x - L)/L & 0 < x < L \\ 0 & x > L. \end{cases}$$

Determine $\rho(x, t)$.

**74.3.** Consider the following partial differential equation:

$$\frac{\partial \rho}{\partial t} - \rho^2 \frac{\partial \rho}{\partial x} = 0 \quad -\infty < x < \infty.$$

(a)   Why can't this equation model a traffic flow problem?

(b)   Solve this partial differential equation by the method of characteristics, subject to the initial conditions:

$$\rho(x, 0) = \begin{cases} 1 & x < 0 \\ 1 - x & 0 < x < 1 \\ 0 & x > 1. \end{cases}$$

**74.4.** Consider the example solved in this section. What traffic density should be approached as $L \longrightarrow 0$? Verify that as $L \longrightarrow 0$ equation 74.9 approaches the correct traffic density.

# 75. Wave Propagation
# of Automobile Brake Lights

Before the study of more complex traffic flow problems, let us indicate a simple explanation for the fascinating wave phenomena of automobile brake lights. Have you ever been traveling in heavy traffic on a highway and observed that after someone applies their brake (lighting the taillight) a long distance ahead, succeeding cars apply their brakes? The brake lights appear to travel in your direction. In a short length of time you too are suddenly compelled to apply your brakes. You will apply your brakes at a different position from where the first car applied its brakes; see Fig. 75-1. The lit taillight might have traveled backwards against the traffic (if a bicyclist were to keep up to the brake light, he or she would have to travel opposite to the direction of traffic!).

We model the process of applying brakes in the following way. Assume that a driver applies the car's brakes at some critical density $\rho_c$. Although this might not be entirely accurate, it is a reasonable approximation. Thus when cars are at that density taillights go on. Under this hypothesis, taillights indicate a path of constant density, a characteristic. Its velocity should be

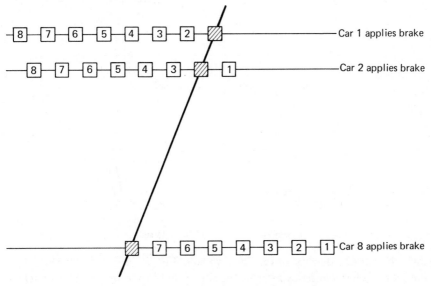

Figure 75-1   Lit brake light moving backwards.

given by

$$\frac{dx}{dt} = \frac{dq}{d\rho}\Big|_{\rho=\rho_c}.$$

If cars brake in "heavy traffic", then $dq/d\rho\,|_{\rho=\rho_c} < 0$ and the wave propagates in the direction opposite to traffic!

We really are not suggesting that this is the exact mechanism by which brake lights are observed. To make an analysis of this situation requires a careful experimental investigation of the conditions under which a driver of a car applies its brakes.

## 76.  Congestion Ahead

Let us imagine a situation in which traffic initially becomes heavier as we go further along the road. The traffic becomes denser or compressed, as shown in Fig. 76-1. The solution we will obtain is called a **compression** wave. For convenience assume that $\rho \rightarrow \rho_1$ as $x \rightarrow +\infty$ and $\rho \rightarrow \rho_0$ as $x \rightarrow -\infty$, where $0 \leq \rho_0 < \rho_1 \leq \rho_{max}$. What does our mathematical model predict? First a few characteristics are sketched in the region of heavier traffic ($\rho \approx \rho_1$) and a few in the region of lighter traffic ($\rho \approx \rho_0$). A density wave for the heavier traffic moves at velocity $dq/d\rho\,|_{\rho=\rho_1}$ which is less than the velocity of

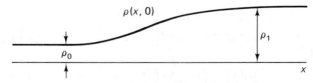

Figure 76-1    Heavier traffic is ahead initially.

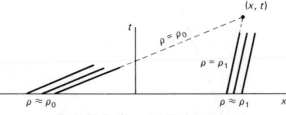

Figure 76-2    Characteristics intersect.

the lighter traffic density wave. Thus we have Fig. 76-2. Eventually these two families of characteristics intersect as illustrated in the figure. The sketched characteristics are moving forward; the velocities of both density waves were assumed positive. This does not have to be so in general. However, in any situation in which the traffic becomes denser further along the road, characteristics will still intersect. At a position where an intersection occurs, the theory predicts the density is $\rho_0$ and at the same time $\rho_1$. Clearly this is impossible. Something has gone wrong!

To explain this difficulty the density is roughly sketched at different times based on the method of characteristics. Let us follow two observers, A and B, starting at positions marked ● each watching constant density. The one in lighter traffic moves at a constant velocity, faster than the one in heavier traffic, as Fig. 76-3 illustrates. The "distance" between the heavier and lighter traffic is becoming shorter. The light traffic is catching up to the heavier traffic. Instead of the density distribution spreading out (as it does after a light turns green), it is becoming steeper. If we continue to apply the method of characteristics, eventually the observer on the left passes the observer on the right. Then we obtain Fig. 76-4. Thus the method of characteristics predicts that the traffic density becomes a "multivalued" function of position; that is, at some later time our mathematics predicts there will be three densities at some positions (for example, as illustrated in Fig. 76-4). We say the traffic density wave "breaks." However, clearly it makes no sense to have three values of density at one place.* The density must be a single-valued

---

*The partial differential equations describing the height of water waves near the shore (i.e., in shallow water) are similar to the equations for traffic density waves. In this situation the prediction of "breaking" is then quite significant!

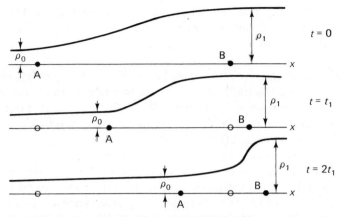

Figure 76-3   Evolution of traffic density as lighter traffic moves faster than heavier traffic.

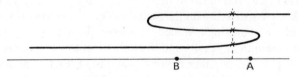

Figure 76-4   Triple-valued traffic density as predicted by the method of characteristics.

function of position along the highway. In the next section we will resolve this difficulty presented by the method of characteristics.

# 77.  Discontinuous Traffic

On the basis of the partial differential equation of traffic flow, we predicted the physically impossible phenomena that the traffic density becomes multivalued. Since the method of characteristics is mathematically justified, it is the partial differential equation itself which must not be entirely valid. Some approximation or assumption that we used must at times be invalid. To discover what type of modification we need to make, let us briefly review the assumptions and approximations necessary in our derivation of the partial differential equation of traffic flow:

1. Assuming that average quantities (such as density and velocity) exist, we formulated the integral conservation of cars.
2. If density and flow are continuous, then the integral conservation law becomes a differential conservation law.

3. By postulating that the velocity is only a function of density, the differential conservation law becomes a partial differential equation for the traffic density.

One or more of these assumptions must be modified, but only in regions along the highway where the traffic density has been predicted to be multivalued. Otherwise our formulation is adequate. We wish to continue using similar types of mathematical models involving traffic density and velocity. Hence we will continue to assume that (1) is valid; cars are still not created or destroyed. Assumption (3) could be removed by allowing, for example, the cars' velocity to depend also on the gradient of the traffic density, $u = u(\rho, \partial \rho / \partial x)$, rather than to depend only on the traffic density, $u = u(\rho)$. This would take into account the driver's ability to perceive traffic problems ahead. As the density becomes much larger *ahead*, a driver could respond by slowing down faster than implied by the density at the driver's position alone. This modified assumption is briefly discussed in the exercises. In particular, the difficulty of multivaluedness associated with the method of characteristics disappears. The traffic variables remain single-valued. However, the mathematical techniques necessary to obtain these results and to apply them to various traffic problems are relatively difficult, possibly beyond the present level of many readers of this text. Hence, we prefer to modify our mathematical model in a different way. Instead, let us consider assumption (2). We will investigate traffic flow removing, where necessary, the assumption that the traffic density and velocity field are continuous functions of space and time. The resulting mathematical theory will not be difficult to understand and interpret. Furthermore, it can be shown (although we do not) that the theory we generate concerning traffic flow with discontinuities can be related to the theory developed by using continuous traffic variables with $u = u(\rho, \rho_x)$ rather than $u = u(\rho)$.

Assume that the traffic density (as illustrated in Fig. 77-1) and velocity field are discontinuous at some unknown position $x_s$ in space, and that this discontinuity might propagate in time $x_s(t)$. We reconstruct the derivation of conservation of cars, since the resulting partial differential equation of traffic

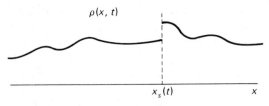

$\rho(x, t)$

$x_s(t)$          $x$

Figure 77-1    Traffic density discontinuous at $x = x_s(t)$.

flow is no longer valid at a discontinuity. Consider the number of cars contained in the region $x_1 < x < x_2$, where we assume $x_1 < x_s(t) < x_2$:

$$N(t) = \int_{x_1}^{x_2} \rho(x, t)\, dx.$$

This integral is still well defined even if $\rho(x, t)$ has a jump-discontinuity.* Since $x_s$ depends on $t$, we allow the two endpoints to move. Consider the rate of change of the number of cars between $x = x_1(t)$ and $x = x_2(t)$,

$$\frac{dN(t)}{dt} = \frac{d}{dt} \int_{x_1(t)}^{x_2(t)} \rho(x, t)\, dx.$$

The rate of change of cars is only due to cars crossing at $x = x_1$ and $x = x_2$. Since the left end $x = x_1$ is not fixed, but instead moves with velocity $dx_1/dt$, the number of cars per hour crossing the moving boundary (the flow relative to a moving coordinate system) is

$$\rho(x_1, t)\left(u(x_1, t) - \frac{dx_1}{dt}\right) = q(x_1, t) - \rho(x_1, t)\frac{dx_1}{dt}.$$

(If the boundary moves with the car velocity, then no cars pass the moving boundary.) A similar expression can be derived for the number of cars per hour crossing a moving boundary at $x = x_2$. Thus

$$\frac{d}{dt} \int_{x_1(t)}^{x_2(t)} \rho(x, t)\, dx = q(x_1, t) - \rho(x_1, t)\frac{dx_1}{dt} - \left[q(x_2, t) - \rho(x_2, t)\frac{dx_2}{dt}\right].$$

Suppose that the jump-discontinuity, which we call a **shock wave** or simply a **shock**,† occurs at $x_s(t)$, called the position of the shock. Let both the

---

*A function $f(x)$ is said to have a **jump-discontinuity** at $x = x_s$ if the limit from the right of $f(x), f(x_s{}^+)$, does *not* equal the limit from the left, $f(x_s{}^-)$. However, both limits must exist. For example, see Fig. 77-2.

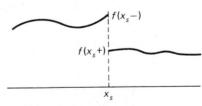

Figure 77-2  Jump discontinuity.

†The terminology, *shock wave*, is introduced because of the analogous behavior which occurs in gas dynamics. There, changes in pressure and density of air, for example, propagate, and are heard (due to the sensitivity of the human ear). They are called *sound waves*. When fluctuations of pressure and density are small, the equations describing sound waves can be linearized (in a manner similar to that discussed in Sec. 66). Then sound is propagated at a constant speed known as the sound speed. However, if the amplitudes of the fluctuations of pressure and density are not small, then the pressure and density can be mathematically modeled as being discontinuous, the result being called a *shock wave*. Examples are the sound emitted from an explosion or the thunder resulting from lightning. If a shock wave results from exceeding the sound barrier, it is known as a *sonic boom*.

left and right boundaries of the region move exactly with the shock, one on one side and one on the other side (as though the two boundaries were two bicyclists riding on a bicycle-built-for-two with the shock between the two riders). Since no cars will be contained in the region $x_1 \leq x \leq x_2$ (it being of infinitesimally small length), $\int_{x_1}^{x_2} \rho \, dx = 0$ and therefore

$$0 = q(x_1, t) - \rho(x_1, t)\frac{dx_1}{dt} - \left[ q(x_2, t) - \rho(x_2, t)\frac{dx_2}{dt} \right].$$

Both ends move at the same velocity, the **shock velocity**. Thus

$$\frac{dx_1}{dt} = \frac{dx_2}{dt} = \frac{dx_s}{dt}.$$

The traffic flow relative to the moving shock on one side of the shock equals the relative flow on the other side. Solving for the shock velocity, yields

$$\frac{dx_s}{dt} = \frac{q(x_1, t) - q(x_2, t)}{\rho(x_1, t) - \rho(x_2, t)}. \tag{77.1}$$

The denominator is the nonzero difference in the densities on the two sides of the shock. This jump in density is denoted $[\rho]$,

$$[\rho] = \rho(x_1, t) - \rho(x_2, t),$$

or equivalently (since $x_1 = x_s^-$ and $x_2 = x_s^+$)

$$[\rho] = \rho(x_s^-, t) - \rho(x_s^+, t). \tag{77.2a}$$

Similarly the numerator is the jump in the traffic flow across the discontinuity $[q]$,

$$[q] = q(x_s^-, t) - q(x_s^+, t). \tag{77.2b}$$

Using this notation, the shock velocity (or velocity of the discontinuity) is given by

$$\frac{dx_s}{dt} = \frac{[q]}{[\rho]}. \tag{77.3}$$

If on one side of the shock the density is $\rho_1$ and on the other side $\rho_2$, then the shock must move at the following velocity:

$$\boxed{\frac{dx_s}{dt} = \frac{\rho_2 u(\rho_2) - \rho_1 u(\rho_1)}{\rho_2 - \rho_1}.}$$   (77.4)

At points of discontinuity this shock condition replaces the use of the partial differential equation which is valid elsewhere. However, we have not yet explained where shocks occur and how to determine $\rho_1$ and $\rho_2$. In the next section a calculation of this kind will be undertaken.

The shock condition can be derived in an alternate manner. Imagine two fixed observers at $x = x_1$ and $x = x_2$, in which case conservation of cars implies that

$$\frac{d}{dt} \int_{x_1}^{x_2} \rho \, dx = q(x_1, t) - q(x_2, t).$$

Suppose the discontinuity occurs at some place between $x = x_1$ and $x = x_2$. We will calculate the derivative of an integral whose integrand is discontinuous. It is best to divide the integral into two parts,

$$\int_{x_1}^{x_2} \rho \, dx = \int_{x_1}^{x_s} \rho \, dx + \int_{x_s}^{x_2} \rho \, dx.$$

In each integral, the integrand $\rho$ is continuous and hence we can differentiate each without any difficulties. However, the limits of the two integrals are not constant since $x_s$ depends on time, $x_s(t)$. As a review the rule for differentiating an integral with variable limits is quoted from calculus (see exercises 60.2 and 60.3):

$$\boxed{\frac{d}{dt} \int_{\alpha(t)}^{\beta(t)} f(x, t) \, dx = \frac{d\beta}{dt} f(\beta, t) - \frac{d\alpha}{dt} f(\alpha, t) + \int_{\alpha(t)}^{\beta(t)} \frac{\partial f(x, t)}{\partial t} \, dx.}$$

This formula is *not* valid if $f(x, t)$ has a jump discontinuity between the two limits of integration. That is why we divided the integral above into two parts. Applying this well-known formula twice,

$$\frac{d}{dt} \int_{x_1}^{x_s} \rho \, dx = \frac{dx_s}{dt} \rho(x_s^-, t) + \int_{x_1}^{x_s} \frac{\partial \rho}{\partial t} \, dx$$

$$\frac{d}{dt} \int_{x_s}^{x_2} \rho \, dx = -\frac{dx_s}{dt} \rho(x_s^+, t) + \int_{x_s}^{x_2} \frac{\partial \rho}{\partial t} \, dx,$$

yields

$$[\rho]\frac{dx_s}{dt} + \int_{x_1}^{x_s} \frac{\partial \rho}{\partial t} \, dx + \int_{x_s}^{x_2} \frac{\partial \rho}{\partial t} \, dx = q(x_1, t) - q(x_2, t).$$   (77.5)

This formula is valid for all time. If $x = x_1$ is infinitesimally near the shock, $x = x_s$, and if $x = x_2$ is infinitesimally near $x = x_s$ at the same time, then both integrals in equation 77.5 vanish. Thus

$$[\rho]\frac{dx_s}{dt} = [q],$$

which is equivalent to the shock condition as previously derived, equation 77.3. Exercise 77.8 derives equation 77.3 from equation 77.5 differently.

   This shock velocity can also be graphically represented on the flow-density curve. Suppose that a shock occurs when lighter traffic with density $\rho_1$ catches up to heavier traffic with density $\rho_2$. The shock velocity is given by equations 77.3 or 77.4. However, note that the slope of the straight line connecting the points on the flow-density curve representing these two traffic situations ($\rho = \rho_1$ and $\rho = \rho_2$) has exactly the value of the shock velocity, as shown in Fig. 77-3. The shock velocity can be positive or negative as illustrated in the figure.

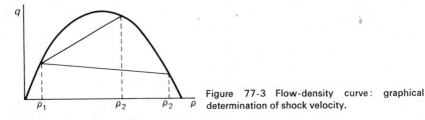

Figure 77-3 Flow-density curve: graphical determination of shock velocity.

   Let us briefly describe the manner in which a very simple traffic shock propagates. Assume that the traffic initially consists of two uniform traffic states of density $\rho_1$ and $\rho_2$, separated by a shock, as shown in Fig. 77-4. In addition, suppose that a short time $\Delta t$ later, the shock moves a distance $\Delta x_s$.

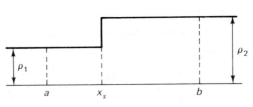

Figure 77-4   Initial traffic density.

   Then we have Fig. 77-5. Consider two fixed places $x = a$ and $x = b$ as indicated in the figures. The change in the number of cars between $x = a$ and $x = b$ is only explained by cars crossing at $x = a$ and at $x = b$. The change in the number of cars, $N(\Delta t) - N(0)$, is $-\Delta x_s(\rho_2 - \rho_1)$. The number of cars

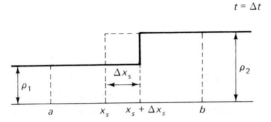

Figure 77-5   Propagating shock wave: caused by two different uniform traffic densities.

that crosses at $x = a$ is $\Delta t q_1 = \Delta t \rho_1 u(\rho_1)$, since the traffic flow is constant there. Similarly the number of cars that crosses at $x = b$ is $\Delta t q_2$. Thus $\Delta t(q_1 - q_2) = -\Delta x_s(\rho_2 - \rho_1)$, or

$$\frac{\Delta x_s}{\Delta t} = \frac{q_1 - q_2}{\rho_1 - \rho_2} = \frac{[q]}{[\rho]}.$$

Therefore the velocity of the shock, $\Delta x_s/\Delta t$, is again the same as derived before.

In the next section we will consider traffic problems in which the partial differential equation predicts multivalued solutions, and hence shocks must be introduced to give physically realistic solutions.

# EXERCISES

**77.1.** If $u = u_{max}(1 - \rho/\rho_{max})$, then what is the velocity of a traffic shock separating densities $\rho_0$ and $\rho_1$? (Simplify the expression as much as possible.) Show that the shock velocity is the average of the density wave velocities associated with $\rho_0$ and $\rho_1$.

**77.2.** If $u = u_{max}(1 - \rho^2/\rho_{max}^2)$, then what is the velocity of a traffic shock separating densities $\rho_0$ and $\rho_1$? (Simplify the expression as much as possible.) Show that the shock velocity is *not* the average of the density wave velocities associated with $\rho_0$ and $\rho_1$.

**77.3.** A **weak shock** is a shock in which the shock strength (the difference in densities) is small. For a weak shock, show that the shock velocity is *approximately* the average of the density wave velocities associated with the two densities. [Hint: Use Taylor series methods.]

**77.4.** Show $[\rho^2] \neq [\rho]^2$.

**77.5.** Suppose instead of $u = U(\rho)$, that a car's velocity $u$ is

$$u = U(\rho) - \frac{\nu}{\rho}\frac{\partial \rho}{\partial x},$$

where $\nu$ is a constant.

(a)   What sign should $\nu$ have for this expression to be physically reasonable?

(b)  What equation now describes conservation of cars?
(c)  Assume that $U(\rho) = u_{max}(1 - \rho/\rho_{max})$. Show that

$$\frac{\partial \rho}{\partial t} + u_{max}\left(1 - \frac{2\rho}{\rho_{max}}\right)\frac{\partial \rho}{\partial x} = v\frac{\partial^2 \rho}{\partial x^2},$$

called **Burger's equation**.

**77.6.**  Consider Burger's equation as derived in exercise 77.5. Suppose that a solution exists as a density wave moving without change of shape at velocity $V$,

$$\rho(x, t) = f(x - Vt).$$

(a)  What ordinary differential equation is satisfied by $f$?
(b)  Integrate this differential equation once. By graphical techniques show that a solution exists, such that $f \rightarrow \rho_2$ as $x \rightarrow +\infty$ and $f \rightarrow \rho_1$ as $x \rightarrow -\infty$, only if $\rho_2 > \rho_1$. Roughly sketch this solution. Give a physical interpretation of this result.
(c)  Show that the velocity of wave propagation, $V$, is the same as the shock velocity separating $\rho = \rho_1$ from $\rho = \rho_2$ (occurring if $v = 0$).

**77.7.**  (a)  A more sophisticated theory of traffic flow assumes drivers do not move at a velocity determined by the density. Instead drivers accelerate in a manner so as to approach a desired velocity-density curve. Formulate such a model. [Hint: See exercise 61.3.] What type of initial conditions would be necessary to solve such a problem?
(b)  The model in part (a) essentially introduces a delay (due to the time a driver takes to accelerate) in a driver's response to the observed density. Unless drivers look far enough ahead to compensate for this response time, this delay process is very unstable. Accordingly, modify the model in part (a). [Hint: See exercise 77.5.]

**77.8.**  Reconsider equation 77.5. Derive the equation for the shock velocity, using the appropriate partial differential equation valid for $x_1 < x < x_s$ and $x_s < x < x_2$.

# 78. Uniform Traffic Stopped by a Red Light

In this section we will investigate what happens to a uniform stream of moving traffic (with density $\rho = \rho_0$) as it is suddenly halted by a red light at $x = 0$. (We assume the first car immediately stops, ignoring the slowing down phenomena associated with a yellow light.) We will only analyze the traffic behind the light, disregarding what occurs in front of the light.

The initial density is a constant, $\rho = \rho_0$, as shown in Fig. 78-1. The red light is mathematically modeled in the following simple way. At $x = 0$ the traffic is stopped (i.e., $u = 0$), and hence $\rho = \rho_{max}$ for all time $t > 0$; see

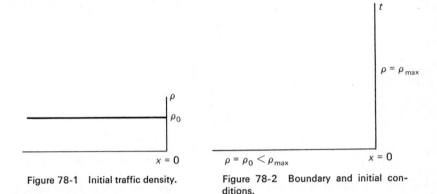

Figure 78-1   Initial traffic density.

Figure 78-2   Boundary and initial conditions.

Fig. 78-2. Characteristics that emanate from regions in which $\rho = \rho_0$ move at velocity $dq/d\rho \,|_{\rho_0}$, while characteristics emanating from the position of the traffic light ($x = 0$, where $\rho = \rho_{max}$) travel at velocity $dq/d\rho \,|_{\rho_{max}}$. The density wave associated with lower densities travels faster. Therefore, the diagrams in Fig. 78-3 indicate that characteristics intersect each other whether the initial uniform traffic is light or heavy:

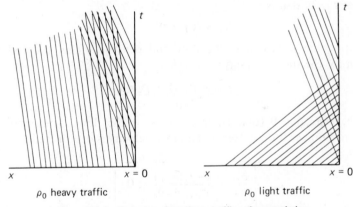

Figure 78-3   Stopping of uniform traffic: characteristics.

In either case there is a cross-hatched region indicating that the method of characteristics yields a multivalued solution to the partial differential equation. We will show that this difficulty is remedied by considering a shock wave, a propagating wave demarcating the path at which densities and velocities abruptly change (i.e., are discontinuous).

Let us suppose that there is a shock wave. In either light or heavy traffic, the space-time diagram is of the form shown in Fig. 78-4. On one side of the shock the method of characteristics suggests the traffic density is uniform $\rho = \rho_0$, and on the other side $\rho = \rho_{max}$, bumper-to-bumper traffic. We do not

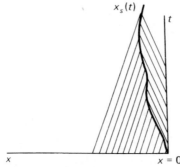

Figure 78-4    Unknown shock path.

know as yet the path of the shock. The theory for such a discontinuous solution implies that the path for any shock must satisfy the shock condition,

$$\frac{dx_s}{dt} = \frac{[q]}{[\rho]}. \tag{78.1}$$

The initial position of the shock is known, giving a condition for this first-order ordinary differential equation. In this case, the shock must initiate at $x_s = 0$ at $t = 0$, that is

$$x_s(0) = 0.$$

Substituting the jumps in traffic flow and density, yields the following equation for the shock velocity:

$$\frac{dx_s}{dt} = \frac{\rho_{max}u(\rho_{max}) - \rho_0 u(\rho_0)}{\rho_{max} - \rho_0}.$$

However, $u(\rho_{max}) = 0$ (that is, there is no traffic flow corresponding to bumper-to-bumper traffic). Hence the shock velocity is determined,

$$\frac{dx_s}{dt} = \frac{-\rho_0 u(\rho_0)}{\rho_{max} - \rho_0} < 0. \tag{78.2}$$

Thus the shock moves at a constant negative velocity. Consequently, applying the initial condition results in the following equation for the position of the shock:

$$x_s = \frac{-\rho_0 u(\rho_0)}{\rho_{max} - \rho_0} t.$$

The resulting space-time diagram is sketched in Fig. 78-5. For any time, $t > 0$, the traffic density is discontinuous, as shown in Fig. 78-6.

This shock separates cars standing still from cars moving forward at velocity $u(\rho_0)$. If this happens, then the cars must decelerate from $u(\rho_0)$ to

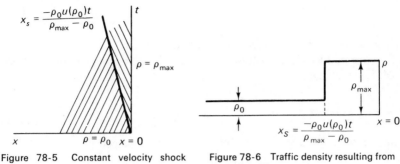

Figure 78-5    Constant velocity shock wave.

Figure 78-6    Traffic density resulting from stopped traffic.

zero instantaneously. Have you ever observed sudden decelerations? Since cars cannot instantly decelerate, this theory predicts accidents at these shocks. However, in a more realistic mathematical model the dependence of velocity only on density, $u(\rho)$, must be modified *only in regions extremely near shocks*, that is regions in which the density is changing rapidly. In such regions a good driver presumably would observe the stopped traffic ahead and slow down before being forced to suddenly brake. One suspects that such a mechanism would prevent shocks. We will not develop the mathematical model to include these effects although such a modification can be accomplished.

Let us show that we can explain the increase of cars in line behind the red light in another way. Instead of using the velocity field equations, consider each car individually. Suppose that each car moves at speed $u(\rho_0)$. At time $t$, how many cars would be forced to stop by catching up to the line of stopped cars? Consider the $(N + 1)$st car behind the light when the light changes to red. Since its velocity is constant, $u(\rho_0)$, and its distance from the light initially (at $t = 0$) is $N/\rho_0$, this car's position is determined by solving the initial value problem:

$$\frac{dx_{N+1}}{dt} = u(\rho_0) \quad \text{with} \quad x_{N+1}(0) = -N/\rho_0.$$

Thus

$$x_{N+1}(t) = u(\rho_0)t - \frac{N}{\rho_0}.$$

When this car is forced to stop it will be $N/\rho_{max}$ distance from the light. How long will that take? Substituting $x_{N+1} = -N/\rho_{max}$, yields

$$-\frac{N}{\rho_{max}} = u(\rho_0)t - \frac{N}{\rho_0}.$$

Thus the $(N + 1)$st car will stop at

$$t = \frac{N}{u(\rho_0)}\left(\frac{1}{\rho_0} - \frac{1}{\rho_{max}}\right). \qquad (78.3)$$

Its position when stopped is

$$x = -N/\rho_{max}. \qquad (78.4)$$

We have determined the position and time at which each car stops. To follow the building line of stopped cars, eliminate $N$ from equations 78.3 and 78.4, in which case

$$x = \frac{-u(\rho_0)t/\rho_{max}}{\dfrac{1}{\rho_0} - \dfrac{1}{\rho_{max}}}.$$

The line of stopped vehicles moves at a constant velocity

$$\frac{dx}{dt} = \frac{-u(\rho_0)/\rho_{max}}{\dfrac{1}{\rho_0} - \dfrac{1}{\rho_{max}}} = \frac{-\rho_0 u(\rho_0)}{\rho_{max} - \rho_0},$$

which is the same velocity as previously derived!

An equivalent space-time sketch is facilitated by using the flow-density curve. Suppose that the uniform traffic stopped by the red light has density $\rho_0$ marked in Fig. 78-7 on the flow-density curve:

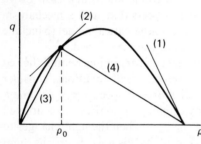

Figure 78-7  Fundamental Diagram of Road Traffic: various important velocities.

Also sketched on the diagram are lines associated with (1) density wave velocity corresponding to $\rho_{max}$; (2) density wave velocity corresponding to $\rho_0$, (3) car velocity corresponding to $\rho_0$; and (4) shock velocity between the uniform flow $\rho_0$ and bumper-to-bumper traffic $\rho_{max}$. The resulting space-time diagram is Fig. 78-8 (in which, as discussed before, the coordinate $x$ and $t$ are reversed from their usual position). A car starting from $x = -L$ is marked

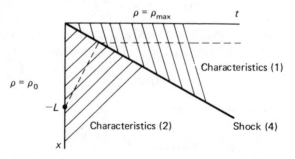

Figure 78-8  Graphical determination of traffic density and car paths.

with a dotted line (showing the car velocity to be faster than the density wave velocity).

# EXERCISES

**78.1.** Suppose that the initial traffic density is

$$\rho(x, 0) = \begin{cases} \rho_0 & x < 0 \\ \rho_1 & x > 0. \end{cases}$$

Consider the two cases, $\rho_0 < \rho_1$ and $\rho_1 < \rho_0$. For which of the preceding cases is a density shock necessary? Briefly explain.

**78.2.** Assume that $u = u_{max}(1 - \rho/\rho_{max})$ and that the initial traffic density is

$$\rho(x, 0) = \begin{cases} \dfrac{\rho_{max}}{5} & x < 0 \\ \dfrac{3\rho_{max}}{5} & x > 0. \end{cases}$$

(a)  Sketch the initial density.
(b)  Determine and sketch the density at later times.
(c)  Determine the path of a car (in space-time) which starts at $x = -x_0$ (behind $x = 0$).
(d)  Determine the path of a car (in space-time) which starts at $x = x_0$ (ahead of $x = 0$).

**78.3.** Assume that $u = u_{max}(1 - \rho/\rho_{max})$ and at $t = 0$, the traffic density is

$$\rho(x, 0) = \begin{cases} \dfrac{\rho_{max}}{3} & x < 0 \\ \dfrac{2\rho_{max}}{3} & x > 0. \end{cases}$$

Why does the density not change in time?

**78.4.** Referring to the problem in Sec. 78, show algebraically that the value of the shock velocity is between the velocities of the two density waves.

**78.5.** Suppose that only a sketch of the flow-density curve is known. Assume that the density is known at $t = 0$,

$$\rho(x, 0) = \begin{cases} \dfrac{\rho_{max}}{4} & x < 0 \\ \dfrac{3\rho_{max}}{4} & x > 0. \end{cases}$$

Determine the traffic density at later times.

**78.6.** If $u = u_{max}(1 - \rho/\rho_{max})$, then at what velocity do cars pile up at a red traffic light, assuming that the initial traffic density is a constant $\rho_0$.

**78.7.**  Suppose that a traffic light turned from green to yellow before turning red. How would you mathematically model the yellow light? (Do not solve any problems corresponding to your model.)

**78.8.**  Determine the traffic density on a semi-infinite $(x > 0)$ highway for which the density at the entrance $x = 0$ is

$$\rho(0, t) = \begin{cases} \rho_1 & 0 < t < \tau \\ \rho_0 & t > \tau \end{cases}$$

and the initial density is uniform along the highway $(\rho(x, 0) = \rho_0, x > 0)$. Assume that $\rho_1$ is lighter traffic than $\rho_0$ and both are light traffic (i.e., assume that $u(\rho) = u_{max}(1 - \rho/\rho_{max})$ and thus $\rho_1 < \rho_0 < \rho_{max}/2$). Sketch the density at various values of time.

**78.9.**  Do exercise 78.8 if $\rho_0 < \rho_1 < \rho_{max}/2$.

**78.10.**  Assume that $u(\rho) = u_{max}(1 - \rho^2/\rho_{max}^2)$. Determine the traffic density $\rho$ (for $t > 0$) if the initial traffic density is

$$\rho(x, 0) = \begin{cases} \rho_1 & x < 0 \\ \rho_2 & x > 0. \end{cases}$$

(a)  Assume that $\rho_2 > \rho_1$.
(b)  Assume that $\rho_2 < \rho_1$.

**78.11.**  Using the flow-density relationship of exercise 68.2, sketch the traffic density 10 minutes after the traffic density was 30 cars per mile for $x < 0$ and 150 cars per mile for $x > 0$.

**78.12.**  If uniform traffic is stopped by a red light, what is the traffic density in front of the light? [This problem will be answered in Sec. 82.]

# 79.  A Stationary Shock Wave

Before studying more complex traffic problems, let us consider one more simple example. Let us imagine the situation sketched in Fig. 79-1 in which initially

$$\rho(x, 0) = \begin{cases} \rho_{max} & x > 0 \\ 0 & x < 0. \end{cases}$$

This is an initial semi-infinite line of bumper-to-bumper traffic followed by no traffic. The solution to this traffic problem is quite easy. Each car observes bumper-to-bumper traffic and hence remains standing still. There is no

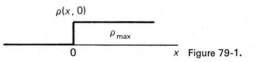

$\rho(x, 0)$

$\rho_{max}$

0                                            $x$    Figure 79-1.

motion. For all time,

$$p(x, t) = \begin{cases} p_{\max} & x > 0 \\ 0 & x < 0. \end{cases}$$

We will show that the method of characteristics (when modified by shock conditions) yields this same result. This problem is discussed in the same manner as for the mathematically similar initial conditions sketched in Fig. 79-2. As before, first the characteristics corresponding to $p = p_{\max}$ and

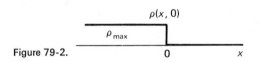

$p(x, 0)$

$p_{\max}$

0      $x$

Figure 79-2.

$p = 0$ are drawn (see Fig. 79-3). The characteristics clearly intersect in a V-shaped region. Furthermore fanlike characteristics can be constructed emanating from the origin (as though the initial density $p(x, 0)$ smoothly varied monotonically between $p = 0$ and $p = p_{\max}$ in a very short distance). Thus, we obtain Fig. 79-4. Consequently, in the region of intersecting characteristics, there are three families of characteristics. On these:

1. $p = p_{\max}$
2. $p = 0$
3. $x/t = q'(p)$.

For the third case if we assume that the linear velocity-density relationship is valid,

$$u(p) = u_{\max}\left(1 - \frac{p}{p_{\max}}\right),$$

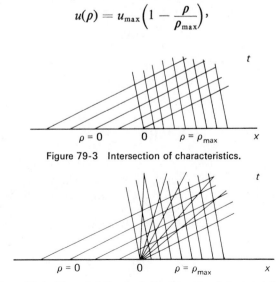

$t$

$p = 0$      0      $p = p_{\max}$      $x$

Figure 79-3   Intersection of characteristics.

$t$

$p = 0$      0      $p = p_{\max}$      $x$

Figure 79-4   Characteristics (including fan-shaped characteristics).

then (see Sec. 73)

$$\rho = \frac{\rho_{\max}}{2}\left(1 - \frac{x}{u_{\max}t}\right);$$

the density depends linearly on position.

In the region of intersecting characteristics, the density of cars is triple-valued—clearly not allowable. In particular, sketched in Fig. 79-5 are some of these triple-valued densities for different values of $t$:

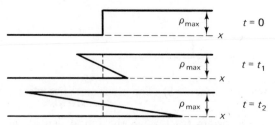

Figure 79-5    Traffic density ignoring shocks.

To remedy this difficulty, a shock is introduced,

$$\frac{dx_s}{dt} = \frac{[q]}{[\rho]}.$$

Using the nonfanlike characteristics, the shock speed between bumper-to-bumper traffic and no traffic is calculated:

$$\frac{dx_s}{dt} = \frac{\rho_{\max}u(\rho_{\max}) - 0u(0)}{\rho_{\max} - 0}.$$

Since $u(\rho_{\max}) = 0$,

$$\frac{dx_s}{dt} = 0.$$

Thus it is concluded that this shock is stationary (i.e., does not move). Since it starts at $x = 0$, it will stay there, as was already known!

# EXERCISES

**79.1.** Reconsider the problem of Sec. 78. Show that using the method of characteristics (ignoring traffic shock waves), the traffic density is triple-valued. Sketch the resulting triple-valued traffic density. Show that the solution with shocks corresponds to cutting off equal areas of the "lobes" of the triple-valued density as drawn in Fig. 79-6. Whitham* has shown this to be a general result.

---

*Reference in Sec. 86.

Figure 79-6. _____

**79.2.** Suppose that

$$p(x, 0) = \begin{cases} p_0 & x > 0 \\ 0 & x < 0. \end{cases}$$

Determine the velocity of the shock. Briefly give a physical explanation of the result.

**79.3.** The initial traffic density on a road is

$$p(x, 0) = \begin{cases} 0 & x \le 0 \\ \dfrac{\rho_{max}x}{L} & 0 < x < L \\ \rho_{max} & x \ge L. \end{cases}$$

Assume that $u(\rho) = u_{max}(1 - \rho/\rho_{max})$.
(a) Sketch the initial density.
(b) Show that all characteristics from the interval $0 < x < L$ (and $t = 0$) intersect at the point $x = L/2$, $t = L/2u_{max}$.
(c) A traffic shock will form at this point. Find its subsequent motion.
(d) Sketch the $x$-$t$ plane, showing the shock and the characteristics necessary to determine $p(x, t)$.
(e) Sketch $p(x, t)$ before and after the shock.
(f) Describe briefly how the individual automobiles behave (do *not* determine their paths mathematically).

# 80. The Earliest Shock

In the past sections, we began to describe the propagation of shock waves in traffic problems. In the examples considered, the density was initially discontinuous; thus the shock waves formed immediately. However, we now will show that the dominant feature of traffic flow problems is that even if the traffic variables are initially smoothly spatially dependent, then shock waves are still generated, but it takes a finite time. Let us illustrate this property by considering a situation in which the initial traffic density is locally larger somewhere along the road, for example, imagine a situation as drawn in Fig. 80-1. The characteristics corresponding to less dense traffic move faster. To be specific, suppose the initial density wave velocity is

$$\frac{dq}{d\rho} = \frac{u_{max}}{4}\left[3 - \frac{6}{3 + 4(x/L)^2}\right],$$

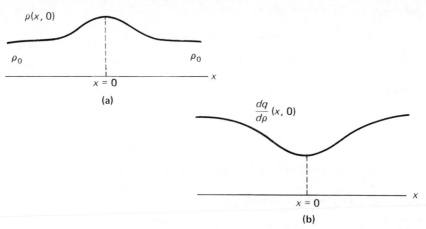

Figure 80-1   Initial traffic density and initial density wave velocity.

in which case we sketch in Fig. 80-2 the characteristics starting from $x/L = 0$, $\pm\frac{1}{2}$, $\pm1$, $\pm\frac{3}{2}$, $\pm2$, $\pm3$:

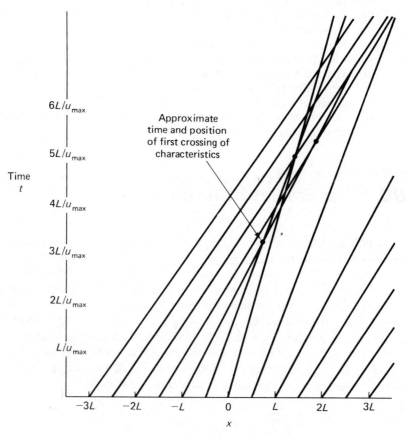

Figure 80-2   First intersection of characteristics.

The characteristics eventually cross due to the region in which the density is increasing. The fast traffic catches up to the slower moving denser traffic. Shocks are expected.

Fig. 80-2 suggests that shocks do not occur immediately. Let us attempt to calculate when a shock first occurs. Suppose that the first shock occurs at $t = \tau$, due to the intersection of two characteristics initially a distance $\Delta x$ (not necessarily small) apart, one emanating from $x_1$, the other from $x_1 + \Delta x$; see Fig. 80-3. If this is the first intersection, then no characteristics could have crossed at an earlier time. However, any characteristics between $x = x_1$ and $x = x_1 + \Delta x$ at $t = 0$ will intersect one of the other two characteristics almost always before $t = \tau$ as illustrated in Fig. 80-4. Thus shocks cannot first occur due to characteristics that are a finite distance $\Delta x$ apart. Instead, the first shock actually occurs due to the intersection of neighboring characteristics (the limit as $\Delta x \longrightarrow 0$). We will show that even though $\Delta x \to 0$, the first intersection occurs at a finite positive time, the time of the earliest shock.

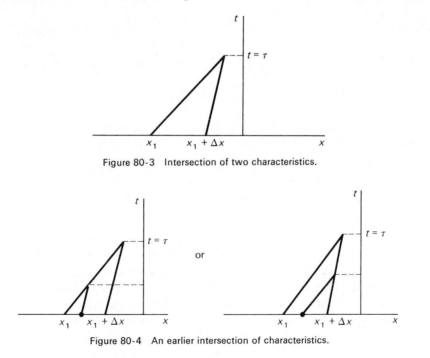

Figure 80-3   Intersection of two characteristics.

Figure 80-4   An earlier intersection of characteristics.

The equation for the characteristics is

$$\frac{dx}{dt} = \frac{dq}{d\rho}. \qquad (80.1)$$

We will analyze neighboring characteristics. Consider the characteristic emanating from $x = x_1$ at $t = 0$,

$$x = \frac{dq}{dp}\bigg|_{p(x_1)} t + x_1,$$

and the characteristic starting from $x = x_1 + \Delta x$ at $t = 0$,

$$x = \frac{dq}{dp}\bigg|_{p(x_1 + \Delta x)} t + x_1 + \Delta x,$$

where $p(x_1) = p(x_1, 0)$ and $p(x_1 + \Delta x) = p(x_1 + \Delta x, 0)$. Assume that $\Delta x > 0$, in which case Fig. 80-5 indicates the general behavior of these two

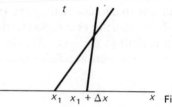

$x_1 \quad x_1 + \Delta x \qquad x$   Figure 80-5.

straight line characteristics. These *characteristics intersect* (in a positive time) only if

$$\frac{dq}{dp}\bigg|_{p(x_1 + \Delta x)} < \frac{dq}{dp}\bigg|_{p(x_1)};$$

that is if the density of traffic is higher at $x_1 + \Delta x$ than at $x_1$. Solving for the intersection point by eliminating $x$ yields

$$\frac{dq}{dp}\bigg|_{p(x_1)} t + x_1 = \frac{dq}{dp}\bigg|_{p(x_1 + \Delta x)} t + x_1 + \Delta x.$$

Therefore the time at which *nearly* neighboring curves intersect is

$$t = \frac{\Delta x}{\dfrac{dq}{dp}\bigg|_{p(x_1)} - \dfrac{dq}{dp}\bigg|_{p(x_1 + \Delta x)}}.$$

Consider the characteristics as paths of observers following constant density. Then this equation states that the time of intersection of the two observers is the initial distance between the observers divided by the relative velocity of the two observers (i.e., how much faster the one on the left is moving). Although the distance in between is small, the relative velocity is also small. Thus we shouldn't be surprised that as $\Delta x \to 0$, the time does not approach zero. To consider neighboring characteristics, the limit as $\Delta x \to 0$ must be calculated:

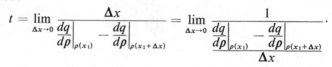

Consequently from the definition of the derivative,

$$t = \frac{-1}{\dfrac{d}{dx_1}\left(\dfrac{dq}{d\rho}\right)}.$$  (80.2a)

Since $dq/d\rho$ only depends on $\rho$,

$$\frac{d}{dx_1}\left(\frac{dq}{d\rho}\right) = \frac{d\rho}{dx_1}\frac{d}{d\rho}\left(\frac{dq}{d\rho}\right) = \frac{d\rho}{dx_1}\frac{d^2q}{d\rho^2},$$

and hence an alternate expression for the time when neighboring characteristics intersect is

$$t = \frac{-1}{\dfrac{d\rho}{dx_1}\dfrac{d^2q}{d\rho^2}}.$$  (80.2b)

Let us determine the conditions under which neighboring characteristics actually intersect; in other words, when is the time $t$ given by equation 80.2a or 80.2b positive? Since the Fundamental Diagram of Road Traffic is always concave downwards (i.e., $d^2q/d\rho^2 < 0$), it follows from equation 80.2b that only if $d\rho/dx_1 > 0$ will neighboring characteristics intersect. The condition $d\rho/dx_1 > 0$ means that the traffic density is increasing at the point where the neighboring characteristics start. Thus we conclude that neighboring characteristics which emanate from regions where the density is *locally* increasing further along the road will always intersect. When sketching characteristics, we cannot show the intersection of "exactly" neighboring characteristics. Instead, in Fig. 80-2, we have marked the intersection of the "nearest sketched" characteristics (for example, the position where the characteristic starting at $x = 0$ intersects the one starting at $x = -L/2$).

Perhaps the initial density is such that it is locally increasing at many places along the roadway, indicated in Fig. 80-6 as (〜〜〜):

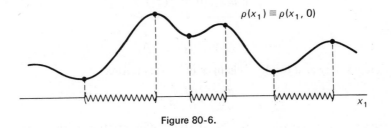

$$\rho(x_1) \equiv \rho(x_1, 0)$$

Figure 80-6.

For all characteristics emanating in regions where $d\rho/dx_1 > 0$, neighboring characteristics intersect. To determine the first time at which an intersection (shock) occurs, we must minimize the intersection time over all possible neighboring characteristics, i.e., find the *absolute* minimum of $t$ given by equation 80.2a. This can be calculated by determining where

$$\frac{d^2}{dx_1^2}\left(\frac{dq}{d\rho}\right) = 0,$$

(and $(d^3/dx_1^3)(dq/d\rho) < 0$).

These results concerning the earliest occurrence of a shock can be derived in an alternate manner. In Fig. 80-7 we sketch the density as a function of

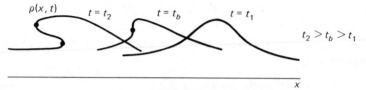

$\rho(x, t)$    $t = t_2$        $t = t_b$        $t = t_1$

$t_2 > t_b > t_1$

$x$

Figure 80-7    Evolution of traffic density ignoring shocks.

space for various times, ignoring the possibilities of shocks. We observe from the figure that $\partial\rho/\partial x$ first becomes infinite at the time of breaking $(t = t_b)$. Thus, let us calculate $\partial\rho/\partial x$. From the method of characteristics,

$$\frac{d\rho}{dt} = 0 \quad \text{along} \quad \frac{dx}{dt} = \frac{dq}{d\rho}(\rho).$$

The equation for the straight line characteristics is

$$x = \frac{dq}{d\rho}(\rho(x_1, 0))t + x_1. \tag{80.3}$$

$x_1(x, t)$ depends in a complicated manner on $x$ and $t$ (see Sec. 74). Since the traffic density is constant along the characteristic

$$\rho(x, t) = \rho(x_1, 0).$$

If the initial condition is prescribed,

$$\boxed{\rho(x_1, 0) = f(x_1),}$$

then

$$\rho(x, t) = f(x_1(x, t)).$$

$\rho$ changes only as a result of changes of $x_1$. Therefore,

$$\frac{\partial\rho}{\partial x} = \frac{df}{dx_1}\frac{\partial x_1}{\partial x}.$$

However, from equation 80.3 by partial differentiation with respect to $x$ (holding $t$ fixed, but certainly not $x_1$)

$$1 = \left[\frac{d}{dx_1}\left(\frac{dq}{d\rho}\right)t + 1\right]\frac{\partial x_1}{\partial x}.$$

Finally we obtain

$$\frac{\partial p}{\partial x} = \frac{\dfrac{df}{dx_1}}{\left[1 + \dfrac{d}{dx_1}\left(\dfrac{dq}{dp}\right)t\right]}.$$

$\partial p/\partial x$ becomes infinite at the same time neighboring characteristics intersect (see equation 80.2a). Before $t = t_b$, no neighboring characteristics intersect and $\partial p/\partial x$ is never infinite. When $t = t_b$, $\partial p/\partial x = \infty$ at the position of breaking, the first place where neighboring characteristics intersect (see Fig. 80-2). After $t = t_b$, a shock should be introduced to avoid the triple-valued solution. However, let us continue to investigate the method of characteristics. At $t = t_2 > t_b$ there are two positions at which $\partial p/\partial x = \infty$. This means that one set of neighboring characteristics intersects at the same time as another set, but at a different position (see Fig. 80-2).

Equations 80.2a and 80.2b imply that no shocks occur only if $dp/dx_1 < 0$ for the entire highway; the initial traffic density must be steadily decreasing. No shocks occur only if the initial traffic density is of the general form shown in Fig. 80-8, in which case traffic will thin out, rather than shock. Consequently, traffic shocks are almost always predicted by this theory of traffic.

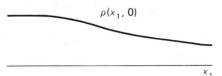

$\rho(x_1, 0)$

$x_1$

Figure 80-8 Traffic situation such that a shock will not form.

# EXERCISES

**80.1.** Assume that $u = u_{max}(1 - \rho/\rho_{max})$.

(a) Show that the time of intersection of neighboring characteristics (corresponding to the collision of two observers moving with constant density) is

$$t = \frac{\rho_{max}}{2u_{max}\dfrac{d\rho}{dx_1}}.$$

(b) If at $t = 0$,

$$\rho(x, 0) = \rho_{max} \exp\left(\frac{-x^2}{L^2}\right).$$

(1) Sketch the initial density.
(2) Determine the time of the first shock.
(3) Where does this shock first occur?

**80.2.** Calculate in general $\partial p/\partial t$. Show that $\partial p/\partial t$ tends towards infinity as the time of the earliest shock is approached.

**80.3.** Geometrically construct the shock wave if initially the density is as sketched in Fig. 80-1 (with $p_0 = 15$ and $p_1 = 45$), where the flow-density curve is given by Fig. 68-2. [Hint: Since the shock velocity is approximately the average of the two density wave velocities (see exercise 77.3), the velocity of the shock can be approximated by taking an "eyeball" estimate of the average slope!]

**80.4.** Using the result of exercise 71.9, calculate $\partial p/\partial x$ and $\partial p/\partial t$. Show that both tend towards infinity as the time of the earliest shock is approached.

**80.5.** For the problem roughly sketched in Fig. 80-2, show that the first shock occurs at $t = 8L/3u_{max}$. Briefly explain how we can improve the accuracy of Fig. 80-2.

**80.6.** Suppose the initial traffic density is such that at $t = 0$

$$\frac{dq}{dp} = u_{max}\left[\frac{1}{2} - \frac{3}{3 + (x/L)^2}\right].$$

(a) Using graph paper, sketch the characteristics corresponding to $x/L = 0$, $\pm\frac{1}{2}, \pm1, \pm\frac{3}{2}, \pm2, \pm3$. From the sketch, estimate the time and position of the first breaking.

(b) Illustrate in your sketch the space-time region in which the method of characteristics predicts the density is triple-valued.

(c) From the results of this section, when and where does the first shock occur? Compare your answer to part (a).

# 81.  Validity of Linearization

One of the first traffic problems we considered was one in which the initial traffic density is nearly uniform, $p(x_1, 0) = p_0 + \epsilon f(x_1)$. If the process of linearization is a valid approximation, then in Secs. 66–70 we showed the traffic density at later times can be approximated by

$$p(x, t) = p_0 + \epsilon f(x - ct),$$

where $c = dq/dp|_{p=p_0}$. The characteristics are approximated by parallel straight lines. The density wave moves forward for light traffic and backward for heavy traffic. However, we will show that this linearization process is usually *not* valid for large times. For nearly uniform traffic, the exact solution obtained by the method of characteristics (see Sec. 80) indicates that the characteristics are not parallel, but are nearly parallel. Thus characteristics

may intersect. A shock first forms at the smallest value of $t$ such that

$$t = \frac{-1}{\dfrac{d}{dx_1}\left(\dfrac{dq}{dp}\right)}.$$

Since,

$$\frac{d}{dx_1}\left(\frac{dq}{dp}\right) = \frac{d^2q}{dp^2}\frac{dp}{dx_1} \approx \epsilon \frac{df}{dx_1}\frac{d^2q}{dp^2}(p_0),$$

a shock will occur at some large (positive) time, $O(1/\epsilon)$, if somewhere $(df(x)/dx) > 0$ (assuming $d^2q/dp^2|_{p=p_0} < 0$). This time at which characteristics cross is quite large. For times less than that, no shocks occur and the slopes obtained by the method of characteristics are approximately the same as the constant value for the density wave calculated by the linear theory. However, for large times a shock will occur not predicted by the linearized theory. We thus conclude that linear theory is valid for limited times, not all times. This conclusion also frequently holds for nonlinear problems in other areas of study where a linearized analysis is utilized.

# EXERCISES

**81.1.** If initially $p(x, 0) = p_0 + \epsilon f(x)$, show that the exact density wave velocity differs only slightly from that predicted by the linearized theory. Approximate the difference in velocities. Under what circumstances will the exact solution differ substantially from the linearized approximation?

**81.2.** Reconsider exercise 67.2. Determine $p(x, t)$. You may assume that $u = u_{max}(1 - p/p_{max})$. Discuss differences between the exact answer and those predicted by the methods of Sec. 67.
(a) Assume that $\epsilon > 0$.
(b) Assume that $\epsilon < 0$.

**81.3.** Consider a situation in which traffic is initially nearly bumper to bumper, $p(x, 0) = p_{max} + \epsilon f(x)$.
(a) Why will we assume that $f(x) \le 0$?
(b) Determine the density for all times (using the linearized theory).
(c) Assuming that $u = u_{max}(1 - p/p_{max})$, calculate the velocity field.
(d) What equation determines the motion of a car starting at $x = L$?
(e) For times that are not too large, *approximately* solve the differential equation of part (d). [Hint: The car velocity is small and hence the car does not travel very far for times that are not too large.]

**81.4.** Reconsider exercise 81.3. Describe the motion of a car starting at $x = 0$ i $f(x) = -1 + \sin(x/20L)$. Does this correspond to your experience travelin in a car?

# 82.  Effect of a Red Light or an Accident

In this section, we will analyze a problem of practical interest. Assume that traffic is moving at a constant density $\rho_0$, and then traffic is stopped at a point $(x = 0)$ *for a finite amount of time* $\tau$ (for example, because of a red light or an accident). We will determine the effect of traffic being momentarily stopped.*
The initial density is a constant $\rho_0$,

$$\rho(x, 0) = \rho_0.$$

After the light turns red, cars line up behind the light in a manner we have already investigated (Sec. 78); see Fig. 82-1. The shock velocity is

$$\frac{dx_s}{dt} = \frac{[q]}{[\rho]} = \frac{\rho_{max}u(\rho_{max}) - \rho_0 u(\rho_0)}{\rho_{max} - \rho_0} = \frac{-\rho_0 u(\rho_0)}{\rho_{max} - \rho_0}, \tag{82.1}$$

the velocity at which a line of stopped cars increases.

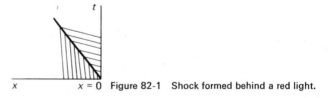

$x$        $x = 0$    Figure 82-1    Shock formed behind a red light.

In front of the light, the initial traffic density is also $\rho_0$. The traffic light gives a boundary condition (in front of the light) of zero traffic. It is as though the light separates traffic of *zero density* from traffic of density $\rho_{max}$, as illustrated in Fig. 82-2. In this configuration the lighter traffic ($\rho = 0$) is behind heavier traffic ($\rho = \rho_0$) and hence a shock forms between the faster moving density wave with density zero and the density wave with density

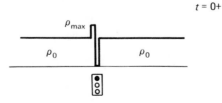

Figure 82-2    Uniform traffic density as instantaneously effected by a red light.

---

*This problem was analyzed by P. I. Richards, "Shock Waves on the Highway," *Operations Research 4*, 42–51 (1956).

$\rho = \rho_0$. The last car that traveled past the traffic light before it turned red moves at velocity $u(\rho_0)$. Thus the position of this car is where the shock occurs, since behind this car $\rho = 0$, while ahead of it $\rho = \rho_0$. Mathematically, the velocity of this shock on the "right" can be obtained using the shock condition:

$$\frac{dx_{sr}}{dt} = \frac{[q]}{[\rho]} = \frac{\rho_0 u(\rho_0)}{\rho_0} = u(\rho_0). \tag{82.2}$$

As we know, this shock wave travels at the same velocity as each car (of density $\rho_0$). Thus if the light stayed red forever, then we obtain the characteristics sketched in Fig. 82-3. At any fixed time (before the light returns to green), the density is as shown in Fig. 82-4.

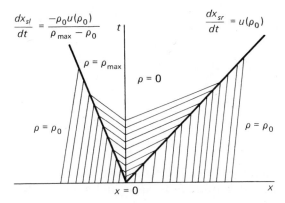

Figure 82-3    Red light stopping traffic—method of characteristics (note two shock waves).

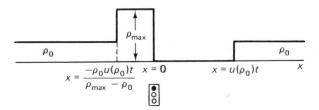

Figure 82-4    Traffic density after a red light stops traffic (note again two shocks).

At some time $\tau$, we assume that the light changes from red to green. Immediately near the light, the problem is one already solved (see Secs. 72–73), yielding a situation in which traffic gradually accelerates through the signal. Far behind the light, the cars at density $\rho_0$ continue to pile up at the line of stopped cars even though the light has changed (this continues to occur until the line of cars completely dissipates). The velocity at which the line continues to increase remains the same; it is again the shock velocity between $\rho = \rho_0$ and $\rho = \rho_{max}$, equation 82.1.

These results have been obtained for any velocity-density relationship. In the rest of this section for convenience we will assume

$$u(\rho) = u_{max}\left(1 - \frac{\rho}{\rho_{max}}\right),$$

as discussed in Sec. 73. Using this linear relationship, we note that the density wave velocity is

$$\frac{dq}{d\rho} = u_{max}\left(1 - \frac{2\rho}{\rho_{max}}\right).$$

Furthermore the general expression for the shock velocity may be simplified as follows:

$$\frac{dx_s}{dt} = \frac{[q]}{[\rho]} = \frac{q_2 - q_1}{\rho_2 - \rho_1} = \frac{u_{max}\left[\rho_2\left(1 - \frac{\rho_2}{\rho_{max}}\right) - \rho_1\left(1 - \frac{\rho_1}{\rho_{max}}\right)\right]}{\rho_2 - \rho_1},$$

or equivalently

$$\frac{dx_s}{dt} = u_{max}\frac{\rho_2 - \rho_1 + \frac{\rho_1^2 - \rho_2^2}{\rho_{max}}}{\rho_2 - \rho_1}.$$

Dividing through by $\rho_2 - \rho_1$ yields a simpler expression for the velocity at which a discontinuity between densities $\rho_1$ and $\rho_2$ propagates:

$$\frac{dx_s}{dt} = u_{max}\left(1 - \frac{\rho_1 + \rho_2}{\rho_{max}}\right). \qquad (82.3)$$

An alternate interpretation of this result is discussed in exercise 77.1. Thus the "left" shock, separating the uniform density $\rho_0$ from bumper-to-bumper traffic, moves at the velocity

$$\frac{dx_{sl}}{dt} = \frac{-\rho_0 u_{max}}{\rho_{max}}. \qquad (82.4)$$

Far ahead of the light, there is no effect from the light. There, the cars continue to move uniformly at velocity $u(\rho_0)$. Thus for some time shortly after $t = \tau$, the density is as sketched in Fig. 82-5.

The first car after the light travels at the fastest velocity $u(0) = u_{max}$, and hence catches up to the traffic of density $\rho_0$. The line of stopped cars decreases at the *speed* $u_{max}$, but the line is being increased at the speed

$$\left|\frac{-\rho_0 u_{max}}{\rho_{max}}\right| = \frac{\rho_0 u_{max}}{\rho_{max}},$$

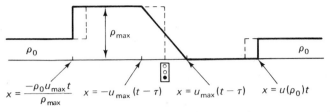

Figure 82-5   Traffic density a short time after stopped cars are restarted. (The dotted line indicates the density at $t = \tau$).

which is less than $u_{max}$. Hence the total line of stopped cars eventually dissipates. Which occurs first:

1. the lead car catches up to the uniformly moving traffic, at $t = t_u$ or
2. the line of stopped cars completely dissipates at $t = t_d$?

We will solve for the time at which each event occurs.

The lead car catches up to the uniformly moving traffic at time $t_u$, when

$$u_{max}(t_u - \tau) = u(p_0)t_u,$$

(following from Fig. 82-5) or thus when

$$t_u = \frac{u_{max}\tau}{u_{max} - u(p_0)} = \frac{u_{max}\tau}{u_{max} - u_{max}\left(1 - \dfrac{p_0}{p_{max}}\right)} = \frac{p_{max}\tau}{p_0}, \qquad (82.5)$$

a very long time for light traffic, a shorter time for heavier traffic. $t_u$ can also be computed as the distance the lead car is behind the trail car of the uniform traffic at $t = \tau$, $(u(p_0)\tau$, the constant velocity times the length of time the light was red), divided by the relative velocity, $u_{max} - u(p_0)$. Thus

$$t_u = \tau + \frac{u(p_0)\tau}{u_{max} - u(p_0)},$$

which is equivalent to equation 82.5. The line of cars dissipates at time $t_d$, when (see Fig. 82-5)

$$\frac{u_{max}}{p_{max}} p_0 t_d = u_{max}(t_d - \tau).$$

Hence,

$$t_d = \frac{u_{max}\tau}{u_{max}\left(1 - \dfrac{p_0}{p_{max}}\right)} = \frac{\tau}{1 - \dfrac{p_0}{p_{max}}}. \qquad (82.6)$$

The time it takes to dissipate the line after the light turns green is the length of stopped cars at $t = \tau$, $(p_0 u_{max}/p_{max})\tau$, divided by the velocity at which cars dissipate, $u_{max} - (p_0 u_{max}/p_{max})$. Thus

$$t_d = \tau + \frac{p_0 u_{max}\tau/p_{max}}{u_{max}(1 - p_0/p_{max})},$$

which is equivalent to equation 82.6.

By comparing equation 82.5 to equation 82.6, it is seen that for heavy traffic, in which $\rho_0 > \rho_{max}/2$, the lead car catches up first; see Fig. 82-6(a). For light traffic, in which $\rho_0 < \rho_{max}/2$, the line dissipates first, as seen in Fig. 82-6(b). At maximum traffic flow (if the uniform density corresponds to the capacity of the road), $\rho_0 = \rho_{max}/2$, both phenomena occur simultaneously; see Fig. 82-7.

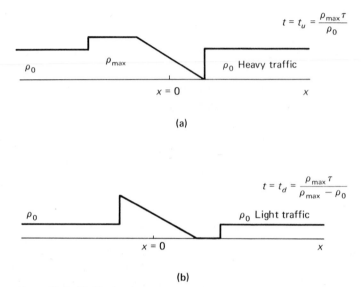

(a)

(b)

Figure 82-6   Traffic density:
(a) in heavy traffic, a lead car catches up before line of stopped cars completely dissipates; (b) in light traffic, vice versa.

Figure 82-7   Traffic density when lead car catches up at the same time as line dissipates.

The space-time characteristic curves are sketched for light and heavy traffic in Fig. 82-8(a) and (b). The shocks are marked in heavy lines. After the time of each previously mentioned event, a shock occurs resulting from the intersection of the fanlike characteristics (emanating from the light turning green at $x = 0$ at $t = \tau$) and the characteristics corresponding to the uniform density $\rho_0$. For example, as depicted in Fig. 82-9(a), certain cars far in back of the light do not notice that the light has changed from green to red, back to green. These cars move at velocity $u(\rho_0)$. Eventually they catch up to the thinned out waiting line as the stopped cars have all started again. In addition,

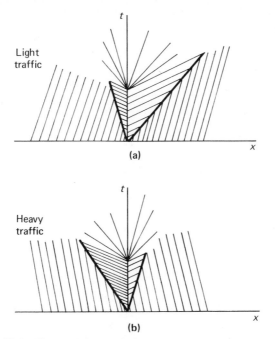

(a)

(b)

Figure 82-8   Characteristics: preliminary sketch for both light and heavy traffic.

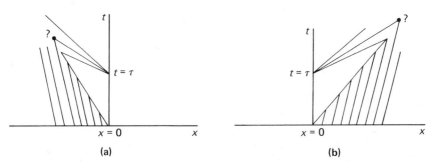

(a)

(b)

Figure 82-9   Intersection of characteristics:
(a) behind light after line dissipates; (b) in front of light after lead car catches up.

Fig. 82-9(b) indicates that, for the "right" shock, eventually the cars accelerating from the traffic light overtake the uniformly moving traffic of density $\rho_0$. Before the first of these two events occurs, the density distributions are as previously sketched. After the "left" shock occurs, we see Fig. 82-10, while after the "right" shock occurs we have Fig. 82-11. In both cases the **shock strength** (that is the difference between the two traffic densities) is decreasing! We now determine the paths of these two shocks. In either case,

$$\frac{dx_s}{dt} = \frac{[q]}{[\rho]} = \frac{u_f\rho_f - u(\rho_0)\rho_0}{\rho_f - \rho_0},$$

**377**

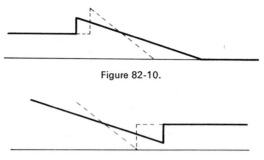

Figure 82-10.

Figure 82-11.

where $\rho_f$ and $u_f$ stand for the density and velocity in the fanlike region (either thinning or accelerating regions),

$$u_f = u_{max}\left(1 - \frac{\rho_f}{\rho_{max}}\right) \quad \text{and} \quad u(\rho_0) = u_{max}\left(1 - \frac{\rho_0}{\rho_{max}}\right).$$

Using equation 82.3 yields

$$\frac{dx_s}{dt} = u_{max}\left(1 - \frac{\rho_0 + \rho_f}{\rho_{max}}\right).$$

However, $\rho_f$ depends on $x$ and $t$. Using the results for fanlike regions (with a linear velocity-density relationship-see Sec. 73) starting at $t = \tau$,

$$\rho_f = \frac{\rho_{max}}{2}\left[1 - \frac{x}{u_{max}(t - \tau)}\right],$$

yields

$$\frac{dx_s}{dt} = u_{max}\left(\frac{1}{2} - \frac{\rho_0}{\rho_{max}}\right) + \frac{x_s}{2(t - \tau)}. \tag{82.7}$$

The velocity of this shock is not a constant. It is not a uniformly moving shock, since it represents the moving jump-discontinuity between a constant density region and a nonconstant density region. However, the ordinary differential equation describing the path of the shock, equation 82.7, is quickly solved, (see equation 73.5),

$$x_s = B(t - \tau)^{1/2} + u_{max}\left(1 - \frac{2\rho_0}{\rho_{max}}\right)(t - \tau), \tag{82.8}$$

where $B$ is the integration constant. The two different shocks ("left" and "right") correspond to different values of $B$.

The shock strength could be measured as $[\rho]$ or $\rho_f - \rho_0$,

$$[\rho] = \frac{\rho_{max}}{2}\left(1 - \frac{x}{u_{max}(t - \tau)}\right) - \rho_0.$$

Using equation 82.8,

$$[\rho] = -\frac{\rho_{max}B}{2u_{max}(t - \tau)^{1/2}}.$$

The shock strength (of either shock) tends to zero as $t - \tau \to \infty$. Furthermore we have determined the rate at which the shock strengths tend to zero. More general discussions, beyond the scope of this text, show that in other situations the shock strength tends to zero: it is usually also proportional to time raised to the $-\frac{1}{2}$ power. The velocity of the shock is

$$\frac{dx_s}{dt} = u_{max}\left(1 - \frac{2\rho_0}{\rho_{max}}\right) + \frac{B}{2}(t - \tau)^{-1/2}.$$

As the time increases after the light turns green, both shock velocities tend to the same constant, i.e., as $t - \tau \to \infty$

$$\frac{dx_s}{dt} \longrightarrow u_{max}\left(1 - \frac{2\rho_0}{\rho_{max}}\right). \tag{82.9}$$

This asymptotic shock velocity is just the density wave velocity corresponding to $\rho_0$. If traffic is heavy ($\rho_0 > \rho_{max}/2$), from equation 82.9 both shocks go backwards, while if traffic is light ($\rho_0 < \rho_{max}/2$), both shocks eventually travel forwards. Although both shocks are approaching the same velocity, interestingly enough, the distance between the two shocks is tending towards infinity since

$$x_{sl} - x_{sr} = (B_l - B_r)(t - \tau)^{1/2}.$$

The initial condition for the right shock is the position and time at which the first car catches up to the uniform traffic, namely at

$$t = t_u = \frac{\rho_{max}}{\rho_0}\tau, \qquad x_{sr} = u(\rho_0)t = u_{max}(\rho_{max}/\rho_0 - 1)\tau.$$

From this condition, $B_r$ can be determined for the right shock. The initial condition for the left shock is the position and time at which a car far behind the light catches up to the last remnant of the stopped traffic, that is at

$$t = t_d = \frac{\tau}{1 - \rho_0/\rho_{max}}, \qquad x_{sl} = -u_{max}(t - \tau) = -\frac{u_{max}\rho_0}{\rho_{max} - \rho_0}\tau.$$

To study the effect of the stopped traffic, the traffic behind the light will be thoroughly investigated. For this reason we determine the value of $B_l$, the integration constant for the "left" shock. From equation 82.8

$$-\frac{u_{max}\rho_0}{\rho_{max} - \rho_0}\tau = B_l\tau^{1/2}\left(\frac{1}{1 - \rho_0/\rho_{max}} - 1\right)^{1/2}$$
$$+ u_{max}\tau\left(1 - \frac{2\rho_0}{\rho_{max}}\right)\left(\frac{1}{1 - \rho_0/\rho_{max}} - 1\right).$$

Multiplying by $\rho_{max} - \rho_0$, yields

$$(\rho_{max} - \rho_0)^{1/2}B_l\tau^{1/2}\rho_0^{1/2} = -u_{max}\rho_0\tau - u_{max}\rho_0\tau\left(1 - \frac{2\rho_0}{\rho_{max}}\right).$$

Thus

$$B_l = \frac{-2u_{\max}\rho_0\tau}{[\rho_0\tau(\rho_{\max} - \rho_0)]^{1/2}}\left(1 - \frac{\rho_0}{\rho_{\max}}\right) = -2u_{\max}\left(\frac{\rho_0\tau}{\rho_{\max} - \rho_0}\right)^{1/2}\left(1 - \frac{\rho_0}{\rho_{\max}}\right).$$

If the traffic is heavy ($\rho_0 > \rho_{\max}/2$), then from equation 82.8 the shock never returns to the position of the traffic light, but travels backwards indefinitely. For heavy traffic, the traffic congestion caused by the momentary stoppage of traffic never disappears. For large $t$, its velocity is approximately constant

$$\frac{dx_{sl}}{dt} \approx -u_{\max}\left(\frac{2\rho_0 - \rho_{\max}}{\rho_{\max}}\right)$$

$$= -\frac{u_{\max}}{\rho_{\max}}\rho_0 + \frac{u_{\max}}{\rho_{\max}}(\rho_{\max} - \rho_0) > -\frac{u_{\max}}{\rho_{\max}}\rho_0.$$

Thus this asymptotic shock velocity is greater than (not as negative) the shock directly due to the red light; the speed of the shock slows down, as illustrated in Fig. 82-12.

Figure 82-12   Shock wave behind light slows down.

If the traffic is light ($\rho_0 < \rho_{\max}/2$), then from equation 82.9 the shock eventually reverses its motion. The shock returns to the origin when,

$$0 = B_l(t - \tau)^{1/2} + u_{\max}\left(1 - \frac{2\rho_0}{\rho_{\max}}\right)(t - \tau),$$

or equivalently when

$$(t - \tau)^{1/2} = \frac{-B_l}{u_{\max}\left(1 - \frac{2\rho_0}{\rho_{\max}}\right)} \quad \text{or} \quad t = \tau + \frac{B_l^2}{u_{\max}^2\left(1 - \frac{2\rho_0}{\rho_{\max}}\right)^2}.$$

Using the expression for $B_l$, yields

$$t = \frac{\tau}{(1 - 2\rho_0/\rho_{\max})^2}. \tag{82.10}$$

This phenomena is sketched in Fig. 82-13. The accelerating line of cars (due to the light changing from green to red, back to green) has completely dissipated at this time. At this moment, the traffic density at the position of the traffic light suddenly drops from $\rho_{\max}/2$ (the value at the origin for all time since the

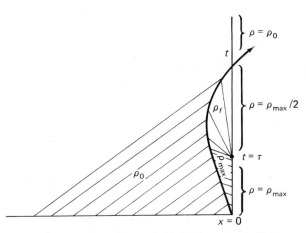

**Figure 82-13**   Shock wave behind light passes the light.

traffic started) to the uniform density $\rho_0$. An observer at the traffic light would mark this as the time when the traffic jam has finally cleared away. This time can be quite long. As Richards noted, if $\rho_0 = \frac{3}{8}\rho_{max}$ (light but not very light traffic), then the time of the elimination of the congestion is

$$t = \frac{\tau}{(1 - 3/4)^2} = 16\tau.$$

The traffic jam lasted from $\tau$ to $16\tau$, or fifteen times the length of the light. As an application, an accident which halted traffic for five minutes would, under these conditions, produce a traffic jam requiring an additional hour and a quarter to clear!

A simpler way to determine the time at which traffic clears is to note that the number of cars having gone through the light is $(t - \tau)q_{capacity}$, where $q_{capacity}$ is the capacity of the road. However, the first car that passes the light *after* the traffic jam clears has been traveling at the constant velocity $u(\rho_0)$ for time $t$. Thus the total number of cars that passed the light is the product of the initial density $\rho_0$ and the initial distance $u(\rho_0)t$ the "first" car is behind the light, $u(\rho_0)t \cdot \rho_0$. Since these two expressions must be equal, we see that the time for the traffic jam to clear is

$$(t - \tau)q_{capacity} = q(\rho_0)t.$$

Therefore

$$t = \frac{\tau q_{capacity}}{q_{capacity} - q(\rho_0)}, \tag{82.11}$$

which is equivalent to equation 82.10.

After the strengths of both shocks have started to diminish, a sketch of the density as a function of position would be Fig. 82-14. This figure is called an

N-wave. In summary, the space-time diagram for a momentary stoppage of uniform *light* traffic is sketched in Fig. 82-15.

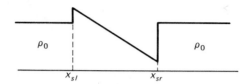

Figure 82-14    Traffic density after both line dissipates and lead car catches up.

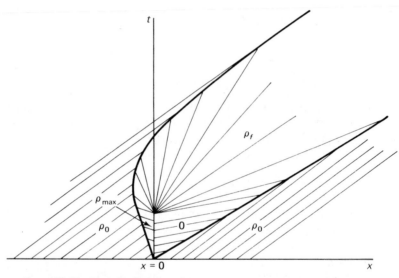

Figure 82-15    Method of characteristics showing shocks resulting from a temporary stoppage of light traffic.

# EXERCISES

**82.1.**    Assume that $u = u_{max}(1 - \rho/\rho_{max})$. If the initial density is

$$\rho(x, 0) = \begin{cases} \rho_1 & x < 0 \\ \rho_2 & a > x > 0 \\ \rho_3, & x > a \end{cases}$$

with $0 < \rho_1 < \rho_2 < \rho_3 < \rho_{max}$, then determine the density at later times. [Hint: See exercise 77.1. Calculate the shock between $\rho_1$ and $\rho_2$. Show that this shock moves faster than the shock between $\rho_2$ and $\rho_3$. What happens after these two shocks meet?]

**82.2.** Assume that $u = u_{max}(1 - \rho/\rho_{max})$ and that the initial traffic density is

$$\rho(x, 0) = \begin{cases} \rho_1 & |x| > a \\ \rho_0 & |x| < a, \end{cases}$$

where $\rho_1 > \rho_0$. Determine the density at later times.

**82.3.** Assume $u = u_{max}(1 - \rho/\rho_{max})$ and the initial traffic density is

$$\rho(x, 0) = \begin{cases} \rho_1 & |x| > a \\ \rho_0 & |x| < a, \end{cases}$$

where $\rho_1 < \rho_0$.
(a) Determine the density at later times.
(b) Consider a car starting from $x < -a$. How long is that car delayed in passing the increased density? [Hint: Find the time it would take to travel the same distance without the increased density.]

**82.4.** Analyze the traffic flow caused by a traffic light temporarily stopping heavy traffic if $u(\rho) = u_{max}(1 - \rho/\rho_{max})$.

**82.5.** Consider a short transition between a two-lane and three-lane highway, as sketched in Fig. 82-16. Let $\rho_2$ and $\rho_3$ be the traffic density per lane and

Figure 82-16.

$q_2$ and $q_3$ be the traffic flow per lane in the two- and three-lane roads respectively. Assume that the velocity-density relationship is still the same for each segment of the highway. (Is this reasonable?) If the number of cars in the transition region is always small, show that

$$3q_3 = 2q_2.$$

What happens to cars as they go from a two-lane highway into a three-lane highway and vice versa?

**82.6.** Assume that the transition region between a two- and three-lane highway is of a negligibly small distance, so that we can assume that there is a two-lane highway for $x < 0$ and a three-lane highway for $x > 0$. Using the results of exercise 82.5, calculate the density per lane of traffic at later times if initially the density (per lane) is a constant $\rho_0$ everywhere. Assume that $u(\rho) = u_{max}(1 - \rho/\rho_{max})$ and that
(a) $\rho_0 < \rho_{max}/2$
(b) $\rho_0 > \rho_{max}/2$
(c) $\rho_0 = \rho_{max}/2.$

**82.7.** Reconsider exercise 82.6 with a three-lane highway for $x < 0$ and a two-lane highway for $x > 0$.

    (a)  Assume that the initial density is such that the total flow (moving at density $\rho_0$) in the three-lane highway is less than the two-lane road's total capacity.

    (b)  Assume that the initial density is such that the total flow (moving at density $\rho_0$) in the three-lane highway is more than the two-lane road's total capacity. (Hints: A shock must occur, starting at $x = 0$. A moving line of traffic waiting to enter the narrower highway will develop.)

**82.8.**  Consider the two highways in Fig. 82-17, one which has a **bottleneck** in which for some distance the road is reduced from three to two lanes:

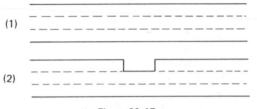

Figure 82-17.

Compare highways (1) and (2) with the same initial traffic density (per lane) $\rho_0$ under the condition in which the total flow (moving with density $\rho_0$) in the three-lane highway is more than the two-lane road's total capacity (refer to exercise 82.7). Consider a car a distance $x = L$ behind the bottleneck. How long is it delayed?

**82.9.**  Consider the traffic congestion caused by a slow-moving truck in the following problem. The initial density on a single-lane highway is $\rho_0 < \rho_{max}/2$ (and the corresponding velocity $u(\rho_0)$). Suppose that a construction truck enters the road and travels at $u(\rho_0)/2$ for a quarter of an hour before leaving the roadway. Calculate the resulting density as a function of time.

**82.10.**  Show that if $u(\rho) = u_{max}(1 - \rho/\rho_{max})$, then equation 82.11 is equivalent to equation 82.10.

**82.11.**  Assume that $u(\rho) = u_{max}(1 - \rho/\rho_{max})$ and traffic is coming to a traffic light at a light density $\rho_0$, $\rho_0 < \rho_{max}/2$. If the traffic light stays red for time $\tau$, how long must the light stay green in order for traffic not to back up behind the light?

**82.12.**  Redo exercise 82.11 if $u(\rho)$ is known but $u(\rho) \neq u_{max}(1 - \rho/\rho_{max})$.

**82.13.**  Assume $u(\rho) = u_{max}(1 - \rho/\rho_{max})$. Determine the traffic density if initially

$$\rho = \begin{cases} \rho_{max} & x < 0 \\ 0 & 0 < x < H \\ \rho_{max} & H < x < L \\ 0 & L < x, \end{cases}$$

where $H < L/2$. In particular, determine the paths of all traffic shock waves.

## 83.  Exits and Entrances

Let us now relax the assumptions concerning no exits or entrances on the segment of road being investigated. Exits and entrances are now allowed, as Fig. 83-1 represents. We reconsider conservation of cars. The rate of change

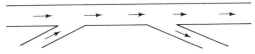

Figure 83-1   Exits and entrances.

of cars between $x = x_1$ and $x = x_2$ results not only from cars crossing at $x = x_1$ and $x = x_2$, but also from cars entering or exiting the road between $x = x_1$ and $x = x_2$. Let $\bar{\beta}(x_1, x_2, t)$ be the net number of cars per hour entering the region between $x = x_1$ and $x = x_2$. (The net number is the difference between the number entering and those exiting. It might be possible for example for $\bar{\beta}$ to be negative.) Thus conservation of cars implies

$$\frac{\partial}{\partial t} \int_{x_1}^{x_2} \rho(x, t)\, dx = q(x_1, t) - q(x_2, t) + \bar{\beta}(x_1, x_2, t).$$

It is more convenient to introduce the net number of cars per hour entering *per mile of roadway*, called $\beta(x, t)$, where

$$\bar{\beta}(x_1, x_2, t) = \int_{x_1}^{x_2} \beta(x, t)\, dx.$$

Taking a derivative with respect to $x_2$ (and replacing $x_2$ by $x$) yields the partial differential equation for **conservation of cars** (allowing exits and entrances),

$$\boxed{\frac{\partial \rho}{\partial t} + \frac{\partial q}{\partial x} = \beta.}$$
(83.1)

If $u(\rho)$, then $q(\rho)$, and consequently

$$\boxed{\frac{\partial \rho}{\partial t} + \frac{dq}{d\rho}\frac{\partial \rho}{\partial x} = \beta.}$$
(83.2)

The partial differential equation expressing conservation of cars, equation 65.3, is modified by the introduction of the term $\beta$ on the right hand side representing the effect of entrances and/or exits.

The method of characteristics can be used to solve this equation if $\beta$ is either known or has known dependence on the traffic density. The expression

$$\frac{\partial \rho}{\partial t} + \frac{dq}{d\rho}\frac{\partial \rho}{\partial x},$$

again represents the time derivative moving with the velocity $dq/d\rho$, i.e., if

$$\boxed{\frac{dx}{dt} = \frac{dq}{d\rho},} \qquad\qquad (83.3)$$

then this conservation equation implies

$$\boxed{\frac{d\rho}{dt} = \beta.} \qquad\qquad (83.4)$$

The curves such that $dx/dt = dq/d\rho$ are again called **characteristics**. The *density is no longer constant in the characteristic direction.* Hence the *characteristics* themselves are *no longer straight lines*! The density waves do not move at a constant velocity. The partial differential equation has been reduced to a system of two ordinary differential equations. In the next section, an example will be discussed that illustrates the solution of this system.

# EXERCISES

**83.1.** Consider a two-lane highway going in one direction which allows cars to pass. Let $\rho_1$ be the density in the slower lane, and $\rho_2$ be the density in the faster lane. Assume that it is possible for cars to change lanes.

(a) Show that

$$\frac{\partial \rho_1}{\partial t} + \frac{\partial}{\partial x}(\rho_1 u_1) = F$$

$$\frac{\partial \rho_2}{\partial t} + \frac{\partial}{\partial x}(\rho_2 u_2) = -F.$$

Assume that $u_1 = u_1(\rho_1)$ and $u_2 = u_2(\rho_2)$ are different, and $F$ represents the effect of lane changing.

(b) What qualitative dependence on $\rho_1$ and $\rho_2$ do you expect for $F$? Postulate a simple mathematical model of this.

**83.2.** Consider a highway with one lane of traffic density $\rho_+$ and velocity $u_+$ going in one direction, and a second lane of density $\rho_-$ and velocity $u_-$ going in the opposite direction. Passing is allowed enabling the average velocity to increase at the same density. Formulate a model of this highway with passing.

What qualitative dependence on $\rho_+$ and $\rho_-$ will $u_+$ and $u_-$ have? Assume $U$-turns are not allowed. [Hint: See exercise 83.1.]

**83.3.** Traffic problems which are more complex than those previously analyzed can be formulated. Suppose that the road itself is not uniform. For example, the road surface may vary affecting the cars' velocity. Thus it is no longer appropriate to assume $u(\rho)$, but the same kinds of approximations suggest $u(\rho, x)$.

    (a)   What is the formula for the traffic flow?

    (b)   Assume cars enter at the rate of $\beta$ cars per hour per mile of roadway. What partial differential equation describes conservation of cars?

    (c)   The method of characteristics, reduces the partial differential equation to what system of possibly nonlinear ordinary differential equations?

# 84. Constantly Entering Cars

If the net rate per mile of cars entering a highway is a constant $\beta_0$, then the traffic density at all times must satisfy the following partial differential equation:

$$\frac{\partial \rho}{\partial t} + \frac{dq}{d\rho}\frac{\partial \rho}{\partial x} = \beta_0, \qquad (84.1)$$

as derived in the previous section. The equations for the characteristics are

$$\frac{d\rho}{dt} = \beta_0, \qquad (84.2)$$

if

$$\frac{dx}{dt} = \frac{dq}{d\rho}. \qquad (84.3)$$

    The density is not constant along the characteristic. Instead, integrating equation 84.2 shows that

$$\rho = \beta_0 t + \rho_0, \qquad (84.4)$$

since we assume $\beta_0$ is a constant. The density depends linearly on time along the as yet unknown characteristic curve. The constant of integration $\rho_0$ is the traffic density at $t = 0$. For each characteristic curve the constant $\rho_0$ may be different. If the characteristic emanates from $x = x_0$, then

$$\rho_0 = \rho(x_0, 0). \qquad (84.5)$$

    In order to determine the density at a given position and time, it is necessary to know the characteristic curve as illustrated in Fig. 84-1. If the characteristic going through the point $(x, t)$ was curve $A$ in Fig. 84-1, then the

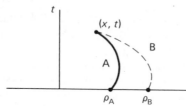

Figure 84-1    Density determined by unknown characteristic.

density at $(x, t)$ would be from equation 84.4 $\rho = \beta_0 t + \rho_A$. However, if the characteristic was curve $B$, then $\rho = \beta_0 t + \rho_B$. Even though the density is given by equation 84.4, we are unable to know what value $\rho_0$ should be unless the characteristics are known.

To determine the characteristic curves, equation 84.3 must be solved. For convenience, we assume that the linear velocity-density relationship, $u = u_{max}(1 - \rho/\rho_{max})$, is valid, in which case (see Sec. 73),

$$\frac{dq}{d\rho} = u_{max}\left(1 - \frac{2\rho}{\rho_{max}}\right).$$

Thus from equations 84.3 and 84.4, the characteristics satisfy the following ordinary differential equation:

$$\frac{dx}{dt} = u_{max}\left(1 - \frac{2\beta_0 t + 2\rho_0}{\rho_{max}}\right).$$

By integrating this equation, the characteristics obtained are not straight lines. However, in this case, the characteristics are parabolas as

$$x = u_{max}\left(1 - \frac{2\rho_0}{\rho_{max}}\right)t - \beta_0 \frac{u_{max}}{\rho_{max}}t^2 + x_0,$$

where $x_0$ is the initial position of the parabolic characteristic. Thus we obtain Fig. 84-2. These parabolic characteristics can be sketched knowing the

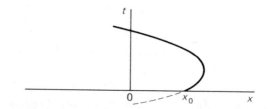

Figure 84-2   Constantly entering cars: parabolic characteristics.

initial distribution of traffic density. Along each parabola, equation 84.4 is satisfied. As time increases, the density increases as traffic builds due to the constantly entering cars (assuming $\beta_0 > 0$). If neighboring parabolas intersect, a shock forms, in which case a shock condition is necessary,

$$\frac{dx_{shock}}{dt} = \frac{[q]}{[\rho]},$$

as may be derived in the exercises. The shock condition is the same as that which occurs without exits and entrances.

# EXERCISES

**84.1.** From the integral conservation of cars, derive the shock condition when cars are constantly entering a highway.

**84.2.** Show that the neighboring parabolic characteristics of Sec. 84 first intersect at the same time as the first traffic shock occurs without entrances or exits. Show that the position of the first shock is further along the road if cars are constantly exiting than if no cars enter or exit. [Hint: See Sec. 80.]

**84.3.** Assume that there are some exits but no entrances along a roadway. Suppose that we approximate the rate of exiting cars as being proportional to the density, i.e., $\beta = -\gamma\rho$. Assume that $u = u_{max}(1 - \rho/\rho_{max})$. Under what conditions (if any) will a traffic shock occur? [Hint: See Sec. 80.]

**84.4.** Suppose that cars are entering an infinite highway ($-\infty < x < \infty$) at a constant rate $\beta_0$ per mile. If the initial traffic density is a constant $\rho_0$, determine the traffic density for all later times. At what time is this model no longer valid? Briefly explain.

# 85. A Highway Entrance

In this section, we will solve a problem involving traffic entering a highway. If we assume a linear velocity-density relationship, then traffic density satisfies

$$\frac{\partial \rho}{\partial t} + u_{max}\left(1 - \frac{2\rho}{\rho_{max}}\right)\frac{\partial \rho}{\partial x} = \beta. \tag{85.1}$$

Suppose initially that there are no cars on the road

$$\rho(x, 0) = 0.$$

However, suppose cars are entering the road (in some finite region $0 < x < x_E$) at a constant rate $\beta_0$ per mile for all time,

$$\beta(x, t) = \begin{cases} 0 & x < 0 \\ \beta_0 & 0 < x < x_E \\ 0 & x > x_E. \end{cases}$$

What is the resulting traffic flow? We expect that the first car enters and accelerates to the maximum speed. Thereafter each car's velocity is limited.

The method of characteristics implies that

$$\frac{d\rho}{dt} = \beta,$$

when

$$\frac{dx}{dt} = u_{\max}\left(1 - \frac{2\rho}{\rho_{\max}}\right).$$

In sections of the highway in front of (and behind) the region of entering cars, $\beta$ is zero, and the characteristics are straight lines corresponding to a constant density wave velocity (equal to the maximum car velocity if there are no cars); see Fig. 85-1.

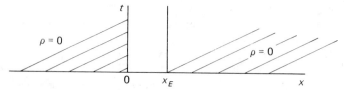

Figure 85-1   In regions without entrances, the characteristics are straight.

In the entrance region of the highway ($\beta = \beta_0$), the characteristics are parabolas. Some of these parabolas start at $t = 0$ at $x = x_0$ from regions of zero traffic density in which case

$$\boxed{\rho = \beta_0 t} \tag{85.2a}$$

$$x = u_{\max}t - \beta_0\frac{u_{\max}}{\rho_{\max}}t^2 + x_0. \tag{85.2b}$$

These parabolas differ from each other by a constant translation in $x$. The density is increasing in time as cars enter, equation 85.2a. Other parabolas emanate from $x = 0$ at some values of $t = \tau$ at which $\rho = 0$. For these characteristics, while they are in the region in which $\beta = \beta_0$,

$$\rho = \beta_0(t - \tau) \tag{85.3a}$$

$$x = u_{\max}(t - \tau) - \beta_0\frac{u_{\max}}{\rho_{\max}}(t - \tau)^2. \tag{85.3b}$$

In this region, by eliminating $\tau$ from equations 85.3a and 85.3b,

$$\boxed{x = \frac{u_{\max}\rho_{\max}}{\beta_0}\left(\frac{\rho}{\rho_{\max}} - \frac{\rho^2}{\rho_{\max}^2}\right).} \tag{85.4}$$

These parabolas are all translations in time from the parabola corresponding to $x_0 = 0$. At $x = x_E$, the density is the same value. Thus, we obtain Fig. 85-2; that is we will show these parabolas do *not* turn back; see Fig. 85-3.

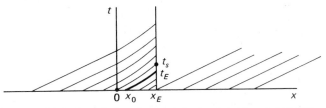

Figure 85-2    Straight line characteristics bend due to entering cars.

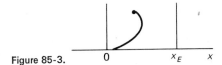

Figure 85-3.

For the parabola emanating at $x = 0$ at $t = 0$, the maximum value of $x$ occurs when

$$\frac{dx}{dt} = 0 \qquad \left(\frac{dx}{dt} = u_{max} - 2\beta_0 \frac{u_{max}}{\rho_{max}} t\right).$$

Thus $t = \rho_{max}/2\beta_0$, in which case $x = u_{max}\rho_{max}/4\beta_0$. If $(u_{max}\rho_{max}/4\beta_0) > x_E$, then the vertex of the parabola starting from $x = 0$ (at $t = 0$) would occur outside the region of entering cars. Since $\beta_0 x_E$ is the total flow of cars coming in the entrance, we will assume that this flow is less than the maximum capacity of the road,

$$\frac{u_{max}\rho_{max}}{4} > \beta_0 x_E.$$

Since $dq/d\rho > 0$, it can be shown that the densities are all less than $\rho_{max}/2$ and hence correspond to light traffic.

After leaving the region of entering cars, these parabolic characteristics become straight lines. The traffic density is constant along each straight line characteristic. However, for different characteristics, the constant value of the traffic density is different. For the characteristics emanating at $t = 0$ (for $0 \le x < x_E$), the density at $x = x_E$ is

$$\rho = \beta_0 t_E,$$

where $t = t_E$ is the time that the characteristic intersects the end of the entrance region, $x = x_E$ (note that $t_E$ depends on $x_0$—see Fig. 85-2). In general

$$x_E = u_{max} t_E - \beta_0 \frac{u_{max}}{\rho_{max}} t_E^2 + x_0.$$

Thus

$$t_E = \frac{1 - \sqrt{1 - \dfrac{4\beta_0(x_E - x_0)}{\rho_{max} u_{max}}}}{2\beta_0/\rho_{max}}.$$

At $x = x_E$, the traffic becomes denser and hence moves more slowly until $t = t_E(x_0 = 0) \equiv t_s$. After leaving the entrance region, the velocity of the characteristic is

$$\frac{dx}{dt} = u_{max}(1 - 2\rho/\rho_{max}),$$

but $\rho$ is the constant $\beta_0 t_E$. Consequently,

$$x = u_{max}(1 - 2\beta_0 t_E/\rho_{max})(t - t_E) + x_E.$$

These straight lines fan out since heavier traffic occurs after the lighter traffic, as shown in Fig. 85-4. In this region of straight line characteristics $\rho = \beta_0 t_E$ and hence

$$\boxed{x = u_{max}(1 - 2\rho/\rho_{max})\left(t - \frac{\rho}{\beta_0}\right) + x_E.} \qquad (85.5)$$

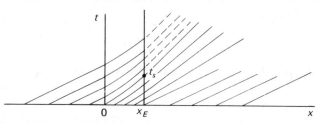

Figure 85-4  Parabolic characteristics straighten upon passing through entrance region.

At $x_E$, for $t \geq t_s$, the density is the same,

$$\boxed{\rho = \frac{\rho_{max}}{2}\left(1 - \sqrt{1 - \frac{4\beta_0 x_E}{\rho_{max} u_{max}}}\right).} \qquad (85.6)$$

Hence, these characteristics for $x > x_E$ are all parallel straight lines, as shown in dotted lines in Fig. 85-4.

In Fig. 85-5 we sketch for fixed times the traffic density.

**(a)** For $0 \leqslant t \leqslant t_s$

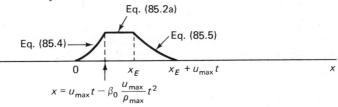

Eq. (85.2a)

Eq. (85.4) ———

Eq. (85.5)

0     $x_E$     $x_E + u_{max}t$     $x$

$$x = u_{max}t - \beta_0 \frac{u_{max}}{\rho_{max}} t^2$$

**(b)** At $t = t_s$ (and earlier)

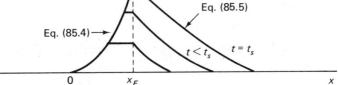

Eq. (85.5)

Eq. (85.4) ———

$t < t_s$     $t = t_s$

0     $x_E$     $x$

**(c)** At later times $(t > t_s)$

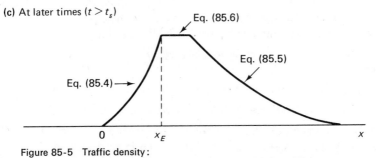

Eq. (85.6)

Eq. (85.5)

Eq. (85.4) ———

0     $x_E$     $x$

Figure 85-5   Traffic density:
(a) slowly increases; (b) continues to build; (c) reaches its maximum.

Thus the diagram in Fig. 85-6 illustrates the traffic density for all times:

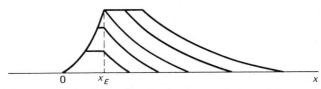

0     $x_E$     $x$

Figure 85-6   Traffic density continues to increase in front of the entrance region.

# EXERCISES

**85.1.** Show that neighboring parabolic characteristics do not intersect if $u_{max}\rho_{max}/4 > \beta_0 x_E$.

**85.2.** Consider the case of constantly entering cars for which $u_{max}\rho_{max}/4 < \beta_0 x_E$.
   - (a) Determine the traffic density for $x > x_E$.
   - (b) When does a shock first occur?
   - (c) What differential equation describes the path of a shock?
   - (d) Determine the density everywhere before the shock occurs.

**85.3.** Consider a highway entrance with $x_E \longrightarrow 0$, $\beta_0 \longrightarrow \infty$ such that $\beta_0 x_E \longrightarrow Q$, a constant.
   - (a) Give a physical interpretation of this situation.
   - (b) Determine the solution corresponding to $\rho(x, 0) = 0$ by considering a limit of the problem analyzed in Sec. 85.
   - (c) Solve the initial value problem $\rho(x, 0) = 0$ directly.

# 86.  *Further Reading in Traffic Flow*

The mathematical models we have analyzed postulate the importance of the traffic variables, density and velocity. We have then pursued deterministic models. Probabilistic models are primarily discussed in

HAIGHT, F. A., *Mathematical Theories of Traffic Flow*. New York: Academic Press, 1963.

A collection of four thorough review articles has been edited by D. C. Gazis:

GAZIS, D. C., *Traffic Science*. New York: John Wiley & Sons, 1974.

I highly recommend this book because of the excellent presentation by L. C. Edie which includes some of the material we have discussed. In addition, other authors in Gazis' book discuss a wide variety of traffic problems including traffic delays, control, generation, distribution, and assignment. These two books are excellent sources of additional references mostly contained in the research literature, many of which are accessible to the reader of this text.

A third book which I must recommend is

WHITHAM, G. B., *Linear and Nonlinear Waves*. New York: John Wiley & Sons, 1974.

This was written by one of the developers of deterministic traffic theory. Although this book only discusses traffic problems briefly, it does contain significant developments of the theory. [Furthermore, this book expertly presents various other applied mathematics problems involving wave motion (most from areas of physics).]

# Index